GLOBAL
SOUTH
ASIA

PADMA KAIMAL, K. SIVARAMAKRISHNAN,
AND ANAND A. YANG, SERIES EDITORS

The Gender of Caste

REPRESENTING DALITS
IN PRINT

Charu Gupta

UNIVERSITY OF WASHINGTON PRESS
Seattle and London

Printed and bound in the United States of America

20 19 18 17 16   5 4 3 2 1

PUBLISHED IN SOUTH ASIA BY PERMANENT BLACK
Delhi, India
http://permanent-black.blogspot.com/

UNIVERSITY OF WASHINGTON PRESS
www.washington.edu/uwpress

LIBRARY OF CONGRESS CATALOGING-IN-PUBLICATION DATA
Names: Gupta, Charu.
Title: The gender of caste : representing Dalits in print / Charu Gupta.
Description: Seattle : University of Washington Press, 2016. | Includes bibliographical references and index.
Identifiers: LCCN 2015035762 | ISBN 9780295995649 (hardcover : acid-free paper)
Subjects: LCSH: Dalit women—India, North—Public opinion. | Dalit women—India, North— History—Sources. | Caste—India, North. | Sex role—India, North. | Public opinion— India, North. | Dalits in literature. | Dalits—India, North—Social conditions. | India, North—Social conditions.
Classification: LCC DS422.C3 G864 2016 | DDC 305.48/44—dc23
LC record available at http://lccn.loc.gov/2015035762

The paper used in this publication is acid-free and meets the minimum requirements of American National Standard for Information Sciences—Permanence of Paper for Printed Library Materials, ANSI Z39.48–1984. ∞

for

PETER ROBB
my teacher and guide

Contents

Abbreviations

BSP	Bahujan Samaj Party
CMS	Church Missionary Society
Deptt	Department
EPW	*Economic and Political Weekly*
Home Poll	Home (Political) Department
IESHR	*Indian Economic and Social History Review*
JAS	*The Journal of Asian Studies*
Judl	Judicial
MAS	*Modern Asian Studies*
NAI	National Archives of India, New Delhi
NICTBS	North Indian Christian Tract and Book Society
NMML	Nehru Memorial Museum and Library, New Delhi
NNR	*Native Newspaper Reports of UP*
NWP	The North Western Provinces and Oudh (later United Provinces)
OBC	Other Backward Castes
OIOC	Oriental and India Office Collection, British Library
PAI	(*Secret*) *Police Abstracts of Intelligence of UP Government*
UP	The United Provinces of Agra and Oudh (later Uttar Pradesh)
UPSA	Uttar Pradesh State Archives, Lucknow

Preface and
Acknowledgments

This book grew out of an auto-critique of my first monograph, *Sexuality, Obscenity, Community* (2002), in which I had examined the interface between Hindu nationalism, gender, and the Hindi print-popular archive in colonial India. I realized that while highlighting representations of Hindu women, and positing social difference as an enduring aspect of modern gendering, I had inadvertently neglected Dalit women. Though I follow similar methodologies and archives, I have made gender and caste distinctions my focus in the present book.

The present work having come to fruition, I wish to acknowledge all those who made it possible. Among institutions, my primary debt is to the Nehru Memorial Museum and Library (NMML), New Delhi, which granted me a fellowship to pursue this research. I also thank the South Asia Council at Yale University, where I was "Visiting Faculty"; the University of Hawaii, for selecting me as a Rama Watamull Distinguished Scholar; and the Charles Wallace India Trust for a travel grant. A special thanks to the History Department at the University of Delhi for support and encouragement. I owe a great debt to the libraries and staff of the National Archives of India, the NMML, the Central Secretariat Library, and the Marwari Library, Delhi; the Bharti Bhavan Library and the Hindi Sahitya Sammelan Library, Allahabad; the Nagari Pracharini Sabha Library, Banaras; the Uttar Pradesh State Archives and the CID Office, Lucknow; the British Library, London; and the Divinity Library, Yale University. A warm thanks to Rupali Ghosh, Jaya, Sadhana Chaturvedi, and Ram Naresh Sharma, who gave all possible assistance in locating material.

Some of the ideas and material in this work were presented at conferences and seminars in a number of places: in India at the NMML, New Delhi; University of Delhi; Jawaharlal Nehru University, New Delhi; the Indian Council of Historical Research, New Delhi; the National Archives of India, New Delhi; the India International Centre, New Delhi; Kolkata University; Jadavpur University, Kolkata; Banaras Hindu University; the Govind Ballabh Pant Institute, Allahabad; and the Institute of Advanced Study, Shimla. In the USA at Yale University; the South Asia Studies Conference, Madison, 2008; the Sexuality and the Archive Colloquium, Duke University, 2009; the Conference of the Association of Asian Studies, Hawaii, 2011; the Conference on Engendering Rights in India, Chicago University, 2012; and the Berkshire Conference on the History of Women, Amherst, 2011, and Toronto, 2014; in Australia at the UNSW, Sydney; Macquarie University, Sydney; and the Conference on Subaltern Studies, Australian National University, 2011; in Scotland at the International Conference on Mutiny at the Margins, Edinburgh, 2007; in Nepal at the Exploring Masculinities Seminar, Kathmandu, 2008; in China at the Conference of the International Association for Feminist Economics, Hongzhou, China, 2011. I am grateful to the organizers, discussants, and participants for feedback and criticisms which have contributed greatly towards shaping my arguments.

My heartfelt thanks to many Dalit activists, writers, and friends who shared their invaluable insights with me, especially the late Bhagwan Das, a walking encyclopedia who lived very close to my home; and to Ashok Bharti, Anita Bharti, Rajni Tilak, Darapuriji, Daya Shankarji, and Mata Prasadji. My colleagues and friends in the History Department at the University of Delhi have extended deep warmth and constant help. I wish especially to thank Sunil Kumar, Sanghamitra Mishra, Aparna Balachandran, Biswamoy Pati, Amar Farooqui, Anshu Malhotra, Seema Alavi, Upinder Singh, Nayanjot Lahiri, Prabhu Mohapatra, and B.P. Sahu. My students, especially Vidhya Raveendranathan and Sharmita Ray, offered constructive ideas on various chapters, and I have learnt much from many of them in the course of my teaching.

Words are always insufficient when thanking friends who have provided unstinting support, and with many of whom I had stimulating discussions on parts of this book. Their warmth, along with constant encouragement and valuable suggestions, are integral to this book. Among them: Anand Swamy, Brinda Bose, Lata Singh, Anjali Arondekar, Ram Rawat, Badri Narayan, Crispin Bates, Geeta Patel, Neloufer de Mel, S. Charusheela, S. Shankar, Jayeeta Sharma, Sonia Sikka, Manuela Ciotti, Assa Doron, Kama Maclean, Debjani Ganguli, Kalpana Ram, Rochona Majumdar, Rahul Roy, Mary John, Nandini Sundar, Raj Kumar, Tapan Basu, Prathama Banerjee, Ravikant, Shahana Bhattacharya, Shohini Ghosh, Aditya Nigam, Nivedita Menon, and the late Sharmila Rege. My sincere thanks also to Majid Siddiqui, Philip Lutgendorf, Gautum Bhadra, Uma Chakravarti, Prem Chowdhry, Manager Pandey, Sumit Sarkar, Mrinalini Sinha, Barbara Ramusack, and Sudha Pai for sharpening my understanding and inspiration. My dear friend Jeremy Seabrook has read every part of this book and tightened it greatly. Anupama Rao and Peter Robb provided critical comments and insights, as only they could, which have distinctively shaped the book. K. Sivaramakrishnan contributed in innumerable ways and my heartfelt thanks to him. I offer my warm appreciation to Mahesh Rangarajan, who provided unfailing support at every stage. My acknowledgments would be incomplete without including Tanika Sarkar, whose role in my work is pivotal. I greatly admire her scholarship and she has been a pillar of strength and encouragement. Anonymous readers appointed by Permanent Black and the University of Washington Press offered astute comments that provoked significant revisions in the manuscript. Lorri Hagman of the University of Washington Press at Seattle offered many valuable suggestions which helped me sharpen focus and clarify issues that I had assumed were clear, but which were not. And, finally, Rukun Advani, who has spoilt me completely, so that I cannot now think of publishing any book of mine without his editorial support.

Parts of this book have been published in earlier versions in the *Journal of Asian Studies, Modern Asian Studies,* the *Indian Economic and Social History Review*, and in Crispin Bates (ed.), *Mutiny at the Margins, Volume V.*

My family—my mother Damyanti Gupta, my father Lalit Gupta, my sisters Ritu and Diksha, and many others—have given me tremendous warmth, love, and happiness. My son Ishaan has provided unforgettable moments of sharing and laugher.

Above all, to Mukul. My best friend and companion. My most remarkable partner. With my love.

Using late-nineteenth and early-twentieth-century sources on Dalits poses a problem: how to be accurate to the vocabulary and language usages of an earlier time without sounding abrasive to people reading them now. Most of the print literature by revivalists, reformers, and nationalists—one of the main sources for this book—did not use the term "Dalit." Much more frequent were the terms *achhut*, depressed classes, and Harijans. Sometimes in these writings the distinction between Shudra and *achhut* was blurred and the terms were used interchangeably, with many a *jati* finding its way into both categories. Some *jatis*, such as the Pasis, were stigmatized as criminal tribes. Many words, including caste names for Dalits, were (and are) used as insults and were deeply casteist. When I use such words—for example, untouchable—and caste names, it is in the context of their use at the time and is not intended to hurt or offend. At the same time, as convenient shorthand and to indicate personal political sympathies, I often deploy the term Dalit when expressing my own views. A related caveat is in order: while not taking away from the complexities, internal fissures, and specificities of different castes, I use the term Dalit in a generic, broad, and inclusive sense.

Proper names and caste names are not italicized, but other Hindi words are. Such words, as well as caste names, appear in the Glossary.

To enhance readability I have avoided diacritical marks and transcribed Hindi terms phonetically. All translations from Hindi to English, unless otherwise indicated, are my own. Translations of Hindi book titles are given in the Bibliography, and of articles from period journals in the footnotes. Such translations are not always exact, they often simply provide the subject of the material. When in book citations the names of publishers are not in evidence, it is because the source does not carry them. All Vikram Samvat dates have been converted to Gregorian dates by the standard method of deducting fifty-seven years from the former to arrive at the latter.

All references to unpublished documents state the file number first, followed by the year, other details, and finally the department and archival location.

Introduction

Gendering Dalits

I n May 1927, *Chand*, the leading Hindi journal of early-twentieth-century colonial North India, published an *Achhut Ank*, a special issue on Dalits. Though overwhelmingly androcentric, it had a distinct perspective on Dalit women, encapsulated in the following:

> It is the story of days and nights of fasting; it is the story of those mothers who leave the dead bodies of their beloved children in their broken huts and go to do *begar* in the homes of demonic landlords; it is the story of those wives who leave their essence of being, their godlike husbands and their life-wealth on the deathbed, and in the face of the naked sword of oppression go to do *begar* with their heads bent; it is the story of those sisters who are subject day and night to the sexual passions of oppressors in front of their parents and brothers; . . . it is the horrifying story of extreme poverty; . . . it is the moving story of the desolation of Hindu religion and Hindu society, and it is also the story of the rise of Islam and Christianity in India; *it is the heart-rending story of silent tears, soundless weeping, and speechless suffering.*[1]

This poignant account of Dalit women was emblematic of a critical shift in their representation within a segment of upper-caste reformist-nationalist Hindi literature in early-twentieth-century North India. The dominant precolonial image of the Dalit woman as a site of evil

[1] Editorial, *"Paap ki Granthiyan"* (Records of Sin), *Chand*, May 1927: 5 (2–6). Special issue on untouchables, emphasis mine. *Chand* (1922–41), a Hindi monthly published from Allahabad, proved to be extremely popular in the 1920s under the editorship of Ramrakh Singh Sahgal. For details, Orsini 2002: 267–74; Nijhawan 2012: 79–89.

and pollution gave way to images of her anguished, victimized body. Yet inasmuch as it framed its portrayal largely through an upper-caste lens, the *Achhut Ank* also strengthened certain stereotypes of Dalits and carried the inherent contradiction of embracing Dalits within a hierarchized Hindu fold. Noticeable too is the holding up to view an idealized image of subservient and silently suffering Dalit women. While weaving their labor and sexuality into a singular identity of the oppressed woman, the special issue also reveals anxieties around the conversion of such women to Islam and Christianity. The specific context for this *Achhut Ank* was perhaps a series of interrelated factors—the incipient emergence of the Adi Hindu movement and worries about the increasing assertiveness of Dalits in Uttar Pradesh (UP), necessitating responses from reformers and nationalists; the propagation of *shuddhi* and *sangathan* by the Arya Samaj, which en-compassed attempts to draw Dalits into the larger politics of a unified Hindu nation by, among other things, constructing a homogeneous Hindu identity; and fears of the conversion of Dalits, linked to an imagined decline in Hindu numbers.

The print-public sphere in colonial North India, however, was deeply heterogeneous, and there were varied representations of Dalits, including Dalit women, which jostled with these tropes of victim-hood. Nor were Dalits passive recipients of these representations: they contested them with their own versions and renditions.

The Gender of Caste invites readers to rethink the history of caste from a gendered perspective in colonial North India, specifically UP. It foregrounds "representations in print" as its critical tool, addressing print as a significant if ambivalent site for the reproduction, transformation, and contestation of caste and gender ideologies. Exploring imaginative possibilities within structures and languages of representation through visual print culture and archival material, it navigates through a contentious associational discourse around caste and gender which developed amongst colonizers, national-ists, revivalists, reformers, and Dalits, permeating the social fabric in contradictory ways. Juxtaposing a series of historical narratives, it tries to "unread" dominant inscriptions on gendered caste bodies while highlighting emancipatory possibilities through counter-voices and agencies.

The aim of this book is twofold: first, to examine practices of distinction and hierarchy within the Hindu community, and posit how social difference was an enduring aspect of caste gendering. It interrogates dominant modern narratives on gendered untouchables, including erudite enunciations of liberal reform, to demonstrate how—to paraphrase Jacques Ranciere—representations of Dalits were often "embodied allegories of inequality."[2] The second aspect is to approach the regulation of caste and gender at the level of the quotidian while unveiling the hidden archives of Dalit resistance. Towards this end I mobilize a rich and understudied vernacular archive of popular and didactic writings in Hindi newspapers and journals, cartoons, and missionary publications to highlight how social practices and relations left their mark on print and the literary: the two drew from, and fed into, each other. Simultaneously, I look at ideas of intimacy and body history to understand the terribly material, embodied character of caste–gender dynamics, its representational density, its divergent receptions in public life. I examine the social practices and representations of intimacy in everyday life that put the peculiar and pervasive imprint of caste upon the Dalit woman's body. Alongside, by teasing out Dalit women's individual needs and desires I attempt to disrupt the neat folding of the self into the collective.

The images included resonate with conjunctions between gender and caste. The first three chapters discuss representations of Dalit women as vamps, victims, and *viranganas* in a variety of print genres. I begin by telling the story of how, in diadactic literature and in portrayals of the Chamar *dai*, Dalit women were recast through new forms and idioms into vamps and stigmatized bodies, as unhygienic and lascivious. I then describe how, in a section of reformist literature, images of the permanently polluted, evil, and grotesque Dalit woman's body give way to suffering figures, redefined therein as victims deserving redemption. This move also allows for a conceptualization of the ideal Dalit woman as epitomized in the figure of Shabari, the low-caste woman worshiper of Ram in the *Ramayan*.

Simultaneously, contesting such representations through a multi-pronged critique of caste in the public sphere, in present-day popular

[2] Ranciere 2009: 12.

Dalit writings Dalit women come to be marked as militant figures in the revolt of 1857: these contestations are explored in Chapter 3. Through such symbols these chapters probe different representations of Dalit women, characterized by condemnation, romanticization, victimhood, and heroism.

Since the book is about the gender of caste, it also shows Dalit men as gendered subjects and addresses constructions of Dalit masculinities. In the fourth chapter I suggest that Dalit men were constituted as effeminate or criminal by colonizers and upper castes but reclaimed by Dalits themselves as men with distinct identities, rights, and manhood through their assertions at work, in the army and in politics, and by their attitudes to food and women.

The fifth chapter examines religious conversions by Dalit women to Christianity and Islam. It studies them through the lens of sartorial desires, romances, and the language of aspirations and individual intimate rights. The construction of an alternative Dalit mythology is the subject of Chapter 6, which focuses on the reinterpretation of goddesses such as Lona Chamarin and Sitala—venerated by Dalits in particular—and a genre of song called *kajli* sung largely by low-caste women.

Finally the book analyses representations of indentured, transnational, subaltern women in caste and Hindi literature, showing how they came to be constructed as both innocent victims and guilty migrants.

The seemingly incongruous locations and subjects of this book's chapters are in fact closely linked and intertwined, revealing throughout the entanglement and co-constitution of attempts to regulate Dalit bodies, the new socialities of caste, and the texts and acts of Dalit women's (and men's) self-expression, whereby the representations of Dalits were both enabled and transformed.

Historiographies of Caste and Gender

Both "caste" and "gender" are forms of social difference and systems of inequality that have, typically, been addressed in isolation from each other. While caste is seen as a uniquely Indian form of hierarchical stratification to be treated empirically, gender has been viewed as a

universal conceptual category central to the reproduction of patriarchies.[3] Perceptive regional histories of Dalits,[4] particularly of colonial Maharashtra,[5] have provided critical redemptive narratives on
Dalits.[6] With the meteoric rise of the Bahujan Samaj Party (BSP)
and Dalit movements in UP, significant studies have centered on a
quest for new identities among the Jatavs of urban Agra in the early
twentieth century;[7] the politics of laboring urban Dalits and the
activities of the Adi Hindu movement and Swami Achhutanand in
inter-war UP;[8] critiques of the assumptions traditionally made about
Chamars being leatherworkers when in fact the majority of them
were agriculturists;[9] the changing meanings of Dalit ideologies for the
Chamars of Lucknow in the 1970s and 1980s;[10] the contemporary
Dalit politics of the BSP;[11] and the claims of Dalits to a dynamic
counter-print public and political space in the region.[12]

Rich and insightful as these studies have been, in them Dalits have
largely appeared as a male category. At the same time, feminist writings
on colonial India have written of patriarchy and oppression principally
with a focus on representations of and by high-caste, middle-class

[3] Rao 2012: 239.

[4] Juergensmeyer 2009 (1982); Bandyopadhyay 1997; Dube 1998; Prashad
2000.

[5] O'Hanlon 1985; Omvedt 1994; Rao 2009. Particularly exciting are
studies on the caste question *vis-à-vis* Ambedkar and Gandhi: Zelliott 1992;
Nagaraj 2010; Jaffrelot 2004; Rodrigues 2002. In histories of modern India,
what Bengal has signified for gender, Maharashtra has meant for caste, each
providing much of the theoretical constructs. Perhaps Rammohun Roy and
Vidyasagar here and Jotirao Phule and Ambedkar there have played a critical
role in this.

[6] Also significant are works on South India: Pandian 2007; Basu 2011;
Geetha and Rajadurai 1998.

[7] Lynch 1969. Chamars/Jatavs are the largest Dalit caste in the region,
and most studies have centered on their experiences.

[8] Gooptu 2001. Also Joshi 2003; Bharti 2011.

[9] Rawat 2012: 54–84.

[10] Khare 1984.

[11] Pai 2002; Chandra 2004.

[12] Narayan 2001, 2006, 2011; Brueck 2014; Amardeep 2012; Naimishray
2014; Hunt 2014.

women.[13] These, while also significant in their own right, tacitly imply via the conspicuous absence of Dalit women that their portrayal does not merit a separate study since they can be subsumed within the category "women."[14] The depiction of Dalit women as a major area of feminist examination has remained on the fringes, particularly in the context of colonial UP, a shortcoming from which my own earlier work is not exempt.[15] The implicit conclusion has been that in colonial India most women were upper caste and middle class, while virtually all the lower castes and Dalits were men.[16] However, while in the gendered politics of power women are always subservient to men, in the caste politics of power upper-caste, middle-class women often collude with men. So this book questions both the presumptive maleness of most Dalit studies, and the presumptive upper-casteness of many feminist writings of the colonial period. It points out how the differentials of caste and gender between women and men, and among colonized women, were critical in structuring patterns of domination and subordination.

In the past two decades the intersectedness of anti-caste thought and gender has emerged as central in the work of some feminists, specially among those with a West India and South India focus. They have shown how caste radicals—be it Jotirao Phule, B.R. Ambedkar, or E.V. Ramasamy Periyar—distinctly drew and challenged connections between sexual regulation and caste reproduction.

[13] Sangari and Vaid 1989; Forbes 1996; Sarkar 1999, 2001; Bannerji 2001; Engels 1996. One reason for this has been that the concern of most social reform movements was largely about Hindu middle-class women rather than caste: Sarkar 2002: 61.

[14] While feminist historians in India have effectively critiqued the homogenized and hegemonic representation by and of white, Western feminism, they have unwittingly privileged upper-caste women over women of the lower castes by obscuring the latter. For further critiques: Rao 2003: 1–47; Rege 2006.

[15] Gupta 2001.

[16] It is often assumed in the West too that "racism is what happens to black men. Sexism is what happens to white women": Hull, Scott, and Smith 1982; Smith 1998. In India, the trivialization of the identities of Dalit women not only obscures the double jeopardy of caste and gender that they face, but also limits our understanding of both caste and gender.

They have demonstrated the contradictory contours of sexuality, marriage, and family in the anti-Brahmin politics of Maharashtra.[17] They have reclaimed some of Ambedkar's writings—which imagined new caste–gender codes and trenchantly critiqued endogamy—as feminist classics.[18] They have unveiled the radical embrace of marriage as a partnership of two political comrades outside the family, and contraception as a means of sexual pleasure as posited by Periyar and the Self-Respecters of Tamilnadu.[19] Yet, because the annihilation of caste, rather than sexual freedom *per se*, was the focus of male anti-caste reformers, there was an obvious lacuna in the otherwise radical connections they drew.[20] Further, although caste radicals challenged caste ideology, "they were by no means immune to the extension of novel patriarchal practices into their own households."[21] Many of the issues addressed in this book, while deeply influenced by, and drawing from, such caste and feminist studies, fall in between the signposts of these gender and Dalit historiographies. It also draws inspiration from contemporary Hindi writings by Dalit feminists who have brought new complexities to debates around Dalit women,[22] and from a rich body of work by black feminists on representation.[23] As Carol Henderson says: "In exploring the various imaginings of the

[17] Rao 2009: 50–68. Uma Chakravarti has emphasized the intimate relationship between the consolidation of Brahmanical patriarchy and traditional caste hierarchy during the Peshwai in eighteenth-century western India: Chakravarti 2003: 107–11.

[18] Rege 2013: 13–56.

[19] Anandhi 1991: 24–41, 1998: 139–66; Geetha 2003; Veeramani 1992.

[20] They thus often limited themselves to marriage and its protocols.

[21] Rao 2009: 53. Feminist anthropologists too have revealed how Dalit women repudiate elite norms: Kapadia 1995; Franco, Macwan, and Suguna 2000; Jogdand 1995.

[22] Besides a rich yield of creative writing, including poems, stories, and autobiographies, many essays, for example by Anita Bharti and Vimal Thorat, have explored innovative ways for reconsidering representations of Dalit female bodies in social and cultural imaginations, along with scathing critiques of Dalit patriarchies: Bharti 2013: 209–52; Thorat 2008: 63–70.

[23] hooks 1992; Gilman 1985; Collins 2000; James and Sharpley-Whiting 2000; Bennett and Dickerson 2000; Wallace-Sanders 2002; Henderson 2010; Willis 2010.

black female body in print and visual culture, it is hoped that the contradictory impulses of using a body that is marked and likewise coded, will give way to an alternative symphony of voices that honor the legacies of black women—both real and imagined."[24]

Representations, Archives, and Print

Intricate and inextricable connections existed between caste, gender, representation, and the emerging print-public-popular culture in late-colonial UP. Histories of representation pose afresh the relationship between myth and memory, the oral and the written, rhetoric and everyday reality.[25] Representations of Dalits by the upper castes and liberal reformers not only showed the prejudices embedded in power relations, but also rendered perceptions, hidden anxieties, and practices into words and images. However, the process of transmission, or the transition from representation to reception, is never straightforward: castes, communities, and individuals can perceive the same thing quite differently. This work sees the representational battle, with all its ambiguities and flexibilities, as a sign of power and contestation. While comparing gendered representations of Dalits by "self" and "others," it attempts to alter the fundamental division of power between touchable–untouchable and caste stigma. The circuits of production and the available repertoires of representation expose the prose and image wars inaugurated in this period by conservatives, reformists, and Dalits, whereby the relationship between caste and gender as categories was constantly made and unmade. The pervasive, clichéd, and stereotypical images of Dalit womanhood and manhood were reified and mediated through certain representations. However, they also opened up the possibilities for subversive appropriations and challenges through counter-images and defiant identity formations. Even when not overtly visible, even when not always speaking, representations can thus provide spaces for readings of Dalit subjectivities and allow us to engage with the paradoxical social, political, and literary constitution of Dalit selves.

[24] Henderson 2010: 17.
[25] Amin 2005b: 2.

Grappling with a range of positions and possibilities around Dalit representations, this research collates them with the heterogeneity of caste experiences, events, practices, and discourses. It recasts disjunctive forms of representation in portrayals of Dalit women, Dalit masculinities, and depictions of conversions, popular culture, and indenture. It deploys didactic manuals, reformist magazines, women's periodicals, missionary propaganda, police reports, cartoons, and popular Dalit pamphlets to create an archive where representation is about replication *and* innovation.

In the process I rely on different archival registers, motivated by what Anjali Arondekar calls archival "romance" and "desire,"[26] through which I reconstitute my historiographical perspectives. Recalcitrant histories of gendering caste are gleaned by including, and indeed centering, materials that are often elided in archival research. While historians have been convinced of the authority and authenticity of the archive, scholars, particularly feminists, have questioned seeing the archive as verifiable, as having a fixed entity, as a sign of historical subjectivity, and as the most important basis for the production and institutionalization of knowledge. Focusing on silences and erasures, they have sought to read between the lines, recover and record omissions, and point creatively to the permeability and mutability of the archives.[27] This book similarly attempts to not only re-read the standard archives and expand their components, but also insists that we revisit what constitutes a peripheral and/or central archival source. Rooted in a cross-referential feminist counter-archive, I rely on different techniques of dealing with sources that determine the deep structures of historiography itself. Texturing and highlighting the materials present in the archives, I study a rich repertoire of vernacular imaginative texts, in dialogue with other hegemonic texts, to explore the place of gender in caste. An expanded vernacular archive indicates greater access to social life and diversity

[26] Arondekar 2009: 1, 6.

[27] Ibid.: 5–6; Derrida 1995; Cvetkovich 2003; Gupta 2011. Many feminist historians in India have, for example, used gossip, memories, fictions, and visual representations to present a gender-sensitive history: Sarkar 1999, 2001, 2009; Burton 2003; Ramaswamy 2011; Sinha 2006.

of representation, enabling new ways of studying gender and caste. These sources, spread in the bylanes and small local libraries of Allahabad, Lucknow, and Banaras, help us refocus on conversations amongst local inhabitants on gendered Dalits in the period. Derrida has referred to the principles of *commencement*, where archives and history begin; and to *commandment*, the prescriptions offered by those who construct and interpret, i.e. the "archons." These then become their "archontic" functions.[28] In the present work, through its immersion in the Hindi print archive, the home team often provides the starting point. Because they were central to the local textual representations of Dalits, vernacular materials have become my constitutive rather than supplementary archives. Such materials were often embedded within non-archival genres, and yet contained elements which permitted them to be recognized as archival. The turn towards the twentieth century in relation to the print culture of UP creates a revised conception of the archive.

In colonial India, writing and print were social and cultural practices, and in spite of low literacy rates came to be viewed as important agents of change, attracting diverse authors and readers. From the late nineteenth century there emerged a vibrant public culture in urban UP, and print became a commodity; this was facilitated by the rapid growth of public institutions, libraries, publishing houses, printing presses, newspapers, and books.[29] Print aided both the standardization of languages and literatures as well as their democratization.[30] The low cost and ubiquity of print, combined with urbanization and the growth of a middle class in UP, strengthened vernacular publishing, which helped fashion as well as contest gender, caste, and religious identities.[31] By the early twentieth century Hindi became the dominant print language of a large section of middle-class, upper-caste

[28] Derrida 1995: 1–3.

[29] For the multilayered impact of print: Eisenstein 1979; Chartier 1989; Anderson 1991 (1983). In the Indian context: Orsini 2002; Naregal 2001; Ghosh 2006; Stark 2007: 1–28; Blackburn 2003; Venkatachalapathy 2012; Gupta 2001: 30–4.

[30] Blackburn 2003: 10–11; Venkatachalapathy 2012.

[31] Freitag 1989; Gooptu 2001; Gupta 2001; Hansen 1992; Orsini 2002.

reformers, and nationalists in UP.[32] These publicists created a new indigenous Hindi public literary sphere and an expansive vernacular archive, including chapbooks, magazines, and newspapers.

Hindi also became the dominant public language in UP for the discourse on caste. With the emergence of the pioneering presence of Ambedkar and Gandhi, the figure of the untouchable became a ubiquitous subject in Hindi writings.[33] Seeing themselves as flag-bearers for the social transmission of knowledge, revivalists and reformers evolved their own idioms, codes, and practices to express, write, debate, and shape ideas about untouchables and untouchability. Didactic literature, reformist magazines, propaganda material, and cartoons published by orthodox Sanatani Hindus and reformist Arya Samajis, nationalists and missionaries, authors, and journalists were saturated with debates and images of Dalit women and men; they included discussions about "difference" and "sameness," pollution and victimization, antagonism and sympathy, distancing and wooing.[34] These landscapes became troubled sites where divergent readings of the stigmatization and suffering of Dalit womanhood came to be staged, suggesting continuities—although couched in different idioms—as well as significant shifts from the earlier period. However, in spite of the heterogeneous and fragmented nature of the Hindi

[32] Before the 1860s, most vernacular magazines and newspapers in UP were in Urdu. The 1870s and 1880s saw the emergence and flourishing of many newspapers and journals in Hindi, such as *Kavi Vachan Sudha* (Banaras, 1867), *Hindi Pradeep* (1874), and *Bharat Mitra* (1877). Caste journals also began appearing, with *Brahman* and *Kshatriya Mitra* starting in 1880. Some 150 papers and journals in Hindi either began or were restarted between 1884 and 1894. Newspapers like *Abhyudaya* (1907), *Vartman*, and *Pratap* (1913), and magazines such as *Saraswati* (1900), *Madhuri* (1922), and *Chand* (1922) had considerable runs. For details, Gupta 2001; Orsini 2002; Natarajan 1954: 183–7.

[33] Novels, plays, and stories were published on the *achhut*. For example, Srivastava 1928; "Ram" 1926; "Komal" 1934; "Viyogi" 1943.

[34] For example, there were sharp disagreements between the Sanatani Hindu *pandit*s and the Arya Samaj; the former vociferously emphasized a fundamental difference between upper castes and Dalits, and the latter stressed pan-Hindu unity, transcending caste differences.

print-public sphere, it was, in as late as the 1920s, largely controlled by the Hindi literati, by men and women who belonged to the Brahmin, Bhumihar, Kayasth, Agarwal, Khatri, and Thakur castes.[35] Amidst the sharp differences there were convergences in their voices, expressed around the fear of conversions, a putative decline in Hindu numbers, and anxieties about the increase in Dalit protests and movements—all of which made a section of writers, reformers, and nationalists respond with alacrity and adopt a more humane language.[36] But even amidst the rhetoric of liberal reform and sympathy, there was an "erasure of caste as an analytic."[37]

Equally, by the 1920s, urban, elite, and middle-class women were making forceful claims for space in the dynamic print world of Hindi, with a resultant flowering of such women as readers, writers, editors, and educators. They carved new roles for themselves by thinking through novel idioms, questioning domestic norms, articulating political participation, finding ways of self-expression, and forging a collective identity.[38] And yet, even when conceiving homogeneous unities and seamless narratives of sisterhood, their voices and writings were undercut by implicit exclusions, embedded within frameworks of caste.[39] Around the same time, urban, literate Dalits in UP also began writing in Hindi, viewing print and publishing as critical tools to claim upward mobility and dignity.[40] Two recent Dalit anthologies show how Dalit writers have made strategic interventions in the field of print and knowledge.[41] In the Hindi world of the 1920s, too, as part of a vernacular reading and writing public, Dalit caste spokespersons started making, through their associations, journals, and tracts, forceful claims to rights. Writings by Achhutanand, Ramcharan

[35] Orsini 2002: 4.

[36] Rawat 2012: 136–44; Joshi 2003: 247.

[37] Gajarawala 2013: 35

[38] Nijhawan 2012: 3; Thapar-Bjorkert 2006.

[39] Mirroring their male counterparts, these women were almost exclusively Kayasth, Brahmin, Thakur, or Khatri: Orsini 2002: 245, 249; Nijhawan 2012: 10.

[40] Amardeep 2012; Brueck 2014: 23–42; Bharti 2011; Hunt 2014: 35–42; Naimishray 2014: 39–60; Narayan 2006, 2011; Rawat 2012.

[41] Satyanarayana and Tharu 2011, 2013.

Kuril, Swami Bodhanand, Chandrika Prasad Jigyasu, Ramnarayan Yadavendu, and many other male Dalit activists attacked social and religious stigmas, articulated a distinct Dalit identity, and demanded education, jobs, and increased political participation and representation.[42] Print journalism helped nurture a Hindi Dalit counter-public, the boundaries of which were "located squarely in the interpretive framework of caste."[43] This created a new sense of Dalit identity, characterized by novel ways and practices of representing Dalits. This new muscular flexing of vernacular print culture offers us different ways of approaching dissenting voices in colonial UP, even as it allows fresh challenges against colonial, nationalist, and Hindu accounts. This is notwithstanding the fact that Dalit writings were themselves largely driven by male agendas. The subject of Dalit politics, and its print-public culture, came to be imagined as principally male by the first decades of the twentieth century. However, with the meteoric rise of Dalit politics in UP, there has over the longue durée been a flowering of Dalit popular literature which is deeply invested in history, and in distinctive gendered representations: to provide just one instance at this point, it decodes the Indian Rebellion of 1857 through innovative expressions of gender.

Unlike most Dalit histories, which have either focused on upper-caste Hindi literary print-public culture, or the Dalit counter-print sphere, I work with both to show their proliferation around gendered castes. Also, many works tend to focus on polemical texts and systematic treatises on caste, where male radicals in particular outline arguments about the relationship between sexual and social reproduction. I, however, am invested in print and material culture studies, and representation–reception histories as a method. Alongside print, I work with visual materials as they were illustrative of, contributed to, and were themselves shaped by debates around caste and gender.[44] Embedded in a dense world, visuals of

---

[42] Jigyasu 1965 (1937); Mahasatveer 1930; Yadavendu 1942.

[43] Brueck 2014: 50.

[44] For example, visuals of Dalit women, ever-present in reformist magazines, especially *Chand*, provide illuminating windows to their representation and are open to divergent receptions and interpretations. Scholars have pointed to

*achhut*s in mainstream reformist magazines offered varied forms of subjectification as they simultaneously and ambivalently played on three tracks: of lamenting upper-caste behavior; of claiming a shared space between upper castes and Dalits; and sometimes inadvertently transgressing normative discourses on caste and gender.

Intimacy, the Everyday, and the Individual

Gendering Dalits also raises other questions located in intimacy, the everyday, and the individual. Studies on Dalit life testimonies and autobiographies stress that narratives of pain and suffering are often their cultural capital.[45] Others argue that it is not so much experiences of pain that undergird Dalit resistance as those of quotidian and routine caste violence, through which stigma is perpetuated in, on, and through Dalit bodies and becomes a constant source of humiliation. Violence also becomes the principal basis for the production and reproduction of Dalit female bodies.[46] Most works on Dalits have rightly recognized exploitation, violence, victimhood, stigma, pain, suffering, upward mobility, and assertiveness as motifs critical to Dalit studies. However, I fold caste and gender into histories of intimacy and the body.[47] Intimacy is experienced in love and pleasure, but also expressed through touch and clothing, relationships and representations, associations and exclusions. Located in politics and the everyday, intimacy is constantly in a flux, contestable, and rewritable, disrupting the boundaries between the individual and the community, the private and the public, the personal and the political. Ann Stoler remarks that "the notion of the 'intimate' is a descriptive

---

the richness of the visual in comprehending Indian colonial pasts, including of women and Dalits: Guha-Thakurta 2004; Pinney 2004; Ramaswamy 2011; Tartakov 2012.

[45] Ganguli 2009: 429–42; Hunt 2014: 176–208; Kumar 2010: 157–256; Pandey 2013: 162–93.

[46] Rao 2009: 216.

[47] In this I am motivated by a workshop organized by Anupama Rao and myself on "A Social History of Caste and Intimacy," December 9–10, 2011, NMML, New Delhi.

marker of the familiar and the essential *and* of relations grounded in sex."[48] Anthony Giddens observes how "the possibility of intimacy means the promise of democracy."[49] And according to Alex Lubin "intimate matters" are inextricably related to "civil rights activism in the public sphere."[50] Intimacy provides us with a new way to talk of caste, not only through identity categories, politics, and structural and institutional inequalities, but also as an idea made material through the physical body. It allows us to see the subtle manner in which caste functions as body history and body language, the politics of which permeates the most intimate spaces of our lives.[51] Gender, in any case, brings our attention to questions of intimacy and the body. Dalit women are made to inhabit a social place of extreme moral ambivalence, and their bodies are repeatedly brought into focus through questions of sex and sexual promiscuity. This work reflects on embodied representations of Dalit femininities and masculinities, of conversions and indentured labor through critical engagements with caste intimacies, addressing regulations of Dalit female (and male) bodies through language, images, and etiquette on the one hand, and through practices of control and discipline on the other.

I ponder on the adjacencies of gender, caste, and intimacy through the rhythms of daily life. I do not equate the history of Dalits in colonial UP solely with the Adi Hindu movement, prominent figures like Achhutanand, the writings of first-generation Dalit intellectuals, and the impact of Ambedkar. Nor do I focus on cataclysmic public events and the leading Hindi literati. Rather, I concentrate on the everyday and the anecdotal, both in terms of writings and events, in print, and in public and intimate spaces, to ascertain engaged perspectives on Dalit women and men. Peter Robb stresses the significance of discovering routine, transitory, and non-consequential histories by showing how "trivia" and the study of what "does not matter" matters.[52] This quotidian ordinariness often conceals deep

---

[48] Stoler 2002: 9.
[49] Giddens 1992: 188.
[50] Lubin 2005: xi.
[51] Chatterjee 1994: 194–7.
[52] Robb 2011: 210–11.

structures of inequality. I attempt to see how everyday life reproduces a hegemonic caste order as well as creates the possibilities for practices of dissent. Everyday life is a multi-accentual concept which "consists of transformed and transforming meanings of materiality"; a "social space" that "enables and constrains the actions and interactions of daily life." It exists "in a continuous process of making and remaking," "always unfinished, always ongoing, always in a state of becoming."[53] Methodologically, the focus on the everyday is critical from a gender perspective. Dalit women, while often not vital players in many of the public, political, and evident struggles of the period, were ubiquitous subalterns in the mundane world of work, home, and family, in daily interactions in the social, public, and ritual spheres, and in the figuring of sexualities and patriarchies.

Further, the overwhelming focus on the collective/community identities of Dalits creates difficulties in examining the gender of caste. In many of the autobiographies and testimonies penned by Dalit women, individual needs, desires, and resistances are often subsumed within the rubric of community struggles. Dalit conversions have also been largely examined as mass movements and group strategies. In the wider caste politics, this has proved significant as collective Dalit claims have often taken precedence over gender identities and individual protests. Dalit women too have often identified more with community and family than gender. It is important, however, to move beyond this routine approach. While examining the collective and mass representation of Dalits I also try to mark the individual Dalit woman. I bring Dalit women's individual desires to my readings of conversions, and single out Dalit women's migration as indentured labor in order to reshape the ways in which we usually look at the gender of caste. These personal and intimate histories not only reveal how Dalit women stood at times as individual subjects—following distinct trajectories, embodying personal needs and desires—but also how they implicitly questioned both caste hierarchies and Dalit patriarchies through accounts of intensely material realities. Such individual acts heightened anxieties among caste ideologues, nationalists, and Dalit men, often provoking everyday violence framed

[53] Storey 2014: 135–6.

around the bodies of Dalit women. Through this vindication of Dalit woman as an individual in her own right, I connect caste, gender, and intimacy with sexuality and everyday violence.

The structure of the book is episodic rather than chronological. It discusses discrete events and narratives, different genres, moments, and moves, the in-between, to show mutabilities in the constructions of Dalit women. Nonetheless, my work tends to concentrate on the first half of the twentieth century, this being the period of efflorescence of Hindi print cultures. Further, the inter-war period was a moment not merely of imperial reform and redirection, but also of a creative redefinition of a rights discourse, enabling the imagination of political utopias. It was a time when sexual, gender, and caste differences evolved into their modern shapes, with emergent notions of reform, nationalism, and Dalit activism.

Caste and Gender in the Socio-Political Economy of UP

The contentious socio-political economy of UP at the turn to the twentieth century left its imprints on the gendered representation of Dalits and provides the context for this book. A growing body of scholarship has carefully and relentlessly interrogated caste, highlighting the distinct yet overlapping ways in which configurations of caste changed, gained legitimacy, and were challenged in colonial India. Urban morphology, municipal laws, orientalizing perceptions, ethnographic accounts, missionary activities, the opening of new educational institutions, uniform judicial systems, different employment opportunities, and the decennial census initiated by the British, while "secularizing" caste, also helped strengthen the politicization of Hindu religion.[54] Caste became a protean category for colonial capitalism, social reform, and Hindu nationalism.

After 1857 there was a rapid expansion in UP of new and improved means of organization and communication, market production, law

[54] Banerjee-Dube 2010: xv–lxiv; Cohn 1987: 224–54; Inden 1990: 56–66; Dirks 1987, 2001: 3–18; Pinch 1996: 17–20; Sarkar 1997: 358–90; Bayly 1999: 1–96, 144–86.

courts, education, libraries, the press, and print, all coinciding with the flourishing of a vital upper-caste Hindu mercantile culture and the emergence of a dynamic new middle class in towns.[55] New job openings and professions—such as law, teaching, and journalism— provided new arenas for upward mobility which benefited a section of the upper and intermediate castes. By the end of the nineteenth century a new group of landholders appeared in the region.[56] These substantial gains, borne along by Western influences on lifestyles and corresponding to judgements of propriety, civilization, and modern-ization, gave the upwardly mobile a larger stake in the defence of hierarchies; and they thus evolved new ways of strengthening their claims over Dalit bodies, their labor, and sexuality. The construction of Dalits as dim-witted yet burly figures capable of menial drudgery was carefully fabricated by colonizers and the upper castes alike.

Alongside, there were growing economic insecurities for some, as the colonial onslaught in UP posed a serious challenge to many of the conventional occupations and dislocated existing relations. Traditional sources of patronage were considerably reduced and adversity overtook a section of the population.[57] The problems were compounded by a general crisis of employment for the educated.[58] A class of clerks, with low salaries and low status, emerged. Bemoaning the supposed loss of a golden age, the upper castes painted a bleak mental landscape of modern times as a period of social degradation. The trope of Kaliyug signified a loss of manliness, assertive lower castes, and disorderly women.[59] The breaking down of taboos and "caste-specific" behavior and dispositions was lamented.[60] Brahmins, abandoning their vocation of rituals and prayers, were seen as falling prey to indolence; Kshatriyas, instead of being valorous and displaying fortitude, had it was believed become sexually debased and enervated; and Shudras, having abandoned their obligation of servitude, were

[55] Bayly 1983: 180–1, 386–93, 427–30; 1996: 338.

[56] Cohn 1987: 384.

[57] Kumar 2000; Carroll 1977.

[58] *Report of the Unemployment Committee UP 1935*: 19–20, 33–7, 261–73, 391–4.

[59] Sarkar 1997: 186–215.

[60] Editorial, "*Hindu Samaj aur Jatibhed*" (Hindu Society and Caste Differences), *Chand,* May 1932: 5 (2–7).

imperiously proclaiming their rights.[61] Grieving over the status of Brahmins, a poem in a Brahmin journal reads:

> Many [Brahmins] are servants of prostitutes, and roam about beating
> small drums.
> Our daughters-in-law have become beggars at pilgrimages, and many
> [Brahmins] eat in Shudra homes!![62]
>
> [*bahut kanchnin ke chakar hain, table firat bajate.*
> *bani bahu tirthan firat bhikhari, bahut shudra ghar khate!!*]

Modern developments, such as the railways, made it difficult to maintain caste separations and stringent food taboos.[63] This offended orthodox Hindus.[64] The customary demarcation of gendered spaces was being rendered impossible with the spread of education among women, new ideals of the companionate marriage and monogamy,[65] and women's increasing participation in the national movement and the print-public sphere.[66] These changes increased patriarchal and caste insecurities: conservative caste-Hindu men felt their control over the ranking of caste and gender was waning, so there was a renewed emphasis on maintaining and strengthening social order, caste status, and domination. Caste distinctions came to be marked through women's bodies. Caste and gender inequalities reinforced each other, and women emerged as a powerful means for Brahmanical patriarchal attempts to consolidate social pyramids and express caste exclusivities.[67] Simultaneously, caste associations in UP proliferated, particularly after the 1901 census when a decision was made to

[61] "*Samaj Sudhar*" (Social Service), *Sudha*, April 1929: 318. A regular column by this name was carried in *Sudha*.

[62] Prasad 1911.

[63] Blunt 1931: 332.

[64] *Bharat Jiwan*, December 5, 1898, *NNR*, December 13, 1898: 653; *Bharat Jiwan*, June 17, 1907, *NNR*, June 22, 1907: 751; *Bharat Jiwan*, January 6, 1902, *NNR*, January 11, 1902: 28. Demands for separate carriages and refreshment rooms for high-caste Hindus were raised: *Agra Akhbar*, December 20, 1876, *NNR*, December 23, 1876: 747; *Bharat Jiwan*, June 2, 1902; *NNR*, June 7, 1902: 378.

[65] *Census, 1911, UP*: 31.

[66] Nijhawan 2012; Orsini 2002: 243–308; Thapar-Bjorkert 2006.

[67] Gupta 1907: 128–39. For details, Chapter 1.

rank castes according to "social precedence." Even relatively better-off castes and *jati*s like Kayasths, Khatris, Agarwals, and Marwaris started claiming Kshatriya status, wanting a greater share in public appointments and political representation.[68] Intermediate castes such as Ahirs and Yadavs too launched their caste associations and journals.[69] Print helped foster caste interests: various caste associations published genealogical caste tracts and started their own journals. There were transformations in relationships between castes, and language and customs relating to women became critical to mark one's caste status, counter the claims of other castes, and denigrate low-caste practices.[70]

The vibrant public sphere of UP also grew in response to the meteoric growth of a politics of Hinduization and caste reform that reinforced certain tenets of Hindu praxis while challenging others. Simultaneously, anxieties over Muslim and Dalit figures strengthened debates about caste and its gendering. The cow-protection movement in UP, between 1880 and 1920,[71] sharpened the vilification of Chamars (and Muslims) as cattle killers.[72] Alongside, the activities of the Hindu Mahasabha and the Arya Samaj expanded considerably.[73] Facing Western criticism of Hinduism as severely oppressive towards women and untouchables, movements like the Arya Samaj, while legitimizing caste principles, also began to formulate limited critiques of caste rigidities, deploying a vocabulary of sympathy.[74] There was a shift—from seeing the Dalit woman as herself intolerable, to seeing that her dominant image had become intolerable—resulting in a transformation from perceptions of her as lascivious and stigmatized to someone vulnerable and victimized, even if the change involved a desexualization of the Dalit female body. Simultaneously, reformers

[68] Harishchandra 1918; Deshraj 1934; Das 1914; Bais 1931; Singh and Singh 1936. For details, Ahmad 1971: 172–3; Carroll 1977, 1978.

[69] *Census, 1931, UP*: 544–52; Varma 1907; Yadav 1914; Yadav 1927; Varma 1916, 1939; Agnihotri 1905; Lal 1919. Journals like *Kalwar Kesari*, *Kurmi-Kshatriya Diwakar*, and *Yadavesh* were published.

[70] Varma 1904; Sharma 1928. For details, Gupta 2001: 24–6.

[71] Pinch 1996: 119–21; Freitag 1989: 148–74.

[72] Rawat 2012: 16–17, 47–8.

[73] Freitag 1989; Jones 1989; Jordens 1978, 1981.

[74] Bayly 1999.

attempted to "improve" the popular practices of the lower castes, especially those relating to women, ostensibly to cleanse them of perceived evils and lax moral standards.[75] Colonial delineations of Dalit gender norms often worked in conjunction with such formulations, creating images of an antagonistic "other"—for example, by labeling castes like Pasis as criminal tribes in UP. Conversely, the use of expressions of compassion and pity implicitly established claims for ostensible champions of caste equality.

By the 1920s the Arya Samaj, with the sharpening of sectarian identities, grew adamant and vociferous, claiming that untouchables were a regular part of Hinduism.[76] They could be redeemed if they renounced their depraved lifestyles and reclaimed to the righteous paths of Hinduism through *shuddhi*, the movement which flowered in UP in the 1920s.[77] In constructions of Dalits, the rubric of purity–pollution was now overtaken by a politics of numbers, violence, and claims to an illusionary cohesive Hindu identity whereby the "other" came to be identified with Muslims, this in turn helping to foster unity between "progressive" Hindu reformists and "conservative" neo-traditionalists. By a grotesque twist Muslims were even blamed for untouchability, one reformer contending that there had been no untouchability before the Muslims arrived in India, and after which all cow killers had come to be branded as untouchables.[78] Another argued that "There was no caste system in the Vedic period . . . With the coming of the Muslims, untouchability got a boost. Since it was argued that Muslim were untouchables [*mlecch*], those who touched them also became untouchables."[79] Anxieties around Dalit conversions increased among reformers, forcing them to support inter-caste marriages, at least rhetorically. However, daily caste tensions

[75] It is not insignificant that many of the leading members of the Arya Samaj and orthodox Hindu bodies were also active members of various caste associations in UP, which helped to maintain the hierarchical dominance of the upper castes.

[76] Mendelsohn and Vicziany 1998: 27–8.

[77] Gupta 2001: 222–32.

[78] "*Hindu Samaj ka Punarnirman*" (Reconstruction of Hindu Society), *Chand*, January 1928.

[79] Gaurishankar Singh Chandail, "*Asprishyata ki Kahani*" (The Story of Untouchability), *Chand*, January 1934: 329 (321–30).

could not be wished away, and in fact took on new lineaments. There was little to show that the rules of touch were falling into desuetude, except insofar as they had become incompatible with the routines of everyday life. For example, though supposedly no questions were asked at railway stations by porters, the men who supplied drinking water to passengers were still Brahmins. Postmen refused to deliver letters to untouchables.[80]

The relationship between Dalits and Hindu reformers was fraught in UP. The Arya Samaj and the Hindu Mahasabha were wary of the Adi Hindu movement, which from the 1920s was gaining strength among the Dalits of UP. In a resolution unanimously passed by the 11th session of the Hindu Mahasabha in April 1928, it was stated: "The Hindu Mahasabha emphatically protests against the so-called Adi Hindu movement started by some self-seeking persons with a view to create division between the Hindu community and warns the so-called untouchable brethren against the dangers of falling a victim to this harmful propaganda and calls upon them to remain faithful to the well wishers of their ancestral Hindu faith."[81] While some Dalits were initially attracted to the Arya Samaj, they soon realized its limitations and became critical of such reformist movements from above. A pamphlet titled "Dalit Brothers Protect Yourself from Danger" (*Dalit Bhaiyon Khatre se Bacho*) exhorted Jatavs, Chamars, Khatiks, Dhobis, and Mehtars to beware of the superficial reforms being launched in their name and poignantly asked the upper castes if they had done the following:

> (1) Removed separated taps from *pyaus* (2) Made any effort to open occupations like putting stalls of milk, curd or betel and various other shops (3) Is there any example of the twice-born-caste girl breaking caste taboos and marrying a Dalit boy (4) Can any Dalit claim himself to be a Dalit and eat food at a *dhaba* (5) Can anyone rent a house in the name of a Dalit (6) Can any Dalit have his own *pyaus* and give water to others (7) Can any one of our caste become an office bearer of upper-caste reformist organizations? None of this had been achieved.[82]

[80] L/PJ/9/108, OIOC.

[81] "Hindu Mahasabha Resolutions on Removal of Untouchability," Subject File 18/1931, Moonje Papers, NMML.

[82] Subject File 37/I/1934, Moonje Papers, NMML.

Dalits constituted around 22 per cent of the total population of UP, with Chamars being the largest, followed by Pasis.[83] They were dispersed in both rural and urban areas and lived in separate ghettos.[84] A substantial portion of Dalits, particularly Chamars, were agricultural peasants and agrarian laborers.[85] Many continued to perform *begar* for the *zamindar*s, which became increasingly common between the 1870s and 1920s. Alongside, Dalits were confronted with economic dislocation caused by growing land hunger, extreme poverty, agrarian depression, rural indebtedness, evictions, the impoverishment of ancestral holdings, and the decline of cottage industries.[86] Many found their means of livelihood in jeopardy.[87] The substantial increase in the population of UP, especially from the early twentieth century, multiplied pressures on jobs and employment.[88] However, many Dalits continued to live in villages, with some acquiring land. A few became active in the Kisan Sabha movement of Awadh in 1919–22. A considerable number of Dalit men saw urban areas as better pastures and migrated to the towns. Migration often disturbed the domestic balance of power, and Dalit women became subject to new patriarchal negotiations.[89] However, some Dalit women posed as single women to work as indentured laborers and escape the oppression from within.

Increasing migration provided some impetus to several somewhat alleviating factors: the weakening of hereditary employment, the loosening of traditional caste ties, the gaining of urban employment,

[83] Singh 1947; *Census, 1931, UP*: 535; In certain regions, Chamars outnumbered Brahmins, for example in Meerut, where there were 15.6 per cent Chamars and 10.08 per cent Brahmins: Kitts 1885: 68.

[84] "Provisional and Confidential Note: Depressed Classes in UP," Mss Eur F77/44, OIOC.

[85] Singh 1947; Rawat 2012: 54–84; *Royal Commission on Agriculture*: 390–1, 472.

[86] *Royal Commission on Labour*: 138–9; *Census, 1931, UP*: 396, 404; *Report of the Unemployment Committee UP 1935*: 264; Whitcombe 1972; Siddiqi 1973.

[87] Shilberrad 1898: 45.

[88] *Report of the Unemployment Committee UP 1935*: 24–6; *Census, 1931, UP*: 24.

[89] Parmar 2011: 71–104.

small extensions of leisure time, the expansion of petty trade, the acquisition of modern education, and the forging of new alliances and peer solidarities. In some measure, these allowed Dalits partial escape from day-to-day exploitation by the upper castes.[90] Maren Bellwinkel-Schempp describes the late nineteenth century as "golden days" for Kanpur's Dalits. The development of Kanpur as a burgeoning industrial town after 1857 opened up opportunities: Dalits were needed as coolies, laborers, and mechanics to construct and later to work in the factories.[91] From all over UP, Chamars migrated to Kanpur—the Kuril from the nearby districts, the Ahirvar from Bundelkhand, and the Dhusiya and the Jaisvara from eastern UP.[92] There was considerable industrial expansion in the urban economy of UP in the first half of the twentieth century. Between 1922 and 1927 the number of regulated factories in the region rose from 255 to 354, an increase of 39 per cent, and factory workers increased from 72,545 to 88,319, an increase of 22 per cent.[93] More new jobs were created, with Dalits being appointed in railways, mines, and factories, as manual servants of British families, as peons in offices, and as municipal sweepers and scavengers.[94] Though urban spaces too were segregated along caste lines and Dalits largely continued being relegated to squalid neighborhoods, confined to the worst jobs, and ghettoized into hereditary occupations,[95] they began to perceive even these arduous and inferior urban paid jobs as somewhat empowering. Many now regarded themselves as government employees, not as the servants of high-caste individuals, and this gave them a degree of self-esteem.[96] Sweepers, for example, felt more secure and preferred municipal jobs to which no traditional stigma was attached. Limited forms of capitalism opened out some opportunities for some members of castes—such as the Doms, Telis, and Kalwars—to acquire wealth in

[90] *Royal Commission on Labour*: 138–43; Siddiqi 1973; Whitcombe 1972.

[91] Bellwinkel-Schempp 2006: 23. Also Joshi 2003: 79–81.

[92] Bellwinkel-Schempp 2007: 2177.

[93] *Royal Commission on Labour*: 133.

[94] Gooptu 2001: 145; *Report of the Unemployment Committee UP 1935*: 137–64.

[95] Gooptu 2001: 146.

[96] Ibid.; Sarkar 2013.

trades such as liquor, oilseeds, and metals.[97] Chamars, significant in
the economic hierarchy of UP, diversified into various jobs; some took
to the profitable trades of shoemaking and saddlery, others found new
opportunities in large tanneries, especially around Kanpur, where they
earned relatively high wages.[98] In Agra some families of the Chamar
caste came to be accepted as creditworthy merchants.[99] Many Dalits
renewed their efforts to enrol in the British army, claiming warrior
origins for their castes. The Shilpkars of Kumaon were particularly
successful in these endeavors, especially during World War II. Dalit
women also seem to have found job opportunities diversifying. In
1921, 735 women per 1000 men among the Bhangis (the largest
number being female scavengers) and 707 women per 1000 men
among the Pasis were reported as part of the workforce.[100] In 1931
the percentage of women in the total population of urban earners and
working dependents was 21.8 in Allahabad, 9.2 in Kanpur, 17.7 in
Banaras, and 8.2 in Lucknow.[101] It was also a time when Chamar midwives began demanding more money for their work.

In the religious sphere, too, there came mixed responses from Dalits
in colonial UP. A flowering of religious and social movements grew
visible among them, many of these tracing their genealogies to a pre-
Aryan period. Dalits attacked caste inequalities and untouchability
through an assertion of *bhakti* devotionalism, the rejection of Vedic
Hinduism, and the construction of a pre-Aryan identity for Dalits as
the original inhabitants—the Adi Hindus—of India.[102] They evolved
a language of egalitarian *bhakti* by embracing anticaste sects such as
the Kabirpanthis, the Shivnarayanis, and the Raidasis.[103] At times they
even incorporated themselves into *bhakti* sects hitherto dominated by

[97] Mencher 1974.

[98] Walton 1903: 25–8; Blunt 1931: 237; Briggs 1920: 226–9; *Cawnpore:
A Gazetteer*: 104, 117; Joshi 2003: 79–81.

[99] Bayly 1983: 340, 445.

[100] *Census, 1921, UP*: 181–2; Dayashankar Dube, "*Kuch Achhut Jatiyon
ki Dasha*" (The Condition of Some Untouchable Castes), *Chand*, May 1927:
18, 20 (16–24).

[101] *Census, 1931, UP, Part II*: 382.

[102] Gooptu 2001: 144.

[103] Ibid.: 145–52; Lorenzen 1995:1–32; Schomer and McLeod 1987; Lele
1981; Kshirsagar 1994: 31–5; Wakankar 2010.

the upper castes, thereby gaining some exemption from upper-caste exploitation, as was the case with the Shivnarayanis in eastern UP. Bihari Lal, a rich Khatik building contractor, constructed a beautiful Shivnarayan temple in Kanpur in 1870.[104] Many Chamars became devotees of Ramanand and of the Dalit saint Ravidas, also known as Raidas. Some became followers of the Kabirpanth movement, or of the Nath Yogis and the Nath Panthis who revered, respectively, Gorakhnath and Namdev. Most important, in the 1930s the Adi Hindu movement, led by Achhutanand, acquired a huge Dalit following.[105] History became a major weapon in the hands of these Adi Hindu Dalits, who claimed that not only were they the original inhabitants of India who thus had prior rights over its land and territory, but also that there had been a Adi Hindu monarchy without caste which was destroyed by Brahmanical Hinduism. Dalits were in short giving voice to myriad conceptions of their religious identity by claiming to be Raidasis, Shivnarayanis, Kabirpanthis, and Adi Hindus, all challenging Brahmanical notions in diverse ways. Conversion to Christianity and Islam became other ways to escape Brahmanical hierarchies, and for Dalit women to express intimate desires. Such religious contention served to reclaim old spaces while simultaneously laying claim to new ones.

Colonial rule was seen by Dalits as initiating certain democratizing processes.[106] The efforts of government functionaries, missionaries, the Arya Samaj, and Dalits paved the way for a partial educational opening up for Dalits in UP,[107] leading to the emergence of the first generation of Dalit intellectuals, who increasingly saw education, knowledge, and language as central to their capacity for further assertion. Dalits also now questioned upper-caste religious and symbolic monopolies in the intimate sphere by arguing, for example, their right to enter temples, draw water from any and every well, sport

[104] Bellwinkel-Schempp 2006: 23; many temples were refurbished by Dalits in the urban areas of UP at this time: Gooptu 2001: 149–50.

[105] Rawat 2012: 144–50, 155–74; Gooptu 2001: 152–84; Khare 1984: 83–5.

[106] Jaffrelot 2004.

[107] *Census, 1901, NWP*: 170–5; *Census, 1911, UP*: 143–8, 255; *Census, 1921, UP*: 126–7; *Census, 1931, UP*: 478–507.

footwear, carry umbrellas, and wear gold in the presence of persons of high ritual status. Their struggles often took the form of associational politics, with new alliances and organizations being made possible by the increase in opportunities and means, rise in wealth, new ideas, the print media, and postal communication. Decennial colonial census operations were seen as positive opportunities for upward mobility. Petitions were submitted to the government by Dalit castes in UP asking for a higher ritual ranking. Western claims and ethnographic studies were constantly cited or refuted as part of the self-assertion. With the strengthening of the Adi Hindu movement, their presence grew politically. They tried to bargain with the colonial state, not only for educational and professional concessions but also for increased representation in electoral processes. In these efforts they often found the state a better ally than the Congress, which was dominated by caste-Hindus. These developments made a section of Dalits perceive colonial rule as a period of change and openness, offering them some limited sense of liberation and security.[108] There was also a social restructuring of the caste-specific functioning of patriarchies, as altered practices in relation to women became an important means for the upward mobility of Dalits. The entanglements of Dalits with modernity were layered: they often used its rubric to argue for more rights, greater dignity, diverse means of livelihood, less unethical portrayals of the body, *and* the reconstitution of patriarchies.

While revealing this broad social context this book attempts to show in the ensuing chapters how the gendered representations of Dalits by colonizers, reformers, nationalists, and Dalits themselves constituted, were reflective of, and contested dominant motifs and embodiments. I will also try to show how distinctive yet sometimes aligned positions on caste gendering by various players upset archival predictability, and make room for a more robust history of the gender of caste.

[108] Gooptu 2001.

1

Dirty "Other" Vamp
(Mis)Representing Dalit Women

This and the next two chapters collate contradictory representations of Dalit women as vamps, victims, and *viranganas* in the Hindi print-public sphere. Interweaving textual-literary expressions and visual images, they unpack the intricate narratives and lexicons that came to stand for Dalit women. The foundational role of semantic and representational presuppositions around Dalit women's bodies provides the key to understanding the complexities of caste, gender, and sexuality in North India. Through words, sentences, topics, and illustrations each chapter asks how and why certain images of Dalit women have been epistemically privileged in different contexts and archives. Embodying and unmaking prejudices, representations of Dalit women became potent symbols and critical grounds for identity formation as well as social positioning for upper castes, reformers, and Dalits.

Among the literary genres of the period was one comprising didactic literature and domestic manuals in Hindi, these principally addressing middle-class, high-caste Hindu women. Such advice books were aimed at creating and strengthening insidious segregations and asymmetrical relations between women and men, with women representing the heart and emotion and men the brain and intellect. Masculine spaces endorsed socially valued knowledge of theology, law, and medicine, while the feminine cosmos contained devalued varieties of learning such as childcare, cooking, and cleaning.[1] An

---

[1] Hancock 2001; Walsh 2004; Gupta 2001: 123–61; Stark 2007: 413–20.

exploration of this genre through a Dalit-feminist lens, however, puts a question mark on binaries such as male versus female, and suggests the simultaneous active management of gender, caste, and class power. Managing the domestic was crucial to caste. The codes of behavior suggested in domestic manuals simultaneously implied control over women by men and over outcastes by the higher castes. The domestic performances of the internalized "other" are evident in representations of gendered caste bodies in these writings.[2]

While Dalit women never appeared as actors in didactic manuals, the genre constructed them in particular ways and circulated ideas about them, providing a perspective on (mis)representations that came to signify Dalit women as a body (in both senses of the term). This location of Dalit women's barely legible images, filled with silences regarding the inferiorized, renders the often hidden operations of gender and caste that are nonetheless present as defining forces in the organization of hierarchies. The unvoiced, unseen Dalit woman was critical to upper-caste constructions. She was referred to here not as a woman but identified with her caste and stigmatized occupation: for instance, *chamarin, dhobin, bhangan, dai, malin, nain,* and *kaharin.* She was not just a footnote, but a constitutive footnote, perceived in binary opposition to the upper-caste woman. Caste and gender were not only constitutive of the social, caste was in fact central to how gender was reproduced. In distinct ways this literature and the material culture around it were involved with a gendered casteist discourse committed to institutionalizing stable categories comprising *pativratas* and *kutnis.* Such stereotypes were apparent in caste manuals, composed mostly by spokesmen of the high and intermediate castes, in which the figure of the woman became important to underscore caste distinctions. Descriptions of the Chamar midwife in writings of the period strengthened the typecasting of Dalit women as vamps.

[2] The impetus for this chapter also comes from writings by African-American feminists who have shown how the black female body was seen as embodying savagery, irrationality, ugliness, inferiority, and "excessive" sexuality, while the white body was marked by the obverse, i.e. civility, rationality, beauty, and superiority: Wallace-Sanders 2004; Morrison 1992; hooks 1992; Jordan 1968; Hunter 2005; Gilman 1985; Sharpley-Whiting 1999; Roberts 1994; Collins 2004.

Taken together, these writings are meaningful for a historian not because they are about "facts"; rather they are evidence of dominant discourses and beliefs that encoded norms relating to caste and gender. An examination of the way Dalit women were constructed here tells us much about the describers and the imaginers. We know as much about the subject as the object.[3] Foucault argues that all representations are by their very nature insidious instruments of surveillance and oppression—both tools and effects of power. While this view over-looks how representation can also provide contingent modes of resistance, the figuring of the Dalit woman, steeped in cliché in a large part of this literature, seems to show the correctness of Foucault's view. Relying largely on writings by men, I interrogate invasive readings of gendered caste bodies and show how Dalit women were decoded and recoded into a "comfortable" system of representation. Carlo Ginzburg tells us that any analysis of representation cannot overlook the principle of reality.[4] Structures of gender-caste oppression, and the material conditions of Dalit women in colonial India, impinged on identity formation and representation—as partially reflected in these genres.

Taken together, these representations also signify continuities in images of Dalit women from the past, but taking new shape at this time, especially because of the flourishing of mass print culture. Ancient texts and epics, be they the *Manusmriti*, the *Ramayan*, or the *Mahabharat*, often depicted Dalit and Dravidian women as vulgar, treacherous, dangerous, polluted, and evil "others." The figure of Surpanakha (literally "sharp, long nails") in the *Ramayan* was referred to as that of a "savage," embodying all that was ugly and fearful. Researchers have read the mutilation of Surpanakha's body at the hands of Lakshman as punishment by an Aryan male to a Dravidian woman. In the *Mahabharat*, Hidimbi, a low-caste woman, epitomizes female lustfulness. The *Manusmriti* dehumanizes the Dalit woman as the "fierce, untouchable woman," as one permanently and constantly polluted.[5] The repetitive transmission of negative and false images

[3] Morrison 1992.
[4] Ginzburg 1999: 17.
[5] Bharati 1995; Doniger 1991; Erndl 1991: 67–87; Singh 2004: 22–71.

of Dalit women had its roots in ancient cultural traditions.[6] In some writings of colonial North India such images returned, taking on new forms and meanings.

Didactic Literature: The Reification of Caste–Gender Difference

It has been shown that during colonialism the real battle for ideal upper-caste womanhood was waged in the home. The domestic domain was the inner core of a national, caste-Hindu order and the woman was perceived as the harbinger of its spiritual essence.[7] Simultaneously, it has been claimed that colonial laws and social reforms centering on women and marriage reimprisoned women into new patriarchies and renewed domestic discipline.[8] While these perspectives marginalize women who creatively appropriated reforms and nationalism to their advantage, didactic and caste manuals did become an important means to refurbish indigenous patriarchies and upper-caste norms.

In colonial UP the print explosion and the emerging vernacular press helped produce a large amount of didactic Hindi books, mainly from the late nineteenth century. Written overwhelmingly by the Hindu middle-class male literati of the upper and intermediate castes, they were often conformist in orientation and became part of the cultural resources that helped fashion female identities and notions of respectable domesticity.[9] These edifying tracts facilitated the public dissemination and consumption of normative images and prescriptions of behavior. In such guides to etiquette, constructions of sexuality, educational reform, thrift, childcare, and household management became arenas of grave social concern, scientific investigation, and reformist endeavor. Claiming to deal with the conditions and problems of principally middle-class, high-caste Hindu housewives,

[6] Chakravarti 1989, 2004.
[7] Chatterjee 1994: 120–1.
[8] Sangari and Vaid 1989; McClintock 1995: 1–4; Stoler 1995.
[9] Gupta 2001: 123–76. The production of such manuals has been linked the world over with the explosion of print and middle-class women have particularly been their focus: Langland 1995.

they contained within them precise and detailed instructions which grew into symbols, imposing definitions upon what existed and what ought to. In the process they reflected discursive practices, producing and strengthening constructions of the woman as detached from productive resources and activities. Scores of primers spread a masculinist image of the ideal woman as one lacking all independence and economic power, and thus wholly subservient in a predominantly male world. Middle-class, upper-caste "good" women were asked to be *pativratas*, competent largely as household workers distanced from earning and financial health.[10] Their energies were to be garnered towards moral upliftment and the advancement of souls within the home.[11] These primers taught women how they ought to behave, how to think, how to feel and act. Even tracts written with some sensitivity to gender had these ideals marked out.

The crafting of an ideal upper-caste woman in these manuals, validating ideas of "self" and "other," required a repeated denigration of the perceived practices of low-caste women. Such mediated representations helped consolidate caste barriers, police caste borders, contribute to a rhetoric that "naturalized" gender–caste differences, and perpetuate the status quo. As Terry Eagleton puts it: "A dominant power may legitimate itself by promoting beliefs and values congenial to it; naturalizing and universalizing such beliefs so as to render them self-evident and apparently inevitable; denigrating ideas which might challenge it."[12]

The caste identities of readers and writers of this literature helped determine and sharpen their differences from women of the lower castes in terms of social status, lifestyle, dress and deportment, and general behavior. Prejudice, as argued, often parades as difference, with difference becoming a mark of the subordinated and the marginalized.[13] Such representations attempted to disseminate a collective

[10] There were scores of books of this kind, for example: Poddar 1929: 24–5; Vajpeyi 1934; "Pagal" 1921; Goyandka 1937; Garg 1930; Girdavar 1922; Joshi 1918; Kannomal 1923; "Mani" 1935.

[11] Vidyavati Seth, *"Prachin aur Navin Bharat ki Mahilaen"* (Women of Ancient and Modern India), *Madhuri,* October 1922: 339–42; *Swarajya,* March 21, 1908, *NNR,* March 28, 1908: 306.

[12] Eagleton 1992: 5.

[13] Pandey 2013: 34–60.

worldview, a hierarchical construction of womanhood. Though it was usually upper-caste male writers who constructed Dalit women as deviants from prescribed norms, upper-caste women too often helped map the terrain of Dalit women's (mis)representations.[14] These manuals directed high-caste women to adequately clothe their bodies against the male gaze, to speak with a becoming softness, and never to quarrel or gossip. These were precisely the traits that identified the Dalit woman. The image of the morally virtuous upper-caste woman was conjugated against negative portrayals of the Dalit woman, who was seen as loud, raucous, unfeminine, uncultured, and shameless.[15] One such tract, *Kanyaon ki Pothi ya Kanya Subodhini*, meant for girls and women, while retailing appropriate behavior to them, distinguished between high and low caste by emphasizing that upper-caste women refrained from battling and abusing each other (giving "*galis*"), these being specified as the traits of low-caste women.[16] Gendered casteist stereotypes were reinforced via literary tropes, as exemplified in a regional saying:

> Is the washerwoman any less ferocious than the oil-miller's wife? She has a pestle, the other a washing bat.[17]

> [*telin se kya dhobin ghaat? iske musal uske laat.*]

The use of an "obscene" vocabulary spoken at a piercing pitch was the sign of low-caste women, their inferiority being manifest as anger during fights with other women. Episodes of these were seen as frequent and violent occurrences within Dalit communities generally. The presence of Dalit women helped in the creation of binaries, in the portrayal of polar opposites, and in improving the social image of upper-caste women. Caste difference was marked in profound ways through such constructions of gender difference. Reformist rhetoric too sometimes succumbed to such stereotypes. Purportedly sympathetic, an article on the Mallah *jati* had this to say about its

[14] Some of the domestic manuals penned by upper-caste women reflected similar biases: for example, Devi 1919; Devi 1910, 1925; Devi 1948; Hukmadevi 1932.
[15] Chatterjee 1994: 127.
[16] Gaur 1927: 19.
[17] Gautum 2007b: 103.

women: "Mallah women are champions when it comes to hurling abuse, fighting, and screaming. Over every small issue they remind you of [women of the] past seven generations. No one has succeeded in controlling their tongues."[18] Colonial language could bristle with descriptions of Dalit women as loud, coarse, and vulgar. Narrating a fight between two Chamar women, one report stated:

> The lung capacity of low-class village women and their staying power, when they are once provoked, pass belief. They usually possess harsh, rasping voices. They begin shouting abuse, at once, at what seems, but is not, the top of their power. This immediately provokes a similar outburst from their opponent and is followed by a rapidly rising crescendo, until it seems that one of them must, before long, break a blood vessel. Their fluency is extraordinary. They are never at a loss for a word. Nothing will stop them and they seldom pause to take breath.[19]

Didactic literature fortified such metaphors. Through rhymes and anecdotes, a tract labeled low-caste women as cheater (*thagini*), greedy (*chatori*), deceitful (*kapati*), uncultured (*phuhar*), and home breaker (*kutni*).[20] A tract had its last—and stated to be its most significant—chapter titled "Warning from Dangers" (*Jokhimon se Chetavni*).[21] Addressing itself to middle-class, high-caste girls and women, it stated:

> In households, *kutnis* come and go. We have to engage daily with women like the *malin, nain, kaharin, chamarin, dhobin, pisanharin, maniharin,* and *dai*. All these women also indulge in forms of pimping. They provoke quarrels in peaceful homes. They roam around criticizing others. They tell tales about the depraved conduct of husbands and corrupt the minds of brides. They cause fights between husband and wife. When they feel a particular bride is not of sound character, they make her fight with others in the house and sometimes even make her run away with them . . . These *kutnis* work hand in glove with other wicked characters. They take money from them to trick women of decent homes. And they do it so cunningly that it is impossible to detect them. Dear daughter, be very careful of

[18] Mahendra "Raja," "*Bharat ki Mallah Jati*" (Mallah Caste of India), *Vishal Bharat*, August 1952: 106.

[19] Walsh 1929: 98–9.

[20] Bankelal 1909.

[21] Gaur 1927: 220–8.

these women. They are notorious for their false and unwholesome tales. You must clearly tell them you have no time for their dirty stories. Only the *Ramayan* and *Mahabharat* are worth listening to.[22]

Mediating between street and home, and bridging the borders of public and private, many outcaste women entered the inner recesses of upper-caste homes, especially occupationally, as *mehtaranis* and *dais*. Befriending them was perceived as dangerous, revealing upper-caste anxieties. One tract argued that Dalit women, particularly the *dai* and the *bhangan*, were largely responsible for spoiling upper-caste women; it was because of them that jealousy (*irsha*), quarrels (*dvesh*), and tension (*kalah*) prevailed in the family.[23] Upper-caste women were warned of the need for constant vigilance against these perceived adulterous (*vyabhicharini*), degenerate (*patit*), and perilous women.[24] Upper-caste neighborhoods needed to be cleansed of such evil women for they caused grave harm to character.[25] Another tract warned upper-caste women: "Be most cautious of the dangers lurking in interactions with *nain, maniharin, chamarin* and *kaharin*. They are the ones who are mainly responsible for a large number of misdeeds and harm done in the past and being done at present . . . If you interact with and listen to them, the demon will enter your pure hearts."[26]

A significant tract, *Stri Shiksha*, written by an Arya Samajist and later proscribed, attempted to remap gender boundaries in the 1920s by giving minute instructions to upper-caste Hindu women, asking them to keep away from Muslim men, and from symbols, customs, and cultures perceived as "Muslim."[27] While paralleling arguments for a putative Hindu community, it sought to extend it to high-caste exclusivities. Revealing anxieties about the behavior of widows, it warned them not to seek support from any *kaharin, nain, dhobin, pisanharin, maniharin,* and *bhangan*.[28] Such admonitions were tied

[22] Ibid.: 222.
[23] Chaturvedi 1946: 68–9.
[24] Sharma 1938: 235.
[25] Thakur 1932: 70.
[26] Pandey 1931: 38.
[27] Gupta 2001: 278–9.
[28] Mahopdeshak 1927: 12.

to the fear of conversion. While Western missionary women had been effectively brought under surveillance, it was feared that, since outcaste women were converting to Christianity or Islam, they might persuade upper-caste women to do so as well. Their interactions could not be easily regulated since they went into houses to do various kinds of work and had access to informal conversations with upper-caste women. Particularly feared was the idea that they would encourage widows to elope, convert, and remarry.[29]

The devaluation of Dalit women increased because they departed from the conceptions of "true womanhood" as defined by the cult of high-caste women. In these tracts, Dalit women were denied the status of "women" and classified by their supposedly degrading occupations. Tied to ideologies of domesticity, such portrayals viewed femininity as devoid of labor, denying its economic importance for the household. The work of elite women was often invisibilized, strengthening the derogation of Dalit women's paid work.[30] Promoting claims of middle-class women to the prized domain of housewifery and childcare as a mark of status, these manuals maligned Dalit women who worked outside: they were perceived as unable to devote their lives exclusively to the virtuous path of wifehood and motherhood. Such women had "polluted" characters, did not look after their children properly, could not make their husbands happy; all their "soft" traits had disappeared, destroying their "womanliness."[31] They were charged with drugging their children with opium to work long hours, gravely harming the health of their own children. Two stereotypes of women were thus simultaneously constructed. Women who could afford not to work were defined as ideal, while Dalit women remunerated for their services were denigrated via a pervasive devaluation of all manual labor. This strengthened the private/public dichotomy.

In conjunction, the upper-caste male world often drew the Dalit woman's body as flagrantly sexual, this trait being juxtaposed against the secluded demeanor of the high-caste woman's body. Dalit women were identified as shameless, as prostitutes (*randis*) lacking

[29] Ibid.; Gupta 2001: 298–320.
[30] Sen 1999: 9.
[31] Poddar 1929.

all modesty (*lajja*).[32] There was a symbiosis here with British cultural consciousness. Colonial rule saw the sexual behavior of Indians as marked by "passionate unreason," "unruliness," and "loose" sexual mores.[33] This became more pronounced in their constructions of Dalit women. Medical histories and theories about sexuality became interlaced with bodies that were both Dalit and female. Nudity and relatively darker skins were seen as characteristics of their bodies. There was also an association of hot climates and open public spaces with sexual promiscuity, which took symbolic shape in the form of the Dalit woman, who was seen as immoral and openly licentious, indulging in premarital sexual liberty and infidelity, living in temporary marriages and going through frequent divorces. Coded as synonymous with prostitution and availability, this was sometimes used to castigate the incivility of lower castes in general. Dalit gender practices around premarital sexual life, marriage, widowhood, divorce, and women's public mobility were also invoked to mark their schism from the upper castes.[34] In orientalist reportage the dependent status of unclean menial groups was defined by superior landed people in relation to the sexual availability of their womenfolk.[35] Paradoxically, thus, the Dalit female body, while represented as unwomanly and unfeminine, was also perceived as lustful. Her body was at the same time ugly and alluring, repulsive and desirable, untouchable and available, productive and reproductive. The everyday caste-based sexual violence on Dalit women's bodies was camouflaged in terms of the alleged easy virtue of Dalit women themselves,[36] both by upper castes and colonizers.[37] Even William Crooke, the ethnographically inclined and observant colonial civil servant, often judged the sexual practices, marriage customs, and sexuality of Dalit women from a caste perspective: "It is needless to say that the records of our courts swarm with examples of the association of men of the Rajput class with women of the lower races and in this stratum of village society

[32] Vajpeyi 1941: 76; Devi 1919: 28.
[33] Levine 2003.
[34] Kolenda 1987: 289–356.
[35] Bayly 1999: 196.
[36] Mendelsohn and Vicziany 1998: 11; Dube 1998: 171.
[37] Guha 1987: 144.

there is not even a pretence of moral continence. The effect of this state of things is obvious and requires no further illustration."[38] At another place he casually remarked, "As a rule Bhangi women bear an indifferent character."[39] Such public markings of Dalit women's bodies as profane were exacerbated by the fact that most of them were active in the non-segregated workforce and worked as agricultural laborers along with men. A tract stated: "If you look at the personal life of many of these lowly and laborer women who work around our household, then you too will say along with us that 80 out of 100 of these women have extremely degenerate characters. Even the census reports state that many of these women laborers are actually prostitutes in reality. Many of the women peddlers who sell things or sit in shops proclaim their lewd behavior loudly. Only 2 out of every 1000 such women can be said to have a chaste character."[40]

Ironically, many manuals entrusted upper-caste women with the responsibility of ensuring decorous behavior among low-caste women and servants.[41] Tied to domestic governance, this was part of her household duty. As she was to educate her children, so she was to ensure the "correct" conduct of low-caste women with whom she associated. It was argued that, in the company of high-caste women, low-caste women could acquire some cleanliness and civilization. Many manuals had instructions on how to behave with servants and outcaste women and how to get them to work. Upper-caste women were repeatedly tutored to extract adequate work from such women, and to keep them under constant surveillance when at work.[42] It was also stressed that upper-caste women should try and do most of the work themselves and, as far as possible, prevent outcaste women from entering their homes.[43] The fear of sexual liaisons between upper-caste men and outcaste women was much expressed. Upper-caste women were warned to beware of women who might entice their husbands; they were enjoined vigilance to ensure that *their* men stayed a safe

---

[38] Crooke 1896b, I: xxiv.
[39] Ibid.: 291.
[40] Sehgal 1922: 77.
[41] Banerjee 2004.
[42] Sharma 1938: 234; "Pagal" 1921: 83; *Chand*, January 1932: 386.
[43] Kannomal 1923: 29.

distance from low-caste working women. While critiquing men for their frivolous nature, biases against outcaste women emerged: "The licentious tendencies of men are very visible in public spaces—on streets, roads, narrow lanes, markets, fairs and festivals . . . They will not talk with their wife at home but will laugh and talk with the *jamadarin* who comes from outside to clean bathrooms and streets. They will flirt with the *maniharin* and the *chamarin* on the street, completely neglecting their wife. Women must be careful of their husbands' dirty minds and beware of these women."[44]

Didactic treatises for men, especially on *brahmacharya* and the preservation of semen for the service of the nation,[45] listed contact with sexually "domineering" low-caste women as among the reasons for sensual excitement and sexual excess. A tract stated that to prevent semen loss and avoid sexually rampant notions it was imperative that upper-caste men keep away from the *tambolin, malin, kunjri, bhatiyarin, paniharin, dhobin, nayin, gvalin,* and *telin.*[46]

Sometimes, though rarely, Dalit women appeared as bearers of traditional knowledge, with mythical powers and strong, healthy bodies. For example, in debates on purdah, one of the arguments was that upper-caste women were unhealthy because they kept themselves veiled. Or, when making the case that upper-caste women ought to increase the household chores of low-caste women, it was argued that the latter were in better health because they did more physical work, such as getting water from the well, grinding grain, and performing housework.[47] Dalit women's laboring body was at times romanticized as robust, with the capacity for continuous and hard physical labor. This could be a way to get more work out of her and domesticate her labor for practical use in the household and the field. British discourses, which signaled complexities of revulsion and attraction, abetted such constructions of Dalit female subjectivity through history, travel narratives, and "scientific" racism. Outcaste women were occasionally contrasted with high-caste women who lived a

[44] Thakur 1930: 105–6.
[45] Gupta 2001: 66–83.
[46] "Gaur" 1929: 10.
[47] *"Stri Samaj"* (Women's Society), *Sudha,* July 1929: 659.

veiled life amidst *zenana* households which, according to the British, meant unhealthy lives. By contrast, outcaste women did not observe purdah, did hard physical labor, lived in the open air, ate simple food, and were healthier, producing better milk for their children.[48] This was extended to conceptions of Dalit women's propensity for easy deliveries and breastfeeding: apparently they experienced no pain during childbirth because daily physical labor had toughened them up. A manual certified this: "Most upper-caste women experience unbearable labor pains. However, low-caste village women have in particular been spotted working in the fields half an hour before the birth of a child. They have no difficulty or pain during labor and do not even need a midwife."[49]

It has been persuasively argued that the experience of pain—and thus the materiality of the body—lends a sense of reality to a society in times of crisis.[50] Upper-caste women were so defined by their experience of pain in childbirth that an inability to feel pain was almost evidence of witchcraft. In such portrayals the upper-caste woman was in a more "sympathetic" position. By deflecting power on to Dalit women, a false image was promoted of upper-caste women as powerless and passive victims. This imagery could also lend itself to branding Dalit women as witches, invoking narratives of fear and horror. Images of outcaste women as evil child-eaters were reinforced at times by rumors. For instance, there was a rumor in Kanpur in August 1924, which was widely believed, that a *kaharin* had been caught cooking a dead child to eat. The infant, it was claimed, she had herself murdered. It was reported that the child's father had taken the matter into his own hands and, in one of the three open places of the city, was having her skinned alive on the eve of August 24. This caused a large crowd of about 7000 to collect at various places. Another version was that the cannibal-mother was to be buried up to her waist and torn to pieces by a pair of mad dogs. This was very similar to a rumor spread in Lucknow a year before this.[51]

[48] *Abla Hitkarak* (fortnightly newspaper for women, published by the American Mission Press), October 15, 1887: 88.

[49] "Sumen" 1933: 264.

[50] Scarry 1985: 185–91.

[51] *PAI*, September 6, 1924: 287.

In a substantial part of didactic literature, thus, Dalit women were classified as *kutni*s, as intimidating and evil, as having to be kept away from upper-caste women and men. They were embodiments of disrupted harmony, of the recalcitrant woman who could not be molded into conformity with upper-caste ideals. The construction of "woman" in this literature had two sides: upper caste was what woman ought to be; Dalit was what she had better not be. Such negative portrayals, while suggesting continuities with precolonial images, also signaled an insistence on gende–caste identities as emblems of modernity and civilization. While not evident in official records, such representations were ubiquitous in the didactic literature of colonial North India.

Such attitudes were often reflected in caste manuals and caste associations of the time. These were dominated by spokesmen of the intermediate and upper castes, people who were invested in claiming higher status and upward mobility.[52] In UP, as elsewhere, women's roles affected the status of a caste, as caste respectability was marked by gender.[53] Practices relating to women, and perceived dissimilarities in the everyday life and behavior of women of different castes, became an influential determinant to rearticulate and register caste rankings, to elicit legal recognition of the ceremonial status of castes.[54] Ethnographic surveyors and census enumerators too relied on a cluster of paradigmatic gender practices and the supposed "moral" conduct of women of various castes to fix their place in caste hierarchies.[55] Caste-Hindus particularly dissociated themselves from the envisioned gender customs of Dalits.

Many caste manuals came to be written by advocates of the Sanatan Dharm, by Brahmins and Kshatriyas. They ridiculed the customs of Chamars, sweepers, washermen, and barbers, especially those pertaining to women, to stress how historically deep and unbridgeable were the differences between them.[56] Kumar Cheda Singh Varma, a Rajput and advocate in the Allahabad High Court, wrote an

[52] Galanter 1997; Ahmad 1971: 168–9; Carroll 1977, 1978.
[53] Blunt 1931: 241; *Census, 1911, UP*: 331.
[54] Varma 1904: 91–8.
[55] Sharan 2003: 291.
[56] Sharma 1928.

influential book which branded low-caste practices relating to women as obscene, unfeminine, and uncivilized. Extensively using census reports and the writings of Crooke, Risley, and Todd, Varma made a sharp distinction between Kshatriyas and other castes and went on to argue that widow remarriage and polyandry were two systems "opposed to the true and orthodox system of marriage prevalent among the *dwij* classes of the Hindu community."[57] Intermediate and Shudra castes on the "fringes" in the census—for instance the Ahirs, Kurmis, and Jats—were keen to be recorded as noticeably distinct from Dalits, and women came in handy as significant pointers. Their caste associations and handbooks revealed divergent strains of caste reform and uplift, for they were in the awkward space of resisting Brahmanical notions of caste while also reinforcing patriarchy by trying to impose womanhood in the way it was defined by the upper castes. Thus they advocated a "politics of respectability" characterized by cleanliness, temperance, thrift, polite manners, and sexual purity. They also attempted to stop their women from activities seen as those of low-caste women, while also urging their women to distance themselves from untouchables.[58] It has generally been observed that when a caste upgraded itself, or gained economically, it withdrew its women from the field and introduced stricter veiling practices among them to prove itself worthy of the elevated position.[59] Many *vanshavali*s of these castes forbade their women from the street, the street signifying the male domain, a social-public arena of profane peril and proscribed pleasures—also associated with Dalit women. The Ahirs of Azamgarh and Pratapgarh, calling themselves Yaduvanshis, resolved to forbid their women from going into town or the bazaars to sell milk; their manuals too forbade women from "degraded" work in the public sphere, while simultaneously degrading Khatiks, whose women peddled fruit on the street.[60] Changes in the dress codes of

[57] Varma 1904: 94.

[58] Ghisaram 1920; Yadav 1914; Yadav 1927; Varma 1907; Varma 1916, 1939; Jaghina 1934; Pinch 1996: 124–6.

[59] Srinivas 1998; Tarlo 1996: 166.

[60] *PAI*, April 29, 1922: 783; *PAI*, May 6, 1922: 823; *PAI*, December 10, 1925: 544; *PAI*, June 5, 1926: 309; *PAI*, September 29, 1928: 405; Baldevsingh 1924: 27; Yadav 1927: 7, 9, 30–1, 36.

their women were proposed by Jats; they were told to don a jacket and blouse which would distinguish them from low-caste women.[61]

Simultaneously, a consistent discourse around purdah began to emerge in caste manuals. Dalit women did not observe purdah, but to raise their social status it was often resorted to by many intermediate castes. Percival Scott, while travelling in the countryside of UP, noticed that "The purdah seems to raise the social status of a family. Among the common classes the purdah is not observed, as the women work at manual labor; but as soon as a man finds himself possessed of sufficient means to enable him to dispense with his wife's assistance out of doors, he puts her into purdah."[62] Like the upper and middling castes, lower- and Dalit-caste spokespersons and associations were engaged in a politics of respectability and social recognition. These were led often by men who had gained economically and were literate, who perpetuated parallel ideals, claiming propriety through the manners and morals of their women. Negative descriptions of Dalit women were, however, most visible in the case of the Chamar *dai*.

Constructing the Chamar *Dai*

The denunciation of the Dalit woman was perhaps most blatantly reflected in colonial North India through the Chamar midwife. Many scholars have shown how, with the coming of modernity and industrialization in the West, traditional midwives and home births came to be largely replaced by the medicalization of childbirth and deliveries in hospitals. Women's reproductive bodies became the objects of a male medical gaze and midwives were marginalized in favor of modern biomedical knowledge.[63] In the context of India, too, it has been argued that with the coming of colonialism and Western medical practices, traditional midwives came to be increasingly attacked,[64] even if childbirth remained largely in the hands of women,

[61] Jaghina 1934: 131.

[62] O'Connor 1908: 48.

[63] Oakley 1984; Duden 1993; Ehrenreich and English 1973; Borst 1995; Armstrong 1983; Hobby 2009; Martin 1987; Leavitt 1986; Davis-Floyd and Sargent 1997.

[64] Hollen 2003: 36–56; Ram and Jolly 1998; Jeffery, Jeffery, and Lyon 1989; Rozario and Samuel 2002; Chawla 2006.

and mostly within the home. The shifting imagery of midwives was intricately linked to caste. Colonial voices found corresponding echoes among upper-caste reformers and nationalists, but even amidst their condemnation Dalit midwives attempted to make a space for themselves by demanding rights and proving themselves "uncontrollable."

In precolonial North India pregnancy and childbirth were seen as natural and controlled by *dais*. Women at the time of childbirth were seen as ceremonially polluting and impure. Thus, it was largely Dalit, especially Chamar, women who practiced midwifery.[65] They were in a sense both outside and within the pale of Hinduism: outside in that they were denied all the privileges of caste-Hindus; within in the sense that their labor was essential for the maintenance of social structures.[66] Dalit midwives were the gatekeepers of gender and caste distinctions, which by their very presence they also transgressed. The profession was often hereditary;[67] and the skill and labor involved in midwifery were of a fairly high standard. A popular saying went:

You cannot hide your pregnancy from a Chamar midwife[68]

[*chamain se pet na chipela*]

However, Dalit midwives were usually paid in kind; or else their wages were dismally meager.[69] Moreover, as an earner the *chamarin dai* was often required to pay half a rupee yearly to the landlord as a manorial due.[70] Chamar midwives had to perform menial and "impure" duties for upper-caste women: for example, by cutting the umbilical cord and disposing of the placenta and blood—"defiling" themselves all the more. Yet, in spite of this exploitative system, the Chamar midwife had some leverage: she mediated between male

[65] Briggs 1920: 24–6, 53–4; Blunt 1931: 242; Nesfield 1885: 22; Rozario and Samuel 2002: 7–11; Jeffery, Jeffery, and Lyon 1989.

[66] Ouwerkerk 1945: 8–9.

[67] E.A. Foster, "The Untrained Midwife in India," *The American Journal of Nursing*, 12 (1), October 1911: 34–5.

[68] Singh 2011: 195.

[69] Chaturvedi 1947: 16; Balfour and Young 1929: 126–7.

[70] *Barabanki: A Gazetteer*: 134–5.

authority in a patriarchal society and female reproductive power within the family. Each Chamar midwife usually had a certain number of families whom she served, and she had a near monopoly over childbirth in them.[71] She worked intimately with the pregnant woman and was a critical part of the upper-caste household. Often, until some of her demands were met, she could refuse to perform her duties, creating situations of crisis because, during the delivery period, which sometimes meant miscarriage and abortion, her curative skill and knowledge were indispensable. If a son was born she negotiated hard to get a higher fee. Due to the nature of her work she was also frequently attributed with extraordinary healing and supernatural magical powers.[72]

With the coming of colonialism, while Chamar women continued to practice midwifery, the imagery surrounding them saw significant shifts. In the early years of British rule in UP, midwives were regarded as having a hand in female infanticide.[73] They were also viewed as an important group of informal native informants who could leak vital information about the private quarters of elite households.[74] From the second half of the nineteenth century, with the firming up of colonial rule and the establishment of Western allopathic medical practices, British official records, medical discourses, scientists, and doctors made serious attempts to dislodge the Chamar *dai* from her hereditary occupation and increasingly came to construct her as unintelligent, ignorant, dirty, filthy, and debased, burdened with the inability to learn new methods. Systems of surveillance thus came to appear around Dalit female reproductive technologies.[75]

If colonial reports explicitly attacked the Chamar *dai*,[76] Hindu middle-class reformers and nationalists were not far behind. The caste of the midwife became central to her censure in didactic manuals,

[71] Crooke 1896b, II: 190.

[72] Parmar 2011: 92–102.

[73] 27–28/August 1877, Police, A, Home Deptt, NAI; Singha 1998: 130–7; Kasturi 2002.

[74] Bayly 1996: 54, 92, 164–5, 177.

[75] Lang 2005; Forbes 2005: 70–100; Gupta 2001: 177–85; Jeffery, Jeffery, and Lyon 1989; Engels 1996: 129; Arnold 1993: 257–9.

[76] Gupta 2001: 179–81. Also, Foster, "Untrained Midwife."

vernacular newspapers, and upper-caste reformist literature. It was repeatedly stated that during confinement upper-caste pregnant Hindu women were at the mercy of Chamar midwives who had no regular training in midwifery and were extremely dirty in their habits.[77] A long article in *Chand* attempted to transform the "morally and sexually polluting" Chamar *dai* into a dirty, evil, and dangerous witch of progressive India:

> No low-caste woman can be a good midwife . . . It has become a business . . . Even the mere expression of desire by a low-caste woman to practice midwifery makes people avail her services. These women are very dirty. They come in with dirty clothes, full of disease and germs. The *dai* does not allow fresh air to enter the room . . . Her face resembles that of a witch, her hair is full of lice and she has dirty, soiled hands . . . She pulls out the child by force, often breaking the child's limbs . . . Many a time, her sharp nails injure the pregnant woman. She carries with her strange packets of herbs . . . She uses the hair of goats and the heads of monkeys . . . It is imperative that other castes take on this work.[78]

Another issue of *Chand*, which especially focused on newborn children, carried a color picture titled "Our Midwives" (*Hamari Daiyan*), which not only typecast the native Chamar *dai* but also criminalized her. It carried a detailed message (below the caption) to make the reader feel doubly sure (Fig. 1).

This vilification of the Chamar *dai* as barbaric, as extremely dangerous for women, as the killer of children, as a witch, as usually very old and rigid in her ways, as basing her practice on non-scientific beliefs and popular superstition, as inherently dirty, unsanitary, vermin-ridden, evil, and immoral—all combined the logic of caste with a modern civic discourse. It was an attempt to strengthen hierarchies of gender, caste, and class and involved a complex range of social and cultural beliefs, created and propagated by the dominant castes. Clean/dirty, ordered/disordered were symbolically charged values, characterized by an interplay among the categories of the moral and the physical, and directly related to caste and the social

---

[77] Girdavar 1922.

[78] Bhavanidayal Sanyasi, "*Stri aur Seva*" (Women and Service), *Chand*, October 1928: 650–5.

हमारी दाइआँ

1. "Our Midwives"

In this period of progress also, due to the lack of educated midwives, thousands of children, as soon as they enter the world, see their life end . . . We find in many regions the detestable custom of cutting the umbilical cord with a sickle. In the picture, see a very old *chamari* of sixty years, whose hands are trembling, using a sickle for chopping vegetables to cut the umbilical cord. Because of her trembling hands, it has been cut excessively. Blood is oozing out and the poor, innocent child has become quiet forever. The poor woman who has recently given birth is suffering alone and silent. Who will touch the *chamari*! Readers please also notice the torn mat, the floor bed, and the burning fire by the side.

Source: Chand, December 1924, between pp. 144 and 145.

organization of space. "Clean" signified moral purity while "dirty" was symbolized by the central figure of the Chamar *dai*.[79] Such portrayals also reflected continuities with earlier images of Dalit women, though strengthened now by the vocabulary of science and civilization.

"Common sense" understandings and critiques of the Chamar midwife fed smoothly into those of biology, medicine, and Western

[79] Briggs 1920: 24–6, 53–4; Blunt 1931: 242.

science. Her trenchant censure was used, in colonial and reformist literature, to legitimize elite interventions in the domain of childbirth. Both emphasized the need for the professionalization of the midwife through the dual process of marginalizing the hereditary low-caste *dai* and/or by training and disciplining indigenous midwives in modern standardized formats.[80] In the name of protecting women and children, regulations on midwives were passed by the UP government, with minute details.[81] Municipalities were urged to get legal power over the registration of midwives, make them follow rules, forbid those who did not register to practice the profession and impose penalties.[82] A bill on these lines was introduced in UP in 1933. P. Mason, secretary to the government, argued its necessity: "Owing to the large number of unqualified or partially qualified nurses and midwives now practicing in UP, the necessity of an Act to provide for the registration of nurses and midwives, in order to protect from these untrained and incompetent women both the public and such practitioners as are properly qualified, has recently been stressed both in the press and by the Inspector-General of Civil Hospitals. The attached bill accordingly provides for the registration of nurses, midwives, assistant midwives and health visitors and for a Council to control them."[83] Under the proposed act, "midwife" meant a person who held a diploma in midwifery from an institution recognized by the medical council, or who had been registered by the government.[84] The act was finally passed by the UP Legislative Council on February 20, 1934. Known as the UP Nurses, Midwives, Assistant Midwives and Health Visitors Registration Act, 1934, it stated:

> Only those persons could be registered (a) who have undergone the courses of training and have passed the examinations prescribed by the Governing Body of the UP State Medical Faculty for nurses, midwives,

[80] "Review: Report of the Royal Commission on Labour in India, 1929–30," *The Journal of the Association of Medical Women in India*, XIX (4), November 1931: 54 (51–5); Gupta 2001: 180.

[81] 68–9/June 1900, Medical, A, Home Deptt, NAI.

[82] 25–26/October 1919, Legislative Deptt, NAI.

[83] 1248/1933, Judl, Home Deptt, NAI.

[84] Ibid.

assistant midwives and health visitors respectively and who fulfill such other conditions as may be prescribed; (b) who although not entitled to registration under clause (a) above, are already in the active practice, of their professions as nurses, midwives, assistant midwives and health visitors respectively at the commencement of this Act, subject to such conditions and restrictions as may be prescribed.[85]

The new nationalist Hindu elites and reformers endorsed and incorporated such actions. An article titled "The Need for Good Midwives" (*Achchi Daiyon ki Avashyakta*) stressed the importance of "respectable," educated women, especially widows of "good" families, taking up midwifery. They were asked to undertake systematic training and obtain a proper license through the municipality, medical colleges, and government hospitals.[86] By the early twentieth century some urban middle-class families started seeking the help of professional female doctors and trained midwives. However, a constant lack of finances, an overwhelming urban, middle-class bias, and much more expensive officially trained midwives made their reach limited, suggesting that for a large section of the population the traditional Chamar *dai* was still the only choice at childbirth.[87] It was noted that in urban areas too, women industrial workers preferred to be attended by the indigenous *dai* who understood their ways and did not worry them overly about the need for cleanliness.[88]

Chamar *dais* continued to make their presence felt through other ways—by resisting training imposed from above, by refusing to do the work if not paid adequately, and by claiming rights. Most Chamar *dais* were openly hostile to all training and licensing.[89] Many of them, recognizing that childbirth was still largely dependent on their labor, started demanding payments in cash and a fee for services

[85] 124-II/1934, Publication, Legislative Deptt, NAI.

[86] Dr Prasadilal Jha, "*Achchi Daiyon ki Avashyakta*," *Stri Darpan*, September 1923: 476–8; Ishwardutt Sharma, "*Atm-tyag*" (Self-Sacrifice), *Saraswati*, September 1916: 182.

[87] Gupta 2001: 182–3; Premchand 1984, II: 204.

[88] Miss M.I. Balfour, "Indian Women in Industry," *The Journal of the Association of Medical Women in India*, XX (4), November 1932: 12 (5–18); *Royal Commission on Labour*: 157.

[89] Gupta 2001: 184.

performed.[90] Chamar associations and *panchayats* reacted in two
ways. Some Chamars, particularly those who had gained financially,
passed resolutions forbidding their women from practising the stigmatized and degraded work of midwifery. For example, a meeting
of Chamars at Jaunpur urged that Chamar women should not work
as midwives.[91] Others, however, insisted on better fees for the work.
A *panchayat* of Chamars at Basti resolved that their women should
demand wages in cash and accept not less than Rs 1.40 a day when
functioning as midwives.[92] In Banaras the Chamars passed a resolution
in July 1926 that not less than Rs 5 should be charged for cutting
the umbilical cord of a newborn baby at the time of delivery by their
women. It was reported from the region that a Chamar midwife
refused to attend the delivery of a child unless she was first paid
Rs 5.[93] In the early decades of the twentieth century there were
increasing "complaints" from various regions of UP that the labor
services of Chamar midwives were no longer easily available—unless
they were well paid for.[94] Midwifery continued a remunerative
profession for Chamar women and their rates rose considerably
during this period.[95]

In consonance with the didactic literature being published in late-
nineteenth and early-twentieth-century North India, the image of
the Dalit midwife also came to be further vilified in this period. The
discourses emanating from the colonial state were actively supported
by the upper castes. Medical discourse around childbearing excluded
dais, even as it gave them the means to claim their occupation as
services for a monetary fee. At the same time, Chamar *dais* were
active agents who attempted to make the best of the situation and
who drew sustenance from the growing protests and movements by

[90] Briggs1920: 54, 65.

[91] *PAI*, October 9, 1926: 544.

[92] *PAI*, May 20, 1922: 880.

[93] *PAI*, August 7, 1926: 417.

[94] Dalit women from other castes too were making similar demands. It
was stated that "the *kaharin*, who till 15 or 20 years ago had thought herself
well paid at 3 annas and a couple of chapattis, now demanded 8 annas and
a rupee": *Census, 1911, UP*: 399.

[95] Briggs 1920: 54.

Dalits in general in this period. It was difficult to bring the Dalit midwife under constant vilification and surveillance.

Conclusion

In a large part of the didactic literature, and in representations of the Chamar midwife generally, Dalit women emerged as the perverse muses of various writers. Dogmas about evil, immoral, primitive, polluted, and dirty Dalit women found their way in once more through new arenas and idioms deployed in novel forms and new kinds of literature, even as caste–gender distinctions merged with some of the incoming notions of modern civil society. The demonizing of Dalit women became a surrogate for "naturalizing" their inferiority, for outlawing certain aspects of women's behavior, for strengthening caste patriarchies, for glorifying upper-caste norms, and for marking one's position in the civilizational ladder. Reinforcing and reinventing myths about Dalit women to suit upper-caste truths, such pictures provided a way of contemplating chaos and civilization, desire and fear.[96]

The assault of this literature revealed that the representation of women, even when spoken to or spoken about, as both objects and subjects, was sharply divided along caste lines, reinforcing not just a caste hierarchy but also a female hierarchy among upper-caste and Dalit women. Such dichotomous characterizations of both upper-caste and Dalit women had a far-reaching impact on both sets of women. Through such coding, Dalit women were symbolically split into polarized selves, transformed into signs of wicked, dirty, sexual, and dangerous; upper-caste women remained pure, undifferentiated, and whole. At the same time, it needs to be asserted that Dalit women were not passive onlookers; they implicitly contested such imagery, this being reflected in the actions taken by Chamar midwives. While the dominant positioning in most didactic manuals was of Dalit women as vamps, there were reformist expressions in print which, for a complex set of reasons, attempted to arouse sympathy for the Dalit woman through the frame of victimhood—to which we now turn.

[96] Morrison 1992: 7.

2

Paradoxes of Victimhood
Iconographies of Suffering, Sympathy, and Subservience

This chapter discusses how and why representations of Dalit women as stigmatized were transformed into liberal sympathy in a section of upper-caste reformist-nationalist writings in Hindi in the early twentieth century. Historically, the change was a need of the times, for reformers faced the challenge of reclaiming and incorporating the untouchables within a putative Hindu community and nation. The rubric of victimhood and suffering proved expedient, often functioning in tandem with sentimentality, sympathy, and subservience. At the same time, there were limits to such portrayals, as they were inextricably bound within limited frameworks of charitable benevolence and spectatorial pity, within which Dalit women appeared as mute sufferers, as romanticized and submissive beings. I try to see here how such idioms were invoked to evade questions of structural inequality, and thereby I show up the limits and ambiguities of reform of this variety.

Social scientists have been concerned with the causes and consequences of human suffering. Veena Das and others argue that a degree of emotional healing takes place among suffering individuals once they feel the world around them is making an effort to recognize their pain by representing them sympathetically.[1] Intricate links between the problem of suffering and the politics of compassion are

[1] Das 2001: 1–30.

particularly evident in modern societies.[2] These are often interwoven with sentimentality which, combined with humanitarian impulses, has been a strong motive for social reform.[3] Feminists have theorized sentimentality and its usages within representations of African-American women and the marginalized. Rebecca Wanzo argues that sentimental politics shapes the rhetoric around victimization; it frequently presents itself as progressive about social justice while eventually merely helping to preserve the status quo.[4] The political theorist Wendy Brown puts it in other words: when we substitute emotional and personal vocabularies for political ones, she says, we replace the justice project with a therapeutic or behavioral one.[5] In relation to media ethics, the philosopher Lilie Chouliaraki outlines the nature of public discourses around suffering and the politics of pity, showing the production and systematic distribution of ethical sensibilities to distant others, along with hierarchies of place and human life. This is a process in which one "uses image and language so as to render the spectacle of suffering not only comprehensible but also ethically acceptable for the spectator."[6] In early-twentieth-century North India this logic of sentimental and spectatorial telling was crafted over Dalit women's bodies, privileging a language of personal and domestic betterment from within. As Arundhati Roy argues, appeals to an inner voice, moral righteousness, and a reformed heart were often posited by the upper castes to underplay brutal, institutionalized injustices of caste.[7] Vocabularies of sympathy and sentimentality were also meant to provide a sedative for wounds that were centuries old, and, in turn, expected to stimulate feelings of gratitude and obedience among the untouchables. Symbols of deference, embodied in specific Dalit figures, came to epitomize the "ideal" untouchable, exemplified by the figure of Shabari. As Wanzo explains it, sentimental texts and practices of story-telling

[2] Boltanski 1999; Wilkinson 2005.
[3] Wilkinson 2005: 111–16.
[4] Wanzo 2009: 9.
[5] Brown 2006: 16.
[6] Chouliaraki 2006: 3.
[7] Roy 2014.

around suffering bodies often make the body of color iconographic, leading to the "crafting of generic heroes for the moment."[8]

Deploying literary-visual materials and mundane anecdotal popular writings, this chapter explores the new spaces within which Dalit women, by being made to appear as figures of sympathy, provided the stamp of historical legitimation for reformers claiming to "eradicate" caste. Invoking sentimental melodrama, this conjunctural moment was marked by a move from one set of representations to another—from the woman as lascivious to the woman as vulnerable. Dalit women emerged here as victims of caste exploitation, cricumscribed employment, and poverty. Metaphors of sympathy, however, were marked by incongruity: they coalesced with images of acquiescence and superiority to regulate Dalit women's bodies. This is characterized in the present chapter through examining the reallocation of focus from Surpanakha to Shabari, and the fraught debates around inter-caste marriages. Reformist narratives often embedded untouchables within a male paradigm. I situate representations of Dalit women as victims within this larger milieu.

Upper Castes and Dalits:
Ties and Tensions

In mediated representations upper-caste reformist-nationalists were speaking on behalf of Dalits and helping shape attitudes and beliefs about them, creating a variety of inferential caste-ism. At the same time, such representations cannot be simply dismissed as hypocritical. The print culture of the period reflected continuing discussions among nationalists and reformers on caste inequities, with serious attempts to transform "polluted" bodies into suffering Hindus, entailing a redefinition of untouchability. They were helped by a substantial section of Hindi writers who developed similar idioms and, in a limited way, contested the traditional representation of Dalits. They critiqued the cruelty and oppression that had once gone unquestioned, arguing that hoary practices of this variety were now unacceptable.[9]

[8] Wanzo 2009: 17.
[9] Shastri 1916.

Their relatively compassionate view coincided with a wider cultural attack on Brahmins and upper-caste religious preachers by reformers, especially the Arya Samaj. The figure of the Brahmin priest *vis-à-vis* the untouchable emerged, in particular, as that of a scoundrel.[10]

◆ ग्राम विचारतो ◆   ३५

द्वैध नीति

पंडितजीसे यह पूछनेपर की आप जब अन्य धर्मियों को मन्दिरमें घुसने देते हैं तब अछूतों को क्यों मना करते हैं ?
इसपर पंडितजीने चट उत्तर दिया, भाई ! एक बात ले ली ह और एक छोड़ दी है ।

2. "Dual Policy"

A Brahmin priest was asked why he allowed people of other religions to enter the temple but not the untouchables. The priest promptly replied, "Brother! I have accepted one thing and rejected the other."

Source: Kedia 1933: 35.

Lampooning Brahmin priests, reformers argued that they allowed "cow-killing prostitutes" and tobacco smokers to enter "our" temples, but objected to "our" Bhangi or Chamar brothers from following suit (Figure 3).

Parodying the Brahmin priest was often combined with a hierarchy that viewed untouchables as higher than Muslims. Brahmins were

[10] *Saraswati,* December 1904: 402; Chatursen 1930.

नाच हिश है मन्दिर में, आई है रण्डी, भडुए सझ !
दुलकारा जाता अछूत है, पण्डों का कैसा यह ढझ !!

3. Brahmin, Prostitute, and Untouchable

Dancing is going on in the temple, with prostitutes and pimps!
The untouchable is driven away—what a way among Brahmins!!

Source: *Chand*, May 1927: 133.

कुत्ता 'बाबा है प्रसाद' और मार खा रहा ऊपर चमार !
देखो तनिक पुजारी जी का, है कितना सुन्दर व्यापार !!

Fine Art Printing Cottage, Allahabad.

4. Brahmin, Dog, and Untouchable

The dog is "receiving a propitiatory offering" while the
Chamar is being beaten up!

Take a look at the wonderful trade of the priest!!

Source: *Chand*, May 1927: 77.

criticized for allowing and accepting Muslims in temples and homes
while rebuffing "our very own untouchables" (Figures 5, 6).

5. Brahmin, Maulana, and Untouchable

Brahmin to Untouchable: The Lord is insulted at the sight of untouchables!
Go, go Chandal! Else religion will be destroyed!!
Brahmin to Muslim: Come, Maulana Sahib, yes, come in wearing shoes!
It will be Shivji's good fortune to have sight of your feet!!

Source: *Chand*, May 1927: 61.

6. "Curtain over Sense"

Believers of Ram-Krishna are being shooed away by hitting them with stones
and people following other religions are being welcomed.

Source: Kedia 1933: 33.

The Congress was not spared by some reformers, who claimed it was an organization of the rich with no space for untouchables. Madan Mohan Malaviya was depicted as the face of this upper-caste mentality of a party which had proposed separate wells and temples for untouchables.[11] Simultaneously, strenuous attempts were made to win over and reform untouchables through correction, care, and control. Temples, feasts, food, festivals, marriages, and wells provided important arenas for these.[12] Swami Shraddhanand, the leading Arya Samajist, proposed to the Hindu Mahasabha that the "depressed classes" be allowed to draw water from common public wells; that water be freely served to them at drinking posts, as was done for the highest among other Hindus; that all members of the depressed classes be allowed to sit with the higher castes in public meetings and other ceremonies; and that their children be allowed to enter freely, and at teaching time sit with other Hindu and non-Hindu children in government, national, and denominational institutions.[13] The Hindu Mahasabha, in its 11th Session held at Jabalpur in April 1928, unanimously adopted a resolution: "This Hindu Mahasabha declares that the so-called untouchables have equal rights with other Hindus to study in public schools, to take water from public wells and other sources of drinking water, to sit with others in public meetings and to walk on public roads."[14]

Swami Vishwanand went to a feast given by Chamars in Buland-shahr in June 1922.[15] In 1928, during Holi time, the Arya Samaj held a meeting of untouchables at Pilibhit and directed the sweepers present to distribute sweets.[16] There were reports of untouchables

[11] "Congress aur Achhut" (Congress and Untouchables), Chand, January 1930: 638–41.

[12] M-3, Hindu Mahasabha Papers, NMML; Editorial, "Paap ki Granthiyan" (Records of Sin), Chand, May 1927: 2–6; Prasad 1916: 38; "Harijan Sangh—A Resolution," Subject File 22, Ist Installment, Baba Ramchandra Papers, NMML; "Correspondence between Patel and Swami Shraddhanand on Depressed Classes," 10/1922–3, All India Congress Committee (AICC) Papers, NMML; "Samachar Sangrah" (Collection of News), Chand, May 1927: 188–92.

[13] Jordens 1981: 137.

[14] Subject File 18/1931, Moonje Papers, NMML.

[15] PAI, July 1, 1922: 1087.

[16] PAI, March 31, 1928: 124.

participating in public processions during Holi in Aligarh and Bana-ras.[17] Congress members smoked with Chamars during Holi at Mora-dabad.[18] Here some Arya Samajists allowed Chamars to draw water from their wells and even partook of water from their pots.[19] Some Bhangis and Doms were taken by the Hindu Mahasabha to bathe at Sangam on the occasion of the Ardh Kumbh Mela at Allahabad in 1924 and were photographed upon their return.[20] Dalits were particularly wooed *vis-à-vis* Muslims. In Pilibhit the local Arya Samajists took part in a sweeper's marriage ceremony. They made speeches informing the sweepers that they were the descendants of Valmiki *muni* who had been forced to become a sweeper by the conquest of Hindustan by the Muhammadans![21] In Saharanpur, on May 18, 1923, a *dhol* was placed in a well and labeled "Hindu *dhol* for the use of Chamars," which angered Muslims.[22] Reformist maga-zines published cartoons showing that relative equality had been

7. "Lion and Lamb on the Same Riverbank"

Look at the pilgrimage site of Triveni at Prayag:
How the touchable and the untouchable bathe together.

Source: Kedia 1933: 34.[23]

[17] *"Sarvajanik Juluson Mein Achhut"* (Untouchables in Public Processions),
"Samachar Sangrah," Chand, May 1927: 189; *Chand*, November 1926: 36.

[18] *PAI*, March 25, 1922: 597.

[19] *PAI*, April 21, 1923: 265.

[20] *PAI*, February 23, 1924: 75.

[21] *PAI*, May 26, 1928: 193.

[22] Ibid.: 309.

[23] It takes no guessing who is the lion and who the lamb!

achieved between caste-Hindus and untouchables, with scenes of them bathing together on the same riverbank (Figure 7), and collectively drawing water from a well (Figure 8).

8. Water from Well

High-castes and untouchables are filling water from the same well.

[*kulin aur achhut ek kuen se pani bhar rahe hain.*]

Source: Stri Darpan, August 1924: 453.[24]

New public spaces like railway stations, platforms and carriages, jails and restaurants, editorial rooms and publishing houses, were seen in reformist literature as the great equalizers, encouraging Brahmins and sweepers to sit on the same bench, drink from the same tap (Figure 9), and promote inter-dining (Figure 10), thus blurring caste distinctions.[25]

An article claimed that all Hindus were the same, as the various varnas were like the five fingers of a hand, efficient only when working

[24] Note how the image of the well is molded with the figure of a high-caste man, who looks from above and pulls the strings.

[25] Hiralal, "*Chhua-chhut*" (Pollution Taboos), *Chand,* May 1927: 73 (72–4).

9. "Thirst for Water"

The train has two minutes left to leave.
Brahmin and untouchable drink water from the same tap.

Source: Kedia 1933: 34.

10. Interdining

The chief editor of this issue, Mr Pandit Nandkisore ji Tiwari, B.A., who is a
Saryu Brahmin, is dining in person with Banshilal Kori (Chamar), a compositor
in the Hindi department of the press.

Source: *Chand*, May 1927: inside cover picture.[26]

[26] This picture appeared on the first page (after the Contents) of a special
issue of *Chand* on untouchables. While celebrating interdining, notice how the
two figures are portrayed and the hierarchies in ways of addressing them.

together.[27] Another argued: "Unlike cows, buffaloes and trees, Brahmins, Kshatriyas, Vaishyas, and Shudras are not separate *jati*s. If these ancient Sanskrit names are referred to in today's language, they will be called teachers, soldiers, merchants, and workers. They are all brothers and belong to the same *jati*."[28]

However, such images and arguments, even while criticizing untouchability, maintained occupational distinctions. They were caught in other contradictions as well, for even within supposedly sensitive accounts a condescending language was deployed showing Dalits as defiled and debased. The "dirty bodies" of untouchables were a physical and moral problem for the reformers. *Chand* stated that *achhut* women and men had so many deplorable traits that educated people, even while sympathetic to them, hesitated to interact freely with them: "They [untouchables] are completely indifferent to personal cleanliness. They do not bathe for months together. Their hair is a jungle-house of lice. Their clothes are a bundle of filth and their teeth show half an inch of grime deposit. Muck has seeped into their very veins; that is to say, they have made dirt their everyday and constant companion."[29]

Annie Besant provided clarity of expression to this general disdain:

> The children of the depressed classes need, first of all, to be taught cleanliness, outside decency of behaviour and the earliest rudiments of education, religion and morality. Their bodies, at present, are ill-odorous and foul, with the liquor and strong-smelling foods out of which for generations they have been built up; it will need some generations of purer food and living to make their bodies fit to sit in the close neighbourhood of a school-room with children who have received bodies from an ancestry trained in habits of exquisite personal cleanliness and fed on pure food-stuffs. We have to raise the depressed classes to a similar level of physical purity, not to drag down the clean to the level of the dirty and until this is done close association is undesirable.[30]

[27] *Abhyudaya*, November 21, 1925: 6.

[28] Santram, "*Samaj Sudhar,*" *Sudha*, September 1927: 222 (219–22).

[29] Editorial, "*Shiksha aur Kusanskar*" (Education and Bad Rituals), *Chand*, May 1927: 11–12.

[30] Vatsa 1977 (1912): 46–7.

Describing untouchables as dirty was not a socially neutral enterprise: cleanliness and hygiene were labeled characteristic upper-
caste values to be aggressively espoused as the aspirations of lower
castes.[31] Notions of dirt and cleanliness were located within and
constitutive of space and social relations.[32] Camouflaging structural, occupational, and physical constraints faced by Dalits, criteria
of cleanliness became a means to impose dominant value systems,
strengthen cultural, spatial, and social boundaries, and paint untouchables as in need of constant reform. One reformer from UP argued:
"There are certain bad customs among these backward classes which,
if removed completely, will soon bridge the gulf between them and
the Dwijas. These are the eating of carrion, filthy habits, as well as
their mode of living."[33]

Emulation was advised to untouchables while stressing the "superiority" of upper-caste social practices. The Hindu Mahasabha and
Arya Samaj distributed free soap in Dalit neighborhoods (*achhut
mohallas*).[34] One reformer scribbled this:

> If you are neat and clean, who can despise you?
> Fragrance will light up all your ten prospects.[35]

> [*jo saaf aur suthre ho tau hogi kise ghrina.*
> *khushboo se mehek jayegi teri disha dason.*]

Reformers believed that untouchables could evolve to higher stages
of civilization if directed away from "vice" and molded in upper-caste
ways. Besides being trained in hygiene, health, and refined religious
practices, untouchables had to be prevented from drinking liquor and
eating beef and made vegetarian.[36] A poem published by the Harijan
Sevak Sangh recommended:

[31] "*Hindu Samaj ki Unnati ke Sadhan*" (Means for Progress of Hindu
Society), *Chand*, August 1926: 386–7; "*Dalitoddhar Sammelan*" (Conference
for the Uplift of Untouchables), *Chand*, March 1930: 874–5; "*Samaj Sudhar*,"
Sudha, January 1930: 699–707.

[32] Campkin and Cox 2007: 1.

[33] *The Indian Social Reformer*, January 28, 1933: 341.

[34] Subject File 52/1939, Moonje Papers, NMML; Joshi 2003: 247.

[35] "Sant" 1933.

[36] *Chand*, January 1932: 387; *Abhyudaya*, November 21, 1925: 5.

Give up meat entirely, this will benefit all.
Sell no cow to the butcher, this is what religion teaches.
Think of drink as sin, break your bond with arrack.
Stop the sale of dope and weed, save yourself from them.
Do away with the hookah ritual—if you wish to be called a Hindu.[37]

[maans khana bilkul chodo, ismen sab kalyan hai.
gau na becho haath kasai, yahi dharm sikhlata hai.
sharab pina haram samjho, taadi taad katana hai,
bhang-charas ki bikri roko, inse to bach jaana hai.
hukke ki ab rasm mita do, gar hindu kehlana hai.]

The emphasis on cleanliness and purity, and the "improvements" recommended in eating habits, legitimated the power of the upper castes by conferring religious and social sanctity. Proclaiming the achievements of reformers, it was said: "The Depressed classes will see that they are now passing through a stage in their history when they begin to adopt and adapt such Hindu customs . . . People bathe, dress cleanly, and wear marks of religious devotion, and this is due to the influence of a reformed Hinduism."[38] A reformist tract poetically stated on its front cover:

Who likes falling and bruising one's feet?
It is our duty to uplift ourselves and everyone else alongside.[39]

[pairon mein gir thokar khana yeh kab kisko pyara hai,
uthna aur uthana sab ko, yeh kartavya humara hai!]

Upper-caste norms were the unquestioned standard by which the lower castes were judged. Whatever the "virtues" of untouchables, they could never achieve the level of civilized behavior of the upper castes because they could only mimic the "original." Though reformers claimed to be sympathetic to Dalits, they were in their eyes only entitled to "differential" equality and rights.[40] This revealed a shared subconscious in the dominant culture, often masquerading as common sense, of prejudice against Dalits.[41] For all their progressivism, liberal

[37] Dube 1933: 13.
[38] The Indian Social Reformer, November 16, 1935: 169.
[39] Mishra 1922: cover.
[40] Sarkar 1997: 368–9.
[41] Pandey 2013: 2–3.

reformers were complicit with the casteist edifice. By enhancing upper-caste norms and ideals, this had the effect of maintaining upper-caste hegemony. Sanatan Dharmis expressed it more blatantly. Damodar Shastri, a Sanatanist, wrote in an article in *Chand*:

> Those who are called untouchables are called so because of their dirty occupation and the absence of differentiation amongst them of purity from pollution. Though sweepers keep our homes clean, in their personal lives they are very dirty . . . We too clean the shit of our children but we do not become untouchable because we clean ourselves properly. However, sweepers are dirty in their habits and mentality. They clean toilets and then eat bread with the same hands . . . If we allow them access to our wells, they will become polluted, for untouchables will spit in them and put dirty utensils in them . . . Untouchability will persist till these people educate themselves and give up their undesirable rural customs and learn the language of cleanliness.[42]

Equally prickly within an ostensibly sympathetic framework was the question of how to maintain purity of caste.[43] This was recorded: "It is necessary to maintain purity in food and eating habits and boundaries of untouchability, so that the Hindu community is not harmed . . . We are bound to feel hatred if we pure upper castes are asked to consume food cooked by impure castes like the Dom and Chamar . . . We of course should aim at getting rid of boundaries of touch between the twice-born castes."[44] While reformers had conceded some ground to Dalits, underlying tensions could not be wished away. The examples of hostility were innumerable. It was reported in 1923 from Saharanpur that feelings were running high as a result of Arya Samajist efforts to bring Chamars within the pale of orthodox Hinduism.[45] In Moradabad, well-water drawn by Chamars aroused opposition amongst tradition-bound Hindus.[46]

[42] Damodar Shastri, "*Kuch Vicharniya Baten*" (Some Noteworthy Thoughts), *Chand*, March 1928: 575–7 (572–8). Also, Gopaldamodar Tamskar, "*Sanatandharm ka Sanatanatv*" (The Sanatan Essence of Sanatandharm), *Chand*, February 1934: 440–6.

[43] Baijnath 1905: 45.

[44] Krishnanand, "*Anuchit Chhua-chhut*" (Improper Pollution Taboos), *Stri Darpan*, September 1922: 156 (155–7).

[45] 25/May 1923, Home Poll, NAI; *PAI*, April 21, 1923: 265.

[46] *PAI*, May 5, 1923: 279.

Many protested against the proposals of the Hindu Mahasabha to allow Dalits to draw water from the same wells.[47] Low-caste boy scouts were forbidden to bathe in a tank located near a temple in Almora which had been specifically filled by the municipal board for the use of scouts.[48] Riots were reported in Bijnor between Dalits and caste-Hindus over the use of wells in 1938.[49] In a village of Agra district, an untouchable purchased some *puris* from a *halwai* and, instead of departing with them, began eating them at the shop. The *halwai* thrashed him on the grounds that he was supposed to have eaten on the roadside near the public drain.[50] At another place in Agra a *halwai* was outcasted for cooking *puris* for Chamars.[51] The festival of Holi, supposedly seen as an occasion to reconcile with the untouchables, was fraught. On March 11, 1922 a procession of sweepers in Muttra (Mathura), out to celebrate Holi, was not allowed to enter the city and was attacked on the grounds that the sweepers had plans to defile sweetmeat shops.[52] When Dr Babu Ram urged the people of Meerut, at a meeting during Holi, to embrace men of the untouchable castes, many Hindus hurriedly left the meeting and it soon broke up completely.[53] There was friction between Banias and Chamars over the Holi festivities when the Chamars demanded performing cremation ceremonies with the Banias; this was of course refused.[54]

The hostility of the orthodox Brahmins of Banaras towards untouchables was expressed with special vehemence. It was resolved by the Varnashram Sudhar Sabha there that no Brahmin should perform any ceremonies, particularly the *janeu* ceremony, for people of the lower castes.[55] When one Mesuriyadan Pasi decided to wear the *janeu*, he, along with two other Pasis, was attacked by Brahmins.[56] Banaras'

[47] *Abhyudaya*, March 20, 1926: 5.
[48] *The Indian Social Reformer*, August 22, 1925: 809.
[49] Mss Eur E251/1, Hallett Collection, OIOC.
[50] Verma 1971: 11.
[51] *PAI,* September 9, 1922: 1386.
[52] *PAI*, March 18, 1922: 350; *PAI*, March 25, 1922: 597.
[53] *PAI*, March 10, 1923: 155.
[54] *PAI*, April 5, 1924: 126.
[55] *PAI*, June 10, 1922: 967.
[56] Editorial, *Chand*, August 1934: 450.

pandits objected strongly to readings of the Vedas by the depressed classes.[57] When Madan Mohan Malaviya asked Behari Lal, a depressed class representative, to speak at the Hindu Mahasabha session at Banaras in 1923, many of the orthodox *panda*s of Banaras walked out, terming Malaviya an Arya Samajist and not a Sanatan Dharm Hindu.[58] In a meeting of their own they protested against proposals in relation to untouchables put forward at the Hindu Mahasabha gathering. Malaviya expressed regret at having allowed untouchables to speak from the Mahasabha platform. In its meeting held at the Kumbh Mela in Allahabad in January 1924, it was declared that the lower castes were not entitled to wear the sacred thread, learn the Vedas, and inter-dine.[59] Sanatan Dharm publicists in particular argued that although Dalit uplift was needed, upper-caste welfare required that Dalits do their traditional work.[60] Myths of the superiority and purity of the upper castes were constantly used to limit Dalit access to resources and spaces. Within the frame of sameness and sympathy, a veiled language of difference and animosity was sculpted. Such contradictions were reflected in the attitude towards, and writings on, Dalit women as well, with some additional features.

"Polluted" to "Suffering" Body

For the protection of our untouchable sisters, for the protection of their virtue, their character, their morality and their divine sweetness, we will have to foil the attack from all three directions! We will have to protect our helpless untouchable sisters from the hands of the twice-born castes, from the blows of heretics [Muslim *goonda*s and Christian missionaries], and from the onslaught of untouchable men themselves . . . The chastity, the character, the virtue of both untouchable woman and Brahmin *devi* are equally worthy of protection and respect.[61]

The sharp demarcation between upper-caste and Dalit women, evident in didactic manuals, was seeming untenable to many reformers

[57] *PAI*, May 5, 1928: 165.

[58] Interview with Ganpat Rai, Oral History Transcript, NMML: 28–9.

[59] 66/VI/1924, Home Poll, NAI; Sharma 1983. Also, *PAI*, September 15, 1923: 483; Subject File 42/1935, Moonje Papers, NMML.

[60] Lajjaram, "*Samaj Sudhar,*" *Sudha*, January 1928: 704.

[61] "*Achhut Nari ki Durdasha*" (The Pathetic Condition of the Untouchable Woman), *Chand*, May 1927: 175–8 (177).

and nationalists. Images of Dalit women as different, polluted, and evil were relegated to the peripheries and replaced in a substantial segment of reformist Hindi literature with discourses of sameness, sympathy, and victimhood. Alongside, the "burden" of safeguarding Dalit women was seen as falling upon the shoulders of upper-caste women and men with a "conscience." Memories of oppression were reorganized around this new notion.[62] Speaking of male social behavior in eighteenth-century England, the historian Karen Halttunen remarks on how, "in the context of the bourgeois "civilizing process," compassion and a reluctance to inflict pain became identified as distinctly *civilized* emotions, while cruelty was labelled as *savage* or *barbarous.*"[63] This, she believes, became an integral aspect of the humanitarian sensibility of the times, the aim being "to teach virtue by softening the heart and eliciting tears of tender sympathy."[64] A similar point is made by James Carson, who shows how nineteenth-century social reformers conceived of the power of sympathetic identification as the product of high civilization, and thus as characteristic of modernity, and more specifically as the possession of those social classes above the "brutal mob."[65] In early-twentieth-century colonial North India, upper-caste reformers too trenchantly criticized exploitation that had once gone unquestioned, expressing a sense of historical guilt and moral horror at caste-Hindu cruelty. Heralding modernity and nation-building, they appealed fervently to the "innate" virtue of caste-Hindus. This was also a way of challenging colonial notions of "barbarism" and the lack of civilizational ethics among the colonized.

Such writings were accompanied by cartoons depicting the pitiful sufferings of untouchables. Public spaces such as temples and wells, where significant struggles were taking place, were especially associated in these illustrations with Dalit women, since it was chiefly they who drew water, and were perceived as the more frequent temple-goers.

Premchand's social-reform fictions too captured the pathos of the Dalit woman's victimhood. In his story "*Mandir*" (Temple: May 1927),[66] a *chamarin* widow, Sukhiya, goes to the temple to pray for

[62] Mohan 2011: 537.
[63] Halttunen 1995: 303.
[64] Ibid.: 307.
[65] Carson 2010: 11.
[66] Premchand 1984, V: 5–13.

11. "The Rage of the Priest"

"Enough, I have told you so! You cannot enter the temple!"

Source: Kedia 1933: 32.

12. Brahmin, Dalit Woman, and Well

"Oh wicked untouchable! Since when have you the right to touch the tap"—
saying this the Brahmin scolds the old woman!

Source: *Vyanga Chitravali* 1930.

her very ill son but is denied entry by a Brahmin priest. The pain
of her unfulfilled wish, and the abuse she is subjected to, leads to
the death of both child and mother. Before her death Sukhiya rails
against upper-caste men and priests: "My touch will make the God
untouchable! Keep him locked, guard him. You have not an iota of
sympathy in you . . . And you claim to be protectors of *dharm*! You
are murderers, undiluted murderers!"[67]

The story seems largely inspired by the temple-entry agitation,
which was at its peak around this time, and mirrors its several ambiguities. Choosing a Dalit woman as his protagonist, Premchand embraces Sukhiya within a Hindu paradigm, portrays her silent suffering
and sacrifice, scorns the Brahmin priest, and suggests reform from
above and within, the whole story being cast in a Gandhian mold.
Similarly, choosing the other dominant issue of the times—the drawing of water from wells by Dalits—his brief story "*Thakur ka Kuan*"
(The Landlord's Well; August 1932),[68] puts a gendered perspective
on the issue by giving Gangi, a Dalit woman, the lead role. Gangi
fails in her attempt to draw water from the well of a *thakur* for her
extremely ill husband Jokhu, reaching home to find Jokhu drinking
dirty water from a pot. She reflects on both *thakur* and moneylender:
"They're up to their necks in theft, cheating, false cases . . . They
get work done and pay no wages. How are they higher than us,
then? . . . If I happen to come to the village, they look at me with
the eyes of lechers."[69]

Another story, "*Dudh ka Daam*" (The Price of Milk),[70] is about a
bhangan midwife, Bhungi, who is also surrogate mother to the son
of an upper-caste landlord. She keeps her own child hungry at the
cost of her employer's son but receives nothing except his leftovers.
These stories reflect Premchand's critique of the caste prohibitions to
which Dalit women were subject at the hands of priests and landlords,
the oppressors appearing in the full panoply of their villainy. His
repugnance for them and their customs is, however, intertwined

---

[67] Ibid.: 13.
[68] Ibid., I: 141–4.
[69] Ibid.: 142.
[70] Ibid., II: 204–14.

with respect for the taciturn endurance of the Dalit woman, thereby arousing the reader's sympathy for her but also allowing little room for any suggestion of the desirability of decisive action or collective protest. Premchand's turn towards Dalits requiring redemption has provoked incisive criticism, sometimes downright denunciation, by many leading Dalit writers. The critiques have been framed around debates on "authenticity," that is, who can represent or write for whom; and as exemplifying the intermeshing of fractured social realism, popular Gandhian idealism, and liberal reform, all revealing the limits of sympathy.[71]

While strengthening a sense of outrage against the upper castes, these appalling images of caste cruelty captured and popularized a new culture of spectatorial pity and pathos. In a different context, Sheila Moeschen has investigated how "disabled" people's performance was pulled into a net of "charitable sentiment" in nineteenth-century America, which marked such benevolence as seemingly legible, compelling, and uncomplicated.[72] In representations of Dalit women, too, which were accompanied by the humanitarian spectacle of suffering, lay the image of the unfortunate, innocent, poor, weak, helpless, and silent Dalit woman, uncomplainingly enduring every pain.

These images, while critiquing upper-caste women and men for their hierarchical mindsets and indifference, simultaneously construct passively suffering female untouchables as perennial victims of silence, reduced to using body language and gesture to communicate their emotions and to draw attention to their pitiable state. Dalit women appear here as metaphoric sites of passive, ageless endurance. The larger political, economic, and social struggle of Dalits is implicitly

[71] For details, Brueck 2014: 43–60; Gajarawala 2013: 32–53. However, some Dalit women writers hold a different gendered perspective. Thus Anita Bharti, a celebrated Dalit feminist writer, remarks: "If we compare Dalit [women] characters of Premchand with those depicted by many Dalit [male] authors, we will definitely find that Premchand's characters are much more vocal, argumentative, fearless, rebellious and ready to challenge Brahmanism . . . Like Ambedkar, Premchand too advocated *roti–beti* ties and inter-dining": Bharti 2013: 107.

[72] Moeschen 2013.

देती है टुकड़े सेठानी, बैठा कर जूते के पास !
यही इज्जतों का आदर है, जो होते तन-मन से दास !!

13. Suffering Untouchable Woman

The prosperous woman offers meager morsels, making her sit near her shoes!
This is the respect given to untouchables, our slaves body and soul!!

Source: Chand, May 1927: 40.

transformed into a "domestic tragedy," a "suffering from within" which can be recuperated by purging Hinduism of some of its evils. Sentimentality and pity thereby trivialize political engagement with the caste question and the material realities of Dalit lives. The politics of pity is very different and distinct from the politics of justice.[73] As Wendy Brown puts it, "When suffering as such is reduced to a problem of personal feeling, then the field of political battle and political transformation is replaced with an agenda of behavioral, attitudinal, and emotional practices."[74]

Witnessing the pain of the "other" could also make the upper castes aware of their own good fortune, with a privileged person feeling compassion for a less privileged other. Karen Halttunen says: "Humanitarian reform was a major cultural vehicle for the growing unacceptability of pain; it was also, inescapably, an expression and even a demonstration of the new obscenity of pain."[75] Sympathetic

[73] Boltanski 1999: 3–5.
[74] Brown 2006: 16.
[75] Halttunen 1995: 330.

representations of Dalit women brought out the limits of such discourses. The language of sympathy and sentimentality, says Toral Gajarawala, was "a failed project of knowing, a valiant attempt perhaps, but too underscored by hierarchical relations to offer much affectively."[76]

Surpanakha to Shabari: Grotesque to Submissive

Sentimental politics is often, as so frequently noted, accompanied by romanticization, with reformers adopting a paternalistic and patronizing attitude; this is certainly obvious in relation to Dalits at this time. It was reasoned that the Hindu community was powerful precisely because the outcastes addressed the upper castes with the deference that was their due. Even though they were declared as one within the entire Hindu community, many reformers continued to regard Dalits as "the feet" of society.[77] To serve the upper castes was seen as the "natural" trait of the low castes, this being best encapsulated in the image of the obsequious and compliant Shabari.[78] Moreover, it was construed that Dalits should be grateful to the upper castes for the sympathy showered on them, for the benign recognition of their suffering. Upper-caste "kindness" was expected to arouse humility, submission, and *seva* among the untouchables. In an enchanting reading of Shabari and the gastronomical delights of her jujubes, Philip Lutgendorf remarks:

> The identity of this woman and the precise nature of the foodstuffs she places before the brothers has been a matter of no small interest to *Ramayan* tellers and audiences over the last two millennia and in the popular Hindi parlance of recent times, at least, the expression "the tribal woman's jujubes" (*bhilni ke ber*) has become a proverbial designation for a humble but loving offering that pleases God, and the verbal signifier of a highly emotional tableau often represented in popular religious art.[79]

[76] Gajarawala 2013: 66.
[77] Hazarilal Jain, "*Sanatan Dharm aur Achhut*" (Sanatan Dharm and Untouchables), *Chand*, May 1931: 62–6.
[78] Lutgendorf 2001: 119–36, 376–9.
[79] Ibid.: 120.

Lutgendorf goes on to show how, in modern interpretations
of the Shabari episode, marked usually by orthodox or reformist
Hindu leanings, one can detect a tension "between more popular
and liberal, and more elite and conservative orientations; between
the enthusiastic savoring of the sweet and 'juicy' essence of collective devotion, and a more sour perspective that finds such egalitarian impulses unappetizing and indigestible."[80] While agreeing with
his analysis, I extend it by showing how even humane portrayals of
Shabari were marked by incongruities, making the reformist project
suspect.

In a section of upper-caste reformist literature of the early twentieth
century, previous images of Surpanakha as the evil one were replaced
by the figure of Shabari, who came to symbolize the "ideal" low-caste
woman. The image of Shabari was now constantly invoked as a new
icon for low-caste and tribal women, they being advised to emulate her
selfless devotion and sense of rendering service. Books were published
praising Shabari, and many poems came to be composed around her
figure.[81] A book titled *Shabari* linked its publication directly to the
achhutoddhar movement, portraying her as the ideal Dalit woman.[82]
Upholding her model, a reformist poem went:

> How could you forget the jujubes of Shabari, the *bhakti* of the *bhil*,
> How have you treated the worshipers of Ram?[83]
>
> [*ber shabari ke, bhakti bheel ki bhuli kaise,
> ram ke bhakton se kya apne vyavhar kiya.*]

The image of Shabari was particularly useful in presenting a critique
of food taboos and interdining, since Shabari and Ram had shared
food. Yet hierarchy remained embedded in this partaking of victuals.
She represented a low-caste woman who serviced and worshiped
God—and implicitly all upper castes—quietly, submissively, freely,
without inhibition. Her virtuous reverence provoked a facile moralizing whereby it became possible to elide the idea of loving untouchables

[80] Ibid.
[81] "Vachanesh" 1936.
[82] Ibid.: 1.
[83] "Sant" 1933: 4.

such as her into loving God.[84] Her offerings epitomized selfless
devotion, eliciting nothing but affection.[85]

> Why have they come to Shabari's house? To meet her!
> The affection of great people recognizes no inequality!! . . .
> [She,] whose feet pollute the stairs of the temple!
> Her home today has become like the hearts of ascetics!! . . .
> After tasting them, Shabari said she had some sweet jujubes left!
> I wish to offer you my core [she said, and] what is wrong in that!![86]

> [aye hain shabari ke ghar par, kyun? isse karne ko bhent!
> bhed bhav ko nahin janta, maha janon ka sneh amet!! . . .
> jiske charnon se hota hai, kalushit mandir ka sopan!
> bana usi ka bhavan aaj hai, yogijanon ke hriday saman!! . . .
> boli shabari rakh chode hain, chakhke thode meethe ber!
> tumhen chahti arpan karna, hridya, use yeh kya andher!!]

Although outwardly polluted, Shabari was portrayed as inwardly
pure, a woman of childlike simplicity and deep reverence. Admonish-
ing the upper castes, appeals were made via her image, asking that
Dalit women be treated humanely. Ram's treatment of Shabari became
a point of reference and the upper castes were asked to follow his
example.[87]

> God ate blemished jujubes from the hands of Shabari.
> The poet "Ganga" asks: why this change in your attitude now?[88]

> [shabari kar se khaye prabhu ne, van mein jhoote ber.
> "ganga" kavi kyun pada tumhari, mati mein ab hai pher.]

[84] "Achhutoddhar," Sudha, February 1931: 33–40.
[85] We come across some other examples, which were cited in this period to
show the affection of the gods towards low-caste women. Krishna was shown
to have developed a great fondness for Kubja, a hunchbacked woman from a
low caste: Kannomal, "Hindu Dharm mein Achhuton ka Sthaan" (The Place
of Untouchables in Hinduism), Chand, May 1927: 55 (55–6).
[86] Anandi Prasad, "Uphaar" (Gift), Chand, May 1927: 133.
[87] Chandiprasad, "Devi Shabari," Chand, September 1927: 552–62;
Chadrikaprasad 1917: 5.
[88] Dube 1933: 5.

Godly magnanimity did nothing to overthrow the picture of low-caste obsequiousness, with condescension layering the whole. A picture printed on the back of the first page of the special issue on "untouchables" published by *Chand* captured this effectively:

14. "Shabari and Shri Ram"

Say, O Hindu community, where has the idea of purity-pollution gone now! Or tell Shri Ram that he is not the incarnation of God!!

Source: *Chand*, May 1927: behind the first page.

It was important to accept and approve of Shabari since the claim was that through her the status of Ram was enhanced. Dalits had to be embraced for one's own elevation. The Dalit woman was no longer sinful but devout; she could aid the upper-castes' trip to heaven:

Had Ram not eaten fruit from the hands of Shabari,
Would he have been called *Maryada-Purushottam* today?[89]

[*shabari ke kar se le kar yadi, ram nahin phal ko khate,
maryada-purushottam phir ve—kaise aaj kahe jaate?*]

[89] Ramcharit Upadhyay, "*Parirambh*," *Chand*, May 1927: 74–5 (75).

The paternalism of the relationship is constantly in evidence. Shabari is always full of gratitude and humility; to reach out to her, to uplift her, the benevolent needed at times to "stoop" to conquer:

[He] whom we call God—Ram—he uplifted the downtrodden . . .
Forgetting his own pride, He ate the jujubes offered by Shabari, a *bhil* woman.[90]

[*prabu kehte jinhen ve –ram patiton ko uthate the . . .*
bhula kar maan, shabari –bhilni ke ber khate the!]

The image of Shabari became a core symbol of the liberal-reformist literature of this time, sympathy for her being always capped by the image of her subservience. Shabari exemplified spiritual integrity, reverence, austerity, and heartfelt devotion, while also functioning very much within a Hindu paradigm. She provided an emotional and personal vocabulary to Hindu reformers which could blindside the structural and institutional nature of caste inequality. The language of suffering and sympathy helped to shape, regulate, and position Dalit women. Shabari became, for upper-caste reformers, the "truly representative" face and embodiment of a Dalit woman.

Thresholds of Sympathy: Ground Strains and Inter-Caste Marriages

Sympathy, it has been argued, always needs an object of pathos, and it is often a form of sociality and governmentality, a mechanism of differentiation and normalization that ensures stability and facilitates power relations.[91] One scholar contends that a rigorous examination of the faculty of sympathy "reveals that it cannot be wholly divorced from the spectacle and theatre through which an older form of hierarchical power operated."[92] Sympathy for the untouchable woman was garnered by social reformers through the deployment of literary, visual, and rhetorical devices. A sense of historical guilt helped in the reproduction of such images. In the process, however, terms of

[90] Shobharam, "*Achhut Avedan*" (Request of an Untouchable), *Chand*, May 1927: 13–15 (15).
[91] Rai 2002: xi–xxi.
[92] Carson 2010: 12.

upper-caste privilege were subtly reworked and reinstated. Examining the historical guilt of white people, which leads to a cathartic and redemptive alleviation, Joy Wang remarks that it is often guided by "self-indulgent forms" that "merely activate melancholy and morbid stagnation."[93] Likewise, there were dilemmas in the sentimental sympathy of Hindu reformers. The depiction of Dalit women as tragic and submissive figures confined them into being the objects of charity, people in need of the benevolent intervention of upper castes from above for their improvement.[94] Upper-caste and Arya Samaj women were entrusted with leadership roles for inculcating in untouchable women sanitized tropes which would "make them competent enough to be in the company of upper castes":

> First of all, our upper-caste sisters will have to catch their [untouchable women's] hands and with this support lift them up; the dust which has accumulated on their bodies, the dirt and grime that has entered their every pore, will have to be cleansed through sympathy . . . It is only the upper-caste woman who can make the untouchable woman clean, refined, and pure . . . Can an untouchable woman bathe in front of us men? Will it be possible for us to cleanse the filth of her heart and body? . . . Certainly not! Thus, it is our belief that the salvation of untouchable women . . . rests with upper-caste ladies . . . Without our upper-caste educated sisters participating in this sacred rite, there can be no solution to this pathetic situation.[95]

Stri Darpan, a leading women's journal, praised upper-caste women for their efforts to uplift and educate untouchable women.[96] A meeting of *achhut* women was held on March 26, 1928 at Agra in which women from the Arya Samaj spoke about cleanliness and education.[97] The Arya Samaj lauded the role of upper-caste women

---

[93] Wang 2009: 45.

[94] For example, Lakhanpal 1941; Satyavati 1932; Sharda 1925; "Prakash" 1934; Shraddhanand 1919.

[95] *"Achhut Nari ka Samuddhar"* (Rescue of Untouchable Woman), *Chand*, May 1927: 178–80 (178–9).

[96] *"Neech Jatiyan"* (Degraded Castes), *Stri Darpan*, November 1919: 273–4.

[97] *PAI*, April 21, 1928: 135.

such as Pushpa Devi, Vishnu Devi, and Shakuntala Devi in Meerut for their work among untouchable women.[98] Even when decked up in sympathetic rhetoric, the model of womanhood reiterated the terms of upper-caste privilege, deifying Brahmanical patriarchal codes and morals. It was against this, as Uma Chakravarti says, that Dalit women were habitually judged.[99]

There were other problems in the language and idioms of reformist writings. For example, with the growth of communalism Dalit women were privileged over Muslims. A reformist publication stated: "It is amazing that we do not mind worshiping *tazia*s and even send our women to the *pir*, but we hate the *mehtarani* who does the work of a midwife in almost every village of UP."[100] Again, while advocating widow remarriage, social reformers argued that many upper castes were opposed to the practice since it was prevalent among Dalits. The upper castes believed that if they were to practice it, their caste status would be debased. To refute this logic, and in support of widow remarriage, some reformers gave a double-edged argument: "Can gold be transformed to iron merely by the touch of untouchables? If not, widow remarriage cannot be polluted by the touch of untouchables. We also want to ask where this custom came about amongst the untouchables? *Untouchables, after all, are not capable of inventing any custom themselves.* They are actually always aping the upper castes. So this custom of widow remarriage too must have come from the upper castes."[101]

Reformist rhetoric faced other strains, as tensions on the ground remained. For example, a Hindu woman in Agra was subjected to a social boycott for exhibiting sympathy with the cause of outcaste women.[102] In a municipal girl's school of Kanpur, the admission of a Mehtar's daughter created a sensation and many parents withdrew

[98] Upadhyay 1930, 1941. Going a step further, just before Gandhi's fast in 1932 many prominent Hindu women appealed to the depressed classes to drop their demand for separate electorates: *The Indian Social Reformer*, September 24, 1932: 58.

[99] Chakravarti 2003: 109–11.

[100] Sharda 1925: 30.

[101] Joshi 1928: 193–4. Emphasis mine.

[102] *PAI*, July 1, 1933: 333.

their daughters. Harijan girls were thereafter discouraged from seeking admission to the school.[103] In Hapur, Chamar women were not allowed to draw water from wells.[104] Some fifty Chamar women intending to bathe at Garhmukteshwar were prevented from doing so at the usual ghat by Brahmins. The *dola-palki* movement symbolized such tensions. The issue became deeply contentious in the early twentieth century in the Garhwal region. Here, upper castes had traditionally not allowed the Shilpkars or Doms from bringing their newly wedded wives in the *dola-palki*. They were constantly beaten up if they tried to. Resentment against this was growing. In 1924 a marriage party of Dalits decided to go to a village near Bijnor with their *dola-palki*. They were attacked and the *palki* set on fire. In 1940–1 many incidents were reported of attacks by upper castes on the conjugal parties of Dalits, of flogging them and destroying their palanquins.[105]

Sympathy was particularly complicated when it became a question of *roti-beti* ties, which proved to be the most contentious of issues; it caused heated debates, while remaining largely unresolved. *Roti-beti* taboos were central to caste practices of spatial and bodily exclusion. Arguments around inter-caste marriages are discussed briefly in this context. Ambedkar linked the maintenance of endogamy with the strengthening of caste. He argued that inter-caste marriage was the hallmark of Dalit progress and the most important solution to annihilating caste, since it recognized the relationship between maintaining caste purity and controlling women's sexuality on the one hand, and powerfully challenging it on the other.[106] In UP, Swami Achhutanand exhorted Dalits to abolish sub-casteism through inter-sub-caste marriages, proposing that Muslims and Christians too

[103] *Dainik Vartman*, September 12, 1938: 4.

[104] *PAI*, March 17, 1923: 170.

[105] Dalits lanched various protests on this issue in the early twentieth century. The Arya Samaj and Gandhi lent their support to this movement. Finally, the British government issued an order that those preventing Dalits from using palanquins would be penalized. See Rawat 2002: 270–1; Viyogi 2010: 477–8.

[106] Rege 2013: 59–64; Rao 2009: 232–3.

could help such an enterprise.[107] Some social reformers like Santram also advocated inter-caste marriages. Replying to objections, Santram contended that one Amritlal Rai had said that these would lead to unnecessary romances and elopements with the woman domestic servant or low-caste male. Santram replied, albeit in a patronizing tone, that even the *dasi* could be beautiful, talented, and virtuous, that there were in fact many fair and attractive Chamar women. He went on to repudiate the argument that such alliances would greatly lower the ideal of women's purity and honor.[108] In a letter to B.S. Moonje, Surendranath Mahey asked: "Can there be any reality to the Harijan uplift when people are denied the right of mixing freely with the lowly? . . . Our only remedy lies in legal change—in legitimizing inter-caste marriages without the disadvantages of the Civil Marriage Act."[109] Given the fear of conversions, the Hindu Mahasabha, in its 17th Session at Poona in 1935, resolved "in favour of complete liberty of inter-marriage between all sections of the Hindu community," including with Harijans.[110]

Yet, as Prem Chowdhry shows, a more rigid and caste-oriented social pattern was being reinforced in the colonial period, a development particularly disadvantageous to low-caste women. Inter-caste marriages took on new contours and became much more contentious, there being growing anxieties around sexual liaisons with caste groups other than one's own.[111] Caste and gender inequalities reinforced each other as the regulation of women's movement and sexual disciplining emerged as powerful instruments for consolidating caste and community exclusivities. Endeavors to reconstitute the subjectivities of Dalit women led to the creation of fresh norms in conjugal relations, secured through endogamy and the containment of sexuality. Caste endogamy was increasingly observed and often became legally enforceable, even for Dalit caste groups, whose customs

[107] Jigyasu 1968; Kshirsagar 1994.
[108] Santram, "*Antarjatiya Vivah*" (Inter-Caste Marriage), *Sudha*, July 1929: 596–608.
[109] Subject File 37/I/1934, Moonje Papers, NMML.
[110] M-3, Hindu Mahasabha Papers, NMML.
[111] Chowdhry 2007.

were very different. Sanatani Hindus had been vociferously arguing that inter-caste marriages were disastrous and could neither reproduce nor support a thriving Hindu civilization. A popular saying in North India reflected the stereotypes of caste and the deep mistrust of inter-caste marriages:

> A dark-skinned Brahmin and a fair Chamar (both assumed to be born of inter-caste alliances) are never to be trusted, and get no respect.[112]

> [*kala brahmin gora chamar,*
> *inke saath na utre paar.*]

A Sanatani Hindu said:

> Reformers emphasize that it is important to nurture *roti-beti* ties. However, in no society has this been possible . . . People argue that equality between the upper and lower castes is necessary. Again, on this earth, nowhere does such equality exist . . . The noble quality (*abhijat gun*) of Brahmins is a sore thumb for the English . . . The main basis of caste distinction is marriage distinctions and nothing else . . . Somewhere a man is superior and somewhere a woman, but when they are equal on the basis of caste, their child is good . . . If we try to make all one by lifting caste taboos, all castes will face a decline and there will be restlessness and enmity.[113]

Even reformers tended to limit their arguments to allowing untouchables to enter "their" temples and fill water from "their" wells. This was more than enough and it was all they wanted. They did not expect *roti-beti* ties.[114] A reformer contended:

> We are not sure it will be any good making intermarriages a plank in the national platform. Married happiness largely depends on how much wife and husband can take for granted each other without having to thrash out every little question as it arises. As Gandhi observes, while there should be no legal bar or social odium attaching to inter-marriages between persons of different castes or sects, most marriages will continue to be celebrated between persons of analogous upbringing. To make out that a man or woman who marries out of the customary group does more to advance the national interest than another who is content to choose a

---

[112] Gautum 2007a: 107.
[113] Shiromini Sharma, "*Samaj Sudhar*," *Sudha*, August 1927: 100–2.
[114] Chatursen 1930: 171–2.

partner in his or her own class is to look at the question from a wrong perspective. There is no demerit attaching to intermarriages nor is there any special merit either.[115]

In similar vein, Gandhi stated: "Though there is in Varnashrama no prohibition against intermarriage and interdining, there can be no compulsion . . . If the law of Varnashrama was observed there would naturally be a tendency, so far as marriage is concerned, for people to restrict the marital relations to their own Varna."[116]

Still others promoted inter-caste marriages between twice-born castes but fell far short of proposing them between high castes and Dalits, often stating that it should be particularly discouraged with Bhangis and Chamars.[117] Instead, they declared, Kayasth and Vaishya should marry amongst each other, as should Malis and Dhobis. Horizontal, not vertical, alliances were being encouraged in the name of inter-caste marriage.[118] Criticisms and hesitations around inter-caste marriages were reflected in stories, plays, letters, and novels composed at this time. Kanwal Bharti argues that the iconic Hindi writer Nirala was extremely unhappy when Santram formed the "Jaat-Paat Torak Mandal"; Nirala wrote a long article whose title translates as "The Current State of the Caste System" (*Varnashram Dharm ki Vartman Stithi*), scathingly criticizing both inter-caste marriage and inter-dining. Even where inter-caste romance was depicted, it usually ended in tragedy.[119] Narratives by Dalits used the opposition to inter-caste marriages in a different way—to censure upper-caste norms. A powerful play, *Achhuton ka Insaf*, was written by one Nandlal Jaiswar "Viyogi," an active member of the Adi Hindu movement, in 1943.[120] His play depicted an inter-caste romance between a Chamar boy, Vimal, and Malina, the daughter of a Hindu priest, and ended with both committing suicide. In the process, however, it launched

[115] *The Indian Social Reformer*, November 23, 1935: 179.
[116] Ibid.: 186.
[117] Jain 1937.
[118] Editorial, "*Bharat ke Kalank*" (Stains on India), *Chand*, November 1926: 121; "*Antarjatiya Vivah-Pratha ki Avashyakta*" (The Need for Inter-Caste Marriages), *Chand*, September 1934: 525–6.
[119] "*Smriti Kunj*" (Letters), *Chand*, January 1927: 339–42.
[120] "Viyogi" 1943.

an incisive critique of upper-caste hypocrisy. The issue of inter-caste marriage continued highly contentious.

These examples indicate that the language of sympathy was also a paradoxical and protean mode of power,[121] where it often reproduced the very inequalities it decried and sought to bridge. They also reflect the mutable, fluctuating positions of the time, showing reformers caught in a vortex of destabilizing change. Such rhetoric fulfilled many other roles: it revealed to the nation the "humane" face of reformers and nationalists; it had a wider appeal among the Hindu middle classes because such reforms were initiated from above and entailed no radical change; it rallied moral sentiment with a new propriety outlined for Dalits; its deployment simultaneously helped in identification with and differentiation from Dalits; it aided the logic of a wider Hindu unity; it transformed the political and the structural into the social and the domestic; and it deflected people from thinking through the deeper links between caste, hierarchy, sexuality, and patriarchy.

Conclusion

Expressed in the language of sentiment and satire, part of the creative endeavor of reformers in colonial India was aimed at provoking a sense of outraged morality at the behavior of upper castes towards Dalits. Earlier representations of Dalit women's polluting bodies gave way to a deep concern for, and an emotional investment in, her suffering. Frames of victimhood became characteristic of the way she was portrayed, appealing to "innate" and "elevated" feelings of sorrow, sadness, pity, and sympathy among the upper castes. While guided by a sense of the humane, there were problems in the language and idioms propounded. Dalit women often remained powerless and pitiably helpless in these representations, silently suffering within pathetic conditions. Sympathy for them was also clothed within a valorization of their subservience, and a hypothesized gratitude among Dalits was symbolized by the idealization of the figure of Shabari. There were further limits to how effective upper-caste reformist guilt could be. The accent on upper-caste women's leadership in "improving" the social and cultural habits of Dalit women—by their mimicking

---

[121] Rai 2002.

upper-caste ways—and incongruities around inter-caste marriages, always diluted criticisms of caste. Exclusionary terminologies were often built into liberal-reformist lexicons. Vocabularies of suffering and victimhood grew into a way of controlling Dalits, and, at the same time, depoliticizing the social. Feelings of outraged moral sentiment and heightened pathos detached caste from the political economy and eclipsed the deeper levels of their exploitation, thus reducing structural and systematic oppression to token gestures. Amalgamated iconographies of suffering, sentimentality, and subservience often left the larger dominant narratives intact; public policies were rendered essentially private matters and the political transformed into the personal.

In the previous chapter we saw how didactic and caste manuals usually went out of their way to prove the *difference* between lower- and upper-caste women. A part of reformist literature, however, by incorporating the former into a Hindu reformist-nationalist fold, stressed the sameness and homogeneity of Dalit and upper-caste women. In the process, both these viewpoints, not always mutually exclusive, often shared the same logic, and mutually influenced each other, since each was imbued with a casteist lens and upheld similar assumptions about the habits and behavior of Dalit women. Discourses of derogation and co-option were contingent and uneven, and yet upheld a social pragmatism around normativity, disciplining caste-marked bodies. The substitution of pollution by suffering, of paranoia by romanticization, of vamp by victim, of difference by sameness, of stigma by sympathy, of condemnation by subservience, was almost as iniquitous and susceptible to casteist interpretation. These illustrations often worked together, in different yet similar ways, and their ascriptions were often analogous. The paradoxes in conservative and liberal currents of thought were constitutive of the construction of Dalit women in colonial India, where delinquency and condemnation went hand in hand with victimhood and sympathy. At odds with such representations, Dalits in present times have deployed Dalit women icons from colonial North India to declare altered gendered identities.

My next chapter focuses on this Dalit counter-print popular literature.

3

Dalit *Viranganas*

(En)Gendering the Dalit Reinvention of 1857

Normative constructions of Dalit women as vamps and victims have found their nemesis in the present-day Dalit Hindi popular literature composed around 1857's Dalit *viranganas*. Through the recuperation and analysis of such representations of positively militant Dalit women in colonial North India, we see some of the trajectories along which Dalit female subjectivity came to be transformed. Unlike the Dalit print culture of colonial UP, which did not really address women, this literature did—by coding within itself distinct meanings of gender and history. By looking at 1857 from a Dalit feminist perspective we see layers within Dalit voices that were conducive to writing new histories of Dalit women and pointing to alternative resources for self-making. These transformed gendered representations work as critical metaphors, destabilizing conventional constructions of Dalit women. They convey complex messages, colluding with and subverting patriarchies. They throw up the possibilities of a radical gendered Dalit politics which goes well beyond the rubric of "vamp or victim," the discursive frame of "reform and nation," and even the "tyrannies of 1857."

In his extensive analysis of Dalit popular literature, Badri Narayan reflects astutely on how the role of Dalit women heroes of 1857 has aided proclamations of a distinct Dalit identity and politics in UP.[1] While drawing from his work, the attempt here is to examine

[1] Narayan 2006. Also, Hunt 2014: 110–18.

86

the issue through a different frame. Narayan is mainly concerned with the relationship between cultural politics and the democratic participation of Dalit communities whereby Dalit heroines are used by the BSP to construct an aura around a contemporary political icon, Mayawati. My interest on the other hand is in analysing Dalit *viranganas* through a gendered Dalit politics of history-writing. Are these popular histories only an exercise for Dalit claims to power, or do they aid in writing feminist histories of Dalits?

Condemnation and Commemoration: Ambiguous Dalit Genealogies of 1857

The festivities in 2007 around the 150th anniversary of 1857 provoked heated debates over the position of Dalits during the revolt. There were two lines of argument. On the one hand there was condemnation of the 1857 revolt from a Dalit perspective, and on the other there was commemoration of the Dalit contribution, particularly of Dalit *viranganas*. Both viewpoints need to be placed in a larger context. Scholars have argued that subaltern political consciousness reveals a degree of autonomy or distance from mainstream nationalism.[2] Dalits had an ambivalent relationship with Indian nationalism and colonialism, often in opposition to the views of the dominant Hindu communities.[3] A Dalit intellectual argues that the British liberated Dalits from the oppressions of Hindu society by abolishing the laws of Manu and providing them opportunities of education, the most important tool of liberation.[4] In UP, Dalit activists had articulated similar ideas as early as the 1920s.[5] The Adi Hindu movement, for instance, adopted resolutions expressing loyalty to the British government. In their conference at Lucknow in September 1931 they thanked the British for liberating them from Hindu domination, for opening the doors of knowledge to them, and for instituting the "rule of law."[6] In UP the British government set up forty-one schools for

[2] Hardiman 2006.
[3] Zelliot 1992; Rawat 2012: 12–18.
[4] Chandra Bhan Prasad 2004: 92–4.
[5] *PAI*, January 14, 1922: 93; *PAI*, January 28, 1922: 202.
[6] *Report of the Special Session of the All India Adi Hindu Conference*: 1, 4.

the depressed classes who were not allowed entry into general schools by caste-Hindus.[7]

The revolt of 1857 cannot be isolated from these positionings. The anti-Dalit biases of 1857 are well documented. Birjis Qadr, raised to the throne of Awadh by the rebels on July 5, 1857, under the regency of his mother Hazrat Mahal, proclaimed:

> All Hindus and Mussalmans know that four things are held dear by every human being: (1) religion and faith; (2) honor and esteem; (3) life of self and relations; (4) property. These four were protected under the rule of the Indians, under whose government no one interfered with religion; everyone followed his own faith and everyone's honor was protected in accordance with their position. No *paji*, for example, Churha, Chamar, Dhanuk or Pasi could claim equality with them . . . But the English are the enemies of these four things . . . They have brought the honor of the high classes on a level with that of the lower people—sweepers and leather workers. In fact, the English show preference to the lower-castes over the higher classes. On the complaint of a sweeper or a leather-worker, they seize the person of even a Nawab and a Raja and disgrace him.[8]

The proclamation by Bahadur Shah on August 25, 1857, read:

> It is evident, that the British Government in making zemindary settlements have imposed exorbitant *zuma*s, and have disgraced and ruined several zemindars, by putting up their estates to public auction for arrears of rent, in as much as, that on the institution of a suit by a common Ryot, a maid servant or a slave, the respectable zemindars are summoned into court, arrested, put in gaol and disgraced . . . Such extortions will have no manner of existence in the Badshahi government.[9]

These statements reflect a generally deep contempt for Dalits while also epitomizing the authoritarianism of precolonial caste formations. Such nostalgic yearnings for pre-British pasts have found no favor among Dalits.[10] The standard histories of 1857 stress its upper-caste character. Nationalist historians like S.B. Chaudhuri,

[7] Gupta 1985: 118.
[8] 68–9/25 June 1858, Foreign Secret Consultation, NAI.
[9] From Rizvi and Bhargava 1957: 455–8.
[10] Yadav 2007.

Tara Chand, and R.C. Majumdar insist that the ruling classes and traditional elites were the "natural leaders" of the revolt.[11] Marxists can be seen as falling within the same paradigm, seeing the revolt as the last attempt of an elite medieval order to recover its lost status. It has been emphasized that 1857 was "a traditionalist movement in which those who had the most to lose in the new sought the restoration of the old pre-British order."[12] Scholars have also reflected on the overwhelmingly upper-caste composition of the Bengal Army, in which Ashraf Muslims, Brahmins, and Rajputs secured a near monopoly.[13] Largely recruited from Awadh and Bihar, these soldiers carried their caste prejudices, maintaining caste distinctions in relation to food, apparel, and lodging.[14] As these forces turned against the East India Company, the British mobilized a section of the low castes. The Awadh Police Force had a large component of Pasis, Bhangis, Chamars, and Dhanuks who participated in the suppression of the revolt.[15] It appears that Dalits did not have much to gain and only something to lose by being active allies in the revolt. Purity/pollution ties, the crossing of seas, and the biting into the flesh of cows or pigs—rifle bullets were often cartridges greased with animal meat and had to be bitten before being fired—did not affect Dalits in the same way. Jotiba Phule congratulated the Mahars for aiding the British in suppressing the 1857 revolt.[16] A part of Dalit tradition has celebrated the victory of the British in 1857, which was for some Dalit intellectuals the antithesis of modernity as well as retrogressive and narcissistically upper caste.[17] Pointing to the political illegitimacy, from a Dalit perspective, of support to the 1857 revolt, they have refused to bow down before the powerful and inclusive category of nationalism. However, it would be a partial reading to stop here, for the multi-layered character of 1857 shows contradictory pulls. M.H. Court, Magistrate and Collector of Allahabad, remarked: "The poorer

[11] Chaudhuri 1957; Majumdar 1963; Chand 1967: 42–3.
[12] Metcalf 1964: xiii–xiv.
[13] Stokes 1986: 50–1.
[14] Peers 1991: 551–2; Alavi 1995: 51; Kolff 1990.
[15] Roy 2007: 1725. And see Chapter 4.
[16] O'Hanlon 1985.
[17] Rai 2006; Bharti 2006; Yadav 2007.

classes particularly amongst the Hindoos, are, I believe, indeed, I am certain, at heart favourable to us and would gladly see us confirmed in power but they believe our power is gone and acting on this belief they join in plundering and rebelling against the Government."[18]

Recognizing the popular and low-caste basis of the revolt, the historian Rudrangshu Mukherjee links the seemingly disjointed realms of elite and common masses by stressing the mutual dependence of peasantry and *talukdar*s in Awadh, an interdependence which provided the bases for united action at this tumultuous juncture.[19] Tapti Roy too regards 1857 as a popular uprising wherein sepoys, *thakur*s, and people came together, even though their goals and visions differed.[20] Gautam Bhadra highlights the common leaders of the revolt.[21] Though the focus is not on Dalits, the low-caste and class basis of the revolt is recognized.

Counter-Print-Public Culture: Dalitizing Myths, Memories, Histories

The past three decades, coinciding with the meteoric rise of Dalit movements in North India, have seen a proliferation of popular Hindi Dalit literature which has disentangled received knowledge from the apparatus of control. It is believed that Dalits are now in charge of their own narratives, witness to, and participants in their own experiences, as well as bringing in a new Dalit aesthetic. Mass produced, this literature is sold in the thousands through informal networks—ad hoc stalls at public rallies and *mela*s of Dalits, on pavements, and through Dalit presses and publishers—and reaches a large number of Dalit households. Lacking technical sophistication, most of these books are thin, written by relatively unknown authors in simple colloquial Hindi, reproduced in many editions, priced cheaply between Rs 2 and Rs 50, printed on cheap paper, and encompass diverse genres.[22]

[18] Quoted in Rizvi and Bhargava 1957: 478.
[19] Mukherjee 1984: ix–x.
[20] Roy 1994: 17, 258.
[21] Bhadra 1985: 229–75.
[22] Narayan 2001: 104–12; Narayan and Misra 2004: 13–36; Narayan 2006: 50–69; Kshirsagar 1994: 74, 135–6, 346–7; Gupta 2007; Hunt 2014:

Given the currents of political self-determination among Dalits, there has occurred a paradigmatic shift whereby many have felt the imperative need to declare their nationalist credentials. John Stuart Mill argued that the most important factors which give rise to nationalist consciousness among a people are "identity of political antecedents; the possession of a national history and a consequent community of recollection; collective pride and humiliation, pleasure and regret, connected with the same incidents in the past."[23] Copious booklets have been published along these broad lines, cataloging the Dalit investment in and contribution to the freedom struggle, particularly over 1857.[24] What is being proposed by Dalit writers is the concreteness and almost palpable truth of this history.[25] A counterpoint to hegemony,[26] this literature represents dissident voices, reflecting Bakhtin's notion of dialogics and heteroglossia,[27] and Stuart Hall's concept of "oppositional" decoding, challenging "negotiated" reading positions.[28] It may also be equated with Raymond Williams' paradigm of "dominant," "residual," and "emergent" cultural practices in constant interaction.[29]

The 1857 revolt has been completely transformed and inverted in this literature through a convergence of histories, myths, and retellings of the past.[30] Very different from scholarly historical accounts

---

25–82. The production of such pamphlets can be traced from the 1920s, with the establishment of Bahujan Kalyan Prakashan, one the first Dalit presses, founded in Lucknow by Chandrika Prasad Jigyasu. Jagriti Press of Allahabad was another such. Swami Achhutanand founded the *Adi Hindu* newspaper: *PAI*, October 30, 1926. Donations were collected by Chamars to start another paper from Kanpur: *PAI*, December 17, 1927. These were expressly conceived as Dalit enterprises, whereby Dalits were making use of new technologies of print to propagate their viewpoints and assert their identities. For details, Rawat 2012: 123–31; Amardeep 2012; Hunt 2014: 31–42.

[23] Mill 1964: 2–4.

[24] For example: Dinkar 1990; Naimishray 1999, 2003, 2014.

[25] Narayan 2006: 95–6.

[26] Gramsci 1971.

[27] Bakhtin 1981.

[28] Hall 1980.

[29] Williams 1981: 203–5.

[30] Narayan 2006: 96–106.

or even constructed "popular" perceptions, 1857 has here taken on the
character of protest literature and Dalit resistance where alternative
Dalit rebel heroes—some constructed, some exaggerated, some
"discovered"—are represented as its real symbols. In these accounts
the armies of soldiers against the British consist largely of Dalits.
New Dalit histories argue that Dalits had nothing much to lose in
pre-British times as their condition had been miserable even then. So
it was they who truly fought for independence in 1857, while the
upper castes and rulers fought only to restore their rule.[31] The focus
is no longer on sepoys and greased cartridges but on Dalits groaning
under the foreign yoke. The famous Dalit poet Bihari Lal Harit
writes:

> Barbers, washermen, Kurmis, gardeners, grain-parchers, bards and potters
>   fought.
> Cobblers rolling in dust and cotton-carders fought. All Dalit families
>   fought.[32]

> [*nai, dhobi, kurmi, kachchi/bharbhuje bhaat kumhaar lare.*
> *lare khak rub mochi dhanak/sab daliton ke parivar lare.*]

Inspired by altogether different sentiments, these Dalit narratives
are written in an impassioned language, usually by men not trained as
historians. They are writing history with a mission by claiming a past
and using it for the furtherance of their future. One of their rationales
in writing histories of this kind is to stimulate Dalit nationalism, Dalit
patriotic sentiment, and Dalit pride. They are rewriting history to
provide dignity to Dalits.[33] They say:

> Neglected and brave Dalit warriors will again acquire new respect.
> As time passes, this change will be realized by all.[34]

> [*dalit upekshit virvaron ka, hoga phir se nav samman,*
> *samay chakra ki chaal karti – parivartan ka sabko gyan.*]

[31] Naimishray 2003; "Saras" 1995.
[32] Quoted in Disodiya 2004: 89.
[33] Varma 1996, 2004: 15. The writer is a Pasi.
[34] Varma 2004: 15.

Present-day feelings are ascribed to the Dalit heroes of 1857, and they are seen as teaching a lesson in morality: i.e. that Dalits today need to emulate the heroic deeds of their past heroes and fight for their rights. There is an inspirational quality, a positive conviction in this effort which indicates directions for critical histories of the Dalit political present, leading towards new constructions and hitherto unimaginable possibilities. Through their narration of 1857 Dalits also hope to constitute an arena for themselves in the history of a nation-in-the-making.[35] So, these Dalit histories are not just reinventions of a usable past, they are an impassioned plea to recognize the unsung heroes of the revolt who were often illiterate and could leave no written accounts. Dalits claim to be overturning the inaccuracies and prejudices of mainstream historiography—be it nationalist, Marxist, or Western—by retrieving lost histories:

> Here, there and everywhere, you will find discussions on their deeds, but scorned [Dalit] heroes are never written about in papers.[36]

> [*yatra-tatra sarvatra milegi, unki gaatha ki charcha.*
> *kintu apekshit veervaron ka—kabhi nahin chapta parcha.*]

This Dalit literature has not found its way into canonized histories of 1857 and been kept away from the loci of authority—university departments, literary associations, and syllabi. It is often condescendingly seen as inferior, sensational, mimetic, unintellectual, and as lacking in quality, authenticity, and written records, even if moving and passionate. It occupies a different public–political–knowledge domain, the vocabulary of which stresses the Dalitization of history.[37] It is representative of a Dalit-imagined nation in search of its own historical narration. However, even in its celebratory mode it harbors an inherent tension in that it constantly grapples with the ambiguous genealogies of 1857 and nationalism. Significantly, whether anti- or pro-1857, the constructions of Dalit roles in 1857 have been changed by Dalits themselves in tandem with changing socio-political conditions. Thus, 1857 now offers a moment for the negotiation

[35] Narayan 2006: 86–9.
[36] Varma 2004: 13.
[37] Naimishray 2003: 5; "Saras" 1995: 8.

of Dalit identities, whereby Dalits may emerge as subjects involved in self-constitution and recognition. These animated alterations of received assumptions and revisionist histories underscore the rupture between a codified view of 1857 and a more complex construction. Dalits play from their own viewpoint with the confined genealogies of historical pasts. The contradictory politics of exclusion and inclusion, censure and celebration, shows that Dalits wish to be a part of the nation—and yet cannot fully be. Dalits swing in their stance in relation to 1857 because of political compulsions pertaining to domains of power and nationalist assertion on the one hand, and on the other their autonomy and resistance to a dominant and hegemonic nation. Their discourse is thus marked by shifting and selective appropriations in which they can only have an ambivalent, incomplete, and fragmentary relationship with 1857.

Virangana and the Retelling of 1857

The events of 1857 also emerge from a Dalit perspective as a gendered arena. While stressing the upper-caste biases of 1857, scholars have emphasized that the revolt was an attempt to reinstate feudal patriarchies. The remarriage of widows and the abolition of sati were condemned by many of the leaders of 1857.[38] At another level, historians who have stressed the popular basis of the revolt have ignored its gendered dimensions. Gautam Bhadra, while brilliant in discussing four male common rebel leaders of the revolt, says: "In all these representations what has been missed out is the ordinary rebel, *his* role and *his* perception of alien rule and contemporary crisis."[39] A different lens is visible in Dalit popular literature. When it comes to women, the memory of 1857 is inevitably tied to Lakshmibai, the Rani of Jhansi, with celebrations of her valor in poetry, ballad, folktale, drama, school textbooks, and comic books.[40] Popular Dalit histories, however, emphasize the participation of their own Dalit *viranganas*, foreshadowing Lakshmibai and Begum Hazrat Mahal. In fact, Dalit

[38] Yadav 2007.
[39] Bhadra 1985: 230. Emphasis in the original.
[40] For details, Lebra-Chapman 1986.

female icons engaged in radical armed struggles far outnumber Dalit men in these accounts of 1857, littering the Dalit stories of this past and helping define their present identities. Women like Jhalkari Bai of the Kori caste, Uda Devi a Pasi, Avanti Bai a Lodhi, Mahabiri Devi a Bhangi, and Asha Devi a Gurjari, all stated as having been involved in the 1857 revolt, have become symbols of bravery among particular Dalit castes, and ultimately among all Dalits.

Take the case of Jhalkari Bai, about whom there has been a prolife-ration of popular tracts, including comics, poems, plays, novels, biographies, and *nautankis*;[41] there have even come into being maga-zines and organizations in her name. To name a few: there is a comic book, *Jhalkari Bai*; there are poems titled *Virangana Jhalkari Bai Kavya*, *Jhansi ki Sherni: Virangana Jhalkari Bai ka Jeevan Charitra* and *Virangana Jhalkari Bai Mahakavya*; plays and *nautanki*s have been called *Virangana Jhalkari Bai* and *Achhut Virangana Nautanki*; novels and biographies have been titled *Virangana Jhalkari Bai* and *Achhut Virangana*; and a magazine published from Agra is called *Jhalkari Sandesh*.[42] Dalit magazines have published articles on her.[43] Similarly, on Uda Devi there are *khand kavya*s, stories, and magazines.[44]

Such representations of Dalit women as *virangana*s are an impor-tant source of insight into gender politics from a Dalit perspective, as well as being a site of struggle over the meanings of 1857. While functioning as storytelling mechanisms, they are also symbolic strug-gles to impose definition on what is and what should be, often re-flective of hidden desires in the collective unconscious of Dalits. While highlighting the centrality of these women in the symbolic constitution of Dalit identity, this literature reveals a world turned upside down, showing how resistance to dominant discourses about Dalit women has been coded and lived through by Dalit communities at different historical moments. Dalit women *virangana*s emerge

[41] In the colonial period too, there were *nautanki*s staged around *viranga-na*s (but not Dalit ones), combining myth and history. See Hansen 1988: 25–33.

[42] To name a few: "Anu" 1993; Harit 1995; Naimishray 2003; Mata Prasad 1987; Shakya 1999. Also, Narayan 2006: 113–32.

[43] For example, Sheelbodh 2005.

[44] Varma 2004: 15.

here as not only visible but conspicuous characters, as objects of adulation. These representations can be read in different ways as they signify contradictory voices, simultaneously asserting and subverting patriarchies, stretching the boundaries of both 1857 and of the images of Dalit women.[45]

Jhalkari Bai of the Kori caste comes across as an immortal martyr (*amar shaheed*) of 1857. She hails from Jhansi, her husband Puran Kori being an ordinary soldier in the kingdom of Raja Gangadhar Rao. Jhalkari Bai is depicted as the ideal woman, occasionally helping her husband in his traditional occupation of cloth weaving and some-times accompanying him to the royal palace. She is stated to have been brave from her childhood, having been trained by her husband in archery, wrestling, horse-riding, and shooting. Her face and body structure are said to resemble Lakshmibai's. Gradually, Jhalkari Bai and Lakshmibai become friends. Jhalkari was entrusted with the charge of leading the women's wing of the army (*stri sena*), known as Durga Dal. When the 1857 revolt began, the indigenous rulers were mostly interested in saving their thrones. But it was the Dalits who made the revolt a freedom struggle. When the British besieged the fort of Jhansi, Jhalkari fought fiercely. She urged Lakshmibai to escape from the palace and herself took on the guise of the Rani. Her husband died while fighting the British, and upon learning this Jhalkari acquired the ferocity of an injured lioness (*ghayal singhni*). She killed many British soldiers and managed to deceive them for a long time before they discovered her true identity.[46] According to some versions a bullet, followed by a whole hail, ultimately felled her.[47] Another account states that she was set free to live and struggle for a long time.[48]

Uda Devi is said to have been born in the village of Ujriaon around Lucknow. Also known as Jagrani, she was married to Makka Pasi. Becoming an associate of Begum Hazrat Mahal, she formed

[45] Further, different groups from different social circumstances perceive the same representations differently: Hall 1980.

[46] Naimishray 1999: 133–7; Dinkar 1990: 21–5; Mohar 1976: 314; Visharad 1988.

[47] Dinkar 1990: 25.

[48] Shakya 1999: 51–4.

a women's army with herself as commander. Her husband having been martyred in the battle at Chinhat, Uda decided upon revenge.[49] When the British attacked Sikandar Bagh in Lucknow under Campbell, he faced an army of Dalit women:

> Some called them Black African women, some untouchable. Some called them weak, others strong.[50]

> [*koi unko habsin kehta, how kehta neech achhut.*
> *abla koi unhein batlaye, koi kahe unhe majboot.*]

At this point Uda Devi is said to have climbed over a *peepal* tree and shot dead—according to some accounts 32, and others 37—many British soldiers. One soldier, spotting someone in the trees, shot the person dead, only to discover that he had shot a woman.[51]

Asha Devi Gurjari is portrayed as providing leadership to a number of young girls and women; it is stated that on May 8, 1857 she, along with a large number of other Dalit women like Valmiki Mahabiri Devi, Rahimi Gurjari, Bhagwani Devi, Bhagwati Devi, Habiba Gurjari, Indrakaur, Kushal Devi, Naamkaur, Raajkaur, Ranviri Valmiki, Seheja Valmiki, and Shobha Devi, attacked the British army and died fighting.[52] Narratives on Avanti Bai claim that she was the queen of Ramgarh and belonged to the Lodhi community. In 1857, facing oppression by the British, she retaliated by fighting fiercely. When she was surrounded by British soldiers, she decided to kill herself rather than surrender. Her last wish was that the British leave Indian soil and return to their homeland.[53]

Mahabiri Devi belonged to the Bhangi caste and lived in the village of Mundbhar in the district of Muzaffarnagar. Though uneducated she was very intelligent and opposed exploitation of every kind from an early age. She was born for the poor and fought for them. Slowly,

---

[49] For further details, Narayan 2006: 133–49.

[50] Varma 2004: 36. The siege of Sikander Bagh in Lucknow has invoked many accounts. For example, Gordon-Alexander 1898: 65–107; Forbes-Mitchell 1893: 51–73.

[51] Pasi 1998: 7–20; Varma 2004: 20.

[52] Varma 1992: 18.

[53] "Saras" 1995; Naimishray 1999: 142.

her fame spread. Her father made winnowing baskets and hand-held fans. Mahabiri Devi created an organization of women whose aim was to remove women and children from being involved in "dirty" work, enabling them to live with dignity. In 1857 she formed a group of twenty-two women, attacking and killing many British soldiers. She herself was killed by them along with her twenty-two unknown women followers.[54]

As a historian one cannot but be troubled by the relative absence of "hard-core" and written historical evidence in the archives, and in British official and nationalist narratives, on these *viranganas*. While the actual and the fictional coalesce here, are these basically historical myths and fictive histories, or something more? It is tempting to argue that anything that mesmerizes is worth cherishing, and that magic is ruined by questioning its "authenticity." It may also be asked: How "truthful" are official, canonized histories of 1857? Scholars have questioned the possibility of any single authoritative history.[55] Some have contended that history is a prodigious fiction of the human imagination.[56] These glorified Dalit *virangana*-centered histories hint at larger possibilities as they thrive on culture-specific ideals engineered through myths and realities about the position of Dalits and their marginalization. They stand as persuasive accounts, reaching towards their own "realities" and establishing a coherence and consistency for members of the Dalit communities.[57] Carlo Ginzburg shows how an early manifesto on history "from below" appeared in the form of an "imaginary biography" where the intention was to salvage, through a symbolic character, a multitude of lives crushed by poverty and oppression. The mix of imaginary biographies and historical documents makes it also possible for these Dalit histories to leap with a single bound over a threefold obstacle: the lack of evidence; the lack of importance of the subject according to commonly accepted criteria; and the absence of stylistic models. A multitude of lives that have been destined to count for nothing

[54] Dinkar 1990: 26.

[55] Said 1989: 217, 225; White 1987; Sethi 1999: 180–5; Appleby, Hunt, and Jacob 1994.

[56] MacRaild 2008.

[57] Hosking and Schopflin 1997.

find symbolic redemption in the depiction of immortal characters.[58] Can someone who is investigating the history of subordinate social groups expect to reconstruct individuals in the fullest sense of the term?[59] Context, considered as an array of historically determined possibilities, then serves to provide what documents fail to tell us about an individual. These integrations, however, are possibilities, not necessarily consequences; conjectures, not considered facts.[60]

But this is not enough. Dalits are keen to prove the historical credibility of their *viranganas* and constantly cite sources from literary accounts, British narratives, archeology, and oral histories. They claim their works are "scientific," "truthful," and "detailed." Reiteration and authentication go hand in hand in these mediations. This is a conscious effort to suggest the existence of historical dimensions that are hidden, in part—but not only—owing to the difficulties of documentary access, so that gaps must be filled through memories, folksongs, oral accounts, and elements taken from larger present contexts. To quote one of these writers:

> The whole incident is noted inside historical sources.
> This immortal story of ours is not a figment of imagination.[61]
>
> [*aithihasik sandarbhon bhitar, ankit sari hai ghatna.*
> *nahin kalpana se kalpit hai—amar humari yeh rachna.*]

These accounts take recourse to historical events and mix them up with subaltern renderings. In assembling these historical/cultural scripts, Dalit writers take their cue from multiple lineages. The dim boundary between the imaginary and the real is the home terrain of these writings. They impel us to recognize their validity, particularly within a political and social context. They represent a practice of writing which neither disregards history nor, in its insistence on legitimacy, is completely oblivious of other myths and memories. Such practices do not question how far narratives approximate to what once was real: they consider the adequacy of those representations within

[58] Ginzburg 1999: 111–14.
[59] Ibid.: 115.
[60] Ibid.: 116–17.
[61] Varma 2004: 16.

the circumstances in which they were generated. Dalit writings on 1857 fulfill that necessary criterion. Dalits say they are retrieving lost histories which have been deracinated by mainstream historiography, and creating their own notions of their place in historical processes. And they argue that this points to further possibilities of "truths" about 1857. As noted, while history will always seem more "real" than fiction, what emerges as "truth" will be seen from and conceived by the subject position that the author, reader, teacher, subaltern, or historian occupies.[62] In the words of one historian: "[H]istory is time which has gained sense and meaning. History is meaningful and sense-bearing time. It combines past, present and future in a way that human beings can live in the tense intersection of remembered pasts and expected future. History is a process of reflecting the time order of human life, grounded on experience and moved by outlooks on the future."[63]

Scattered, often thin, evidence is cited and repeatedly quoted by Dalits. On Jhalkari Bai, a constantly quoted source is Vrindavan Lal Varma's *Jhansi ki Rani Lakshmibai*. This was published in 1946 after intense research and historical reflection. It mentioned a dusky-complexioned newlywed Jhalkari Dulaiya of the Kori caste, who bore a striking resemblance to the Rani.[64] Vishnubhat Godse, a traveling Brahmin from Maharashtra who is said to have been present in the fort when the Rani fought against General Rose, had also referred to Jhalkari in his Marathi book *Majha Pravas*.[65] Similarly, on Uda Devi, Amritlal Nagar's *Gadar ke Phool*, and William Forbes-Mitchell's *Reminiscences of the Great Mutiny* are often cited.[66] One paragraph from Forbes-Mitchell's book reads thus:

In the centre of the inner court of the Secundrabagh there was a large *peepul* tree with a bushy top, round the foot of which were set a number of jars full of cool water. When the slaughter was almost over many of

[62] Spivak 1988.

[63] Rusen 2005: 2.

[64] Varma 1987 (1946): 92–5, 324. For analysis of this work, see Orsini 2002: 215–24.

[65] Godse 1974 (1907); Nagar 1981 (1957).

[66] Forbes-Mitchell 1893: 57–8. This is the most often quoted source. For example, Varma 2004: 8.

our men went under the tree for the sake of its shade and to quench
their burning thirst with a draught of the cool water from the jars. A
number however lay dead under this tree, both of the Fifty-Third and
Ninety-Third and the many bodies lying in that particular spot attracted
the notice of Captain Dawson. After having carefully examined the
wounds, he noticed that in every case the men had evidently been shot
from above. He thereupon stepped out from beneath the tree and called
to Quaker Wallace to look up if he could see any one in the top of the
tree, because all the dead under it had apparently been shot from above.
Wallace had his rifle loaded and stepping back he carefully scanned the
top of the tree. He almost immediately called out, "I see him, sir!" and
cocking his rifle he repeated aloud,

> I'll pay my vows now to the Lord
> Before His people all.

He fired and down fell a body dressed in a tight-fitting red jacket and
tight-fitting rose-coloured silk trousers; and the breast of the jacket
bursting open with the fall, showed that the wearer was a woman.[67]

Other historical narratives sometimes substantiate these claims. For
example, W. Gordon-Alexander's account of the storming of Sikandar
Bagh by British troops states:

> In addition . . . there were . . . even a few amazon negresses, amongst the
> slain. These amazons having no religious prejudices against the use of
> greased cartridges, whether of pigs' or other animal fat, although doubtless
> professed Muhammadans, were armed with rifles, while the Hindu and
> Muhammadan East Indian rebels were all armed with musket; they
> fought like wild cats, and it was not till after they were killed that their
> sex was even suspected.[68]

Today these *viranganas* stand as given, visible truths, with stamps
issued in their name, many statues constructed, public rallies and
meetings organized, celebrations and festivities conducted, and even
colleges and medical institutions named after them. A huge public
rally and a *mela* is organized in Lucknow every year near the statue
of Uda Devi at Sikandar Bagh on November 16, the day stated to be

[67] Forbes-Mitchell 1893: 57–8.
[68] Gordon-Alexander 1898: 104.

that of her martyrdom.[69] Through a process of constant evocation, these names have become inscribed in Dalit popular memory. In fact these *virangana*s have come to be indispensable symbols in the electoral campaigns of various political parties, the most successful being the BSP, which has used them to build up the image of Mayawati.[70] The links are established by making Mayawati seem the embodiment of miraculous courage and power—those of a goddess and a *devi*—through these icons.[71]

Reading Popular Dalit Histories
of Viranganas

Popular histories of Dalit *virangana*s are open to simultaneously persuasive and competing readings. The constraints of this literature as a historical source are obvious, and its representation of Dalit women needs interrogation. As the main narrative plots have become more elaborate with time, they have also become more sure of themselves, specially of their connection with the larger purposes of Dalit identity. Elements of exaggeration have seeped in deeper. In the Jhalkari Bai story, one episode repeatedly narrated is of Jhalkari being blamed for killing a cow which had in fact been hidden by a Brahmin; but the truth is revealed.[72] This story challenges dominant colonial and Hindu narratives which have regarded Dalits, along with Muslims, as killers of the "holy" cow. Another example: in some stories Jhalkari and Uda start as the subordinates of Lakshmibai and Hazrat Mahal, functioning under their tutelage, and represent images of "alterity" to these figures.[73] However, these have slowly given way to more authoritative and "mature" Dalit histories in which Jhalkari and Uda acquire a larger-than-life status. Earlier narratives on Jhalkari Bai claim she is an accomplice of Lakshmibai who took on her garb to save the

[69] I was present in the *mela* in 2005, organized by Virangana Uda Devi Smarak Sansthan. Every year they take out a magazine on the occasion: *Smarika*.

[70] Narayan 2006: 30–3.

[71] Narayan 2001: 138–54; 2006: 152, 171.

[72] Naimishray 2003; Shakya 1999: 16–27.

[73] Shakya 1999.

Rani's life. We can discern in these tellings a tentativeness regarding the role of Lakshmibai in the revolt, in which Jhalkari Bai is shown as an accomplice or at best the equal of Lakshmibai.[74] However, this template has given way to a Dalit history in which Lakshmibai, instead of being a model nationalist ruler, appears as a weakling reluctant to fight the British and scared of war.[75] Challenging myths and histories surrounding Lakshmibai, it is argued that she not only managed to escape to the forests of Nepal with the help of the ruler of Pratapgarh, but also that she died only in 1915, at the age of eighty. The real martyr is now the *virangana* Jhalkari Bai. It is her name that ought to be written in golden letters. Jhalkari Bai acquires a distinct moral edge over Lakshmibai, for she gave real credence to the notion of sacrifice by behaving in a completely unselfish way. She was a Dalit woman with no kingdom, no palace, no expensive jewelry, no silken clothes. She was neither a queen nor the daughter of a feudal lord nor the wife of a *jagirdar*. She fought selflessly, only for love of her country, and thus her sacrifice far surpasses every other.[76] Dalits further argue that since their women did hard physical labor, their bodies were strong and sturdy, much more suited to fighting than those of upper-caste women, who were frail and delicate, "getting a sprain by just breaking a cucumber."[77] Amplification and admiration are hallmarks in these stories. Forbes-Mitchell's account has formed the most important source for Uda Devi, but it is selectively appropriated. After describing how the woman was shot dead, he clearly states: "She was armed with a pair of heavy old-pattern cavalry pistols, one of which was in her belt still loaded and her pouch was still about half full of ammunition, while from her perch in the tree, which had been carefully prepared before the attack, *she had killed more than half-a-dozen men.*"[78] Interestingly, Dalit accounts leave this out, and the number of soldiers killed by Uda Devi has kept growing, ranging from 32 to 36![79] There are thus stresses and omissions, additions

[74] Ibid.
[75] Dinkar 1990: 21.
[76] Naimishray 1999: 136; 2003: 5; Dinkar 1990: 21–5.
[77] Singh 2011: 269.
[78] Forbes-Mitchell 1893: 58. Emphasis mine.
[79] Pasi 1998: 10–11.

and subtractions in these tracts. Reflecting the ambiguities of Dalits towards nationalism, there is sometimes a covert admiration for the British. It is said that realizing the brave feat was that of Uda, even British officers like Campbell bowed their heads over her dead body in respect.[80] Forbes-Mitchell is again quoted as saying: "When Wallace saw that the person whom he shot was a woman, he burst into tears, exclaiming: 'If I had known it was a woman, I would rather have died a thousand deaths than have harmed her.'"[81]

Some of these Dalit *viranganas* have become specifically iconic within particular Dalit castes, as Uda Devi is for the Pasis.[82] Jhalkari Bai, on the other hand, has been appropriated and eulogized by all Dalits and become a symbol of their unity. These histories do not privilege individual self-fashioning; rather, they produce a collective record of struggle through these women, as against the interiority of the individual heroine. Mimicry becomes an important tool. Many of these *viranganas* show features similar to those in popular memories of Lakshmibai, and they use analogous language and idioms. All are super-brave. They are physically attractive, "classic" beauties, falling into the stereotype of female good looks. They are described as tall, with pointed noses and beautiful eyes.[83] In these eulogizations, poems and songs occupy a central place. Many narrative poems (*khand kavyas*) have cleverly appropriated the famous poem written by Subhadrakumari Chauhan on Lakshmibai. Not only are the lines and words reinterpreted, giving them new meaning, the lilt of the meter also makes them easy to remember. There is this one on Jhalkari Bai:

> Jhalkari you really fought, your youthfulness was unique.
> You were a man among the brave in ousting the British.
> We heard your story from the mouths of warriors.
> You pledged victory for Jhansi by being a friend to the queen . . .
> Jhalkari, you rode from the Datiya gate, trampling the British.
> You were like Kali, and your strike was like lightning.

[80] Ibid.: 7–20; Varma 2004: 20.
[81] Forbes-Mitchell 1893: 58.
[82] Narayan 2006: 133–49.
[83] Shakya 1999: 2, 6; Varma 2004: 23.

The moment a Briton raised his head, you struck him immediately.
We heard your deeds from warriors reciting tales of your bravery.[84]

[*khub lari jhalkari tu tau, teri ek jawani thi.*
dur firangi ko karne mein, veeron mein mardani thi.
har bolon ke much se sun hum teri yeh kahani thi.
rani ki tu saathin banker, jhansi fatah karani thi . . .
datiya fatak raund firangi, agge barh jhalkari thi.
kali roop bhayankar garjan, mano karak damini thi.
kou firangi aankh uthain, dhar se shish uteri thi.
harbolon ke much se sun ham, roop chandika pani thi.]

Most of these *viranganas* have Devi or Bai suffixed to their name.
They are projected as super-moral Dalit women who were very
"noble," besides being highly brave, fantastic nationalists. They are
emblems of *shakti*. Many of these tracts appear didactic in their en-
dorsement of patriarchal values, being often replete with images of
the obedient daughter, loyal wife, and ideal mother, and of morally
chaste, virtuous, and "ideal" women.[85] The moral language perhaps
also allows Dalit men to police the behavior of Dalit women in
general. There is a fight against oppression and yet hegemonic scripts
get rewritten, whereby Dalits make their rubrics of identity conform
to definitions drawn from dominant modes.

Almost all histories of Dalit *viranganas* are written by male authors
catering in no small measure to masculinized political–public spaces.
Very few Dalit women have penned these pamphlets. The gendered
subaltern rarely speaks about herself in these histories, the voices of
Dalit *viranganas* appearing in them like faint discursive threads. It is
the Dalit male author who provides narrative coherence, filling in the
gaps and slipping into the present tense to add dramatic flourish to
the stories. The written word about and visual images of *viranganas* in
these texts and on the covers of the pamphlets spectacularize them by
showing them clad in "masculine" attire, their bodies all covered up.
In all of them they are shown as expert in horse-riding, swimming,
archery, and sword-fighting.[86] They are depicted as born brave, and

[84] Shakya 1999: 1, 44.
[85] Ibid.: 4.
[86] Varma 2004: 23.

the 1857 revolt becomes the turning point that sparks them into
accomplishing great deeds against all the odds. Working through
these women, the tracts are infused with militaristic versions of
1857, the female warrior now a symbol of pride for mainly masculine
political articulation. Through the construction of what might be
termed the Dalit Amazonian, an embattled Dalit masculinity can
be seen as professing itself in the public–political sphere. It may
be argued that the leadership of Mayawati provides a corrective to
this, but she too often fits similar molds. Further, Uda Devi, for
example, has become a figurehead mainly for promoting the political
aspirations of Ramlakhan Pasi, who is stated to have discovered" her.
He has established the Uda Devi Smarak Sansthan which, through
its reverence for Uda Devi, has emerged as a symbol of Pasi honor,
dignity, mobilization, and rights.[87] At the same time, this is utilized
by Ramlakhan Pasi to harness political–public spaces in which there
is as much praise of him as of Uda Devi.[88] In short, while there are
Dalit Amazonian heroines, the leadership and voices propagating
them are largely of Dalit men.

Even as these Dalit *viranganas* are portrayed as superwomen
performing "impossible" acts, the glorifications do not extend to
Dalit women in general. Victimhood is replaced by a new archetype
of heroism which distinguishes only the very few women that are
constructed as heroic. Jhalkari Bai is shown as killing a tiger single-
handedly, scarcely the kind of thing that can be extended into an
image of possibilities for the ordinary Dalit woman.[89] Although empowering, these images are thus not representative of Dalit women.
They often remain simplistic, rarely revealing the diversity, complexity,
and multidimensional facets that make up Dalit women's lives. Therefore, while one may be susceptible to the lure of these images, they
often appear through a filtered vision carefully manipulated by their
male creators.

It may be argued from a Dalit feminist perspective that the emergence of popular Dalit male literature on 1857 has not greatly altered

[87] Narayan 2006: 133–49.

[88] For example, a number of poems and write-ups are devoted to Ramlakhan Pasi in *Smarika*.

[89] Naimishray 2003.

the images of Dalit women. Though different in their scope, arena, and portrayals, these presentations fail to offer a more intelligent and meaningful portrayal of such women. Save for who controls the representations, has anything much changed for the Dalit woman? As bell hooks puts it, this may signify a mere transference without any radical transformation.[90] A truly liberating potential can only be realized when Dalit women themselves create and represent their own histories and images through a collage of identities, and when they sing their own songs.

At the same time, if we argue that representations of these Dalit *viranganas* are constructed only to support dominant male ideology, and that their aim is ultimately coercive, how may this space be also used for confrontation? Does their representation also contain the possibility of carving out more contingent, varied, and flexible modes of resistance?[91] Can they provide oppositional perspectives about Dalit women and about the 1857 revolt? For example, in these stories does the very act of speaking back, of mimicry, impart new interpretations and meanings? As Homi Bhabha says: "To the extent to which discourse is a form of defensive warfare, mimicry marks those moments of civil disobedience within the discipline of civility: signs of spectacular resistance. Then the words of the master become the state of hybridity—the warlike, subaltern sign of the native—then we may not only read between the lines but even seek to change the often coercive reality that they so lucidly contain."[92]

Even the representation of Dalit *viranganas* on a high moral and heroic ground can be seen as an appropriation of respectability and "credibility," imparting new meaning to Dalit participation in past histories. Moral codes have a completely different valence here. Through such portrayals Dalits hope to garner greater respect, opportunity, and dignity for these *viranganas*, and thereby for all Dalits. Such portrayals thus acquire layered meanings. They embody an inspiring picture centered in claims about the neglect of Dalit women warriors of 1857, a marginalization that can no longer be tolerated

[90] hooks 1992: 126.
[91] Rajan 1993: 11, 129.
[92] Bhabha 1994: 121.

by Dalits.[93] Dalit *viranganas* not only carve Dalits into a nation, they also refuse the dominant narratives of humiliation. Here the subalterns are conspicuously vocal, showing a reversal of Spivak's proposition.[94] As has been pointed out, "While Spivak is excellent on the 'itinerary of silencing' endured by the subaltern, particularly historically, there is little attention to the process by which the subaltern's 'coming to voice' might be achieved."[95]

The portrayal of Dalit *viranganas* also interrogates the typecasting of Dalit women as sexually deviant, loose, and unfaithful, and questions the putative relation between history and Dalit women. By shunning outward expressions of sexuality, Dalit women can hope to build a space where they wield more control over their bodies and gain dignity and respect within the dominant culture. Despite the limitations, this dismantles the hegemonic stereotypes of Dalit women which shows them as vamps, or else as passive victims, powerless and subordinated—both of which deny Dalit women any agency of their own. Here, in the new narratives, Dalit women are actors and agents in their own right, active and armed, transformed from victims to victors. Though penned into being by men, they can be appropriated by feminists for strategies of resistance.

The readership of these pamphlets encompasses all Dalits. Jhalkari Bai, Uda Devi, Mahabiri Devi, and alongside them other Dalit women emerge as physically commanding, infused with power, bravery, and sacrifice, locked in violent conflict with the British. The steeping of these narratives within martial valor and violence also implicitly indicates the lived realities of Dalits, which are so frequently marked by violence. Dalit women here become the signifiers of a Dalit identity shaped in part by the experience of violence. In this sense these are not just stories of brave Dalit women but of all Dalits, of their legacy, of their bravery, of their pride, and of their sacrifice in service of the nation.

At places the achievements of Dalit *viranganas* are contrasted with the pathetic condition of Dalit women. Society at large—including

[93] Varma 2004: 5, 17.
[94] Spivak 1988: 287–308.
[95] Moore-Gilbert 1998: 108.

men—is blamed, it being argued that despite their possession of such a brave past and in spite of their being protectors of Dalit dignity, Dalit women have been denied all education, made slaves, and oppressed by men.[96] Some Dalit women are now trying to use these images to their advantage, questioning representations of Dalit women in general, as well as their oppression and exploitation in real life. Thus, Meena Pasi states: "Uda Devi and Jhalkari Bai have shown me that I too can resist all kinds of injustices. I do not have to take things lying down. These figures inspire me to question why I am getting less wages from the landlord, why I am beaten up by my husband when I do equal, if not more, work. I can look up to Uda Devi and say that nothing is impossible if one has the will to resist and fight."[97]

These representations of Dalit women *viranganas* may thus also be seen as a form of "positive engendering,"[98] holding out an appeal to Dalit women generally. The centrality of Dalit *viranganas* in 1857 provokes reflection on the enabling potential for women's real lives via newly ubiquitous icons of Dalit feminine power. It urges Dalits to produce a more critical and self-reflexive account of 1857, reflecting the limits but also the potentialities of gendered Dalit readings. Rather than distilling hegemonic scripts from subversive ones, perhaps it would be more useful to see the lineages of these texts as not singular but layered and hybrid, offering hyphenated meanings of 1857 and of Dalit women participants.

Conclusion

What we are dealing with here are not ordinary academic histories, but histories fashioned in order to challenge conventional modes of thinking about 1857 and Dalit women. While they may not be inherently radical or transformative, they represent dissident voices, coexisting with and simultaneously challenging dominant narratives

[96] Varma 2004: 21.

[97] Interview with Meena Pasi on November 16, 2005 at Lucknow. She, along with many other women, was a participant in the celebration of "Uda Devi Shaheed Diwas," i.e. Uda Devi Martyrdom Event, on that day.

[98] Dehejia 1997: 1–21.

and ideologies. While creating a history of pride, these writers are accruing for Dalits a psychic space and harnessing the resources they need to hold their own on difficult ground. Modernity, memory, and commemoration conjoin to enact this new history of 1857. Dalits are negotiating the tensions of being both within and outside 1857 through processes of positioning and repositioning, denunciation and glorification. They identify 1857 as an arena of Dalit suppression, of attempts to restore feudal patriarchies, of the assertion of Dalit *viranganas*, and of establishing masculinized Dalit political–public spaces. These writings are caught in a dialectics of collusion with and subversion of notions of nationalism, of patriarchal and caste conceptions, of 1857, and of Dalit women. There is no single coherent story here but a dialogical process that stands at the border between disavowal and designation, rejection and valorization. The spaces of Dalits in 1857 are repeatedly lived, deciphered, and renegotiated. They mark a third space where the Mutiny, along with Dalit women's imagery, is simultaneously recovered and transformed, its old boundaries expanded and exploded.

It was, however, not just Dalit women, but also Dalit men and their masculinities that were shaped in multi-layered ways by upper-caste representations. These as well as Dalit men's efforts to reclaim respectability in traditional realms, and through new sites of social freedom, are the subject of exploration in the next chapter.

4

Feminine, Criminal, or Manly?

Imaging Dalit Masculinities

I n India, masculinity studies have burgeoned only recently.[1]
Feminist histories are incomplete without interrogating masculinity: "To understand a system of inequality, we must examine
its dominant group—the study of men is as vital for gender analysis
as the study of ruling classes and elites is for class analysis."[2] In India
the propertied, high-caste, heterosexual Hindu male is at the top
of religious and caste hierarchies, and this is taken as normal, natural, and beyond reproach.[3] Insightful works have revealed how the
male body was constructed in colonial discourse deploying the
dichotomies of the "manly British" and the "effeminate colonial
subject."[4] Links have also been drawn between the growth of the
Hindu Right, assertions of masculinity, and violence.[5] However,
the focus on colonial or upper-caste masculinity leaves unexamin-
ed its appearance in the creation of Dalit identity.[6] While religious

[1] Chopra, Osella, and Osella 2004; Dasgupta 2014.
[2] Connell 1992: 736. Also Connell 1995.
[3] Pandey 2013: 4.
[4] Nandy 1983; Sinha 1995; McClintock 1995.
[5] Banerjee 2005; Chakraborty 2011.
[6] Thus, one source states: "We note with dismay, but a sense of inevitability,
the absence in this polarised picture of the Dalit (ex-untouchable) man,
certainly another of the modern South Asian nation's problematic 'Others'
and hope to find future work addressing this lacuna." See Chopra, Osella,
and Osella 2004: 4. Some anthropological works on India have provided an
important corrective. See Anandhi, Jeyaranjan, and Krishnan 2002: 397–406.

identities have remained an important arena for masculinity studies, the same cannot be said with equal certainty about caste. Dalits have, in discourses around masculinity, remained vexingly invisible or have appeared only as "otherized" negative referents. In other words the entanglements of caste, Dalit identities, sexual ideology, and masculinity have not been much recognized in spite of a growing body of work on Dalits in colonial India. Nonetheless, masculinities are hierarchically structured,[7] whereby the upper castes define their male identities in relation to the subordination of women and other marginalized masculinities. Examining Dalit masculinity destabilizes images of hegemonic masculinity,[8] challenging the rigid links between masculinity, domination, and power. Dalit masculine subjectivity remained ambiguous in its relation with upper-caste masculinity in colonial India. Claiming manhood, for example, could become a way of articulating dignity and rights for Dalits, thereby contesting or creatively appropriating upper-caste ideals of masculinity.

Here I place Dalit masculinity at the center, exploring the diachronic ways in which the Dalit male body was socially manipulated, dismantled, and reinterpreted by colonial authorities, the upper castes, and Dalits themselves, diversely for control and identity-construction in colonial UP. The chapter moves at two distinct yet overlapping levels that repudiate or celebrate Dalit masculinity. First, approaching Dalit masculinity discursively, it shows how the image of the impudent and the delinquent was inscribed onto Dalit bodies by upper castes and colonizers, reflecting the existing dialectics of power relationships and the larger structures of Dalit oppression—such as their lack of education, a discriminatory labor market, a skewed criminal justice system, and technologies of surveillance which resulted in the systematic decimation of Dalit malehood. Second, it attempts to understand the self-fashioning and self-positioning of masculinity in the accounts of Dalit men, shaped by their efforts to claim social respectability in traditional and customary realms—work, women, and

---

Significant works on black masculinity are Collins 2004: 181–212; Wallace 2002; Summers 2004.

[7] Connell 1992, 1995.

[8] Connell 1995.

clothing—on the one hand, and on the other through new sites of social freedom, such as recruitment into the army, re-creating Dalit pasts, labor strikes, and labor protests. The attempt, overall, is to read Dalit histories and the politics of Dalit manhood through a gendered lens.

Dilemmas in Colonial and Upper-Caste Narratives

In colonial India the idea of manhood blossomed into being a national preoccupation. Colonialism justified itself through masculine images, and nationalism worked its own versions, raising individual concerns and collective anxieties over the meanings of masculinity and femininity. Masculinity was expressed in different ways, varying from Vivekananda to Gandhi, from Sanatan Dharmists to Arya Samajists, and from notions of *brahmacharya* to images of Krishna as warrior.[9] Such constructions erased the Dalit male body from the national imaginary. National manhood was overwhelmingly constructed as Hindu and upper caste. However, Dalits could not escape the projection of other versions. The Hindu upper-caste and colonial male gaze froze Dalit bodies into rigid forms, embedding them in power relations. The interface between Western and upper-caste attitudes towards Dalit men reveals that their voices often converged. It was they who controlled the very definitions of masculinity, and while their claims often conflicted, both used similar models to assess their own masculine identities and those of other men, including Muslims and Dalits. Seemingly incongruent images portrayed Dalit men as meek and docile, strong but stupid, ready to serve their masters on the one hand, and on the other as criminal, violent, and threatening. Both sets of contradictory images were framed within and confined to narrow representational fields and fed into each other, the contexts of their invocation contingent and situationally conjured. Such constructions, while making Dalit men publicly visible, bolstered the stereotypes of Dalit male otherness.

[9] Nandy 1983: 1–63; Sinha 1995; McClintock 1995; Banerjee 2005; Chakraborty 2011; Alter 1992, 2000.

Dumb, Dutiful, and Deferential

The Indian male was fashioned by the British as effeminate, lacking in manliness.[10] This was magnified in fabrications of the Dalit male. His body emulated the servile body of the bonded laborer. There was a repeated framing of him as socially meek, politically powerless, economically backward, intellectually stupid, and yet physically strong. Since Dalit men did hard manual labor, justifying the harsh conditions forced upon them required objectifying their bodies as resilient and dim-witted, thus reinforcing their status within domestic subservience. The Chamar male, for example, was often seen as docile, both in colonial and upper-caste literature, ready to do hard work. The Dalit male body was infantilized, tamed, and trained for practical use. Dalits were considered a form of agricultural machinery, valued primarily for their hard work, endurance, and productive capability. Numerous narratives attested to their passivity in servitude, describing them as agricultural laborers par excellence.[11] In several gazetteers of UP it was reiterated that Chamars were good, in fact the best, culti-vators, but were habitually inclined to relinquish and desert their holdings on the slightest of pretexts.[12] The settlement reports too declared that Chamars were hard-working, industrious, laborious, and submissive.[13] M.A. Sherring reported: "They [the Chamars] are willing, obedient, patient and capable of great endurance; yet are apt to be light-fingered and deceitful."[14] There was a widespread feeling that the ignorant Chamar was the only useful Chamar.[15]

Patron–client linkages in villages, and the prevalence of the *jaj-mani* system, and of *begar* particularly in eastern UP, amplified the usefulness of such imagery.[16] This densely populated region suffered

[10] Nandy 1983; Sinha 1995.

[11] *Census, 1931, UP*: 438–42; *Royal Commission on Agriculture*: 391.

[12] *Badaun: A Gazetteer*: 72; *Pilibhit: A Gazetteer*: 89; *Shahjahanpur: A Gazetteer*: 19; *Banaras: A Gazetteer*: 96; *Farrukhabad: A Gazetteer*: 69, 85; *Mirzapur: A Gazetteer*: 99.

[13] For example, *Final Settlement Report on the Bulandshahr District*: 10.

[14] Sherring 1872: 391.

[15] Briggs 1920: 231.

[16] Neale 1962: 21; Mayer 1993: 357–95.

from extreme poverty and heavy pressures on agricultural land. The growth of sugarcane cultivation profited *zamindar*s but offered no economic opportunities for Dalits,[17] 80 per cent of whom were agricultural peasants and laborers.[18] Many Dalits were in debt bondage for generations, receiving awfully low wages.[19] The relationship between the Dalit agricultural laborer and his master was severely exploitative. Local proverbs in UP reflected this position. One proverb on Dalits asserted that as soon as an untouchable had a goblet full of corn he grew proud (*gagri dana, sud utana*), that is to say, he had to be constantly kept living from hand to mouth lest he went on strike. Another helped create the image of perennial servitude: a Chamar must do *begar* even over times of festivity and celebration (*chamar ki diwali par bhi begar*).[20]

Many Dalits had started life as domestic servants in the households of landlords. Even though segregated as agricultural workers, sweepers, and servants, they were in constant intersection with familial spaces. To make them "fit" to serve the upper castes, outcaste men were stripped of their sexuality, their sexual access being conditioned by surveillance. Their masculinity unmade, Dalit men were embodied as asexual, emasculated, and subordinate. Alongside, they were appreciated for their gentleness, childlike simplicity, and affectionate character. This conjectural benevolence, bestowed on Dalit men by their landlords, was one aspect of a devious hegemonic deployment inasmuch as it fed into the suggestion that existing Dalit rural subordination was preferable to their exposure to the "tyrannies of freedom" in the towns. The village was romanticized as an arena of harmony;[21] apparently it was where upper castes behaved with lower castes in

[17] Amin 1984.
[18] *Royal Commission on Agriculture*: 388–91.
[19] Singh 1947: 23, 29, 38; Chaturvedi 1947: 50.
[20] Gautum 2007a: 104.
[21] Various colonial and Western writers, for example Sir Charles Metcalfe, and Indian thinkers and leaders, the foremost being Gandhi, also deemed the Indian village as the epitome of authenticity, the ideal homogeneous location. However, Dalit intellectuals, especially Ambedkar, have provided divergent understandings, showing up the village as a place of oppression and exploitation. For an overview, see Jodhka 2012.

line with customary boundaries (*maryada*), and where Chamar and Pasi men were considerately addressed.[22] *Seva* and fidelity had a much higher status in this version of the world than *naukari*. An article titled "*Hindu Bhangi*," published in the leading Hindi journal *Chand*, while ostensibly expressing sympathy for sweepers, actually strengthened caste hierarchies:

> Bhangi means to serve . . . If sweepers refuse to clean, who will protect the grandeur of the rich and the veiling of high-caste women? . . . Their homes are kept outside the villages and cities so that they get adequate rest and their health remains fine . . . Sweepers are not our servants (*naukar*s) but our attendants (*sevak*s) . . . Sweepers who work for money in government municipalities are to be criticized as they do it for salaries, while their real job is to serve without greed.[23]

While excoriating caste attitudes towards untouchables, the journal delineated the tribulations which the upper castes had to suffer: "If untouchables eschew the protection of Hindus and convert, will you clean your own toilets? Will your women do the work of midwives? Will you do the work of a washerman? Will you do all the work of Chamars?"[24]

Many reformers were categorical in their understanding that untouchables should not give up their traditional occupations, arguing that there was nothing inferior about cleaning out excrement and dirt, and that this was necessary and "natural."[25] It was their physical labor which made Dalits the prize "possessions" of the upper castes, who, naturally, disdained manual work. The Dalit male's intellect was adduced as deficient and childlike.[26] Denied the workings of a normal brain, he was suited to relegation for bodily labor. Binaries of men/women reverberated in the relationship between upper-caste

[22] *Chand*, July 1939: 189–92.

[23] Gaurishankar Singh Chandail, "*Hindu Bhangi*" (Hindu Sweeper), *Chand*, June 1934: 145–9.

[24] Zahurbaksh, "*Samaj ke Agnikund: Achhut ki Atmakatha*" (Fires of Society: Autobiography of an Untouchable), *Chand*, May 1927: 69–88 (88).

[25] "*Antyajon ka Prashn*" (The Question of Younger Brothers), *Chand*, May 1927: 95–7 (97).

[26] "*Dalit Samuday ki Arthik Samasya*" (The Economic Problem of the Dalit Community), *Chand*, January 1940: 133–4.

and Dalit men: intellect/body, rational/irrational, reason/emotion. It was argued that to run society in an efficient manner each caste should be assigned work suited to their capacities, and that this symbolized progress and civilization. An editorial in *Chand* suggested that "Because of Shudras and *dasa*s, many a high caste was relieved of the everyday problems of living, and can devote themselves exclusively to research and thinking, creating philosophy, poetry, and literature."[27]

The Arya Samaj often succumbed to this rhetoric as well. In an article in the magazine *Sudha*, Gangaprasad Upadhyay, a leading figure of the Arya Samaj in UP, pronounced the distinction between "headwork" and "handwork" along caste lines: "The *achhut*s can do no work themselves; they can only obey orders issued by others. If they are with a student, they can keep his books in order; if they are with a soldier, they can dust and clean his sword; if they are with a trader, they can sweep his shop. These men have been referred to as our feet. We must remember that they are not unnecessary but that they can do no original work. They can just follow others' orders."[28]

Dalit men were often visualized in terms used to define women and femininity: small, frail, and docile. It was posited that, symbolically, Dalit labor fostered the same love between landlord and Dalit as marriage did between husband and wife, virtually vindicating inequality as the condition of love. As one reformist tract put it: "We need to be protective towards our *achhut* younger brothers. Just as a husband takes care of his wife and bestows love on her, while also keeping a watch on her movements, we too need to look after *achhut*s and see to it that they are not swayed by external influences. For a harmonious society it is imperative that we maintain such a balance."[29]

Even sympathetic accounts of Dalit men were often cast in the same language. They were seen to possess feminine characteristics—as being more religious, more artful, and more inclined to music.

[27] Editorial, *"Hindu Samaj aur Jatibhed"* (Hindu Society and Caste Differences), *Chand*, May 1932: 2–7 (3).

[28] Gangaprasad Upadhyay, *"Samaj Sudhar," Sudha*, July 1929: 665. Also, Upadhyay 1930, 1941: 11.

[29] Sharma 1923: 24.

There was a romantic casteism here, where the affectionate nature of Dalit men was underlined. An Arya Samaj tract observed: "If we look deeply into the hearts of our *achhut* brother who works around us, we will find a village simpleton who bestows care on us unconditionally. He addresses us as *seth-sahib, babu-sahib*, and *mai-baap*. In return he demands nothing from us except some love."[30] Annie Besant summed it up: "They [the depressed classes] are gentle, docile, as a rule industrious, pathetically submissive, merry enough when not in actual want, with a bright though generally very limited intelligence; of truth and the civic virtues they are for the most part utterly devoid . . . but they are affectionate, grateful for the slightest kindness and with much 'natural religion.'"[31]

Literature in support of and against religious conversions strengthened such imagery. Reformist magazines epitomized Dalits as incapable of independently taking the decision to convert, conjecturing that this was connected to the fact that they were feeble, small of stature, and without a voice or mind in most matters, being manipulated by

15. "Football of the Untouchables"

The *pandit* is scorning the untouchables by giving a call to ostracize them, and the *maulvi* and the *padri* are welcoming the untouchable-like football!!

Source: Chand, January 1929: 455.

[30] Prasad 1915: 8. Also Mishra 1922.
[31] Vatsa 1977 (1912): 31. Lajpat Rai too lamented their "lack of manhood": Rai 1914: 4, 21.

*maulvi*s and missionaries. One cartoon caricatured him as a "football," being kicked by the *pandit*, but being grabbed by the *maulvi* and the *padri* (Figure 15).

Another exhibited him as "unclaimed property" (Figure 16).

Various illustrations reinforced the idea of the meek Dalit body, usually portraying it as dark, set against a white background and an upper-caste, fair, well-built body for enhanced visual contrast.[32] Ironically, these same hues were used to contrast British people from Indians and upper castes from Dalits. A newspaper said: "The word and image of the black (*kala*) created the idea of a helpless, starving and poverty-stricken slave, bleeding in the back owing to gun-shot

16. "Unclaimed Property"

President Maulana Muhammad Ali: Brothers! The question of untouchables is a question of both Hindus and Muslims! It is preferable that Hindus and Muslims together—through compromise—divide them half-and-half. This will lead to Hindu–Muslim unity forever.

Swarajist: Sir, you are absolutely correct. We are in complete agreement with you. After all, these poor untouchables also need some definite place.

Congress Representatives: Ameen! Ameen!!

Source: *Chand*, May 1927: 187; *Chand*, January 1929: 452.

[32] Whiteness is often constructed as analogous with ideals of property, progress, and purity: Dyer 1997; Frankenberg 1993; Hoch 1979; Jordan 1968; Morrison 1992.

wounds and others caused by kicks and strokes of the horse-whip, trembling through fear and standing with hands joined and tears in his eyes."[33]

Such sketches formulated the social and cultural meanings of inhabiting a Dalit body and epitomized the aesthetic values of reformers. They indicated what was sanctioned, often repeatedly, and worthy of being expressed in print. Even benevolent representations of Dalits often used symbols of servility, the Dalit male body being sculpted as semi-nude and kneeling. Through such compromising effigies, the potential power of the male Dalit's body was curtailed, showing his bent legs and outstretched hands, thereby keeping him in "his place."

A segment of British ethnographers strengthened these stereotypes, where a significant marker of distinction was color and physical appearance. Dalit men were often stigmatized as dirty, short, ugly, unclean, and dark. Crooke wrote: "Some Bhangis have the dark complexion, stunted figure and peculiar dark flashing eye which is so characteristic of the Dom."[34] Similarly, Sherring on the Doms: "Dark complexioned, low of stature and somewhat repulsive in appearance, they are readily distinguished from all the better castes of Hindus."[35] Even missionary literature, meant to woo Dalits, could not escape such classifications. Describing the conquest over outcastes by Aryas, one tract stated:

> These Aryans are tall, broad, beautiful, well built and civilized. The non Aryans and low-caste people are ugly, weak, short, wild and uncivilized.[36]

> [yeh arya jati ke log lambe, chaure, sundar, sudaul aur sabhya hote hain. anarya aur neech jati ke log kurup, kudaul, nate kad ke aur asabhya hote hain.]

[33] *Kalidas, NNR*, June 12, 1900: 299.

[34] Crooke 1896b, I: 261.

[35] Sherring 1872: 401. The colonial ethnographer H.H. Risley was in the forefront of grounding caste differences through race. Others like E.A.H. Blunt, J.C. Nesfield, and D. Ibbetson took a different position, arguing that caste was related to occupation rather than an Aryan/non-Aryan divide. For differing perceptions amongst British ethnographers, see Bayly 1999.

[36] *Jati Panti ka Varnan* 1924: 3.

The language used was not a simple reflection of human physiology or customs; it reinforced the assumption that their physical attributes were also an expression of their moral qualities. In the process, these writers were exhibiting a highly charged and socially approved convention.

Defiant and Dangerous

However, these were not the only projections of Dalit men. A repertoire of images also synchronously forged them as lecherous, criminal, violent, and threatening.[37] These socially sanctioned pejoratives were linguistic shorthands in a jumble of casteist semiotics which became potent every time Dalits started asserting their rights. A section of British officials identified Dalits as having criminal attributes because of their genetic inheritance, assigning them the lowest position in the Hindu ranking system.[38] Many of these perceptions were shared by caste-Hindus,[39] who too saw them as aberrations and inferior parts of a homogeneous Hindu identity. Colonial practices drew upon existing Brahmanical frameworks and gave them a further stamp of authority by reifying and confirming such postulations. Images of Dalit men were extended from abstract textual categories into foundational ones. In many British documents and upper-caste perceptions, Dalit men, particularly Chamars, were associated with cattle theft. It was believed that they had an economic motive for poisoning cattle since they were chiefly regarded as tanners and shoemakers.[40] Crooke confidently stated that in numerous cases Chamars had poisoned cattle for hides and flesh.[41] William Hoey, Commissioner of Gorakhpur, was convinced of the diabolical nature

[37] Walsh 1929.

[38] For details, Freitag 1991; Yang 1985; Nigam 1990: 131–64; Mayaram 1991; Singha 1998; Kumar 2004; Rao and Dube 2013.

[39] Singha 1998: 37–46.

[40] For a critique, see Rawat 2012: 24–53. He shows how it was the colonial state that erroneously first singled out cattle poisoning not just as an occasional occurrence but an "organized and professional crime" associated with Chamars. Also, "Forms of Crime," Mss Eur F161/154, Indian Police Collection, OIOC.

[41] Crooke 1896b, II: 190.

of Chamars when it came to poisoning cattle.[42] Elsewhere it was stated that if any single community was utterly addicted to crime, it was the Bhangis.[43] The Pasis of Oudh were identified as criminal tribes under the Criminal Tribes Act of 1871 and thus constituted as hereditary robbers and thieves.[44] The Dusadhs were characterized as drunkards. The Doms of Gorakhpur were decried as always on the "threshold of jail," synonymous with all that was unclean.[45] The terms "criminals" and "low castes" were periodically used interchangeably. As the British discovered a bewildering host of specimens classifiable as "essential types," Dalits were often chronicled negatively in their imaginary.

Once certain Dalits became active in the anti-landlord movements of eastern UP, led by the Kisan Sabha in the 1920s and the spontaneous anti-*begari* agitations of the 1940s,[46] they were perceived as a threat because of their supposed predilection for violence. During riots Dalits were often pinpointed as violent and as a social menace. An officer reported from Kanpur in 1900: "The population of Cawnpore contains a large number of butchers and Chamars engaged in the various tanneries and leather factories, and these classes are notoriously of a turbulent disposition."[47]

Though Muslim men were conceived as the most potent threat to upper-caste Hindu women,[48] sometimes Dalit men were also portrayed in similar ways on account of the fear of intimate liaisons that might be established between them. The anxieties of upper-caste men and their illicit relationships with outcaste women were complemented by greater worries around upper-caste women canoodling with outcaste men. Public places were particularly "dangerous," because they were where outcaste and Muslim men ogled upper-caste women.[49] Didactic manuals ordered upper-caste women to keep away from Dalit men, or observe strict purdah when dealing with them. The treatise *Striyon*

[42] 154 (C)/February 1900, Box 27, Judl (Criminal) Deptt, UPSA.

[43] *Pilibhit: A Gazetteer.* 131.

[44] Hollins 1914: 92–4; Yang 1985: 108–27.

[45] 42–48/November 1916, Jails, A, Home Deptt, NAI; Kitts 1885: v.

[46] Rawat 2012: 175–7.

[47] 291–302/June 1900, Public, A, Home Deptt, NAI.

[48] Gupta 2001: 243–59, 269–98.

[49] Mahopdeshak 1927.

ko Chetavni cautioned: "Never emerge before Dhobis, Chamars, or Bhangis without purdah. Never eat anything offered by them or wear charms and amulets given by them. In public places, never talk to them."[50] Another, meant for Vaishya women, said: "Why do our women observe purdah with righteous men like their husbands and father-in-laws? What they need to do is observe strict purdah in relation to the low castes (*neech kaum*) such as the Dhobi, Chamar, and Bhangi, whose characters are reprehensible; but they often do not."[51]

Fears of illicit relations and exchanges of sensual pleasure between upper-caste women and low-caste men were also illustrated (Figure 17).

These mingled with apprehensions that some upper-caste widows might elope with or marry Muslim and lower-caste men. It was

17. "Tending the Feet"

Prosperous Woman: When you rub my feet with your hands, I am deeply contented.
Servant: I know your pulse.

"Body Paste"

Prosperous Woman: Rub a little more . . .
Servant: I might sprain you . . .

Source: *Vyanga Chitravali* 1930.

[50] Tirathram 1924: 12.
[51] Vaishya 1924: 285.

reported that two upper-caste widows had run away with a Dhobi and Bhangi, respectively. Both men, along with their wives, had converted to Christianity.[52] It was lamented that many Chamars, Nais, and Kahars were eloping with upper-caste widows.[53] Concomitantly, portrayals suggested that Dalit men had to be sexually potent in order to satisfy "hot-natured" Dalit women.[54] They were also imaged as wife beaters and drunkards, unleashing violence in domestic spaces (Figure 18).[55]

Such magnifications, portraying Dalit men as threatening, feral, and bestial, were routinely used by the upper castes to justify Dalit repression and were structural mechanisms for legitimizing an oppressive order.[56] There were two clear inclinations in such fabrications of

18. "Uneducated Husband of Low-caste"

So much time to bring water! I will hit you so hard with the stick that your leg will break!

Source: Chand, January 1941: 125.

[52] *"Samaj ki Chingariyan"* (Fires of Society), *Chand,* November 1927: 151–2.

[53] Dwivedi 1924: 36.

[54] *"Achhut," Chand,* August 1934: 352–9.

[55] *"Bal Patniyon ke Aasoon"* (The Tears of Child Wives), *Chand,* March 1927: 460–1.

[56] Gupta 1997: 120–1.

Dalit men. The exemplary body was one that could be manipulated and measured by its utility, displaying the qualities of industriousness and docility. Woeful were those that not only declined to serve, but defied caste superiority through violent encounters, symbolizing a reversal of entrenched hierarchies.

We Too Are "Men": Dalit Assertions of Manhood

Dalit men were not, of course, just passive screens on which high-caste men and the colonial authorities projected their caste, racial, and gender anxieties. Dalits engaged in a variety of appropriative and subversive strategies. Manhood was a coveted status brutally denied to Dalits, and its restoration in some measure was perceived by them as a prerequisite for rights, equality, and dignity. Through quotidian practices in the spheres of army, political organization, cultural per-formance, work, and private–public spaces, Dalits evolved ways to survive the self-alienating disjunction of caste. Conceiving a gendered sense of self by recuperating their manhood, Dalits were making a case that they possessed as much, if not more, social, cultural, political, and intellectual potential for advancement as the upper castes.

Migration to the cities of UP, while continuing to discriminate Dalits, helped them reconstitute their manhood in limited ways and make visible a variety of Dalit ways of being. Urbanization provided anonymity, making it difficult to enforce caste restrictions in their fullness, and employment opportunities could be sought in more diverse ways. Dalits founded their own movements, journals, caste associations, and temples. Even discourses on better homes and sanitary conditions could be couched in ways requiring that Dalits be considered "men." Urbanization enabled formerly submerged Dalit sub-populations to emerge and make manifest a pre-existing Dalit heterogeneity concerning gender, sexuality, class, and immigrant status. We shall see below some of the spaces where Dalits exerted a different notion of manhood, where they strove to refute subordinated Dalit masculinity by living their own versions of it in specific contexts. Sometimes this effort led to affirmations of their rights, though at other times it strengthened patriarchal formations and prevailing notions of masculinity.

Dalit Men in the Army and Police

Military modernity in colonial India provided many of UP's castes the possibilities of "manhood enhancement." The idiom of martial valor found supporters amongst the urban Shudra poor and the Yadavs and was an effective method for upward mobility.[57] Dalits too used this opportunity to postulate their distinctive military traditions and manhood, in the process drawing from others while giving them their own color. The role and participation of Dalits in the British army and police have been the subject of debate. Scholars, including Dalits, have researched colonial army histories to show that Dalits played a critical part as soldiers in the British armies.[58] The social heterogeneity of the East India Company soldiers, potentially incorporating many low castes, has been noted, as has the fact that Pasis were especially recruited in the earlier period.[59] The performance of Dalit soldiers in the armies of India under different rulers has been written about, as also how they benefited from colonial army services when attempting to emulate the martial traditions of the Kshatriya castes.[60] Mahars were recruited into the Bombay army of the East India Company and it is estimated that they constituted one-sixth of the army up to 1857.[61] The Bengal army led by Clive in the Battle of Plassey consisted largely of Chamars, Dusadhs, Dhusias, Doms, Dhanuks, and Pasis, as was also the case in Bihar and Punjab.[62] It appears that when the English began to transform themselves from an economic to a military power, the low castes provided their first soldiers.[63]

[57] Pinch 1996; Gooptu 2001.

[58] Most of these works have laid particular emphasis on the role of Mahars in the military history of India: Longer 1981; Basham 1980; Constable 2001.

[59] Kolff 1990.

[60] Cohen 1969. He points to the critical role of Dalits in the army during the colonial period. However, Cohen's suggestion that Dalit soldiers could only talk in the language of "Kshatriya-ization" is refuted by Philip Constable, as it does not allow scope for Dalit "sepoys to initiate, interact, and contribute to the formulation of social discourse themselves." Constable 2001: 442.

[61] Cohen 1969: 455.

[62] Basham 1980: 3, 24.

[63] Orme 1758.

However, the recruitment of Dalits into the British army proved fickle, particularly after 1857, when the government decided to stop enlisting them.[64] Theories of able-bodied martial races were approved after 1857 to facilitate a restructuring of the military along caste lines. This meant removing Dalits and Brahmins (as well as South Indians and the communities of eastern India), who were deemed weak, effeminate, and lacking in the martial virtues. Nonetheless, there was much debate on the subject among army officials. As early as 1800 British officers commanding regiments of cavalry had submitted applications for the dismissal of men whom they suspected of belonging to the "objectionable" low castes. Representations were made even to get rid of the low castes when recruiting the native infantry.[65] Some officers, however, condoned their recruitment: "The advantage of introducing low-caste men to a certain extent is that they are more ready to undertake work of a miscellaneous character, frequently such as would be an offence to the caste principles or prejudices of the higher, and further, that there is less danger of religious fanaticism, or of union between such men and the higher castes, on the basis of social and religious sympathy."[66] Brigadier M.G. Dennis, Commanding Officer at Allahabad, wrote to the Assistant Adjutant General, Kanpur Division, in a letter dated February 1, 1860:

> I have carefully inspected about 300 rank and file low-caste men of the Cawnpore Levy now stationed at Allahabad and in point of drill, discipline and apparent efficiency I consider them fully capable of being made quite equal to the high-caste men of the late Sipahee Regiments and from the information I have gleaned regarding the low-caste men, I believe that they possess many desirable qualifications for soldiers—they are anxious to become expert in the use of their arms, they possess much endurance and are ever ready to undertake without murmur the most severe toil assigned to them by their superiors, and for working on entrenchments and fortifications and for making mines and approaches, I believe that they would be found infinitely more willing and useful than high-caste men.[67]

[64] Constable 2001.
[65] F/4/260/5780, 1808–9, OIOC.
[66] L/MIL/7/7236, Military Deptt Records, OIOC.
[67] Ibid.

The most vociferous defense regarding Dalit recruitment in the army and police came from a report submitted in 1860 by Lieutenant Colonel Bruce, Chief of the Oudh Police. Out of a total strength of 4412, most of his force consisted of the low castes, including 462 Bhangis, 252 Chamars, and 764 Pasis. He remarked: "There can be no doubt of the policy of maintaining a portion at least of our soldiers from the lowest orders . . . The Brahmins or Mahomedans may hope that they may be restored as rulers and be always ready to attempt usurpation, but this can hardly be the case with the lower orders, whose ambition would not extend beyond a rise in the social scale, which could only be achieved under our government."[68] Regarding Bhangis, he said:

> There are numerous divisions of the sweeper tribe but all make good soldiers. The men are of good height and fair muscular development and they eat and drink anything with anybody; they are brave, aspire greatly to military service and are fond of the practice of sword exercises in which many of them are expert and are possessed of great shrewdness . . . There are nearly 500 of these men in the Police and they have done good service both as Soldiers and Policemen.[69]

He particularly applauded the Pasis:

> The Passees . . . are extremely hardy and courageous race and furnish most of the village watchmen of Oude and the adjacent NWP, they use the bow and arrow expertly and are said to be able to kill with the latter at wonderful distances; there used to be bodies of these men in the service of every Talookdar and Zemindar of Oude, NWP too—I have no doubt before they came under our rule . . . Although there is hardly a species of theft, robbery and plunder in which they are not experienced and skillful, they have a remarkable name for fidelity when employed, so much so that Bankers employ them to carry their special remittances, householders leave the guard of their property and family to them during their absence and the highest caste Native in the land would not scruple to place them in positions of trust. There are several Regiments of these men employed by the Native Government under the denomination of the Teer Jung Puttans (Regiments of Archers); they are wonderfully active

[68] Ibid.
[69] Ibid.

at all sorts of mining operations and when leading a vagabond life they often commit robberies by mining galleries for considerable distances until they get beneath the position of their prey. Most of the mines against the Baillee Guard were driven by these men under the superintendence of the mutineer Sappers. The Passees alone in Oude, I am sure, number more than 100,000 families and as one or more of these class is employed in almost every family they make the best detectives in the land . . . As soldiers the Passees though of smaller stature vie in courage with the Seikhs—on one occasion the late Captain Dawson, of the Oude Police, was in a position of some danger and his detachment was composed of about half Passees and half Seikhs; he informed me that if possible the former exceeded the latter in fearlessness.[70]

But such advocacy was slowly marginalized and Dalit numbers in the army dwindled steadily after 1857. Most British army officers were opposed to battalions of low-caste men. One said: "If a soldier be chosen only for his soldier-like qualities, courage, strength, endurance, fidelity, obedience, then anything which, like caste, gives a man a feeling of self-respect is a good quality in itself and the higher caste men make the best of soldiers." John Lawrence, in a letter dated January 5, 1861, wrote saying the employment of the lowest castes, such as Chamars and Bhangis, as soldiers alongside Brahmins and Kshatriyas was "like bringing lepers in contact with men of sound health in Europe." Expressing resentment against their recruitment, Brigadier F. Wheeler of Simla stated: "The Bhungees or sweeper castes are very filthy in their habits, as shown by a large proportion of them being ever in Hospital with itch . . . I therefore condemn their caste of men . . . The Chamars and Khutteecks are a shade better . . . But the village cobbler and the tanner of leather, I strongly object to, as I have done to the Bhungee . . . The Kunjur, as a despised race, who feed on rats, mice and other vermin, I utterly reject."[71]

Captain E. Hall, commanding the Aligarh Levy, had this to say about sweepers: "In their habits I consider them as unclean and more than ordinarily liable to sickness, whilst also being generally careless and unthrifty in money matters." Regarding the Chamars he wrote: "As workers of leather they are looked down . . . and in common

[70] Ibid.
[71] Ibid.

with other low-castes are addicted to the use of drugs and liquors."[72]
Brigadier P. Gordon from Banaras recorded of Chamars and Mehtars
their tendency to get drunk; also that they were smallish in appearance
with ill-developed chests and small limbs. Pasis, Chamars, and
Bhangis were repeatedly condemned as drunkards, dirty, and prone
to creating disturbances in the bazaars.[73] Their sense of manliness was
crude and inferior.[74] Many Dalit soldiers were retrenched, forced into
retirement, and excluded from new recruitment.[75] For example, in July
1913 Jamadar Mehr Muhammad in Regiment No. 46 of the Native
Infantry, despite having served for nineteen years, was dismissed from
service since he did not belong to any of the high castes.[76]

However, an increase in manpower requirements during the two
world wars forced a revaluation of the recruitment system.[77] Convict
sweepers from UP were recruited by the government during World
War I to serve in the army overseas, although to do "lowly" work.[78]
In Gorakhpur, Doms were urged to enlist as sweepers,[79] and to go
overseas to serve in the army.[80] A Chamar regiment, including many
Ramdasis, was raised during World War II.[81] Dalit soldiers were
particularly needed for non-combatant services. Dalit spokespersons
renewed the community's demand for army recruitment, especially
during World War II by celebrating their military achievements during

[72] Ibid.
[73] Ibid.
[74] L/MIL/14/216, OIOC; L/MIL/7/12141, OIOC.
[75] Constable 2001; Robertson 1938: 59.
[76] L/MIL/7/12141, OIOC.
[77] Basham 1980: 28–9; Cohen 1969: 458. The late Bhagwan Das, a leading
lawyer and Dalit intellectual, stated that he had been told by many people
in UP and Maharashtra that Ambedkar had written a booklet about the
untouchables in the army. Mahadev Prasad, belonging to the Dhanuk Dalit
caste of UP, and who served as an executive officer in the municipal corpora-
tion of Lucknow, said he had read the book. See Basham 1980: 8–9.
[78] Singha 2007: 424–7. Also 42–48/November 1916, Jails, A, Home Deptt,
NAI; 5/May 1916, Police, Home Deptt, NAI.
[79] 6–7/June 1913, Police, A, Home Deptt, NAI.
[80] 42–48/November 1916, Jails, A, Home Deptt, NAI.
[81] Deshpande 1996: 177, 180–3.

British rule and providing their own martial perspectives. The valor of Dalits was compared to that of Krishna.[82] A conference of the Adi Hindu Sabha in Lucknow in February 1940 stated that the depressed classes would give their full support to Britain in the war and urged that they be recruited.[83] The prestige of enrolling in the military, even in the non-combatant services, was prodigious for the low castes, it being considered a significant means for seeking concessions from the government and claiming superior status. Dalit histories considered enrollment in the army and police a defining moment for social and political affirmation, and for constituting manhood. Notably, Swami Achhutanand (1879–1933), the founder of the Adi Hindu movement in UP, was raised and educated in a military cantonment, where his father was employed.

R.S. Hari Prasad Tamta (1887–1960), President of the Kumaon Shilpkar Sabha and member of the Almora municipality, and a leading member of the UP Adi Hindu Depressed Class Association, pronounced the role that Dalits could play in the British army,[84] and outlined divergent models of masculinity. He underscored the martial role that the Shilpkars of Kumaon had played in the past, pointing to the fluidity of earlier recruitment and the Kshatriya *naukari* traditions of Dalits. On September 7, 1939, he offered to raise a brigade of the depressed classes of Kumaon in service of the British during the war.[85] Many Shilpkars of Kumaon, who were mostly Doms and formed 21.26 and 15.06 per cent of the population in Almora and Garhwal, respectively,[86] enrolled in the army during this time.[87] While they usually went into a labor and not a combatant unit because of the stigma of untouchability, they seized any military designation as a sign of social affirmation. They recalled their military service, even as

[82] "*Harijan aur Sainik Seva*" (Harijan and Military Service), *Chand*, July 1939: 200.

[83] *PAI*, February 24, 1940: 42.

[84] For further details on Tamta and Shilpkars' role in the British army, see Viyogi 2010: 493–501.

[85] L/PJ/10/14, OIOC.

[86] Kitts 1885: 62; *Census, 1931, UP*: 553–63.

[87] Shilpkars were part of the depressed classes in UP: *Census, 1921, UP*, Appendix C, "The Depressed Classes of the Kumaun Hills": 21–2.

porters, to plead for official patronage.[88] Maurice Hallett, the governor of UP, in his address to the Kumaon Shilpkar Sabha in Almora on October 24, 1941, acknowledged their valuable contribution to the war effort, and the readiness with which Shilpkars had come forward to join Pioneer Battalions: "I am particularly glad that the Shilpkars of Kumaon are now recruited to the Army not in hundreds but in thousands. Recently in Lucknow I had the privilege of being taken around the lines of one of the new Pioneer Battalions . . . The Commanding Officer, Major Crawford, was full of praise for their bearing and discipline and from what I myself saw I have no doubt that these men are a worthy addition to the Indian Army."[89]

Writing on March 27, 1942, Tamta linked this to the restoration of manhood and civilization among the Shilpkars:

> I am one of those who stand for unconditional support of the British Government in this struggle which she has taken up for us all . . . You would be glad to hear that from the District of Almora alone I have been able to get about ten thousand Shilpkars (Depressed Classes) recruited in the Army. These Depressed Class men (Shilpkars) are serving in various Pioneer Battalions, Labour Units and as Technicians . . . It is a truth poignantly realized by the Depressed Classes of these Provinces that for centuries preceding the British Rule they were steeped in the abysmal ignorance and unspeakable poverty and the social system as well as the political power then conspired to rob them even of their manhood. Had it not been for the British Government which came to their rescue like a merciful act of God, the Depressed Classes could not hope within any measurable time to emerge from degradation and to share benefits of a civilized world.[90]

Tamta, along with Chandrika Prasad Jigyasu, interviewed the Shilpkar soldiers and gave a spirited speech: "We are immortal souls and these bodies are our garments . . . Just as we feel joy in putting on new clothes in place of old ones, similarly, those who are brave feel joy in entering new bodies after sacrificing old bodies at the altar of duty . . . A coward is afraid of death but a brave person invites it.

[88] Singha 2007.
[89] L/PJ/10/14, OIOC.
[90] Ibid.

He fearlessly enters the battlefield . . . The earth is for the brave to enjoy."[91]

For leaders like Tamta, Shilpkar soldiers personified a sedate peasant brotherhood in arms, a model of simplicity and soldierly masculinity very unlike the luxurious world of upper castes, ready for a variety of tasks that upper-caste soldiers would not touch. The aspiration for military status was continuously reflected during meetings held by Dalits. Resolutions were adopted by the UP Adi Hindu Mahasabha urging the depressed classes to enroll as civic guards, and join the police and military in large numbers. Persistent requests were made to the government to adopt special measures to create scheduled caste regiments and military police forces, as in the Kumaon Division.[92] In a speech made at the Adi Hindu Conference in Allahabad on January 15–16, 1942, Nand Lal Jaiswar "Viyogi" proclaimed that the martial character of Dalits had been proven time and again, especially in 1857, when Dalits helped the British militarily.[93] Dalits mobilized a language of paternalism, accentuating the special bond that they shared with the British government. By repeatedly invoking their tradition of faithful service in the army of the ruling power, they tried to turn that entity into a patron which could be approached for concessions and awards.[94] Land was granted to some Choovail and Chaidah Chamars of UP, paying a *jumma* of Rs 250, as a reward for mutiny services.[95] Some Dalit Jamadars of the British army petitioned for higher pensions, which were granted.[96] The UP government removed the disqualification on the recruitment of Dalits to the police.

[91] "Shilpkar Soldiers," *Pioneer*, August 1, 1942.

[92] L/PJ/8/685, OIOC; "Depressed Classes Urged to Enlist," *Pioneer*, January 18, 1942; *Pioneer*, February 25, 1942; *Samta*, February 25, 1942; Poster in Hindi titled "*UP Adi Hind Mahasabha ke Kuch Pramukh Padadhikari*" (Certain Prominent Office-bearers of the UP Adi Hind Mahasabha): L/PJ/10/ 14, OIOC.

[93] *Report of the Adi Hindu Depressed Classes Kumbh Mela Conference*: 3–4.

[94] Similar idioms were used by prisoners laboring on public works under the British. See Singha 1998: 274–5.

[95] 105–105/6 January 1860, Foreign Consultation, Foreign Deptt, NAI.

[96] L/MIL/7/12141, OIOC.

As a result two Dalits were appointed to the position of Deputy Superintendent of Police in 1937–8.[97]

The All India Scheduled Castes Federation, along with its UP wing, expressed concern at its meeting in October 1945 over the effects of demobilization and peacetime reorganization of the Indian army on scheduled caste troops. It urged not only an acceptance of their present strength in the forces, but also its expansion, so that scheduled castes could reach the highest ranks of the army.[98] Chetu Ram, a Chamar from Azamgarh, wrote a letter to the British government on April 1, 1942, stating that many male members of his caste wanted to form an army battalion to help the British, and that they were entitled to uniforms and good pay.[99] Enrollment in the British police or army, along with uniforms, medals, and military papers, became critical markers for Dalit men to advance their cause for higher levels of political power and equal citizenship, and to project their strength and manhood.

The Pasis and Bhangis of UP recuperated a precolonial, non-Aryan martial race heritage, seeking heroic warriors from the past, but they attached their martial identity to the distinct objective of bidding for continued employment in the British army. Pasis incessantly pronounced that they had been the bravest and the strongest, and were trusted for generations to serve in the army or to be village watchmen (*chaukidar*s), "protecting" people. They worshiped the sword and would rather turn to stone than be defeated. Accusations of criminality were occasionally turned upside down, as when Pasis claimed that in the absence of other outlets some of their community members had resorted to theft as a way of expressing their courage. In order to utilize their strength positively, it was imperative to enroll them in the army.[100] Similarly, Chamars urged the government to absolve them by an act of legislature from the duty of skinning dead animals, and grant them appointments in police and army departments.[101] To mark their military history, an educated sweeper pointed to a cannon used

[97] Kshirsagar 1994: 139.
[98] L/PJ/8/685, OIOC.
[99] L/PJ/10/14, OIOC.
[100] Pasi 1928: 3; Risalsingh 1928: 4–5.
[101] *PAI*, April 2, 1938: 84.

by the sweepers (*bhangiyon wali taup*). It was reported that in 1762 one Harisingh Bhangi had attacked Khwaja Ubaid and captured an armory. He got hold of the cannon, which was named *bhangiyon wali taup*, which then passed to Gujarsingh and Lehnasingh Bhangi.[102] A Dalit writer emphasized the honor of serving in the military, whereby Dalits could fashion for themselves a distinct body, acquire a soldierly bearing, and style their headgear and clothes in a way suited to military service.[103] Appointment in the army had profound implications for the first generation of Dalit publicists, who used it as a language of masculinity, better jobs, and dignity. Dalits seemed to have imbibed a shared strategy of social mobility with other castes, deploying the manhood rhetoric while adding their own distinct arguments to it.

Pasts, Politics, and Public Places

Claims to a Kshatriya identity became an important means for caste associations and the urban Shudra poor of UP to assert themselves and obviate their vulnerability.[104] The decennial census triggered such contentions, with a deluge of writings by various castes professing an upper status. In the early twentieth century a section of Dalit men too wrote their caste genealogies, advancing claims of Kshatriyahood to contest the views of the upper castes against them, and to restore their masculinity and dignity. Accompanied by different, though sometimes overlapping trajectories, the backward castes principally embraced a form of militant Hinduism, while Dalits revitalized *nirgun bhakti*, drawing on the "sant tradition" of uncompromising criticism of caste hierarchies.[105] Simultaneously, Dalit genealogies such as *Chanvar Puran, Suryavansh Kshatriya Jaiswar Sabha, Kshatriya Shilpkar Darpar,*

---

[102] "*Bhangiyon Wali Taup*," *Madhuri*, November 1923: 419.

[103] "*Asprishyon mein Jagriti*" (Awakening among Untouchables), *Chand*, February 1930: 775. Intermediate castes too were making similar claims. For example, Yadavs cited the martial skills of Krishna to emphasize that they made excellent soldiers. See Nathuprasad Yadav, "*British Shasan Kal Mein Yadavon ki Fauji Unnati ka Itihaas*" (History of Military Progress of Yadavs during British Rule), *Yadavesh*, 1 (2), 1935: 21–8; Yadav 1914: 61–4.

[104] Pinch 1996: 81–114.

[105] Gooptu 2001: 185–243; Pinch 1996: 50.

Nishad Vanshavali, Pasi Samaj, Dharuka Kshatriya Vanshavali, Mali Jati Nirnaya, Yadav Jivan and *Yaduvansh Ka Itihas* produced new investments in history.[106] Not concerned so much with economic injustices, these writings centrally proclaimed a Kshatriya identity or a lineage from Krishna, borrowing from a Puranic tradition to retrieve a "pure" historical past and question Brahmanical theories of their origins. However, while relying on "traditional" registers, Dalit genealogies produced something different by challenging a history that defined them as defiled.[107] Raghuvanshi, the author of *Chanvar Puran*, asserted that the word "Chanvar" referred to those who were *suryavanshi* in the *dwij kul*, and they belonged to a renowned lineage dating back to the dawn of life.[108] While many upper castes lamented Kaliyug as a period of destruction, Dalits often used the trope to recuperate their masculinity. *Chanvar Puran* claimed that in this time of Kaliyug their clan (*kul*) would again rise and have the opportunity to re-establish the fame of their ancestors and their lost status.[109]

A subcaste of Chamars in Agra demanded the new nomenclature of "Jatav" to improve their ranking. Sunderlal Sagar contended that the Jatav race was sacred, not untouchable. The Chamars of Meerut, Bulandshahr, and Aligarh submitted petitions to the government claiming they were Jatav Rajputs.[110] Alongside, petitions for a superior rank were submitted to the government by the low castes to stamp their efforts with official recognition. Mookhan Ram, a Kahar from Ballia who worked as a *daftari* in the Home Department of the Government of India, stated that his caste be shown as Chandravanshiya Kshatriya in the official records.[111] Others proclaimed their right to wear the *janeu*.[112] Some took offense at the name "Chamar." A long controversy

---

[106] Raghuvanshi 1916, 1923; Banshidhar 1939; Pasi 1928; Sadhu 1907; Mishra 1911; Gangaram 1935; Sagar 1929; Yadavendu 1942.

[107] Banshidhar 1939: 65–7; Rawat 2012: 123–31.

[108] Raghuvanshi 1916: Introduction.

[109] Ibid.: 46–7.

[110] Lynch 1969: 67–85; *Census, 1931, UP*: 530. Similar trends of naming oneself anew were visible amongst Dalits in other regions: Bandyopadhyay 1997; Dube 1998.

[111] 315/1933, General Adm. Deptt, UPSA.

[112] 209/1918, General Deptt, UPSA.

ensued between the Brahmins of Dehradun and the "Rahtia Sikhs," who were also Arya Samajists settled in the region. The latter were regarded as Chamars by the high castes and not allowed to draw water from wells other than those designated for them. A complaint was lodged by the Rahtia Sikhs in the court against Arjun Dutt and Ram Chander, both Brahmins, who had called them "Ramdasi Chamars." Finally, Arjun Dutt had to pay them a fine of Rs 100.[113]

With the growth of the Adi Hindu movement under the leadership of Achhutanand, Dalits reversed the Aryan theory of race and declared themselves the original inhabitants of India.[114] Dalit genealogies insisted that they had been victims of racial conquest by Aryan Brahmins who had brought with them Brahmanical Hinduism and an "alien" caste system. They claimed an exceptional role for the downtrodden in resisting these invaders, though it was said the Dalits were finally defeated through chicanery and cunningness. Their punishment was to be "demasculinized," banished from society, classified as untouchables, condemned to poverty, and to become consumers of carcasses.[115] At the All India Adi Hindu Conference held at Mayo Hall in Allahabad on December 27–28, 1928, where the hall was packed with Chamars, Doms, and Pasis, Nanak Chand of Allahabad and Achhutanand announced that *achhut*s were the original inhabitants of India. In his stirring speech Achhutanand abused Hindus as tyrants (*zalim*s) and asserted that their religion was that of animals. He detailed the glories of Adi Raj and said that he was prepared to organize a party that would work towards the cessation of the oppression of *achhut*s. Dr Moonje and Madan Mohan Malaviya were declared treacherous enemies. Resolutions were unanimously adopted demanding separate representations for Adi Hindus, the repeal of laws which defined certain tribes and castes as criminal, and urging action against the *Manusmriti*.[116] The Adi Hindu Conference at Lucknow in September 1931 said: "Our degradation and disabilities in this country are not

[113] Bhagwan Singh and Ors. vs Arjun Dutt on May 29, 1920, Allahabad High Court (http://indiankanoon.org/doc/1722120/ downloaded September 19, 2013).

[114] Jigyasu 1965 (1937); Mahasatveer 1930; Sathi 1999; Khare, 1984: 84; Bayly 1999: 127. Other Dalit movements developed similar theories.

[115] Mahasatveer 1930: 50.

[116] *PAI*, January 7, 1928: 7; *PAI*, April 21, 1928: 148.

due to any social or religious reasons but they are due to political and political reasons alone. They are the result of the conflict of the political and economic interests of the Aryans, who came to this country from abroad and whose present descendants are known as *caste-Hindus,* and the original inhabitants of this country, viz. the *Adi Hindus,* who are termed as the depressed classes."[117]

In the words of Chandrika Prasad Jigyasu:

Indigenous brother! Imbibe your glorious history,
which was destroyed by the selfish interest of twice-born Aryans.[118]

[adi-nivasi bandhu! lijiye, yeh nij gauravmay itihaas;
arya-dwijon ne swarth-vivash ho, jise kar diya tha naash.]

In Awadh, Pasis quoted colonial ethnographers and folk traditions to affirm that they had been the lords of the region, that their kings had reigned at Sandila, Dhaurahara, Mitauli, and Ramkot in the districts of Kheri, Hardoi, and Unao. Ramkot, where the town of Bandarmau in Unao now stands, was their chief stronghold.[119] They further claimed: "Our men were the strongest and the bravest. We had powerful bodies and we fought many battles without fear. We were experts in wielding *lathi*s and guns and digging mines was our specialty."[120]

Brahmanical viewpoints on pollution and untouchability were countered by Dalit claims of a true past of "genuine" masculinity in the pre-historical Indian community. Chetu Ram, President of the Chamar Sabha in Sidhari, Azamgarh, addressed two large meetings of more than 5000 Chamars in 1938, in which he stated that six and a half centuries ago they had ruled India, but it had all been snatched from them by *thakur*s and Brahmins. Arabs had in turn snatched it from Hindus, and the British government had snatched it from the Arabs. He urged the government to give them back their "kingdom"

[117] *Report of the Special Session of the All India Adi Hindu Conference:* 3.
[118] Jigyasu 1941: 9.
[119] Risalsingh 1928; *Gazetteer of the Province of Oudh, Vol. II:* 207; Crooke 1896b, IV: 139. Bayly notes that rural Rajput clans had been exogamous in some cases, and married low-caste military people such as Pasis in Awadh. See Bayly 1988: 58.
[120] Pasi 1928: 6.

for they had proved their capacity to rule and fight.[121] While Dalits had no nostalgic yearnings for an Aryan "golden age," they formulated notions of their own glorious pre-Aryan past and civilization with a primordial egalitarian society. Claiming the "lost" culture of the vanquished, Dalits made their lives ethically wholesome. There was a perceptible shift from their earlier erasure of a low-caste past to pride in and reframing of one's caste. Dalits were now avowing that they were proud and accomplished men of knowledge and power.

Dalit genealogies may additionally be read as alternative masculinized discourses nurtured by an emerging counter-print-public sphere of Dalit journalism. The first generation of educated Dalit men in UP realized the importance of print. Achhutanand, born in a Chamar family at Mauja Umari in Mainpuri district, published a booklet, *Harihar Bhajan Mala: Bhagh I*, way back in 1913 from Agra; later he started *Achhut*, a monthly paper, from Delhi in 1922. He also launched the *Adi Hindu Journal* from Kanpur in 1924, which continued till 1932.[122] Tamta started a newspaper, *Samta*, from Almora. Babu Ram Charan (1889–1937) of the Nishad caste launched the newspaper *Nishad Samachar* in 1920 in Lucknow.[123] Dharam Prakash (1900–72), a Jatav born in Bareilly, started a weekly named *Adhikar* which ran over 1935–40.[124] Manikchand Jatav Veer headed the journal *Jivan* from Agra in 1936.[125] Resorting to arguments of science and rationality, these publications addressed the disabilities of caste as contingent and wrong. Shaping a new sense of Dalit identity, they associated their religious and ritual stigmatization with illiteracy, poverty, and social backwardness, and used politics to lay claims to manhood rights.

Modern political arenas have been the "natural" homelands of masculinity.[126] Dalit masculine identity too was politically contingent. Scholars argue that in colonial UP, unlike Maharashtra, politics was

[121] *PAI*, April 2, 1938: 84.

[122] Kshirsagar 1994: 343–6; Jigyasu 1968. For details on the publishing career of Achhutanand, see Amardeep 2012: 74–95; Bharti 2011; Naimishray 2014: 42–9.

[123] Kshirsagar 1994: 74, 172; Mahasatveer 1930: 25–37.

[124] Kshirsagar 1994: 208.

[125] Ibid.: 230; Yadavendu 1942: 238–9.

[126] Dudink, Hagemann, and Tosh 2004.

not a site of action for Dalits.[127] However, the Adi Hindu movement, which dominated UP's Dalit politics in the 1920s and the
1930s, proves otherwise, whereby the manhood of Dalits sought its
ideological expression by equating caste oppression and masculine
subjecthood with political rights. Examples of political assertion by
Dalit men abound in western UP, where their material conditions were
better. The Chamars had, historically, bigger landholdings here and
there was less *begar*. By the late-colonial period, in regions like Meerut,
Muzaffarnagar, and Agra, Chamars had emerged from positions of
servitude, this being reflected in their lifestyle, food, housing, and
clothing.[128] New urban centers developed in the region, providing
some economic development and educational opportunities to the
better-off sections of Dalits. The Jatavs of Agra set up institutions
and movements to challenge upper-caste hegemony.[129] The Adi
Hindu movement started asserting itself in the political–public
sphere, demanding entitlement to full membership in the emerging
nation, more voting rights, and the elimination of the dependency of
franchize on property. Dalit leaders insisted that the liberal rhetoric
of equality before the law, right to education, employment, and political representation knew no caste boundaries.[130] The Adi Hindu
Conference at Lucknow in 1931 adopted as its first resolution the
"right to equal citizenship, free enjoyment of equal rights, and adequate representation in legislatures and services."[131] The UP Adi
Hindu Depressed Classes Association passed resolutions to this effect
at a special scheduled castes (depressed classes) political conference
at Saddar Bazaar on December 10, 1942, further urging 30 per cent
representation through separate electorates for the scheduled castes,
or at least a more equitable distribution of seats. In the 1940s the
UP Scheduled Caste Federation demanded greater representation

[127] Pai 2002: 32.

[128] Singh 1947: 47, 109–24.

[129] Lynch 1969: 35.

[130] L/SG/7/34, Services and General Deptt Collection, OIOC; L/PJ/9/188,
OIOC; *The Indian Social Reformer*, January 17, 1925: 313–14; Blunt
1931. However, there was no question of giving depressed class women any
representation.

[131] *Report of the Special Session of the All India Adi Hindu Conference*: 4.

in legislatures, more jobs in the bureaucracy, and a greater share in political power.[132] Through a male-centered language of resistance and civic rights,[133] an embattled Dalit masculinity announced itself on the political stage, where the public Dalit citizen was imagined within a male paradigm. The implicitly gendered wordings of many of their statements reflected the extent to which Dalit spokespersons had internalized masculine political rhetoric. Quoting Mukunda Behari Mullick, one of the front-ranking leaders of the Namasudra movement in Bengal, Sekhar Bandyopadhyay shows how in his oral deposition before the Indian Statutory Commission in 1928 Mullick demanded voting rights only for men: he argued that their women were not prepared to go to the polling booth.[134] Dalit critiques of the gendered character of caste were constantly subdued by new forms of caste conflict that perceptibly equated the modernization of gender with a reconstitution of caste masculinity. Male political mobilization against caste was determined by the interaction of caste radicalism in a context of colonial modernity and the logical rhetoric of an emerging political nationalism. It was evident that the stage was set for a male-dominated Dalit public–political sphere.[135]

In the cultural realm, myths and heroic traditions of Dalits provided not just models *of* reality but also models *for* reality, which could reveal a motivated urge towards social change. The epic of *Alhakhand*, which appears to have originally been a book of Chandbardai based on the exploits of his master, the ruler Prithviraj of Delhi in the twelfth century, was handed down through centuries to minstrels who chanted various versions of it.[136] Though largely held as a tale of Rajput chivalry, some Dalit minstrels enacted their own accounts of the epic, reinterpreting it not as a tale of Rajput but Dalit heroism. They claimed Alha and Udal, the two brothers whose courageous deeds helped the king Parmal in his war against Prithviraj, as part of their own heroic traditions. In a number of versions the epic referred to Dalit characters, such as the Biria Malin, who carried messages to

[132] L/PJ/8/685, OIOC.
[133] Summers 2004: 2; Wallace 2002.
[134] Bandyopadhyay 2004: 149–50.
[135] Rao 2009: 54.
[136] Grierson 1923; Mss Eur E223/15, Grierson Collection, OIOC.

Alha under the pretext of fetching flowers; or Dhunwa Teli, a leader of the Kannauj forces, a Mallah, and a Kori.[137] Highlighting the connection between the tales of Alha and Udal and the Pasis of Oudh, Carnegy in his *Races of Oudh* stated: "It is affirmed by some [Pasis] that they are a branch of the Kerat tribe of Dwarka. A heroic Pasi named Sen of Bamiya figures prominently in the poetical accounts of the celebrated battle of Ala and Udal; and this gives colour to their asserted connection with Kanouj, where those heroes flourished."[138] Alha and Udal and other Dalit heroes were celebrated in the renderings of the epic by rural Dalits,[139] and by Agra's Jatavs, who claimed Alha and Udal as untouchables. *Alha* and *pachra*, sung by Dusadhs, and *batohiya* songs rendered by Dalits in UP, came to center on such tales. In the 1940s Ambedkar became a part of Dalit performances of the epic in UP, with a recounting of his struggle against untouchability, his fight for an education, and his role as one of the fathers of the constitution of India. He too was delineated as a great leader and a hero who could take his place among the country's leaders with pride.[140] Through such stories Dalits attempted to prove that they were great warriors in heart, word, and deed. Myth and reality, constructions of heroism and valor, combined to provide a language of social rights. In such popular spaces a complex ideology of Dalit masculinity was played out, which was neither heterocentric nor misogynist but developed out of a uniquely Dalit experience. They offered a critical recourse to another language in which different realities of Dalit masculine life were expressed.

However, some Dalits participated in aggressive demonstrations of masculinity in public arenas and in communal violence between Hindus and Muslims, which rocked UP in the early twentieth century. In Allahabad, some Dalits asked to be included in Ramlila committees. They claimed that they could raise a force of men used to

[137] "Notes on the Customs of the Epic," Mss Eur E223/15(ii), Grierson Collection, OIOC.

[138] Quoted in Gayer 1910: 27; Sherring 1872: 399.

[139] Vipinbihari Trivedi, "*Lok Katha ke Nayak Alha Udal*" (Heroes of Folk Tales Alha Udal), *Vishal Bharat,* March 1950: 193–6.

[140] Lynch 1972: 107.

handling *lathi*s that would intimidate Muslims.[141] It was contended that during riots most Muslim *goonda*s were butchers (*kasai*s), *kunjra*s, *bhatiyara*s, and *ekka* drivers. Hindus could win the riots only if Dalits stood against these forces.[142] A serious riot occurred in a village near Banaras in March 1931, when a group of Hindus attacked Muslims over the alleged killing of a cow by one Mohammad Raza. Four Muslims were killed and two seriously injured. Muslims blamed many Hindus in their police report, including one Jeot Kori and one Kallu Chamar.[143] Dalit participation in such riots permitted contrasting interpretations. Feeling an acute loss of material, social, and political power, their mask of toughness perhaps helped Dalits to overcome a sense of defeat and stigmatization. Being sturdy and street-smart was seen by Dalits as making them "normal" and "socially recognizable," as validating their manhood, since they had access to street weapons and their bodies were their weapons.[144] This was their way of being Dalit, male, and adult. Relating physical strength to bravery, even during riots, also facilitated in them a sense of pride in physical labor—to which little social value was ascribed by the upper classes. There could be other reasons for the antagonism of Dalits against Muslims—to prove their Hindu credentials, to think it economically advantageous to fight poor Muslims for lowly jobs, and to save "their" women.[145] A *panchayat* of Chamars at Fyzabad in 1928 decided to lend its full support to the Arya Samaj and to the campaign of *sangathan* and *shuddhi*.[146] At a meeting held at Roorkee in May 1924, under the auspices of the Arya Samaj, it was resolved that Muhammadans should be replaced where possible in menial trades by Hindus and that Hindu masters should get rid of

[141] *PAI*, October 27, 1923: 532.

[142] Sharda 1925: 10.

[143] Shukul and Ors. vs Emperor on January 19, 1933, Allahabad High Court (http://indiankanoon.org/doc/29169/ downloaded September 20, 2013).

[144] For example, a meeting of Dalits in Kanpur resolved to worship Bhim. See *PAI*, September 20, 1946: 146.

[145] Gooptu 2001.

[146] *PAI*, August 18, 1928: 319.

their Muhammadan servants.[147] In Allahabad, Khatiks were employed to sell vegetables in place of Muslim Kunjras.[148] There was a dispute between Chamars and Muslims in Etawah over grazing fields. Some seventy Hindus, including Chamars, attacked a few Muslims on February 1, 1948, killing one Muslim and injuring six others.[149]

Work and the Language of Protest

Dalits' work and ritual rankings fed into each other in a vicious circle: the nature of their work, social status, and stigma had long been inextricably intertwined.[150] Dalits thus attempted to mold stigmatized labor in different ways. They forged caste anew, whereby it sometimes became "the earliest language of class."[151] Despite severe limitations they endeavored to restore some dignity to their work and claim a degree of manhood by negotiating various forms of control over their labor. These ranged from a language of dignity within stigmatized work to shunning such work completely, from expressions of "negative" and customary rights to positive and trade union rights, from evasion and flight to organized resistance, from individual protest to collective struggles and strikes. Through fragmentary examples from urban sweepers, leather workers, and Dalit agricultural laborers, we will see the nature of these assertions.

In UP, as elsewhere in India, sweepers or Bhangis were regarded as most "suited" to scavenging, and remained continuously, exclusively, and universally linked to such work. The notion of scavenging as the customary right of sweepers was widely shared and persistent in rural and urban areas, among the judiciary and state machinery, and even amongst a section of sweepers. They had a virtual monopoly over this indispensable yet devalued work. In UP, urban growth coupled with the expansion of sanitary infrastructure and municipal services created a considerable demand for scavengers, sweepers, and conservancy workers.[152] Though the word "Bhangi" often included caste and occupation, in Awadh Doms were often employed as

[147] *PAI*, May 24, 1924: 174.
[148] *PAI*, April 9, 1938: 91.
[149] *PAI*, February 6, 1948: 23.
[150] Sarkar 2013: 178–81.
[151] Bhattacharya 2013: 79.
[152] Gooptu 2001: 145.

street sweepers.[153] In Banaras too many sweepers were Doms.[154] The Harijan Survey Committee of Kanpur published a detailed and perceptive report on the sweepers of Kanpur city in 1934, high-lighting the nature and problems of their work. Quoting from the 1931 census, it pointed out that there were 29,972 Bhangis in Kanpur district, and unlike industrial laborers they were more or less a settled labor force, keeping their families with them.[155] None of the men had left their wives and children in the rural areas, and the womenfolk also earned as sweepers.[156] Sweepers did the worst jobs, faced severe exploitation, and suffered low earnings and chronic unemployment.[157] The report estimated that the municipality pro-vided employment for 880, or 28 per cent of these, mills for 14 per cent, private bungalows for 13 per cent, private *hata*s and houses for 11 per cent, railways for 3 per cent, the cantonment for 3 per cent; some 12 per cent were underemployed, earning less than Rs 7 per month by private scavenging, and the remaining 16 per cent could find no employment.[158] On the conditions of service of these sweepers, the report remarked:

> Except the railways, some mills and some private employers, the conditions of service are everywhere extremely bad. The worst conditions prevail in the services of the municipality and the cantonment, which together employed about a thousand sweepers . . . Here there is no provision for any holidays, weekly or otherwise, or for any leave. The only leave available is without pay and that on providing a substitute. There was no limitation on the hours of work and not unoften, especially in certain seasons, these sweepers work even upto 13 and 14 hours a day . . . But the worst feature is bribery and corruption with consequent insecurity of service . . . The main cause of this bribery and corruption is virtually the absolute power of the Jamadars and the Sanitary Inspectors over the recruitment and dismissal of sweepers.[159]

[153] Gayer 1910: 67; Cape 1924: 18.

[154] Cape 1924: 17.

[155] *Report of the Committee Appointed by the Cawnpore Harijan Sevak Sangha*: 7–8.

[156] Searle-Chatterjee 1981: 19.

[157] Singh 1947: v.

[158] *Report of the Committee Appointed by the Cawnpore Harijan Sevak Sangha*: 9.

[159] Ibid.: 10–11.

Municipal corporations came to be the largest employers of sweepers, entrusted with ensuring that they did their work continuously and efficiently. It was reported from Banaras in 1925 that sweepers performing "customary" scavenging in households had declined dramatically, while there was a corresponding increase in those employed by the municipality.[160] It was imperative for the cleanliness and sanitation of the cities that sweepers stayed to do this brutal, labor-intensive, utterly filthy, and polluted work, which included street sweeping, drain cleaning, motor lorry filling of rubbish, cleaning public latrines, removing nightsoil in motor lorries and carts at night, sewer cleaning, unloading refuse from carts, cleaning slaughterhouses, destroying stray dogs, removing and disposing of the carcasses of horses, camels, and other dead animals from the streets, and general scavenging.[161] The fear of a filthy and unhygienic city made the municipalities maximize their control over sweepers. In order to ensure their immobility, Section 85 (1) of the UP Municipalities Act made sweepers virtual slaves. This coercive act made any municipal sweeper liable to two months' rigorous imprisonment for mere absence without a reasonable cause, or for resigning and abandoning his employment without the permission of the Board.[162] The courts argued that it was "enacted to meet the grave public danger which may arise from a sudden strike of sweepers in a town."[163] If a municipal sweeper left his employment without a month's notice, he could be sent to prison for four weeks. No extra allowance was granted to sweepers for the extra work they had to perform when someone was absent through sickness, or when the streets were made amazingly clean preparatory to the reception of distinguished visitors to the city.[164] Provisions of section 26 (3) of the Municipalities Act also made sweepers liable to imprisonment for attempting collective bargaining, while permanence of service—including benefits of leave, promotion,

[160] Quoted in Gooptu 2001: 168.

[161] *Report of the Committee Appointed by the Cawnpore Harijan Sevak Sangha*: 21–4; Cape 1924: 17.

[162] *Report of the Committee Appointed by the Cawnpore Harijan Sevak Sangha*: 12.

[163] Angnoo vs Emperor on July 13, 1923, Allahabad High Court (http://indiankanoon.org/doc/576482/ downloaded on October 18, 2013).

[164] Cape 1924: 18.

and provident fund—was denied to them in their employment.[165] They had to work for a full 365 days in the year. In practice, thus, the municipalization of urban facilities severely curtailed sweepers' freedom to bargain with employers.[166]

Even amidst such stringent restrictions, sweepers attempted to fight for their rights. Pushed as they were into a corner, with acute job shortages always looming, they often contested others and claimed their monopoly over "customary" rights and jobs, such as collecting nightsoil, sweeping homes, cleaning private latrines, and sometimes over the possessions of the dead. In relation to these hereditary and customary rights of sweepers in the early nineteenth century, it has been remarked:

> Hereditary sweepers . . . held particularly important rights which were allocated as hereditary "beats" to a particular family. The scavengers made a living by selling "nightsoil" for manure to *zamindars* . . . Nightsoil "shares" were already farmed to bidders under the Nawabi government, but with the value of manure rising again at the beginning of the nineteenth century more and more scavenger families took to mortgaging their beats to outsiders. Their vital domestic position which was reinforced by the fear of pollution made it possible for them to combine against house owners to extort higher fees and a regular system of leasing and sub-leasing grew up in these rights.[167]

From the early twentieth century sweepers increasingly began petitioning the state to let them carry on, or "restore," their "age-old" right over the work of scavenging within their respective areas. Sweepers in the Pilibhit Municipality claimed that they had a customary right to undertake house scavenging and house sweeping and the Board could only undertake it subject to their rights. In the 1920s the sweepers here were at war with the municipality, stating that they had a customary right to collect and sell nightsoil.[168] Two groups of

[165] *Report of the Committee Appointed by the Cawnpore Harijan Sevak Sangha*: 17.

[166] We find a similar account for Delhi scavengers. See Prashad 2000: 3–6.

[167] Bayly 1983: 315–16.

[168] Emperor vs Hori Lal on December 20, 1922, Allahabad High Court (http://indiankanoon.org/doc/587823/ downloaded on October 15, 2013).

sweepers in Muttra (Mathura) clashed in 1928, each claiming that they had exclusive rights over sweeping and cleaning the dharamsala of one Seth Ram Gopal, and the latrines attached to it, each group claiming that the property on which the dharamsala was built had been exclusively served by their ancestors for long, and thus it was their birthright to so continue. Each argued that the other was interfering in the exercise of their rights.[169] In another case, sweepers of the villages of Mauza Karanbas and Mauza Devi clashed, each declaring they were entitled "to take the coffins and ornaments of corpses of Hindus who lived in Mauza Debai and whose bodies were buried or cremated at the burning *ghat* in Karanbas." Both parties therefore set up an exclusive custom.[170] In these contestations, while ratifying their right to livelihood, sweepers were negotiating within a language of what I call "negative" rights. In a situation where other resources of livelihood or other options were unavailable, and where economic compulsions and the inequities of state and law machinery were glaring, sweepers felt compelled to remain scavengers. In paradoxical ways, this was a marker of both subjugation and distinction. While framed within a language of customary rights, such disputes implicitly naturalized caste hierarchies, furthering the existing templates of caste and stigma.

However, stigma could work in polysemic ways. In a slightly later period strikes became a critical means to articulate a language of rights, whereby in partial ways "negative" claims were converted into "positive" rights. Municipal corporations came down heavily on such assertions. On April 10, 1923, the entire sweeping staff of the Allahabad Municipality sent a notice to the Municipal Board demanding an increase in pay. Receiving no reply, they sent a further notice on April 20, threatening to strike on May 1, unless their demands were granted. On the appointed day they abandoned their work in accordance with the notice. The magistrate thereupon sent

[169] Lachman and Anr. vs Bhajan on April 26, 1928, Allahabad High Court (http://indiankanoon.org/doc/1410096/ downloaded on October 15, 2013).

[170] Ganga Bashi and Ors. vs Jamna and Ors. on February 1, 1940, Allahabad High Court (http://indiankanoon.org/doc/1534225/ downloaded on October 18, 2013).

for ten of the ring leaders and on their admitting the facts sentenced them to two months' rigorous imprisonment under Section 85 (1) of the UP Municipalities Act. The order was justified by the magistrate on the grounds that there was extreme danger to the health of the town because of the strike. He pronounced having spoken to the health officer in one case, who had said that there was risk of a cholera epidemic if the town were left unscavenged.[171]

Another case underscored the draconian provisions of Section 85. A group of sweepers in Aligarh gave notice to the Municipal Board on July 6, 1934, saying they would strike work from August 6 if their grievances were not redressed by July 30. The Board considered the matter at a meeting and stated that the grievances of the sweepers would be considered if they withdrew their notice by 8 a.m. on August 3, 1934. After that date the Board began to enlist new sweepers. When the sweepers who had given notices discovered this, they made an application to the Board withdrawing their notices. The recruitment of new sweepers was stopped and the old sweepers were allowed to resume their work, which they did. Some sweepers, including one named Baswa, however, did stop work on August 6 and faced prosecution for the same under Section 85.[172] Despite the laws working against them, the urban areas of UP witnessed continuous, collective, and militant strikes by sweepers and their labor unions, particularly in the 1930s, all demanding better wages and working conditions.[173] Sweepers also wanted an abolition of the system of recruitment through Jamadars, to whom the workers had to pay commission from their wages. Women sweepers too were active in such strikes, demanding three months' fully paid maternity leave, and some baby-care provisions such as the running of crèches and *balwadis*.[174] In March–April 1938 the sweepers of Chandpur in Bijnor

[171] Angnoo vs Emperor on July 13, 1923, Allahabad High Court (http://indiankanoon.org/doc/576482/ downloaded on October 18, 2013).

[172] Baswa vs Emperor on December 5, 1934, Allahabad High Court (http://indiankanoon.org/doc/829374/ downloaded on October 18, 2013).

[173] The early twentieth century witnessed organized strikes by sweepers in many parts of India. See, for example, Sarkar 2013: 174–206. For UP, *Report of the Benares Municipal Board Enquiry Committee*: 178–80.

[174] Verma 1971: x.

struck work and demanded higher wages.[175] In August 1938 the
sweepers' union of Agra threatened a strike if their demands were not
met by the Municipal Board before September 10, 1938.[176] Speakers
at a sweepers' meeting in Lucknow regretted that the Congress government had done nothing tangible for them.[177] The sweepers of
Meerut went on strike in January 1939 as a protest against the harsh
treatment meted out to them.[178] It was reported in March–April 1939
that the sweepers of Aligarh city had been on strike for three days and
those of Muzaffarnagar and Bareilly were threatening to strike if their
demands were not met in the near future.[179] On May 19, 1939 the
sweepers of Jhansi cantonment went on strike to protest against the
sanitary inspector, their working hours, and wages.[180] Another 1000
sweepers of the Municipal Board of Kanpur went on strike on July
3, 1939.[181] It has been argued that such militant actions were linked
to the growth of the Adi Hindu movement. In a charter of demands
submitted to the Allahabad Commissioner in 1939 by the association
of municipal sweepers, it was contended that as an "untouchable Adi
Hindu community" their own representatives should be given places
on the committee set up by the provincial government, to propose
improvements in the working and living conditions of municipal
employees.[182] Apprehending the discharge of a number of sweepers
of the Agra Municipal Board due to a scheme for transport of rubbish
in motor lorries, the local Mehtar Union asked the Board for an
assurance that no sweepers would be dismissed. In the absence of a
favorable reply, the majority of sweepers went on strike and refused to
clean the roads and drains.[183] On June 8, 1940 sweepers employed by
the Board of Gonda district struck work, demanding increased wages.

[175] *PAI*, April 2, 1938: 84.
[176] *PAI*, September 10, 1938: 225.
[177] *PAI*, September 24, 1938: 240.
[178] *PAI*, January 28, 1939: 18.
[179] *PAI*, March 4, 1939: 46; *PAI*, March 18, 1939: 56; *PAI*, April 15, 1939: 79.
[180] *PAI*, May 27, 1939: 121.
[181] *PAI*, July 15, 1939: 177.
[182] Gooptu 2001: 375.
[183] *PAI*, August 5, 1939: 197.

Mirzapur Municipal sweepers went on strike on June 12, 1940.[184] The Lucknow Municipal Board made a new contract for the removal of rubbish, which would throw a number of sweepers out of work. In protest, scavengers of the city threatened a strike from July 1, 1940.[185] Sweepers had an important leverage as their work on an everyday basis was absolutely necessary for urban health and sanitation. Threatening to stop or stopping work, and "flash strikes," became characteristic of sweepers' struggles, whereby they demanded their rights as workers and increased wages, and not just under the rubric of "customary" rights. What was particularly helpful for the sweepers was their caste-based monopoly over this work. Degradation was translated into strength and grievances into demands and rights.[186] During a strike the sweeper was king, ruling the city and robustly marking his presence and importance in urban civic public life. Strikes signified a world turned upside down, with the city at his feet. He was claiming his masculinity through stigmatized symbols, but turning them into statements of power for that short time. Everyone else stood humbled in his presence. An illuminating cartoon by Munro on a successful strike by sweepers in May 1939 in Lahore captured this succinctly and could well apply to any of the cities of UP. Conspicuously, it brought out the "power" of the sweeper, where he stood as monarch, a crown on his head, a broom in his hand, a proud mustache, and staring right at one's face (Figure 19).

Sweepers were not asking to be rid of stigmatized labor, but rather for its recognition and for certain rights and dignity. Similar assertions were visible amongst the leather workers of UP. Leather work involved several categories of workers and different processes—from the removal of the hide from carcasses by flaying, to the tanning and processing of finished leather, and finally the manufacture of leather goods.[187] The

[184] *PAI*, June 22, 1940: 137.

[185] *PAI*, June 29, 1940: 142.

[186] Sarkar 2013: 198. Besides sweepers, Dhobis too deployed similar tactics. When the Dhobis of Banaras were banned by the court from washing clothes on the riverbank, their caste *panchayat* decided not to wash the clothes of any sahibs. This caused grave alarm and the magistrate was forced to promptly reverse his decision. See *NNR* 1902: 611.

[187] Walton 1903.

19. "Monarch of All He Surveys"

Source: *Cartoons by Munro: 104 Cartoons by Munro Culled from the Papers of The Civil and Military Gazette*, Lahore: The Civil and Military Gazette Ltd, 1939.

leather workforce was shaped not only by caste but also gender, with Dalits doing the worst jobs, and amongst them women confined to the lowest. An overview of the establishment and expansion of the modern leather industry in UP reveals that its foundations were laid as a consequence of the 1857 uprising, and its expansion continued right up to the Second World War and beyond. Private tanneries were established under government supervision, which proved an important economic stimulus for Dalits, particularly Chamars, in the urban areas of Agra, Aligarh, and Kanpur.[188] In Kanpur, for example, the family of Rai Sanwal Dass, a Chamar, thrived on hide work, and became amongst the first-class rich families.[189] Leather work, while reinforcing caste degradation, occasionally provided spaces to display Dalit masculinities. Tolaram Chamar claimed that the work of tanning

[188] For the leather industry and leather workers, Rawat 2012: 85–116; Roy 1999; Knorringa 1999: 303–28; Briggs 1920; Lynch 1969; Khare 1984; Bhattacharya 2013.

[189] Mss Eur F77/44, OIOC.

involved a display of strength. It was not because it was stigmatized that Chamars did it, but because they alone were capable of displaying such physical power and hard work.[190] Ramcharan Kuril valorized leather work, claiming that Raidasis alone possessed the special gift of creating beautiful and useful objects out of the hides of animal carcasses.[191] As a mark of respect for their work, many Chamars worshiped the tanner's knife (*rapi*) during Diwali.[192] It was contended that by providing shoes to all, Chamars were responsible for everyone's "physical protection," similar to the traditional work of Kshatriyas.[193] Sometimes, Dalits resisted attempts at weaning them away from leather work. For example, meetings of the Jatia Chamar Sabha were held in rural areas of Meerut, which resolved to cease skinning dead animals, making shoes, and tanning. This, however, was rejected by the Chamars of the city. In this case they used women to put pressure and assert their right over these professions. They threatened that if this was carried out, they would send brides back to their parents and claim back their daughters they had given in marriage.[194]

More pertinent was the language of protest adopted by Dalits to assert their dignity and manhood. A large number of Chamars of Meerut refused to do *begar* in 1922 and the *zamindars* retaliated by refusing them employment, the right of grazing, and cutting grass. They even refused to remove carcasses in the area, making relations between *zamindars* and Chamars extremely strained. The *zamindars* resorted repeatedly to oppressing Chamars one way or the other.[195] It was reported that the Chamars of Bulandshahr were getting restive. There was a revolt against *begar* by the Chamars of Moradabad, who complained to the collector against their local *zamindars*. Chamars here also refused to skin carcasses and repair shoes, even at the cost of

[190] Sharda 1925: 14.

[191] Joshi 2003: 250.

[192] Nesfield 1885: 22.

[193] Raghuvanshi 1916. Similarly, the Pasis claimed to be the best watchmen because of their physical power to keep crime under control. See Crooke 1896b, I: clvi.

[194] *PAI*, November 10, 1923: 545.

[195] *PAI*, March 18, 1922: 350; *PAI*, April 1, 1922: 642; *PAI*, April 8, 1922: 681.

repression and loss.[196] Influenced by them, the Chamars of Badaun too refused to do *begar* and handle dead animals.[197] Similar resolutions were passed in Aligarh, Bareilly, and Mainpuri.[198] A *panchayat* of Chamars at Fyzabad advised its members to resist *begar* and educate their children.[199] These attempts at providing dignity to stigmatized work—by expressing a language of customary rights, by strikes, by highlighting the critical importance of their work, and by protesting against the reprehensible *begar*—show that Dalits were expressing manly dignity and reformulating stigma into a potent source of empowerment.

Conversions, Food, and Women

In UP, as elsewhere, Dalits often attired themselves in clothes from corpses, wore iron jewelry, and ate from broken clay pots. Thus, postures, gestures, and self-embodiment became critical for Dalit positioning. Jigyasu challenged existing pictorial representations of Dalits, saying Dalit intellectuals should pay careful attention to their appearance and present to the world a body which appeared efficiently modern. Educated middle-class Dalits, epitomized in the figure of Ambedkar, often made attempts to imitate Europeans—wearing jackets and trousers, eating seated at a table using a knife and fork—as a way to enhance their status. Scholars remark that such a lifestyle is an adaptation rather than submission, a "survival strategy that makes oneself interesting and attractive to others . . . through making oneself an interesting object, through the cultivation of an aura . . . that elicits rewarding responses from others."[200] Discourses around demeanor and the elevation of male stature were also tied to conversions to Christianity. Missionary literature claimed that conversions provided

[196] *PAI*, March 25, 1922: 597; *PAI*, April 8, 1922: 681; *PAI*, April 22, 1922: 740; *PAI*, May 6, 1922: 823; *PAI*, May 13, 1922: 845.

[197] *PAI*, June 17, 1922: 1003; *PAI*, June 24, 1922: 1045; *PAI*, July 29, 1922: 1231.

[198] *PAI*, June 24, 1922: 1045; *PAI*, July 1, 1922: 1087; *PAI*, March 31, 1923: 203.

[199] *PAI*, August 18, 1928: 319.

[200] Rainwater 1966: 214.

manhood to Dalits by making them into respectable men.[201] The missionary Godfrey Phillips said: "These movements are making the outcaste into a man and giving him a man's place in the world—a place he has never enjoyed before."[202] Rev. R. Hack, working in Meerut amongst Dalit Christians, said: "As far as I can see, they seem to be an industrious and sturdy people and those who have become Christian are becoming more manly and independent and less willing to submit to the unjust conditions which have been imposed on them from time immemorial."[203]

Ironically, while lamenting conversions, reformers too acknowledged that this avenue provided Dalits with an elevated masculine stature, a fact reflected in many cartoons published at this time. One depicted the converted outcaste man dressed in a suit, wearing shoes and walking ahead royally as a sahib. The unconverted Dalit walked behind, barefoot, carrying a load on his head (Figure 20). Conversions ensured white-collar jobs and were economically beneficial. A cartoon had the converted Dalit man flaunting his wealth and giving wages to the unconverted Dalit man (Figure 21). Another had the converted man as the master and the unconverted as his peon (Figure 22). Others depicted converted Dalits playing games (Figure 23) and getting their shoes stitched by the unconverted (Figure 24), thus reversing traditional hierarchies of caste. The elevation of status through conversions was stark, showing increase in height, healthier bodies, erect postures, and better clothes (Figure 25).

It was claimed by some Bhangis and Chamars around Meerut that Christianity gave them a new life through literacy, dignity, and stature. They saw in conversions a way of postulating their manhood, though from a different position than reformers and missionaries.[204] Through the distinct language of conversion they were accessing the advancements of modernity and civilization, denied to them simply because of their caste, and laying claims to a better life.[205]

[201] *Hindu Dharm ke Phal* 1905: 6; *Jotdar ka Brittant* 1898.

[202] Phillips 1912: 83.

[203] *Annual Report of the CMS for the Year 1901–2*: 233.

[204] Forrester 1979: 74–5, 77, 81.

[205] Conversions had implications in particular for Dalit women's clothing.

20. Christian Sahib and Hindu Untouchable

The untouchable who has become a Christian walks
ahead as a sahib. The untouchable Hindu carries a load of chicken
on his head. What an irony!

*[chalta hai age ban sahib, isayi jo hua achhut,
jo hindu, wah murgi dhota, peeche yeh kaisi kartoot?]*

Source: *Vyanga Chitravali* 1930.

21. Untouchable Christian

One curses with arrogance and donates wages. Why such distance
between the same caste—one Christian and one untouchable?

*[ek that se gali dekar daan kar raha mazdoori!
ek jati, achhut isayi, mein rehti kitni doori?]*

Source: *Vyanga Chitravali* 1930.

22. Chaprasi and Sahib

Same color, same blood, same *jati* and yet today.
One is a peon and the other has become a Mister and rules!

[*ek rang hai, ek rakt hai, ek jati the, phir bhi aaj –
chaprasi hai ek, doosra ban sahib karta hai raj!*]

Source: *Vyanga Chitravali* 1930.

23. Sports and Converted Dalit Christians

See the one who is playing with the ball, see the one who is
lifting the ball! Both were of the same caste, do write this
on your hearts!

[*gend khelne vaala dekho, gend uthane wala dekh!
ek jati ke ye donon the, isko bhi lo man mein lekh!*]

Source: *Chand*, May 1927: 165.

24. Dalits and Shoes

He who becomes a Christian, see the stature of that untouchable!
The untouchable who stays a Hindu, see how he stitches shoes!!

*[jo isai ban jaata hai, us achhut ka dekho rang!
jo hindu hai uske joote seene ka bhi dekho dhang!!]*

Source: *Chand*, May 1927: 165.

25. Clothing, Christianity, and Dalit Boys

Untouchable boys are showing pride in their new clothes after
becoming Christians!

Source: *Chand*, January 1929: 451.

Food has been a material and metaphoric obsession for drawing boundaries of caste, religion, and nation.[206] Food was an emblem of purity/pollution, connecting private practices of the body to the social forces of caste supremacy and Dalit subjugation. Particular foods were stigmatized because of their sorority with Dalit diets. Colonizers and caste-Hindus perceived the food of Dalits as synonymous with their bodies, denigrating their eating and drinking habits to brand them as savages, as less than men, and to censure them as dirty, sinful, and unhealthy. This in turn made food another signpost for the Dalits' advocacy of their manhood. Dalits brought to the table and their plates strategies of appropriation, mimicry, parody, and critique as part of their effort to claim self-respect and male selfhood, in which "filth" was displaced through modified food practices. Dalit caste associations and *panchayats* attempted to formulate a novel cuisine and food cosmology, at least at the level of rhetoric. They started making dietary recommendations, forbidding alcohol, tobacco, beef, and pork, outlining their own exegesis of food and drink within social morality. An elevated male status was perceived as being achieved by adopting food and drink reform, and borrowing customs, manners, and taboos from the "superior" castes.[207] The contention here was not a simplistic association of such practices with the upper castes. Rather, caste was seen as playing little role in human improvement and social-cultural accomplishment. The emulation of what were assumed to be upper-caste norms could acquire potentially challenging meanings. A *panchayat* of Chamars at Dildarnagar, a village in Ghazipur, resolved to give up drinking and practice sobriety.[208] A meeting of sweepers on February 17, 1922 at Farukhabad decided to give up drink, and to enforce this decision by boycotts and fines.[209] The sweepers of Kashipur in Kumaon were lectured on the need for abstaining from liquor. The Kahars of Gonda urged their fellow men to give up fishing and eating fish in order to raise their status.[210] The

[206] Alter 2000; Ray and Srinivas 2012; Banerji 2006; Khare 1992; Leong-Salobir 2011.

[207] Srinivas 1998.

[208] *PAI*, February 11, 1922: 304.

[209] *PAI*, March 4, 1922: 471.

[210] *PAI*, April 1, 1922: 642.

Chamars of Aligarh and Badaun agreed to give up meat.[211] A Chamar
conference at Meerut, attended by over 4000 of them, resolved to
abandon meat and alcohol.[212] At a Mathura meeting in March 1923,
Chamars decided against eating the flesh of carrion.[213] A *panchayat* of
Chamars at Fyzabad proclaimed they would give up eating the meat
of dead animals.[214] A meeting of Chamars at Jaunpur proposed the
same.[215] The Bhangis and Chamars of Bulandshahr passed resolutions
in their *panchayat*s forbidding the eating of flesh and the drinking of
liquor.[216] The Chamars of Moradabad decided to start confectioner's
and grocer's shops.[217] A differentiation from Muslims was also signed
through food. In the 1920s, gatherings, *panchayat*s, and conferences
of Chamars in Bulandshahr, Dehradun, Meerut, Mathura, Kanpur,
and Jaunpur decided not to touch, accept, or eat any food, cooked
or uncooked, from Muslim houses. Dining with them was made
taboo, they having resolved to accept food only from Hindus.[218] At
a Chamar meeting in Basti it was decided that they should not eat
beef or kill buffaloes and in no case should they sell cattle to Muslim
butchers.[219] In Bareilly too they distanced themselves from Muslim
butchers and stated that only the latter would henceforward lift dead
animals. They refused to touch the dead calf of one Rahim.[220] The
Nais and Pasis too held *panchayat*s and meetings to discuss the ways
and means of social uplift via changes in their food habits.[221] A Raidas
conference held at Azamgarh in 1930, where over 7000 Chamars
gathered, adopted resolutions on social uplift and prohibition.[222]

[211] *PAI*, June 24, 1922: 1045; *PAI*, July 29, 1922: 1231.

[212] *PAI*, November 4, 1922: 1577.

[213] *PAI*, March 24, 1923: 186.

[214] *PAI*, August 18, 1928: 319; *PAI*, January 10, 1926: 4.

[215] *PAI*, October 9, 1926: 544.

[216] *PAI*, September 29, 1923: 503.

[217] *PAI*, April 1, 1922: 642; *PAI*, May 13, 1922: 845.

[218] *Census, 1931, UP*: 515; *PAI*, April 1, 1922: 642; *PAI*, April 22, 1922:
740; *PAI*, May 20, 1922: 880; *PAI*, November 4, 1922: 1577; *PAI*, March
17, 1923: 124; *PAI*, March 24, 1923: 186; *PAI*, June 23, 1923: 354; *PAI*,
October 9, 1926: 544; *PAI*, March 12, 1927: 92.

[219] *PAI*, April 23, 1938: 105.

[220] *PAI*, July 1, 1922: 1087.

[221] *PAI*, November 10, 1923: 545.

[222] "*Samachar Sangrah*," *Chand*, March 1930: 899.

In a correspondence with Baba Ramchandra, Kaluram Ravidas and Dangu Ram Ravidas reiterated the need to reform the food habits of the Ravidas brothers.[223] Alongside, the sweepers of Kanpur, under the initiative of their *panchayat*, decided not to accept leftover and rejected food as well as the goods of higher castes, which were called *utran* (discarded, used, or second-hand clothes), *jhutan* (leftover or half-eaten food), and *phatkan* (refused or extra bits, literally chaff separated from grain after winnowing). This was reiterated by Achhutanand.[224]

It appears that at the level of rhetoric and resolutions Dalit associations at this time were neither ratifying pride in their traditional food habits and culinary skills, nor exhibiting a distaste for "bland Brahmanical" food.[225] Yet Dalit men were not simply mimicking the ideas, customs, and suggestions of the upper castes, but were actively interpreting and deploying reformist rhetoric for their own purposes. Without losing sight of their distinct social identity, advocating such reforms was their way of saying that they were as capable as the upper castes when it came to cultivating "refined" and "civilized" food habits, while also reversing the signs of their subordination. Such adaptations simultaneously undermined the customary denunciations of Dalits by caste-Hindus.

Control over their women's movements and sexuality also became an important axis for Dalit masculine assertion. Not merely the intermediate castes, even Chamar, Khatik, and Pasi men began putting restrictions on women in intimate spaces.[226] Meetings of Chamars in Moradabad, Meerut, Mathura, Dehra Dun, and Saharanpur decided that they would allow their women less liberty of movement.

[223] "Correspondence with Kaluram Ravidas," Ist Installment, Baba Ramchandra Papers, NMML.

[224] Quoted in Gooptu 2001: 168–9.

[225] The recent controversy over the serving of beef in some hostel messes brings out the different resonances of this process. Dalits have fleshed out the politics of caste-oriented cultural contestations that are embedded within the discourse of food more sharply in the present context: WS 10 Class 2009; Gundimeda 2009; Jalki 2003; Raman 2012: 22–3.

[226] In colonial Bengal too, as the Rajbansis and Namasudras became more socially mobile, they began to emulate stricter gender codes of the gentry: Bandyopadhyay 2004: 152–5.

They forbade them from visiting bazaars and selling grass, and they advocated the wearing of *dhotis* by women when cooking food.[227] Bhangis in Mathura and Bulandshahr passed resolutions in their *panchayat*s forbidding their women from going daily to bazaars and attending fairs (*mela*s).[228] A Pasi *panchayat* in Meerut resolved that their women should not step out for daily labor.[229] The Khatiks of Lucknow decided not to allow their women to peddle fruits on the street and made them sell only in shops.[230] Wealthy urban Chamars began proclaiming a new role for women of their community by putting them under seclusion, particularly stopping them from doing menial work such as removing dung and grinding foodstuff in upper-caste households, while also opposing abuse of their women by Thakurs.[231] A Jatia Chamar Sabha at Meerut, attended by over 4000 Chamars, passed a resolution saying their females ought to go into purdah.[232] The pursuit of respectability could be a source of tension. When a Chamar *panchayat* of Meerut decided that Chamar women should not step out to earn via their daily labor, the *zamindar*s objected and held a meeting to which they summoned Chamars, but the latter refused to show up or change their stance.[233] In a meeting of Chamars at Jaunpur it was suggested that Chamar women should not work as midwives.[234] The seclusion of women thus became the norm wherever it seemed possible. The 1921 Census of UP reported that Pasis, Bhangis, Chamars, and Dhobis all had appreciably more widows than they had ten years earlier,[235] for they too were banning widow remarriage. Many Dalits of UP also opposed the Sarda Act— the Child Marriage Restraint Act 1929. A meeting of Khatiks at Rae

[227] *PAI*, April 1, 1922: 642; *PAI*, May 13, 1922: 845; *PAI*, September 30, 1922: 1466; *PAI*, March 24, 1923: 186.

[228] *PAI*, March 24, 1923: 186; *PAI*, September 29, 1923: 503.

[229] *Abhyudaya*, December 25, 1926: 8.

[230] Blunt 1931: 56, 241.

[231] Raghuvanshi 1916; Briggs 1920: 4, 47; Lynch 1969: 174–81; Cohn 1987: 272–8; Crooke 1975 (1897): 206.

[232] *PAI*, November 4, 1922: 1577.

[233] *PAI*, April 21, 1923: 264.

[234] *PAI*, October 9, 1926: 544.

[235] *Census, 1921, UP*: 104.

Bareilly decided to resist the Sarda Act, and about eighty marriages were performed in contravention of it.[236] Such moves, along with the denial of access to public spaces to Dalit women, have been seen as ways to strengthen claims for upward social mobility through imitative methods.[237] Dalits here were also drawing on dominant norms of manhood, claiming Dalit masculinity not through heterogeneity but through mimicry. They employed the power of mimesis as a means of aping and even magically appropriating the power of the upper castes. These were markers of masculinity in the domestic sphere, in reaction to perceived "emasculation." The Dalit masculinist ethos intersected with patriarchy to produce interlocking sets of power relations. This epistemic blindspot puts a question mark on the relative romanticization that has existed among some Dalit scholars who valorize Dalit culture as being free from sexual controls and much more egalitarian in terms of gender relations.[238] Yet, while broadly falling under the rubric of Sanskritization and assertions of patriarchal control, these measures also signified other meanings.[239] They were also attempts to restore dignity and respectability to their women, countering the accusations of the upper castes, and to protest against the sexual exploitation of their women. The regulation of sexuality was critical for the politicization of caste identity. Dalit reformist masculinity was predicated on the reform of gender within their community and the defense of community honor against the disdain of outsiders.[240] In many ways, Dalits were using the language

[236] *PAI*, December 21, 1928: 711; *PAI*, May 17, 1930: 610.

[237] Scholars have emphasized how women were used by the lower castes to counter their social marginalization: Lynch 1969: 174–81; Cohn 1987: 255–98; Bandyopadhyay 1997, 2004; Dube 1998; Gupta 2010. Uma Chakravarti employs the term *jatikarana* or intensified classification as an explanation for such processes, Chakravarti 2003: 87. For views on how women in turn asserted themselves, Searle-Chatterjee 1981; Jogdand 1995; Jain, Jain, and Bhatnagar 1997; Chowdhry 2007; Rao 2003; Rege 2006.

[238] This view is upheld, for example, by Ilaiah 2005; Kapadia 1996.

[239] The "Sanskritization" model also undermines the conflict that is often generated by the appropriation of upper-caste symbols by the lower castes. See Hardiman 1987: 157–65.

[240] Rao 2009: 49, 61.

of "reforming" practices pertaining to their women to subvert their exclusion. They were drawing on the vocabulary of the upper castes to carve out greater dignity for themselves and their women, and to undermine caste stereotypes reifying their inferiority.

Conclusion

Dominant cultures produced stereotypical representations of Dalits. The attributes of docility, stupidity, and emasculation were mobilized to construct Dalit male bodies. Conflicting, though still formulaic, images also portrayed them as violent, criminal, sexually potent, and habitually drunk. Dalit "othering" was accomplished through a repertoire of caste-marked feminine and masculine tropes. However, Dalits were not passive onlookers. Grappling with lines of authority from marginal social positions, Dalit manhood sought its own ideological equilibrium between caste oppression and masculine subjecthood. Crafting themselves as legitimate political subjects, Dalit publicists staged public battles over the meanings of caste, putting forward claims for dignity and social justice while implementing strategies to ascend the social ladder despite the odds. Politicizing the social, they reframed their manhood by invoking a masculine past, claiming a place in the army, arguing for more political space, and through their work, dress, and culture seeking entry, even if tenuous, into a modern urban public sphere. They deployed the means offered by the colonial economy—for example employment, print, educational opportunities, and religious conversion—for implicit and explicit assertions of Dalit masculinity. Even while the crisis of Dalit life was not consciously perceived or articulated in terms of masculinity, their dissonant discourses and actions became a means of recuperating their manhood, which in turn became a subtle trope for coping with and overcoming to an extent their sense of powerlessness, alienation, and social impotence. It was a performative act, a survival strategy, a form of resistance within limited structures of opportunity, a way to argue for more rights, dignity, and better employment opportunities. Human rights were expressed in these claims to manhood. Protesting against their arbitrary characterization, developing a language of manhood and dignity was their way of stating that moral and intellectual refinement, economic progress, education, better jobs, and dignity of work were not the sole preserve of the upper castes, but principles that applied to all, irrespective of caste.

The function of masculinity, however, is also to control. Even though they came from different backgrounds and perceptions, Dalit men at times colluded with dominant notions of masculinity and their views fed into binaries by acting out a received gendered script. There were shifts in definitions of manhood—from production to consumption, from respectability to bodily assertiveness, from manliness to masculinity. Patriarchal practices were often accentuated by Dalits, particularly in domestic spheres, even while control over women was linked to arguing for greater respectability in relation to them. Dalits also contributed to dominant visions of masculinity when they sometimes emerged as actors of communal violence, even though they did so for contested and varying reasons. At the same time, Dalit framing did produce dislocations and cracks in those very hegemonic embodiments.[241] Theirs often became a non-conformist masculinity, acquiring a dynamic vitality that transformed the mundane into the sublime and made the routine spectacular.

It is not enough to say that Dalit self-representations of masculinity in colonial India were subversive; it is important to place them in the context of and in relation to representations of masculinity by others. Dalit masculinity was not a stable category, but responsive to its cultural, historical, social, and political embeddedness. Ultimately, its construction was neither fully cohesive nor entirely innocent, since gender identities were themselves not immutable. One can only hope that Dalit men will evolve and ultimately dismantle the very ideological fetters that fasten them to a corrosive paradigm of masculinity, using it more as a creative tool to argue for their dignity and rights.

[241] For theoretical inputs, see Derrida 1993: 74–5.

5

Intimate and Embodied Desires
Religious Conversions and
Dalit Women

W e have thus far delineated the dominant varieties of gendered representations of Dalits and counter-constructions
by Dalits themselves. We can now transit to particular
sites and events of religious conversion, popular culture, and indentured labor around which anxieties of caste and gender were especially
evident. Religious conversion has been one of the common expedients
resorted to by those at the bottom of caste hierarchies in India, to
improve their position, reject stratification, reconfigure social boundaries, and register protest as well as social assertion.[1] The figure of
the Dalit convert introduces ruptures in the prevailing ideas of caste,
religion, and nation.

Dalit conversions to Christianity began largely in colonial India
and have provoked a variety of writings.[2] While perceptive, most
scholars have focused on mass movements that show a Dalit male
bias, and within which outcaste women often remain elusive figures.
There has of course developed a considerable literature on Christian
women missionaries, and their position and work within the British

---

[1] Clarke 1998: 4, 125; Fernandes 1994; Galanter 1997; Webster 1994,
1999; Hebden 2011; Mallampalli 2004; Vishwanathan 1998.

[2] Bayly 1999; Forrester 1979; Oddie 1969, 1997; Pati 2003; Philip 1925;
Phillips 1912; Pickett 1933; Vishwanathan 1998; Webster 1994, 1999; Zelliot 1992.

empire.[3] This again, while deeply perceptive, mainly discusses the opportunities and problems faced by missionary women when negotiating new arenas constituted by colonial and mission activity; they do not give adequate space to the possible reception and impact of their work on women at the receiving end. Recently, some works have attempted to fill this lacuna, the most significant being those by Eliza Kent, Chad Bauman, and James Taneti, which discuss the impact of conversion to Christianity on lower-caste women in colonial South India and Chattisgarh.[4] In her landmark study, Kent brings out the complex relationship between caste, gender, conversions, and colonialism by showing how a "discourse of respectability" emerged among Dalit Christian communities which radically transformed the style of femininity to which Indian Christian women were expected to conform.[5] Complementing her work, Bauman shows that conversion did not lead to any straightforward emancipation of Dalit women. Rather, it often implied an adoption of norms consonant with upper-caste Hinduism and Victorian Christian values, leading to a contraction in Dalit women's range of activities. Taneti however highlights how Telugu Dalit Bible women appropriated an alien religious institution by using indigenous resources. While agreeing in part with these perspectives, my effort will be to complicate them by forefronting the relationship of conversion with desire and intimacy. Even while mimicking, Dalits often molded conversions—what has been referred to as the "vernacularization" of Christianity[6]—and even at times used them to subvert the very norms they were supposed to ape. Simultaneously, such acts produced increasing anxieties among caste-Hindus, displacing Dalit female desire.

Dalit conversions in colonial India have been examined largely in the context of Christianity, and as mass movements and collective strategies embedded in community advancement. However, they leave unnoticed the motivations for individual conversion by Dalit

---

[3] Singh 2000; Semple 2003; Brouwer 1990; Flemming 1992; Haggis 2000; Burton 1994; Forbes 1986.

[4] Kent 2004; Bauman 2008; Taneti 2013.

[5] Kent 2004: 4, 240.

[6] Dube 2004: 161–71.

women. It is as if women had no mind or heart of their own; they just followed their families and men. Yet, romance and desire provide a peep into histories of personal conversion to Islam by some Dalit women, moments at which they attempted to stand as individual subjects. This moment was doubly agentive: it signaled an exit from Hindu hierarchy and challenged caste patriarchy.

Here we will concentrate on the representation of the Dalit woman convert by registering a social history of conversion in colonial UP through the lens of caste and intimacy. The effort will be to explore conversions as acts that embodied desires and were accounts of stubborn materialities. I trace police reports, cartoons, popular missionary literature in Hindi, and writings by caste and reformist ideologues to show how conversion, or the possibility of it, produced increasing worries, deeply politicized representations, and resulted in everyday violence framed around the bodies of Dalit women. These were enmeshed in a particular politics of colonial order on the one hand and of incitement on the other, wherein there was both a representational heightening and an erasure of Dalit female desire. Through this context of the overwriting and silencing of Dalit female subjectivity, the attempt is to recover in part Dalit female choice and aspiration. I look at how Dalit women found ways of negotiating codified relations to recast the logic of caste and religious boundaries. To an extent, conversion by Dalit women was an affair of desire which aided the transformative politics of religious rights. They were possibly employing conversion to also contest their association with sexual availability and debased female worth.

Two entry points take us forward. First, a discussion of mass conversion to Christianity and how it was also woven around education and sartorial desires. Second, a focus on individual Dalit female conversions to Islam which were embedded in love and marriage. The tensions between such embodied desires reveal attempts to privilege a language of community rights, which were assigned a greater status, over women's individual choices, which were marginalized and silenced. I also address other concerns. Conversion and its impact on intimacy naturally have a bearing on the sexualities of Dalit women. Ann Stoler has extended Foucauldian paradigms by combining sexualities with social taxonomies of race as formative features of modernity. She agrees with Foucault that discourses around sexuality were activated as discursive incitements facilitating the penetration of self-disciplinary regimes in the intimate domains of modern life. But she argues that sexuality in colonial contexts was predicated on exclusionary principles and could not survive without a racially erotic counterpoint, without reference to the libidinal energies of the primitive, the colonized, which became a marker of critique and desire.[7] Extending this insight, I argue here that it was not just the colonizers; Hindu elite men too underwrote an exclusivist grammar of difference in sexual regimes, be it in relation to clothing or inter-religious romance.

Dalit women's rights are also intricately tied to conversion. Gender historians have highlighted the double-edged meanings of law and a new language of rights for women in colonial India.[8] Religious conversion by women, particularly, produced fraught results in the eyes of the law.[9] In spite of limitations, certain laws did help produce cracks in earlier orthodox mandates and to an extent enabled a new female self-fashioning.[10] I will try to show how disorder crept into the moral order. I do so by extending the language of rights, which have been conventionally and historically defined in terms of codified laws, universal conventions, community needs, and institutional sites. But how does one place rights and their possible expressions in everyday life, which take on not just needs but also desires? Dalit women's embodied desires in the realm of clothing or romance, expressed at times through highly ritualized acts of conversion, imply a language of intimate rights, creating ripples in codified definitions. Caste then becomes an exploration not just of identity categories or questions of political inequality, but also the subtle manner of functioning as body history, and of how everyday life is the site for the social reproduction of a hegemonic caste order *as well as* an enabling ground for generating practices of dissent.

[7] Stoler 1995: 1–54.

[8] Basu 2001; Chandra 1998; Chatterjee 1999; Chowdhry 2007; Nair 1996; Singha 1998.

[9] De 2010; Mallampalli 2010.

[10] Sarkar 2009.

Dalit Religious Conversions in Colonial UP

Persuading and Patronizing: Missionaries and Maulvis

At no stage did the empire challenge caste in the way missionaries did.[11] While there had been earlier conversions by the outcastes, for example to Buddhism in ancient India, the arrival of the British and the impetus it gave to Christian missionary activities proved to be one of the biggest influences in altering their position. The Christian community in India was drawn largely from converts within the depressed classes.[12] There were some Dalit conversions to Christianity in UP,[13] though not as many as in several other parts of colonial India. However, there was a huge discourse, debate, and representation of the issue in popular literature, newspapers, reformist tracts, caste pamphlets, cartoons, and missionary propaganda, especially with the outpouring of print wars between the Arya Samaj and the missionaries. Protestant missionaries, in particular, adopted a variety of techniques for propaganda among the Dalits, including bazaar preaching, itinerant sermons in villages, open services in public places, religious festivals and *melas*, visits to homes, and the distribution of scripture extracts and tracts in mostly the vernacular.[14] The North Indian Christian Tract and Book Soceity (NICTBS), run by the Church Mission of England and headquartered at Allahabad, promoted and disseminated vernacular tracts among the outcastes, including painted story scrolls, books, and a multitude of songs and hymns.[15] Its annual publication and circulation of Christian books reached a staggering 908,000 copies in 1914. A conference on Urdu and Hindi Christian literature held at Allahabad resolved that particular efforts would be made through such literature to influence the lower castes and

[11] Copley 1997: 6.
[12] Webster 1994: 36.
[13] Sharma 1988; Alter 1986.
[14] Sherring 1875: 193; Webster 1994: 36; CMS 1926; *Annual Report of the CMS for the Year 1936–7*: 252–64.
[15] Clayton 1911: 3; Sharma 1988: 92. Lucas n.d.: 3.

servants.[16] Every month between 8000 and 40,000 copies of Hindi tracts were distributed free. Many of these were thin pamphlets of four to six pages, priced cheaply and written in an accessible language.[17] Tracts like *Hindu Dharm ke Phal, Jati ki Chhut-Chhat, Hinduon ki Nirdhanta*, and *Jati Panti ka Varnan* launched vitriolic attacks on Hinduism, particularly on the treatment meted out to outcastes.[18] Hindu practices adversely impacting outcastes were particularly ridiculed, including the absence of inter-caste marriages, unnecessary expenditure on ceremonies and pilgrimages, dirty habits, denying untouchables a dip in the holy Ganga, and the aversion to physical labor among caste-Hindus.[19] By contrast, Christianity was propagated as the ideally egalitarian religion, and conversion as the biggest boon which would give the depressed classes dignity, education, and clean clothes.[20] Mediating on behalf of the outcastes, missionary literature juxtaposed images of the bad effects of Hinduism *vis-à-vis* the positive impact of Christianity (Figure 26).

Deploying the language of benevolent paternalism, it was pronounced that Christians considered physical labor honest and holy; they dined with outcastes, treating them equally before the law and made everyone a part of "one loving brotherhood": "What could not be achieved in thousands of years was being done by the missionaries for the untouchables."[21] At the same time, missionary language was guided by a sense of racial and religious superiority. It was cloaked in a patronizing tone of bringing culture and civilization to the outcastes. For example, a Hindi mission tract stated that "The untouchables are like lost rupees, on which dust, soil, dirt, and mire

[16] *Conference on Urdu and Hindi Christian Literature held at Allahabad*: 4, 15.

[17] Lucas n.d.: 41, 53.

[18] *Hindu Dharm ke Phal* 1905; *Jati ki Chhut-Chhat* 1905; *Hinduon ki Nirdhanta* 1909; *Jati Panti ka Varnan* 1924: 11.

[19] *Hindu Dharm ke Phal* 1905: 3–4, 6–12, 23–4, 33; *Hinduon ki Nirdhanta* 1909: 7–17; *Jati ki Chhut-Chhat* 1905: 1–10; *Ganga ka Vritant* 1905: 14; Bradbury 1884: 110.

[20] *Devi Devta aur Murtipuja* 1923: 24; *Jati Pariksha* 1906: 13

[21] *Jati Panti ka Varnan* 1909: 11. Also Pickett 1938: 36, 38.

UNITED PROVINCES

THE STERNER SIDE
Village Christians who were beaten and not allowed to use the village well and otherwise ill-treated by their non-Christian neighbours.

THE LIGHTER SIDE
Rejoicings at a Christmas mela

26. "The Sterner Side, The Lighter Side"

Source: CMS, *Mass Movement in UP*: 5.

has gathered. But just as dirty and tattered rupees do not lose their actual value, similarly in the eyes of God the value of these people docs not decrease. And we missionaries are here precisely to reform these dirty sinners."[22]

[22] *Jati Panti ka Varnan* 1909: 15. Also *Jati Pariksha* 1906: 8; *Jati ki Chhut-Chhat* 1905.

Islam too carried its teachings among Dalits.[23] Many of the lower castes actively engaged with and creatively reinterpreted Islamic traditions into their lives and cultures during the medieval period.[24] Milind Wakankar argues that Islam provided a radical critique of caste society and offered Dalits an unprecedented way out of institutionalized caste-Hinduism. The Indo-Islamic millennium has been constructed by many Dalits as a long-running low-caste movement against the Brahminical conception of the social.[25] It was stated by colonial officials that a considerable proportion of the cobbler caste of UP had become Muhammadan,[26] and that many Muslim leather workers in the towns were Hindu Chamar converts.[27] Muslim organizations continued to actively seek converts in colonial UP from among the outcastes. In Saharanpur, Moradabad, Bijnor, Bulandshahr, and Dehradun they mobilized resources to preach Islam in villages which contained only untouchables.[28] In Agra and Meerut the Tabligh distributed leaflets welcoming Chamars into Islam as a religion of equals.[29] In 1925 a Muslim *zamindar* of Etah stated that if the outcastes converted to Islam, he would give them 500 *bigha*s of land and also have *roti–beti* ties with them.[30]

Anxieties and Ambiguities: High-Caste Hindus and Reformers

Such campaigns and some actual conversions by Dalits generated apprehensions among high-caste Hindus, the Arya Samaj, and the Hindu Mahasabha. The Arya Samaj effectively utilized the print-public sphere to constantly lament perceived conversions of

[23] Mujahid 1989; Sikand 2004.
[24] Eaton 1993: 113–34.
[25] Wakankar 2010: 114.
[26] Nesfield 1882: 22.
[27] Walton 1903: 12.
[28] *PAI*, April 14, 1923: 241; *PAI*, November 24, 1923; *PAI*, June 7, 1924; *PAI*, May 19, 1928: 189.
[29] *PAI*, October 10, 1925.
[30] "*Etah Zilla ke 400 Chamar*" (400 Chamars of Etah District), *Abhyudaya*, August 22, 1925: 5.

outcastes.[31] This was tied to a number-crunching politics in which a picture of terrible calamity was outlined of rapidly declining Hindu numbers on account of Dalit conversions.[32] It was stated that every week 2000 untouchable Hindus converted to Christianity, which meant 104,000 converts annually. It was also believed that 200,000 untouchables became Muslims every year.[33] A reformist poem urged the upper castes thus:

> Hindus, this is not a time to say, but to do something,
> Hindus, reconstruct the spoilt fate of your community . . .
> Those you were spurning till now, calling them untouchables,
> Hindus, clasp and hug them with love . . .
> Your brothers who have become Christians–Muslims, Hindus,
> make them drink the nectar of Vedic religion . . .
> Because of your negligence you have lost thousands of sons,
> Now do not let the robbers steal from your home.[34]

> [*waqt kehne ka nahin, kuch kar dikhao hinduon,*
> *kaum ki bigdi hui kismet banao hinduon . . .*
> *jinko thukra rahe ho aaj tak keh kar achhut,*
> *pyar se unko kaleje se lagao hinduon . . .*
> *aapke bhai jo ban baithe hain isai-yaman,*
> *unko vaidik dharm ka amrit pilao hinduon . . .*
> *kho chuke ho apni gaflat mein hazaron lal tum,*
> *ab luteron se na apna ghar lutao hinduon.*]

The Moplah rebellion,[35] in particular, provided an opportunity for Hindu organizations to speak about the forcible conversions of

[31] Upadhyay 1930, 1941.

[32] Brahmanand 1934; Chandrikaprasad 1917: 14; Dwivedi 1924: 1, 26, 35; Parmanand 1928; "*Achhut aur Musalman*" (Untouchables and Muslims), *Abhyudaya*, July 18, 1925: 2; Editorial, "*Hinduon ka Haas*" (Decline of Hindus), *Sudha*, June 1929: 541; Editorial, "*Hinduon ka Bhayankar Haas*" (Cataclysmic Decline of Hindus), *Chand*, January 1929: 450–60; Dayashankar Dube, "*Bharat Mein Hinduon ki Dasha*" (Condition of Hindus in India), *Madhuri*, August 1925: 146–53.

[33] Jha 1925: 4.

[34] Dube 1933: 3. Also, "Sant" 1933.

[35] Panikkar 1989.

outcaste women and men by the Moplahs.[36] In North India a large
number of tracts and articles emerged, giving vivid descriptions of
what had supposedly happened in Malabar.[37] Swami Shraddhanand
seized this opportunity to launch the *shuddhi* campaign with rigor
in UP, to reclaim "victims" and protect the "faithful."[38] The Hindu
Mahasabha too joined in, stating that it wanted the depressed classes
not as a separate section of Hindus but in the same body politic.[39] In
1923 the Bhartiya Hindu Shuddhi Sabha was founded, with its head-
quarters at Agra, and Swami Shraddhanand as its president.[40] Organizations like the Achhutoddhar Mandal, the Dalitodhar Sabha,
the Arya Biradri Sammelan, and the Jaat Paat Torak Mandal were
formed at this time. The Harijan Sevak Sangh, Mrs Kamla Nehru,
Mr Bulabhai Desai and several others urged the outcastes not to
convert.[41] Many leading Hindi newspapers and magazines, particularly *Abhyudaya*, *Pratap*, and *Chand*, gave their unequivocal support to these efforts.[42] Simultaneously, a vast literature, including

[36] 156/II/1924, Home Poll, NAI.

[37] Gupta 2001: 225–6; "*Hinduon Ankhen Kholo*" (Hindus Open Your
Eyes), *Abhyudaya*, August 29, 1925: 5.

[38] Though the Arya Samaj had stronger roots in Punjab, the *shuddhi*
movement was more effective in UP: 140/1925, Home Poll, NAI. On the
shuddhi campaign in UP: *Census, 1931, UP*: 501–2; Freitag 1989: 220–48;
Pandey 1978: 115–17; Ghai 1990; Gooptu 2001: 144–57; Jordens 1981:
142–51.

[39] Interview with Ganpat Rai, Oral History Transcript, NMML: 26–7;
140/1925, Home Poll, NAI. Significantly, the Hindu Mahasabha was
not against outcastes converting to Sikhism, as this supposedly provided
masculinity and the martial spirit to Dalits, useful in the fight against Muslims.
Moonje wrote: "As for conversion to Sikhism, I have also been saying from
the time of the Mopla Rebellion of 1921–2 that the Hindus will not object
to conversion to Sikhism, if that will make them soldiers": Subject File
52/1939, Moonje Papers, NMML. Also, *The Indian Social Reformer*, August
15, 1936: 794–5.

[40] *Bhartiya Hindu Shuddhi Sabha ka Sankshipt Itihaas tatha Vivran*;
Shraddhanand 1926: 124; *Pratham Varshik Report*: 1–2.

[41] Subject File 52/1939, Moonje Papers, NMML; *Leader*, June 27,
1925.

[42] *Abhyudaya*, March 13, 1926: 1–2; *Chand*, May 1927: 2–3; *Chand*,

pamphlets, poems, posters, and cartoons, was published to counter conversion attempts by missionaries and Muslims.

Key arguments can be gleaned in this literature against conversions: (1) It is so ironic that we treat untouchables so badly, but once they convert we treat them with respect and equality. (2) In comparison with Muslims or Christians, our Bhangi and Chamar brothers are a thousand times better. They are much cleaner than Muslims and, unlike them, bathe every day. (3) If we do not win back our untouchable brothers, the Hindu *jati* will soon face bankruptcy, as from its treasury will flow a constant expenditure (conversion) but

27. Missionary and Dalits

Abandon, abandon this pathetic state, run away from Hindus!
Come under the protection of Christ, wake up from this deep slumber!!

[*tyago, tyago deen dasha yeh, door hinduon se bhago!
isa ke charano mein aao, is guru-nidra se jaago!!*]

Source: *Chand*, May 1927: 76.

May 1929: 41–51; *Chand*, May 1930: 268–74, 351–3; *Chand*, January 1932: 386–7; *Chand*, May 1932: 2–7; *Pratap*, April 20, 1925; *Pratap*, June 1, 1925.

no earning. It is a matter of life and death. (4) Reconversions are necessary to prevent outcastes from becoming cow-killers. If we are unable to do much in this area, we are handing over a ready harvest to Muslims.[43]

Poems were published by reformers, taking on the voice of untouchables and mourning on their behalf:

> Though I am a worshiper of Ram, you separate me from him.
> Then, when I change my religion and become a Muslim,
> Or I convert into a Christian and adorn the hat and come,
> All pollution vanishes and I am called a "Sahib"!![44]

> [ram bhakt hoon tau bhi, mujhko unse bilag karata hai.
> phir jab dharm badal jaata hai, musalman ban jaata hoon.
> athva isai ban kar ke, hat laga kar aata hoon.
> chut-chat sab mit jaati hai, sahib main kehlata hoon!!]

Reclamation efforts started being made, with meetings held at Hapur, Ghazipur, Meerut, Kanpur, Mathura, Saharanpur, Banaras, Moradabad, Bijnor, and Bareilly to stop conversions and simultaneously reconvert outcastes.[45] In certain sections of UP reconversions by the Arya Samaj were so successful that the Christian population actually declined in number.[46] Hindu leaders like Lala Lajpat Rai, Madan Mohan Malaviya, and Sampurnanand tried to convince orthodox Hindus by threatening them with the idea that "Chamars could leave the Hindu religion and become Muslims and Christians if caste-Hindus did not change their attitudes."[47] Swami

[43] These views were repeatedly expressed: Jha 1925: 5–15; Sharda 1925: 6–9; "Prakash" 1934; Upadhyay 1925; Banprasthi 1927; Chatursen 1930.

[44] Dube 1933: 9.

[45] PAI, January 20, 1923: 38; PAI, February 3, 1923: 69; PAI, March 17, 1923: 170; PAI, April 7, 1923: 226; PAI, April 21, 1923: 266; PAI, May 5, 1923: 278; PAI, June 9, 1923: 332; PAI, June 30, 1923: 367; PAI, March 29, 1924: 118; PAI, February 13, 1926: 84; Shraddhanand 1919: 65; Rai 1914: 27; "Daliton ka Arya Samaj Pravesh" (The Entry of Dalits into the Arya Samaj), "Samachar Sangrah," Chand, May 1927: 191.

[46] Census, 1931, UP: 501–2.

[47] PAI, September 20, 1924; Pratap, July 27, 1925; February 8, 1926; Abhyudaya, March 3, 1928.

Vicharanand declared that the reconversion of a Muslim was equal to the saving of the lives of 500 cows as that was the average amount of beef consumed by a Muslim during his lifetime.[48] Attempts were also made to instill feelings against Muslims among Dalits by urging them, for example, not to celebrate the Ghazi Mian ka Mela, and not to touch food cooked by Muhammadans.[49] Simultaneously, missionaries, Christian priests, and Islamic ideologues were made fun of, and appeared as liars, stupid cow-eaters, and violent.[50] It was stressed that Jesuits particularly were dressing up as Brahmins and converting outcastes under false pretenses.[51] Many Arya Samaj pamphlets carried a picture of Yuddh Prakash, alias Richardson, and his wife Kripadevi, who were reported to be Christian missionaries from Scotland dressing up as ascetics, particularly during the Magh Mela and fairs visited by untouchables, and spreading the word of Christ.[52] The benefits that outcastes were given upon converting were ridiculed as mythical:

> Come drought and hunger, and you [outcastes] abandon family,
>   mother, father, brother.
> The Christian comes with greed and lures, and the world laughs at
>   you.
> You crave the fair-skinned Miss but get only a *chamarin*.
> You desire rides in a car but do not even get a female donkey.
> I just pray to the world, please all beware.
> Christ is nowhere, God save your life.[53]

> [*pada akaal bhukh ke mare, taji kutumb, matu, pit, bhaiya.*
> *aat kristan gahiyon lalach bas, jako jagat hansaiya.*
> *gori miss ki rahi vasna, mili ek chamariya.*
> *lalsa rahi phitan charhan ki, mili na ek gadahiya.*]

[48] *PAI*, June 11, 1927: 217.

[49] *PAI*, June 5, 1926: 308; *PAI*, June 19, 1926: 327; *PAI*, March 12, 1927: 92.

[50] Banprasthi 1927; Upadhyay 1925.

[51] Shraddhanand 1919: 31; Banprasthi 1927: 54; Editorial. "*Hinduon ka Bhayankar Haas*" (The Cataclysmic Decline of Hindus), *Chand*, January 1929: 451.

[52] Upadhyay 1923: 9.

[53] Banprasthi 1927: cover.

main tau gayun din duniya se, bache raho sab bhaiya.]
isu masih nahin kahun, prabhu pran bachaiya.]

Another stated:

A pomegranate can never change into a guava.
Then how can Hindus today become a part of Muslim
    community? . . .
Brahmin, Kshatriyas, Vaishyas, please come forward,
Accept with respect your junior brothers . . .
March ahead oil miller, barber, vegetable seller, bard, beggar,
    washerman, cotton carder.
Kurmi, boatman, Kuril, sweeper—we have faith in you. Become our
    true associates.[54]

[*hota nahin anar kabhi amrud badal ke.*
tab hindu kis bhanti aaj bhaye muslim dal ke. . . .
brahman, kshatri, vaishya kshetra mein aage awo,
antyaj bandhu samaj vishad saadar apnavo . . .
teli nai khatik tamoli bhaat bhikhari. dhobi dhanuk lodh bodh se baarho
    agari.
kurmi kevat kuril jati ke kori bhangi. aasha tumhin se lagi bano sache
    sangi.]

Implicit in such literature was upper-caste prejudice. Moreover,
severe tensions remained on the ground. The attempts at keeping the
boundaries of Hinduism intact by stopping conversion, while simultaneously increasing reconversion, could not be easily reconciled with
maintaining a difference within the Hindu community.

Overpowering and Empowering:
Dalit Responses

Amidst such campaigns by missionaries on the one hand, and Hindu
reformers on the other, Dalits often used conversion as a heuristic
device to signal the achievement of dignity, education, clothing,
employment, political representation, modernity, and "manhood."[55]
Conversions involved complex and varied motivations. It could

[54] Bandhusamaj 1927: 5–14 (poem by Ramavtar Shukl).
[55] Gupta 2010: 309–42; Menon 2006.

be "To escape from cholera . . . Because land owners oppressed us . . . Because our missionary helped us against the Brahmans and the Rajputs . . . Because the love of Jesus won me . . . To get a wife for my younger brother . . . To be saved from forced labor . . . Because I wanted to know God . . . Because the wise men of my caste said I should."[56]

It was not so much the missionaries as Dalits themselves who took the initiative in expressing their attraction towards the missions and launching mass movements for conversion.[57] The census report of 1901 noted that many of the Christians of UP were former Chandals, Doms, Bhangis, and Chamars.[58] By infusing their outlook with a liberal dose of Christian piety, Dalits hoped to influence British humanitarian leanings when seeking concessions from the state. Conversions continued sporadically into the 1920s, when there was once again an impetus to the movement. The American Methodist Episcopal Mission was particularly active among the outcastes in UP and Punjab, gathering 100,000 Christians into its fold.[59] Though by 1931 there were still only 173,077 Indian Christians in UP, a vast majority of them, around 125,000, belonged to the Dalit castes.[60] Conversions usually involved the entire local section of particular outcastes and were not the acts of isolated individuals. Regardless of whether caste *panchayats* or individual families made the decision, evangelism and conversion often followed along family and *jati* lines.[61] Weddings, funerals, and business deals all provided occasions to pass the word; at times conversion could even be a condition for a marriage between Christians and Hindus of the same *jati*. However, conversions were double-edged and the subject position of a convert, especially if Dalit, remained forever "in-between" all ascriptions of place, location, and identity.[62]

[56] Pickett 1933: 159–60.

[57] Sharma 1988: v; Shraddhanand 1919: 42; Rai 1914: 13.

[58] *Census, 1901, NWP*: 68; *Meerut: A Gazetteer*: 79–81; *Pilibhit: A Gazetteer*: 97; Phillips 1912: 100–1.

[59] Phillips 1912: 34.

[60] *Census, 1931, UP*: 500; Webster 1994: 119.

[61] Singh 1947: 178.

[62] Editorial, "*Asprishyata ka Vastavik Swarup aur Kaaran*" (The Real Face of Untouchability and its Reasons), *Chand*, September 1935: 438–43; *The

Alongside, Dalits often used to their advantage the alarm felt by reformers over converting them to demand more rights and as a way of questioning the stigma of untouchability. They played on the fears of Hindu organizations, which responded with alacrity to some of their demands.[63] In Bulandshahr the threat to convert gave Chamars access to a previously restricted public well in a Hindu neighborhood.[64] During an untouchable reform (achhutoddhar) week organized by the Arya Samaj in September 1926 in Agra, Kheri, Allahabad, and Banaras, Dalits demanded that unless Hindus gave them equal rights they would convert to Islam or Christianity.[65] In Farukhabad the threat of conversion to Islam by some Dalits forced a group of Hindus to visit and assure them that if they remained Hindus they would be better treated in future. They invited them to join the prayer (havan) ceremony at Holi.[66] At Moradabad, Chamars threatened to embrace Islam if treated as untouchables.[67] The reasons for reconverting or joining the Arya Samaj could also be very different for Dalits. A Pasi panchayat held in Allahabad said that conversion to Arya Samaj could help them escape the proceedings of the Criminal Tribes Act.[68] The major rebuff that the outcastes gave to the Hindu reformist propaganda was when they actually converted. Many sweepers, Lal Begis, Chandals, Doms, and Chamars of Saharanpur, Jhansi, Badaun, Mathura, Meerut, Roorkee, Etah, Cawnpore, Gorakhpur, Bulandshahr, Moradabad, Pilibhit, Bijnor, and Bareilly converted to Christianity or Islam.[69] Many converted sweepers and Chamars refused to do begar in the households and fields of zamindars.[70]

Indian Social Reformer, November 23, 1935: 186; Das 1969: 143; Ambedkar 1987 (1936): 78.

[63] Rawat 2012: 142–4.

[64] PAI, June 9, 1923: 333.

[65] PAI, March 31, 1928: 135; PAI, April 21, 1928.

[66] PAI, April 10, 1937: 270.

[67] PAI, September 10, 1938: 224.

[68] PAI, November 10, 1923: 545–6.

[69] Allison 1969: 116–27; CMS 1926; Survey of Evangelistic Work: 76; The Indian Social Reformer, February 1, 1936: 349; Mangaldev, "400 Hinduon ko Bachaiye" (Save 400 Hindus), Abhyudaya, August 8, 1925: 4; PAI, May 8, 1926: 251; PAI, June 6, 1925.

[70] Meerut: A Gazetteer: 81.

Against this background, I read representations of Dalit women's conversions through a gendered lens. First, the effort is to underscore conversion to Christianity, its connotations for education, and its sartorial portrayals, done mainly through popular cartoons published in reformist literature. Second, I highlight some police reports to mark individual conversions to Islam and the fears around them.

Conversions, Christianity, Clothes, and Cartoons

It is often argued that the impact of Christian conversions applied equally to Dalit women and men.[71] To an extent outcaste women and men shared similar beliefs, fears, and discrimination. Further, the social system did not generally permit the possibility of female conversion in the absence of a similar change of faith amongst the menfolk.[72] However, it would be simplistic to bracket outcaste women and men together in an undifferentiated fashion. For example, it seems that Dalit women had a more problematic relationship with conversion. Writing in 1896 Robert Stewart stated that "perhaps twice as many men as women had been baptized," a phenomenon he attributed in part to men's greater exposure to new ideas and to women's deeper attachment to familiar customs, religious beliefs, and social ties.[73] Dr Clara A. Swain, a leading woman doctor and missionary who was posted in Bareilly between 1870 and 1885, said: "We were told that some of these men were obliged to give up their wives and children and all their friends when they became Christians, as then they break their caste and it frequently happens that a woman will turn against her husband or son when they change their religion."[74]

Meerut witnessed some of the most intense conversions to Christianity by outcastes.[75] However, it was reported that "the question of

---

[71] Webster 1994: 69.

[72] Sarah Morrison, "Women's Work for Women," *The Foreign Missionary*, XXXIII, 1874–5: 383–5.

[73] Stewart 1896: 243. Also, *Survey of Evangelistic Work*: 80; C.F. Hall, "Village Christians in North India," *Indian Standard*, January 1914: 14.

[74] Swain 1909: 27.

[75] *Annual Report of the CMS for the Year 1936–7*: 252–3, 266–7.

women folk of those converted is causing some difficulty."[76] Cases
were cited where outcaste men were baptized but their wives refused
to convert. In one case the outcaste woman threatened to throw herself
into a well if her husband were baptized. This threat she did not
carry out, but she left him and went away to her own family.[77] Even
Hindu reformers perceived that it was often more difficult to convert
outcaste women to Christianity, as against men. A play published at
this time depicted the world-embracing qualities of Christianity but
ultimately emphasized that the religion of one's own ancestors was
best. It especially urged outcastes to reconvert; an outcaste woman
named Harijani becomes the proponent of this. In the play, Gulabo,
a Dom, condemned by a *pandit* and refused entry into a temple,
converts to Christianity. Harijani is a Chamar woman whose brother
dies of poverty. She is even approached by a merchant to become
his mistress, an offer she refuses. She goes to a well to fill water and
is stopped by upper-caste women. However, even in the midst of
crisis she refuses to convert and decides to commit suicide because
of the calamities that have befallen her. She is saved by Michael, an
outcaste convert who falls in love with her. Ultimately, Harijani is
able to persuade both Gulabo and Michael to reconvert.[78] In the play,
even though upper castes, particularly the priests, are condemned,
reconversions are upheld and outcaste women become the chief
vehicles of this. Shraddhanand remarked: "Eight hundred Chamars
have been converted to Christianity, but the Christian missionaries
commit one basic mistake. They convert the men but leave their
women as they are. Chamar men too convince the missionaries that
their women will automatically follow them but make no serious
attempts for religious conversion of women as well . . . They are left
within their community and the missionaries have not been very
successful with them. Perhaps it is in these women that our hope
lies."[79] While lamenting conversion by the untouchables, another
reformer stated: "If some class deserves credit for clinging to religion

---

[76] *PAI*, March 29, 1924: 116.
[77] *The Indian Female Evangelist*, VI, January 1882: 7.
[78] Natyacharya 1937.
[79] Shraddhanand 1919: 54.

and for upholding the same, it is due to the women-folk in India, who deserve the highest credit in the matter."[80]

Overall, converting women was a difficult enterprise for Christian missionaries. Work among the *zenana* upper-caste households had resulted in the spread of education but was a dismal failure when it came to religious conversion.[81] By comparison, missionaries were more successful among outcaste women.[82] They realized that the Christianization of India depended on winning the women of the depressed classes, while being aware of the difficulties involved in the process. They often expressed exasperation at the trouble of dealing with outcaste women, who were "illiterate," "stupid," "ignorant," prey to "heathen superstition," "primitive," "indifferent," and with "undeveloped minds" because they believed in local demons and strange gods. Even where a Bible woman rather than a male missionary was to be found, teaching outcaste women was constantly a problem because the potential convert was always rushing off towards household duties and the care of children. A missionary women's magazine said that a break with the past was extremely difficult for outcaste women because their lives, even more than men's, were totally absorbed by the constant pre-dawn to dark drudgery of survival.[83] Another stated that while outcaste women were appreciative of "the ministry of friendship" offered by visiting missionaries and Bible women, they had a difficult time learning the new teaching and adopting the novel ways of Christianity. Biblical stories, even though simplified, appeared strange to these women.[84] Babies proved a big hindrance, as one had to teach amidst them crying, laughing, and squabbling. Godfrey Phillips emphasized the importance of working amongst outcaste women in a separate index within his book, which he called "Women's Work for Women among the Depressed."[85] This makes for

[80] *The Indian Social Reformer*, February 29, 1936: 410.

[81] Pitman 1906; Forbes 1986.

[82] Morris 1917: 2, 9; *Annual Report of the CMS for the Year 1936–7*: 257–9.

[83] Quoted in Webster 1994: 69–70.

[84] Rosa T. Wilson, "City and District Work in India," *The Women's Missionary Magazine*, November 1904: 108; "Report of the Foreign Secretary," *The Women's Missionary Magazine*, June 1909: 410–11.

[85] Phillips 1912: 124–8.

interesting reading and alludes to many myths, dilemmas, problems, and concerns among missionaries in relation to the conversion of depressed class women. Phillips believed it was imperative to win over outcaste women, else the results would be disastrous. A missionary authority was quoted as saying that "so long as mother, sister, wife and daughter remain in darkness, so long must husband, brother and son virtually remain so too. None are more ready to drive away from home a Christian convert than the female members of his own household." There was a simultaneous revulsion and compassion for the outcaste woman—revulsion against her "superstitious" beliefs, "filthy" habits, and "ignorance," and compassion for a "fallen" woman, an innocent victim to be redeemed from her low position.

In North India serious attempts at the conversion of outcaste women were only made after 1912, when the mission decided to use the services of one Miss Morris to organize work among outcaste women. Soon some missionary women became active in the rural areas of UP in the early twentieth century, entrusted with the task of converting, teaching, visiting homes, and organizing meetings of outcaste women.[86] The CMS was very effective in the Meerut district, with about eighteen to twenty teachers and Bible women working in the mission area.[87] They mainly focused on visiting and offering instruction in the Christian faith, and in preparing women for baptism or confirmation as members of the church. One missionary in Lucknow said: "We would specially call to your attention the need for Christian women visiting and becoming friends of the women-folk of these local Depressed Classes leaders. Jesus Christ has done much for womanhood and the women of the Depressed Classes need the friendship and teaching of many Christian women whom Christ has redeemed. This is a unique service which only Christians can perform. There is a clarion call to Christian women, both foreign and Indian, in this situation."[88] Mrs Titus, entrusted with working in the Bijnor area, wrote an article, which was read before the Mussoorie Conference on "Woman's Work for Village Women." She said: "Our ideal must be to so permeate the lower strata of Indian Society with the

[86] *Survey of Evangelistic Work*: 80; Sarah Morrison, "Women's Work for Women," 1874–5.

[87] Alter 1986: 63, 74; Pemberton and Perfumi 1915: 47–8.

[88] *The Indian Social Reformer*, August 15, 1936: 796.

Christian religion, that the leaven spreading there from shall permeate the whole lump; to so effectively teach even these low-caste women, whom we call Christians, that we can say that they have been truly won for Christ, that they understand Christian ideals for their lives and are honestly trying to live up to them."[89]

Discussions were also held on subjects like hygiene, sanitation, cleanliness, nutrition, and child nurture. Missionary publications like *Charitra Sudhar, Lara Lari,* and *Ratnmala* were specifically aimed at preaching to outcaste women on these subjects.[90] Inspiring stories, for example *Chandra Lila Sadhuni ka Vritant* and *Mem Sahiba aur Ayah ki Katha,* were published about conversion and the "positive" changes it brought about in the everyday habit and outlook of women.[91] Work among outcaste women was mainly divided into three categories—educational, evangelistic, and medical—which often merged.[92] Orphanages, day schools, and boarding mission schools, even though few and far between, were established; they were perceived as removing outcaste women from a "useless" and "dirty" heathen environment.[93] The Jeyi school in Meerut took pride of place here.[94] The aim of the school was to give girls an education "under the strongest Christian influence" so as to prepare them "to become useful members of the community, as teachers in schools, nurses in mission hospitals, hospital assistants, and eventually as happy wives and wise mothers."[95] Lessons were given on Christian morality and sexual monogamy.

As has been emphasized by historians of gender, conversions to Christianity had contradictory implications for women.[96] On the

[89] Morris 1917: 2.

[90] *Charitra Sudhar* 1910; *Lara Lari* 1905; *Ratnmala* 1869; Lucas n.d.: 93.

[91] *Chandra Lila Sadhuni ka Vritant* 1910; *Mem Sahiba aur Ayah ki Katha* 1896; Campbell 1918.

[92] Swain 1909: 23–4, 105–6.

[93] Campbell 1918.

[94] CMS 1926: 2–3, 8–10; A.M. Stewart, "Education of Village Girls," *Report of the Conference of the Depressed Classes Committee*: 27–30.

[95] Pemberton and Perfumi 1915: 47–8.

[96] Bauman 2008; Haggis 2000; Kent 2004.

28. "Wedding Party at Jeyi"

Source: CMS, *Mass Movement in UP*: 13.

one hand they identify the work done by missionary women amidst their non-Christian "sisters" in the colonial empires as a "mission of domesticity," which schooled them in marriage, education, household work, childcare, cleanliness, and a particular outlook.[97] On the other they stress that it was not a straightforward way of making women good, "clean" Christian wives and mothers, for it opened out a window of opportunities for them. In UP, too, these ambiguities were visible. At times the conditions of Dalit women improved in comparison with the drudgery of their earlier lives. Most converted women refused to do unpaid midwife's work or *begar*. Education, even if limited to sewing, hygiene, and Bible training, was seen as more appropriate than manual work or unpaid public labor.[98] Dalit women were seeking to appropriate the intellectual and political tools of Christianity, using them not so much to mimic British and

[97] Haggis 2000.
[98] Philip 1925: 34–5; Taneti 2013.

missionary culture as to assert a respectable Dalit identity. Mrs Mohini Das, a Dalit Christian convert, addressing the All India Depressed Classes Association in Lucknow on May 22–24, 1936 gave a speech titled "What Womanhood Owes to Christ," where she argued that Christianity opened a new door of opportunity for depressed class women: "Wherever His [Jesus] teachings took root the condition of women began to alter. She became not just a glorified courtesan and housekeeper, but a homemaker, a companion to her husband and a fit mother for bringing up his children."[99] Miss A.M. Stewart, an active missionary in the Jeyi school, stated: "Girls who have passed out of Jeyi School will make a lasting difference in the village communities amongst whom they live, by their lives and examples."[100] Some became Bible women.[101] Though there was a severe shortage of funds and their position remained decidedly low in the hierarchy of the missions, Miss P. Emery had this to say on a depressed class Bible woman in UP:

> Their [converted depressed class men's] wives had been employed as Bible Readers . . . One of the best teachers we have in our district is a woman who has never had but two years schooling in her life, yet she reads the Bible fluently and last year won the prize for the best examination results in the whole district . . . She doesn't know that there is such a word as methods yet she had taught the boys and girls in her village to read with fluency and expression in their Readers and Testaments and they are able to give an intelligent answer regarding the fundamentals of the Christian faith.[102]

Another missionary remarked on how a Christian woman sweeper working in the palace of a local king sold ten gospels to the king's

[99] Mrs Mohini Das, "What Womanhood Owes to Christ," *Indian Witness,* June 11, 1936: 373. This was later also published as a Christian tract. Also, *The Indian Social Reformer*, August 15, 1936: 796.

[100] Stewart, "Education of Village Girls": 277.

[101] Clara Swain too wrote how outcaste women of the orphanage at Bareilly were converted and given training in Bible studies and how some of them later became Bible women: Swain 1909: 33–4, 54.

[102] P. Emery, "The Village Day School," *Report of the Conference of the Depressed Classes Committee*: 15–16.

womenfolk.[103] A Dalit woman, whose ancestors had converted at this time, said in an interview: "My grandmother converted to Christianity because the missionaries gave her hope that her children could receive education and get health facilities."[104]

While the missionaries wished to restructure every aspect of converted Dalit women's daily lives, including their physical appearance, sartorial styles, marital relations, customs, language, and the people with whom they interacted, many of the religious and social practices of these women reflected highly eclectic borrowing and adaptation.[105] As one historian remarks, conversion was not necessarily a movement from one stable identity and discipline to another.[106] Even through processes of mimicry, converted women often selectively appropriated, reconstituted, and at times subverted some of the ideals of upper-caste and missionary life and imbued it with their own sensibilities and practices. Many of these women represented a hybrid identity, practicing syncretic and dual systems in which Christianity merged with, or ran parallel to, other religious beliefs. There were cases where families of sweepers had been converted without the rest of the villagers hearing of it.[107] Even after their conversion, several outcaste women continued to worship, for example, the Sitala (small pox) goddess and other goddesses. At the same time, they went regularly to the church, as it was a place where they could get away for a while from wearisome domestic chores and hard labor in the fields. The missionaries too were challenged by, and had to an extent come to terms with, the beliefs of outcaste women. It was virtually impossible for missionaries to pass on a "pure" form of Christianity: the form was influenced by the context in which they operated. The drive to eradicate the heathen from the native outcaste converted woman, while keeping the native in the Christian, was fraught with contradictions and difficulties. Rev. J.C. Harrison wrote: "As yet none of our Christians have broken

[103] C. Heinrich, "The Church's Responsibility for Evangelism," *Report of the Conference of the Depressed Classes Committee*: 91–6 (94).

[104] Interview with Maya Dass, a Chamar convert to Christianity, Lucknow, September 2, 2006.

[105] Kent 2004.

[106] Sarkar 2014: 53.

[107] *Census, 1901, NWP*: 68.

away from their heathen customs . . . The household gods are still worshipped by the women. The Hindu festivals are kept, charms are retained, *fakirs* are consulted—the Sabbath is not kept, marriages are conducted according to heathen rites."[108]

Sartorial Representations

Conversion to Christianity impacted Dalit women's clothing, as it brought to the fore questions of the body per se *vis-à-vis* caste. Clothes veil the body. They encode modesty and sexual explicitness, they deny and celebrate pleasure. They are a form of social control, a mechanism of inclusion and exclusion, mirroring social hierarchies and moral boundaries. They present an everyday synoptic display of personality, simultaneously communicating and constituting gender, caste, religious, and national identities.[109] Clothing played an active role in the construction of families, castes, classes, regions, and the nation in colonial India.[110] Cloth was inscribed with new meanings by nationalists, particularly Gandhi, and became a key visual symbol of the freedom struggle against British rule.[111] However, it has been argued that there were no singular and stable meanings to clothing choices in colonial India.[112] Feminist historians have argued that attempts at re-dressing women had a distinct relationship to the idealized upper-caste middle-class wife and mother, to a sartorial morality, and to the denigration of sexuality.[113] Sartorial discourses for women by nationalists and Gandhi theoretically encompassed all. For example, in UP it was argued that spinning khadi was beneficial even for lower-caste and poor women working on the street as khadi could cover their bodies and protect their virtue.[114] In practice, however,

[108] Quoted in Alter 1986. Also, *Annual Report of the Meerut Mission of the CMS*: 14–15.

[109] Barnes and Eicher 1992; Gaines and Herzog 1990; Ross 2008: 83–102.

[110] Bayly 1986: 285–322; Cohn 1989: 106–62, 312–13; Tarlo 1996: 23–127.

[111] Bean 1989: 355–76; Ramagundam 2008; Trivedi 2007.

[112] Tarlo 1996.

[113] Bannerji 2001: 99–134; Gupta 2001: 344–9.

[114] Parshuram 1921: 7.

Swadeshi sartorial practices privileged some women over others and were deeply embedded in social, religious, and caste hierarchies, sexual divisions, and moral boundaries, exposing contradictory impulses at the heart of the project.[115]

Clothing hierarchically distinguished women from one another. Dalit women had to endure humiliating dress restrictions which were also ways to mark their bodies as inferior and sexually promiscuous. Her sexuality was there to be seen and consumed, as her private being was made public through what she wore. For example, among the sweepers of Lucknow women were not permitted to wear a bodice, gold ornaments, silver anklets, and a nose ring.[116] In some places Dalit women braved the restrictions and put on silver anklets. Caste-Hindus could not tolerate this breach and, to make an example of such women, some were branded with a red-hot iron. It is worth noting that this was not one exceptional incident.[117] In a village near Agra a caste-Hindu crushed the toes of a Dalit woman because she had rings on her toes. He also forced her to remove her nose ring.[118] There were cases of Brahmin women tearing out the hair of Dalit women because they had taken to dressing it neatly; after which the oppressors would return to bathe in the temple tank to purify themselves.[119] It was reported from various places in UP that Chamars were being beaten up if their women dressed well.[120]

Conversion to Christianity was the enunciation of a divergent association with society through a refashioned and reconstituted caste-marked body. Christian missions in South India encouraged low-caste Shanar women converts in the late eighteenth and early nineteenth centuries to cover their breasts when in public places, associated exclusively with upper-caste women.[121] Such cross-dressing was not only an appropriation of upper-caste dress signifiers that were forbidden to low-caste women, but also represented a resignification

[115] Gupta 2012: 76–84.
[116] Crooke 1896b, I: 290.
[117] Verma 1971: 7.
[118] Ibid.: 11; *Harijan*, June 13, 1933.
[119] Ouwerkerk 1945: 12.
[120] *PAI*, October 16, 1937: 594.
[121] Hardgrave 1968: 171–87; Gladstone 1984; Kent 2004.

of the gendered habitus and improved social standing of the lower castes.

Clothing signaled the distinction between Dalit Christian women and their unconverted counterparts, and a way to garner dignity. Notions of care and presentation of the body were key components informing the conversion mission. Sewing was thus particularly important, as missionaries were keen to see "semi-nude" outcaste women clad in "decent" clothes, fit for clean Christian souls.[122] Pictures appeared in popular literature portraying on the one hand a naked, "dirty," and unkempt outcaste woman, and on the other a fully clothed, sari-clad, "clean" and smiling Christian Dalit woman (Figure 29). John Munro, acting as dewan to Rani Lakshmibai, had issued a proclamation way back in 1812 guaranteeing Indian Christian women the right to cover their breasts.[123] Changes in clothing through conversion became for a section of Dalits a symbolic act, a material marker to transcend systems of inequality, signal upward mobility, write themselves into colonial modernity,[124] acquire respect in the public sphere, fabricate identities, and put the ignominy of their past status behind them.[125]

Reformist iconography, particularly cartoons, also recognized dress as a terrain for contesting social relations and articulating new religious identities. R.K. Laxman, the celebrated Indian cartoonist, testifies that a cartoonist attempts to convey the ironies of everyday life through disapproval and complaint.[126] In colonial UP, *Awadh Punch* was the first Indian newspaper to publish cartoons.[127] Cartoons could make a great impression on a functionally literate population. Soon, many other reformist publications, including those in Hindi, were using them to advocate social reform with a central focus on women.

[122] Swain 1909: 88.

[123] Kooiman 1989: 149.

[124] Menon 2006.

[125] In the present context, a similar point has been made regarding Mayawati's sartorial style: Nigam 2010: 254–5. He states that Mayawati's "ostentatiousness" and her sartorial preferences can be read as her symbolic counter-move, which mocks at Gandhi's attempt at "representing poverty" and mourning through the semiotic transformation of his own body.

[126] Laxman 1989, 1990; Sahay 1998.

[127] Hasan 2007: 9; Oesterheld and Zoller 1999.

29. Clothing and Conversion

Left is the state of being Hindu [untouchable]—
Right is the complete change on becoming a Christian!

Source: *Chand,* May 1929: 51.

In the early twentieth century, cartoons depicting the crisis of
conversion through clothing entered the Hindi print-public sphere
in UP, putting on display the perceived insecurities and sexual unease
of caste- and reformist Hindus. Cartoons published in *Chand* and
various Arya Samaj publications, many of them compiled in *Vyanga
Chitravali,* usually depicted two outcaste women or men together, of
which one had converted to Christianity.[128] These images cataloged
the supposedly alarming results of Dalit conversion to Christianity.
Even while lamenting the occurrence of conversions, they could not
help but acknowledge the change in demeanor and stature that it

[128] Such cartoons were repeatedly published in many newspapers and
magazines, highlighting a broad consensus and opposition to the conversion
of outcastes. For example, *Chand; Vyanga Chitravali* 1930; *Abhyudaya,* March
13, 1926: 9.

brought about among Dalits—in their mode of dressing, walking style, gait, and prestige. One cartoon, for example, visualized the converted outcaste woman walking ahead royally, carrying an umbrella and a purse and wearing a hat, skirt and high-heeled shoes—quite evidently in possession of an elevated status and emancipatory symbols in the public sphere. The unconverted woman walked behind, head bent, barefoot, carrying the child of the converted Dalit woman (Figure 30). Another had the Christian Dalit woman carefully sitting on a chair, looking down, while the untouchable took care of her dog, looking up (Figure 31). Yet another lamented the loss of Hinduism, showing the converted woman again with shoes, a hat, and an umbrella (Figure 32).

30. *Mem* **and** *Dasi*

See the difference between two women of the same species:
One is an English madam and the other a servant-untouchable.
The former walks ahead with an umbrella, while the latter
walks behind with her child.

*[ek jati ki mem, aur dasi-achhut ka yeh antar!
veh chalti chaata le aage, yeh uska bachcha lekar!!]*

Source: *Vyanga Chitravali* 1930.

31. Christian-Hindu Untouchable Woman

The Christian woman is the master of the dog, while the
outcaste woman her servant!
But they both were of the same caste, Hindus please see carefully!!

[*isayin kutte ki malik, hai achhut uski naukar!*
par donon the ek jati ke, dekho hindu ankhen bhar!!]

Source: *Vyanga Chitravali* 1930.

32. Madam Lady and Fish Seller

One has become a madam-lady, the other a fish seller.
Blessed be the religion of Christ, which is all powerful.

[*mem sahiba ek bani hai, aur ek machli wali!*
dhanya dharm isa-masih ka, kitna maha shaktishali!!]

Source: *Chand*, May 1929: 77.

Such cartoons can function as constitutive archives. These banal, everyday, popular, embodied communications are pivotal documents towards an understanding of anxieties among Hindu reformers, while also offering a counter-politics of sartorial desire. Looking beyond the frame, they work multivocally as satires of the educated and of Christian Dalits, while also hitting out at caste-Hindu society within a discursive context of socio-religious reform. Visual imagery, particularly pertaining to clothing, has been recognized as central to Dalit experience.[129] In colonial India these representations encompassed the everyday life of Dalits, at home and on the streets. The rhetoric of such repeated caricaturing of costumes worn and symbols born was meant to manufacture Hindu public opinion against conversion and warn caste-Hindus against treating Dalits badly. Such cartoons did not encompass the "truth" of conversions and its relationship to sartorial styles among Dalit women, as very few dressed in the ways illustrated here. In fact, the dress for Dalit Christian women in missionary schools was very modest—just a sari and a blouse. And it was not as if missionaries tried to impose Western clothes on converted outcaste women. Rather, a good deal of subtle jostling went on between missionaries and women converts, where desires and ambitions were bound up with dilemmas over what to wear.[130] However, as Tarlo remarks, because of its proximity to the body, clothing is particularly susceptible to symbolic elaboration.[131] The very portrayal of Dalit women in such clothes signified an inversion of norms. Their powerful language reflected the traumatized identities of caste-Hindus while making explicit upper-caste perceptions of Dalit women's desires.

It has been proposed that Dalit culture in general does not place any value on an indigenist notion of "authenticity," including in relation to clothing.[132] Discarding the demeaning dress became a code

[129] Tartakov 2012: 92, 268–82.

[130] Kent 2004; Comaroff and Comaroff 1997: 218–73; Harper 2000; Tarlo 1996.

[131] Tarlo 1996: 23–61. Also, Harper 2000: 139–45.

[132] Ilaiah 2003. He goes on to argue that, unlike Gandhi and Nehru, Ambedkar always wore a suit, without facing any problems from his community, whereas Gandhi had to really struggle to de-Westernize himself.

for radical dissent against caste discipline, demonstrating the right to inhabit unmarked bodies.[133] For Dalit women, sartorial changes, even if sometimes mythical, symbolically associated women's clothing with community dignity. Dalits emphasized the right to publicly exhibit dignified bodies, denied to them by the upper castes. As Anupama Rao says, "good clothing, footwear, jewelry, and bodily comportment—standing erect while speaking, refusing to contort the body in an obsequious fashion—was critical to Dalit self-fashioning. Though discourses of sexuality and of female enfranchisement were caste-specific, the focus on the feminized body—how it was experienced and represented—was central to a range of political processes."[134] Clothing representations, which conversion to Christianity provided Dalits, not only questioned upper-caste religious and symbolic monopolies in intimate and public spheres—by arguing for the right to wear footwear, adorn hats, carry umbrellas, and wear the breast-cloth in the presence of persons of high ritual status—it also treated them as matters of collective and direct public action, making them politically radical issues. At the same time, the converted Dalit figure was an internal embarrassment, an "inappropriate other" whose sartorial style defied nationalist logic. It was reported that many Dalit women had abandoned khadi and were buying cheap foreign cloth.[135] These women literally wore their difference on their bodies, signifying an uncomfortable anomaly in the reformist-nationalist discourse.

Romantic Desires and Conversions to Islam

Sartorial representations as a consequence of the mass conversion to Christianity by Dalits, while giving some room for change, embedded women's desires within community boundaries, sometimes even upholding conservative gender constructs. Differing perceptions of conversions were accorded to collective social groups and to individual Dalit women. It has been argued that the political–public

[133] Pandey 2013: 61–96.
[134] Rao 2009: 67–8.
[135] 10/1922–3, AICC Papers, NMML.

Dalit sphere in colonial India was rendered male.[136] One does not wish to overemphasize an "individual versus collective" binary, as these were complex and intertwined issues. At the same time, Dalit men were anxious about individual conversion by Dalit women, particularly to Islam, sans familial and community approval. Such conversion caused disquiet and a collusion of men—Dalits and Hindu reformers—against the personal choices of Dalit women.

By focusing on Dalit women's personal conversion, I wish here to also historicize love and romance, which are mutable concepts,[137] whose meanings are contingent on gender, caste, and religious identities. Tapan Raychaudhuri examines the shifting meanings of romantic love in colonial India, where developments in modern print-public culture profoundly altered intimate concerns.[138] Though reformers treated romantic love as an irrelevant joke, a flourishing popular romantic literature in the period brought new intensity in conjugal relationships, with hardly any precedent available in the pre-modern past. These authoritative archives of intimate histories highlighted the snug connection between marriage, sex, and romantic love (Figure 33).

However, while the literary turn of both Indian feminist studies and postcolonial theory has provided scholars with sophisticated insights into love, desire, and other forms of subjectivities among middle-class women, the same cannot be said about Dalit women. Here I explore how in this climate Dalit women negotiated intimacies beyond their moral and social parameters. Writings from this period provide a window to both sociological realities and their constitution and mobilization for particular political ends, with an inherent politics of exclusion and engagement, reflecting shifting registers of unspoken ambivalence.

One is here also implicitly concerned with everyday violence. The intertwining of gender, religious identities, and violence has been considerably explored by feminist historians of India. While offering deep insight, their works have usually been embedded in cataclysmic

---

[136] Rao 2009.

[137] Collin 2003; Langhamer 2007.

[138] Raychaudhuri 2000: 349–78. Also Orsini 2007: 30–4.

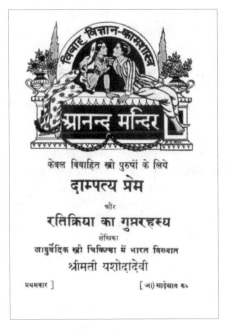

33. Cover of "Pleasure Temple"

Only for Married Women and Men:
Secret of Love and Sex between the Married Couple
by Yashoda Devi, Allahabad, 1933.

events. Other scholars have highlighted the inchoate ways of everyday life.[139] Histories of interreligious intimacy reflect a mundane texture, wherein women were ubiquitous and varied meanings were given to sexual affiliations. Even while reifying heteronormativity, Dalit female desire produced daily policing and everyday violence, along what Foucault calls the alliance model of sexuality, where through the arrangement of marriages the relations and boundaries of caste and religion were policed.[140]

While inter-caste alliances were deeply opposed by caste-Hindus, the thought of women, even if from the lower castes, marrying and converting to Islam or Christianity proved more disturbing.

[139] Certeau 1984: xi–xxiv; Ludtke 1995: 4–30; Heller 1984: 4.
[140] Foucault 1978: 106–11.

Even while rejecting inter-caste intimacies, in certain circumstances lower- and upper-caste men came together to impose constraints on *their* women. This coincided with the growth of militant Hindu assertion in UP, which reached new heights in the 1920s, with unprecedented communal clashes,[141] and aggressive participation from a section of the lower castes.[142] The liberal premise and promise of a reformist discourse was considerably overturned when within it the woman's body became a marker for enthroning communal boundaries. The contentious Hinduization at a moment of threatened conversion rendered Dalit women's conversion precarious as well as courageous, both within their community, in relation to "their" men, and in relation to a hegemonic Hinduism that included them only when it was threatened with losing ground as a political majority.

Hindu reformers and revivalists started making appeals to the upper castes to uplift outcaste women. The Hindu Mahasabha emphasized that there was a need to validate by marriage clandestine amorous relations between a Hindu girl and boy of different castes, even if one of them was an untouchable, to prevent conversions.[143] Cases were cited where the Hindu Mahasabha had prevented a Bhangi or a Chamar woman from converting by marrying her to a higher-caste Hindu boy.[144] Conversions by outcaste women were also represented as a numerical loss: the displacement of potential child-bearing wombs for the Hindu community. A special issue of *Chand* stated that there were millions of outcaste mothers who were full of love but, because of the cruelty of Hindu society, were nurturing wombs for the progeny of Muslims, and thereby producing cow-killers.[145] *Abhyudaya* said: "Many of our Hindu women, whom we consider outcastes, are going into the hands of Muslims and Christians. How can these women, whom we treat so badly, become protectors of the cow and worshipers of Ram and Krishna? . . . We should make

[141] Freitag 1989: 8–9, 230–41; Pandey 1978: 115–17.

[142] Gooptu 2001; 4/1927, Home Poll, NAI.

[143] M-3, Hindu Mahasabha Papers, NMML.

[144] Subject File 42/1935, Moonje Papers, NMML.

[145] Editorial, "*Paap ki Granthiyan*" (Records of Sin), *Chand*, May 1927: 2–6 (4).

every effort to prevent our outcaste women from marrying such men. This is imperative if the number of cow-protectors is not to decline."[146]

Anxieties around conversion to Islam by Dalit women were often expressed in a vocabulary involving abduction. Magazines and newspapers like *Chand, Pratap*, and *Stri Darpan* argued that women, including outcaste women, were being molested and forcibly converted by Muslim men.[147] "*Samachar Sangrah*," a collection of news items regularly published in *Chand*, constructed a profile of Muslims as abductors of Dalit women, using this as a plank to woo Dalit men to the side of caste-Hindus. For example, it was reported in the *Chand* of June 1926 that two girls by the name of Bhuri, a Khatik aged 11–12, and Saza, a Chamar aged 15–16, left their home early morning on April 6, 1926 to glean corn. In the afternoon, two Muslims abducted them. A cloth was tied over their eyes and another forced in their mouth. They took them to a forest and got both the girls drunk. After that they raped them and left. The girls managed to reach a railway station, where the master informed their families, and a Khatik came and took them away.[148] In August 1926 it was reported that some Mallah women were attacked by Muslims; abducted and raped, their bodies were found covered in blood.[149] In November 1926 *Chand* reported how Habibullah, a Muslim *goonda* from Kanpur, forcibly kept a *bhangan* named Rania in his home.[150] Again, in February 1927, reporting from *Pratap*, *Chand* stated that Ramdevi, a Valmiki Hindu woman, was traveling in an *ekka* in which the two *ekkawallahs*, named Bashiruddin and Nazamuddin, took her to a field and tried to rape her. She screamed; many Valmikis working nearby collected and handed over the two *goonda*s to the

[146] Shyambihari Lal, "*Samay ki Maang*" (Call of the Times), *Abhyudaya*, October 31, 1925: 3.

[147] Editorial, "*Deviyon Savdhan*" (Women Beware), *Chand*, May 1924: 8–10; "*Achhut Nari ki Durdasha*" (The Pathetic Condition of the Untouchable Woman), *Chand*, May 1929: 177.

[148] "*Stri Haran*" (Women's Abduction), "*Samachar Sangrah*," *Chand*, June 1926: 215.

[149] "*Samachar Sangrah*," *Chand*, August 1926: 431.

[150] "*Samachar Sangrah*," *Chand*, November 1926: 152.

police. Hindus thus needed to learn from this episode and beware of Muslim *ekkawallahs*.[151] It was reported in *Shuddhi Samachar* that a girl of the Mali caste had been abducted and raped by two Muslim ruffians.[152] *Stri Darpan* mentioned the daughter of a barber as having been abducted by a Muslim in Bijnor.[153] Similar stories were repeatedly conveyed.[154] It was reported in 1938 that while a sweeper woman was cleaning the road near a mosque in Kanpur, attempts to kidnap her were made by Muslim *goondas*. Following this, the Mehtar Sabha resolved to boycott local Muslims.[155] A communal riot occurred in Basti on February 17, 1939, due to the alleged molestation of a Chamar woman by a Muslim, the trouble assuming serious proportions because of the rivalry between the Hindu and Muslim *lathi akharas* in that vicinity.[156] While not questioning the validity of these cases, it is important to see that in almost all of them specifically Muslim names were mentioned, while the Hindu upper-caste sexual exploitation of Dalit women usually remained nameless. These stories helped strengthen the imagery of the Muslim as a rapist of women, including Dalit women. Dalit men often colluded with this rhetoric, helping at times to overpower the realities of caste hierarchization. This touched an emotive nerve, women being crucial to their material existence. At a meeting of sweepers in Dehradun it was resolved not to allow their women to work in Muhammadan households. Similar resolutions were adopted by Chamar, Khatik, and Pasi caste associations in Agra, Allahabad, Banaras, and Kanpur.[157]

More interesting were individual conversions to Islam by some Dalit women on account of love, elopement, and marriage. It has been noted that in many cases of individual conversion, particularly

[151] "*Samachar Sangrah*," *Chand*, December 1927: 312; "*Goondon ki Zyadti*" (The Misdeeds of Scoundrels), "*Samachar Sangrah*," *Chand*, February 1927: 472.

[152] "*Islami Samachar*" (Islamic News), *Shuddhi Samachar*, July 1927: 372–4.

[153] "*Samachar-Saar*," *Stri Darpan*, April 1927: 130.

[154] For example, "*Balaatkaar ka Dand*" (Punishment for Rape), "*Samachar Sangrah*," *Chand*, April 1929: 908.

[155] *Pratap*, March 27, 1938: 8.

[156] *PAI*, February 25, 1939: 40.

[157] *PAI*, March 12, 1927: 92.

by the lower castes, the reason was neither proselytism nor doctrinal conviction but romance.[158] While it is difficult to trace such cases in UP, police abstracts of intelligence provide some glimpses, though with a caveat. Only a few cases merited mention, which led to tensions. None of them were described in sufficient detail.[159] Yet they provide significant insights. In almost all cases reported, it was individual outcaste women (and not men) who were found to be converting. Their romantic involvements were possibly aided by greater mobility. There are many stray examples. In March 1924 a Chamar woman left her husband in Banaras in favor of a Muslim, whom she married.[160] In March 1926 a Bhangi woman converted to Islam and married a Muslim in Aligarh.[161] In the same year, in April, a Muslim of Kanpur had a female sweeper as his mistress, whom he converted.[162] In the next month a Kori woman, kept by a Muslim contractor at Banda, converted.[163] In December 1928 a sweeper woman of Unao married a Muslim and converted.[164] It was reported from Fyzabad in 1934 that an outcaste woman had married a Muslim.[165] In May 1938 a sweeper woman eloped with a Muslim in Dehradun and subsequently converted to Islam.[166] In 1946 a local Muslim brought with him a sweeper woman whom he claimed had embraced Islam.[167] Such cases point to Dalit women's ambiguous relationship to caste and religious identities, hinting at desire and an interest in experimentation. At times they chose to defend their conversion as well. In Basti, a Khatik woman who had been converted to Islam was taken to the Arya Samaj office with a view to reconversion, but she stuck to her decision.[168]

[158] Vishwanathan 1998: 163.

[159] There must have been more cases of such conversions, which remained unmentioned and unreported.

[160] *PAI*, March 29, 1924: 118.

[161] *PAI*, March 27, 1926: 176.

[162] *PAI*, April 3, 1926: 195.

[163] *PAI*, May 1, 1926: 235.

[164] *PAI*, December 1, 1928: 522.

[165] *PAI*, November 24, 1934: 625.

[166] *PAI*, May 21, 1938: 124.

[167] *PAI*, August 2, 1946: 127.

[168] *PAI*, March 6, 1926: 127.

Outcaste women were possibly "using" conversion as a mode of coping with and, within limits, transgressing an oppressive social order.[169] It was a strategic maneuver with social ramifications, combined with elements of choice, desire, and experimentation.[170] It is significant that, unlike conversion to Christianity, which required evidence of baptism and other documents, conversion to Islam merely entailed the recitation of the *kalma* before witnesses. Also, till at least the 1940s the courts recognized that conversion to Islam by women of other religions dissolved their former religion and marriage.[171] This moment of transition may have been perceived by Dalit women as providing some leverage in negotiating personal status and familial, caste, and religious power relations, and reconfiguring social boundaries, even if only partially and temporarily. More often than not they were entering relationships resembling the ones they had left. But is it also possible to see these outcaste women as boundary crossers, with romance offering temporary amelioration? Can we see these as acts of self-expression, or as offering the possibilities for a liberated Dalit woman's body to emerge through alternative religious belongings? Such acts by Dalit women produced a zone of erasure and accommodation in luminal spaces between caste and religion, setting up contingent, in-between identities.

Causing increasing tensions, such crossings were cited by the Arya Samaj and the Hindu Mahasabha to raise a dreaded scenario, and to urge outcaste men to prevent their women from taking such steps. The converted individual Dalit woman was a caste renegade, an "enemy within" whose heart and mind were on the line. It was emphasized that Muslims continually seduced their outcaste women neighbors, ran away with them, and converted them.[172] The outcaste woman's self-consciousness as a woman, as a convert, as a person with sexual agency, was consistently erased. Such individual conversions on their own accord, minus "their men," evoked hostility among Dalit men. The "rule breaking" by these women was seen as an opportunity to

[169] *The Indian Social Reformer*, October 19, 1935: 99.
[170] Guha 1987: 155.
[171] De 2010.
[172] Sharda 1925: 33–4.

reinforce caste, religious, and sexual control. The arc of desire for men outside the community meant that such desire was visceral and tactile, though it could only be acknowledged when it was being regulated as transgression, that is, as going against the dictates of social normativity.

Thus, to extrapolate from the cases above, when the Chamar woman converted in Banaras it caused alarm in Arya Samaj circles. A breach of peace was threatened between them and Muslims.[173] When the Bhangi woman of Aligarh married a Muslim, communal feelings were largely embittered. Large crowds gathered, a case was filed against it, many shops in the city shut, and the city's Bhangis struck work.[174] Trouble arose in Kanpur between sweepers and Muslims when news of the conversion of the female sweeper spread. Arya Samajists seized upon it as a pretext for anti-Muslim propaganda. They succeeded in bringing about a strike of sweepers, who refused to work for Muslims.[175] In Fyzabad the Muslim male was arrested on charges of seducing the outcaste woman. Though he was acquitted when she stated that she was his wife, relations between Muslims and outcastes became strained.[176] The sweeper community threatened to boycott all Muslim houses, following the elopement and conversion of the sweeper woman in Dehradun.[177] The sweepers of Moradabad ceased working for Muslim inhabitants after the "kidnapping" of a sweeper woman by a Julaha.[178] In a village in Meerut a tense situation existed when the sweepers of the locality removed a sweeper woman from the custody of a Muslim.[179] Here, outcaste men colluded in the production of a sense of reality that stigmatized them. While they questioned the dominant order, they also at times identified with it, especially when it came to the question of "their" women. This suggests that we rethink ideas regarding Dalit politics as always radical

[173] *PAI*, March 29, 1924: 118.
[174] *PAI*, March 27, 1926: 176.
[175] *PAI*, April 3, 1926: 195.
[176] *PAI*, November 24, 1934: 625.
[177] *PAI*, May 21, 1938: 124.
[178] *PAI*, February 18, 1939: 35.
[179] *PAI*, August 2, 1946: 127.

or subversive. Instead, expressions of sexuality and desire could also mark the limits of caste emancipation.

Conclusion

Intertwining Dalit women's conversions with clothing and love provides a language of intimate rights. Such conversions were a site of contestation whose meanings shifted at specific historical moments. They inspired a great deal of anxiety and ideological diatribe among Hindu reformers, particularly the Arya Samaj, as they symbolized the possible autonomy and recalcitrance of Dalit women's hearts and minds in intimate arenas of their lives. Social signifiers of caste and religion became tied up with the perceived illegitimacy of desire to produce interlocking sets of power relations. Hindu reformers' sartorial cartoons of converted Christian Dalit women exposed the contradictory impulses at the heart of their project, as, even while lamenting conversions, they paradoxically reflected self-respect through fashion. Foucault's understanding of how bodies are dressed and groomed through both self-discipline and surveillance, and a general panoptic lens, may be pertinent here.[180] However, its disciplinary strength was often diluted, as clothing also became a performative tool for Dalits to adorn dignity and wear themselves into colonial modernity.

Dalit women's individual conversion to Islam evoked a somewhat different response. While opposing inter-caste relationships, Hindu publicists were deeply troubled with fantasies about relations between lower-caste women and Muslim men. The politics of number rendered the thought of inter-caste union palatable, even permissible. There was a complex relationship between caste endogamy and community homogeneity. The contingency of community made the marking of "difference" slippery. Dalit women's conversion for love was an explosive issue. In such a situation, abduction campaigns constructed sedimented discourses on sexual immorality in which the Muslim male was carved out through the repetition of stereotypical motifs. Simultaneously, the figure of the converted Dalit woman had

[180] Foucault 1977: 200–5.

the effect of creating an instrumental and temporary unity across caste, including between caste and outcaste, helping the claims to strengthening a wider Hindu community.[181]

For Dalit men conversions came to be constituted by values derived from specific moral visions, and they came to acquire shifting meanings. They had different norms when it came to mass conversion by community, as against individual conversion by Dalit women. It was applauded as a rational choice representing the "larger" good in one case and condemned as irrational in the other. There was a dissonance between community and political critique on the one hand, and women's individual desires on the other. This helped in marginalizing the possibilities of autonomy within or outside the community, and in the reinstatement of oppressive patriarchies. These politicized entanglements generated "intimate politics,"[182] a form of embodied struggle in which community agendas were formulated, contested, and in some cases transformed through the bodies and practices of these women. Through a politics of representational heightening (as in clothing) and an erasure (as in romance), of telling and not telling, there was a complex playing out of Dalit women's desire.

However, the collective identities and patriarchies thus constructed were unstable. The awkward non-place of Dalit female subjectivity, caught between the claims of community and religion, raises the question of agency as both constituted and subverted by existing structures of power. Through limited but still subversive ways, the localized, quotidian, and embodied practices of Dalit women resituated conversions in a realm of ambiguity, offering a new gendered self. The recalcitrance of desire and the interface between norms and everyday practices threw up the emancipatory possibilities of intimate rights, where highly ritualized acts of conversion, clothing, and marriage could at times become a metaphor for a new vocabulary of selfhood, of the body, and of dignity.

[181] Dube 1933.
[182] Friedman 2006: 3.

6

Goddesses
and Women's Songs

Negotiating Dalit Popular Religion
and Culture

Here I investigate how images of goddesses like Sitala and Lona Chamarin, largely propitiated by low castes, and the song genre of *kajli*, mainly performed by low-caste women, signified continuities and transitions in colonial North India, and how, through these images and songs, gender and caste narratives were dispersed and socially reallocated. I underscore the fluidities within these everyday gendered popular religious and cultural practices, showing how the prejudices of the colonizers and upper castes were unhinged by the resilience and malleability of such social expressions. Researchers who have focused on Indian goddesses,[1] and others who have looked at the oral-performative cultures among women,[2] have noted the shifts that occurred in these fields under the special circumstances of colonial contact, reformist endeavor, nationalist aspiration, and print culture. They have emphasized the marginalization and reinvention of such spaces once they came in for

[1] Hawley and Wulff 1982; Kinsley 1986; Appadurai, Korom, and Mills 1991; Sax 1991; Dehejia 1999; Hiltebeitel and Erndl 2000; Chitgopekar 2002; Pintchman and Sherma 2011; McDermott 2011.

[2] Banerjee 1989; Peterson and Soneji 2008; Jassal 2012; Raheja and Gold 1994; Raheja 2003; Flueckiger 1996; Bakhle 2005; Weidman 2006; Subramanian 2006; Perron 2007; Neuman 1990; Chakravorty 2008; Sampath 2010; Vijaisri 2004; Soneji 2012; Levine 2003; Tambe 2009.

condemnation by the British, who castigated them as signifiers of unrefined practices unworthy of being tolerated in respectable urban middle-class formations, in the propagation of Indian nationalism, in reformist Victorian moralism, and in "civilizing" rhetoric. Alongside, attempts were made by colonizers, reformers, nationalists, the urban middle classes, and caste spokespersons to "improve" the customs popular among low-caste women, ostensibly to wean such women away from what were perceived as lax moral standards, degraded practices, and "Muslim" symbols and rituals.[3] As one scholar has remarked, nationalist criticism "directed itself toward clearing the space of the popular for an elite public ideal of tradition and meaning, a process that involved pushing aside the more obscure and opaque aspects of the popular itself and ignoring its origins in radical low-caste protest and resistance."[4] However, Dalits, the low castes, and women rearticulated their popular idioms from distinct perspectives and for different reasons.[5] By focusing on goddesses and women's songs, respectively, I try to unearth the interplay of caste and gender in the religious and cultural practices of the marginalized. Simultaneously, I examine the possibility of recuperating buried or under-acknowledged counter-archives, and posit different kinds of agency for Dalit women, whether traditional or ritually circumscribed.

Goddesses and Dalits

The cults of goddesses have a long history in Hinduism; they have been manifest in adaptable guises and with sundry connotations over time and space.[6] Feminists have debated their meanings for gender politics—of their enabling or contrary potential[7]—while also recognizing that "Hindu goddess worship is radical in so far as the goddess is not inscribed in the mainstream of deities and her devotees

---

[3] Gupta 2001: 278–81; Rege 1995: 33; Chowdhry 2007; Bayly 1999: 159–60.

[4] Wakankar 2010: 41.

[5] Prashad 2000; Gooptu 2001; Sarkar 1997: 358–90.

[6] McDermott 2011: 39–75.

[7] Hiltebeitel and Erndl 2000; Chitgopekar 2002; Appadurai, Korom, and Mills 1991.

are drawn largely from lower castes, women, and even non-Hindus, thus clearing certain spaces of alternative belief and practice in the monolith of Brahmanical Hinduism."[8] Hindu goddesses were sources of ambivalence—both revulsion and fascination—among the British.[9] One scholar says of Kali: "In the eyes of the early British colonial authorities, missionaries, and scholars, Kali was identified as the most depraved of all forms of modern popular Hinduism, the quintessence of the licentiousness and idolatry that had destroyed the noble, monotheistic spirit of the Vedas and the Vedanta."[10] Conversely, the icons of goddesses, as earthy and militant, were effectively maneuvered by Hindu nationalists to elevate the status of women and Hinduism, for militant articulation, and for inspirational configurations of "Bharat Mata."[11] Goddesses carried distinct connotations among Dalits: as rooted in productive physical labor, and as signifying intimate attachment to earth and nature.[12] One prominent Dalit intellectual believes that, compared to elsewhere, goddesses feature much more than gods in the Dalitbahujan religious pantheon.[13] Of Pochamma, a Dalitbahujan goddess in Andhra Pradesh, he says:

> Pochamma is independent. She does not pretend to serve any man. Her relationship to human beings is gender-neutral, caste-neutral and class-neutral . . . She herself relates to nature, production and procreation . . . They [the goddesses of Dalits] are not known for controlling, exploiting or manipulating their husbands, nor are they known for subordinating men. None of these Goddesses is said to represent delicate femininity. They are not shown sitting on lotus flowers, not shown travelling on peacocks, or on *hamsas* or other birds. Not a single Goddess is shown as a woman

[8] Rajan 2000: 270.

[9] Inden 1986: 401–46.

[10] Urban 2003: 169.

[11] Ramaswamy 2011.

[12] Ilaiah 2005: 91; Wilfred 2007: 129–36. It has been remarked that low-caste religion has a more intimate relationship with gods, there being freedom to scold and criticize them. Du Saraswathi, a Kannada poet and activist among women street sweepers, says: "Dalits in villages scream out to, yell at, hug, their deities." Quoted in Satyanarayana and Tharu 2013: 333. Also, Siddalingaiah 2010.

[13] Ilaiah 1996: 188; 2005: 91; also, Narayan 2006: 28; Siddalingaiah 2010.

pressing the feet of her husband like Lakshmi and Saraswathi . . . They are powerful and independent women.[14]

Though elements of romanticization seem visible in this, the colonial G.W. Briggs too had observed a preponderance of Bhumiya Devi (mother goddess) or *shakti* worship among Chamars in North India.[15] British ethnographers, including Crooke and Briggs, often depicted goddesses worshiped by Dalits as dark in color, and thus as demonic and malign forces delighting in doing damage and harm, their bloodthirstiness placated only by bloody sacrifices and offerings.[16] Such frightful deities were mostly associated with sickness, death, disease, suffering, and witchcraft, and usually absorbed into the Hindu pantheon as lower forms. In her work on witches and goddesses Kathryn Rountree embraces and conflates the debased and the exalted as together symbolizing feminist ritual-makers, or as symbols of female power outside male control, and as representing the sacred, strong, destructive, and dark side of the feminine.[17] Goddesses worshiped by the lower castes too collapsed the dichotomy between goddess and witch. They commanded deep reverence amongst Dalits, while also invoking their awe on account of their destructive prowess. In North India, Sitala and Lona Chamarin symbolized this tradition, and their representations saw modifications during the colonial period.

The Mali Caste and the Reinstatement of Sitala

Sitala, literally meaning "the cool one," and considered the goddess of smallpox, was very popular in many parts of India.[18] Annual fairs around her were held at various places in UP on her special holy

[14] Ilaiah 2005: 92, 96.

[15] Briggs 1920: 154; Singh 2011: 36–7. Besides goddesses, the religious universe of Dalits in North India was embedded in local cults, *pir*s, saints, and Sufi shrines. Ghazi Mian, Guga Pir, and Churhamal were a part of their everyday beliefs: Briggs 1920; Eaton 1978; Fuller 1992.

[16] Briggs 1920: 129–31, 136–9, 154–7, 185–6; Crooke 1896a, II: 263–86; *Census, 1891, NWP*: 220–1.

[17] Rountree 2004.

[18] Crooke 1896a, I: 125–36; Briggs 1920: 136–9; Junghare 1975; Wadley 1980: 33–62; Dimock 1982; Kolenda 1982; Kinsley 1986; Arnold 1993:

day, the eighth day of the Chait month, when winter ceased and summer began. For example, at Mawai near Khurja, at the annual fair in honor of Sitala, around 10,000 women would assemble; very few men partook of this fair.[19] The *neem* tree was the goddess' abode and the donkey was sacred to her, with the animal being often found in association with the shrines of Sitala.[20] There were several of these in the region, for example in Balia, Mathura, Dehradun, and at the Dasatswamedh ghat in Banaras.[21] She was noted as one of the chief deities of Fyzabad.[22] Sitala was associated with cold food and water: during her worship and the festivities surrounding her, "heating" foods and sexual activity were to be avoided. During outbreaks of smallpox, meat, fish, and all food requiring oil and spices were forbidden, and the patient was offered cooling foods such as yoghurt, cold rice, plantains, and coconut, his body being rubbed with cooling *neem* leaves. Sitala was very often served by a Mali, who became very busy when smallpox raged. If the fever was aggravated and delirium ensued, the Mali performed a *puja* of Sitala Mata. When the pustules of smallpox had matured, the Mali used variolation, dipping a thorn of the Karaunda in sesame oil and puncturing each.[23] When the fever had subsided, prayers were offered to Sitala, along with cooling offerings—coconut, rice, and flowers. It was believed that to worship Sitala and pay attention to what she represented was to provide oneself with a more realistic, less fragile view of life, which helped make the frequent outbursts of disease and tragic occurrences seem less devastating.[24]

Low-caste women, especially, venerated Sitala.[25] Among them was the belief that all infant girls represented the band of seven sisters of

---

116–58; Mukhopadhyay 1994; Stewart 1995: 389–97; Katyal and Kishore 2001; Ferrari 2007, 2010, 2014.

[19] Singh 1874: 101–2; Crooke, 1896a, I: 126.

[20] Crooke 1896a, I: 126, 133; Briggs 1920: 122, 124.

[21] Mukhopadhyay 1994: 16–17; Sherring 1868: 65; Crooke, 1896a, I: 127.

[22] Crooke, 1896b, IV: 8.

[23] Crooke, 1896a, I: 95, 131–2.

[24] Kinsley 1986: 211.

[25] Briggs 1920: 137.

the goddess Bhawani, who were Sitala, Durga, Kali, Chandi, Pulmati, Chamariya, and Bhanmati, with Sitala being the eldest.[26] She was also worshiped by sweepers: some Bhangis were hereditary priests of Sitala and arranged the offerings of pigs released at her shrine.[27] Pasis and Khatiks too were Sitala devotees.[28] Chamariya, mentioned by Crooke as a Chamar woman and a leather worker who died an untimely death, and who was also one of the sisters of Sitala, was regarded as causing a very bad form of confluent smallpox, which, it was believed, must be propitiated with the offering of a pig through a Chamar or other low-caste priest.[29] The Mali caste particularly served and invoked Sitala, singing songs in her praise.[30] The main priests who attended to her worship were usually women, Bhangis, and Malis. They were convinced that their acts of piety would help protect their village from smallpox.[31] A story went that once, when Queen Sitala came to earth, she was very thirsty and happened to cross a gardener's grove of flowers. The Malin there gave her water and quenched her thirst. For this Sitala blessed the Malin, pronouncing that whenever her disease afflicted, the Malin's descendants would help the patients through.[32] Invoking Sitala and acting as variolators and folk healers, members of the Mali caste associated themselves with the health and well-being of their area, including the spiritual, emotional, ethical, and material aspects of healing smallpox.

Changes in colonial India in relation to the treatment of smallpox, and its intersections with Sitala have been noted by scholars. In the early nineteenth century the introduction of smallpox vaccination by the British was showcased as another proof of their benevolence, as evidence of the superiority of Western medicine over Eastern "prejudice." However, responses to the vaccination attempts were poor, and hostile reactions were expressed among Indians, especially in the initial phases, a critical reason being that instead of celebrating Sitala

[26] Mss Eur E223/3, Grierson Collection, OIOC; Crooke, 1896a, I: 127–8.

[27] Crooke 1896b, I: 291; Searle-Chatterjee 1981: 81.

[28] Crooke 1896b, III: 261; Crooke 1896b, IV: 147.

[29] Briggs 1920: 136; Crooke 1896a, I: 80–1, 125–6, 129.

[30] Crooke 1896b, III: 455; Ferrari 2010: 156–7.

[31] Katyal and Kishore 2001: 97; Carstairs 1983: 53.

[32] Gangaram 1935: 47–8.

the vaccination was viewed as a violation of her. According to David Arnold: "But perhaps the greatest objection to vaccination was its raw secularity. There was no ritual and dietary preparation; no Sitala prayers or Ganges water; no appeal to the goddess of smallpox to guide the child safely through such a dangerous defile. Since there was 'no preparation of the body or poojah,' no 'blessing could attend it.' Vaccination was seen as an 'irreligious' act, an encroachment on the prerogative of the goddess without any attempt to conciliate her with worship."[33]

While the smallpox vaccine came gradually to be accepted amongst a section of the middle classes and Sitala lost some ground to modern Western cures for smallpox in the colonial period, her importance continued and took new forms, with some transformations, particularly in the hands of low castes such as the Malis. It was reported in the 1920s that the Sitala Devi fair held at the Sirathu Tahsil in Allahabad district attracted 70,000 visitors, only a little less than the Magh Mela.[34] In Agra, the Sitala Mela held in July 1922 became an occasion for assertion by the Bhangis, who arranged a *pyau* there, offering water to devotees, this being an innovation.[35]

With the flourishing of a footpath chapbook print culture in North India, slim pamphlets celebrating Sitala were published. For example, a tract titled *Sitala Gungaan* had *bhajan*s on her, incorporating the importance of Sitala for women of the lower castes and Malis.[36] In the booklet a *bhajan*, while praising Sitala, lamented that the coming of modern medicine, book knowledge, and vaccination had diverted people's attention from her:

> Sitala, I bow before you, you are the goddess of the universe.
> You are the savior, the generous and the knowledgeable . . .
> You are the basis of the earth and the sky.
> You are the one who rids us of all our hardships . . .
> Impudent people with books, modern medicine, and vaccination
> Abandon your worship at their peril.[37]

[33] Arnold 1993: 143.
[34] Vatal 1923: 7.
[35] *PAI*, July 15, 1922: 1160.
[36] *Sitala Gungaan* 1934.
[37] Ibid.: 4–5.

Caste tracts published by the Mali caste in early-twentieth-century North India stressed their critical role in the cure of smallpox. One such tract called *Mali Jati Nirnaya* stated:

> When the anger of Sitala is unleashed, the Mali *jati* bestows good fortune on society. In such a crisis, be it the rich or the poor, the high caste or the low caste, all seek the support of our *jati* . . . Our caste provides great solace and comfort, with lots of patience, to society . . . Besides selling flowers, curing people of this disease is our main occupation . . . We cure the disease and make Sitala Mata happy . . . We are the main priests in temples of Sitala . . . We are the worshipers of Sitala as there is a direct relation between her wrath and us . . . While everyone fears contact with this infectious disease, we provide our service to all. Where else can you see such an example of social service? . . . Sitala is our protector.[38]

The tract went on to say that Malis were much better than doctors at curing smallpox, and other diseases too, so it was unfortunate that their present state was so pathetic.[39] At the same time, calling upon Sitala, they stressed the importance of retaining and carving out their separate identity and taking pride in their profession: "We should remain and retain our identity as Malis and not crave for inclusion amongst Brahmins or Kshatriyas. We are proud of our special role and our past has been glorious."[40] The Mali caste was here not only reinstating its role in the service of Sitala, it was creatively redeploying her and their mythic symbols even while responding to the colonial order. The cult of Sitala has persisted, embodied particularly by the low castes, and she continues to be celebrated in order to fend off disease—including fevers, measles, malaria, and tuberculosis. The sustained popularity of Sitala, in comparison with other goddesses of the low castes, is encapsulated in the following popular saying:

> She is a goddess of the Chamars, but out of fear people call her Sitala *mai*.[41]

[*hui na chamar devi, dare sitala mai kehet baani.*]

[38] Gangaram 1935: 45–51.
[39] Ibid.: 52.
[40] Ibid.: 45–52.
[41] Singh 2011: 195.

Sitala symbolizes the relation between the divine feminine and illness in Hindu culture, and her worship has proved a durable ritual system.[42] Gayatri Spivak provocatively remarks: "There is no great goddess. When activated, each goddess is the great goddess."[43] This "activation" has taken the shape of a flexibility and resilience that has empowered Sitala, in particular, as a goddess of the low castes.

Appropriating Lona Chamarin: Independent Goddess-Witch to Consort

Lona—also known as Nona—Chamarin was a legendary witch-goddess, feared and revered particularly by the Chamars of North India.[44] She was regarded as the most terrible sorceress of the region,[45] and one of the most powerful Siddha practitioners in the early middle ages. The legend of Lona Chamarin has it that Dhanwantari, the great physician of the gods, was bitten by Takshaka, king of the snakes, and, knowing that death approached, he ordered his sons to cook and eat his bodily flesh after his death so that they might thereby inherit all his learning and medical skill. His progeny accordingly cooked his body in a cauldron and were about to eat it when Takshaka appeared in the form of a Brahmin and warned them against this act of cannibalism. So they let the cauldron float down the Ganges. As it floated, Lona the Chamarin, who lived in Unao and was washing on the banks of the river, not knowing that the vessel contained human flesh, fished it out and ate its contents. All at once she obtained the power and wisdom of Dhanwantari and became skilled at curing diseases, especially snake-bites. Then there came a day when all the people of Unao were occupied with the transplanting of rice. Each man brought rice plants in a basket and threw them out towards where Lona Chamarin stood, and upon returning with the next basketful they found Lona had already planted all the saplings cast in her direction. The discovery that Lona could do more work than

[42] Ferrari 2014.

[43] Spivak 1999: 181.

[44] Lona has many literary meanings: salty and savory; an extremely sensuous and attractive woman; a sorceress. All of them capture her representation in parts. See also Thapar 2008: 166.

[45] White 1996: 198, 505 (n.163).

all her companions put together struck them with wonder and they said, "We are two hundred men bringing baskets of plants—how can one woman plant so many all alone?" At last, when the rest went off after emptying their baskets, her brother-in-law stayed behind in hiding. Lona, thinking herself alone, stripped herself naked, took the heap in her hands, muttered some spells, and cast the plants into the air. They descended and all settled in order, each in its proper line and place. Discovering now that she was being observed, she tried to escape. Her brother-in-law followed, trying to reassure her, but she fled all the faster, and as she moved the earth opened before her and behind her, and all the water from the rice fields, gathering into a single wave, pursued her. In this miraculous way was formed the channel of the Loni river in the Unao district.[46]

Lona Chamarin's name was invoked by Chamars in times of trouble and sickness; in the hope of being saved from the fatality of snake-bites; to drive away the diseases that afflict cattle; for a bumper harvest; as a deified ancestor; and as a practitioner of midwifery.[47] In Muzaffarnagar, when it began to hail, Chamars prayed to Lona.[48] They sometimes received gifts from people who saw them as intermediaries with the power to appeal to Lona Chamarin to spare the cattle in their village.[49] Lona Chamarin symbolized a dangerous femininity, those of both a demon and a goddess, with unlimited magical powers and cannibalism. She was the antithesis of the idea of the feminine as inferior, weak, and passive. M.A. Sherring remarked: "The Nona Chamarin is regarded by Hindu families as a witch, whose invisible presence and agency are to be avoided by the performance of certain ceremonies and incantations. Hindu children are bidden to beware of Nona Chamarin and have their imaginations excited by dread of her, in the same way as English children are frightened at the mention of ghosts and goblins."[50]

---

[46] I found this legend, with some minor changes or additions, in three sources: Crooke 1896b, II: 170–1, 185; Briggs 1920: 26–7, 114, 179, 183, 185; *Gazetteer of the Province of Oudh, Vol. III*: 563–4.

[47] Briggs 1920: 26, 179, 183; Singh 2011: 227–8.

[48] Crooke 1896a, I: 79.

[49] Ibid.: 160.

[50] Sherring 1872: 393.

However, the worship of this powerful goddess appears to have receded over time. She finds no mention in recent works on the goddesses and witches of India. While it is difficult to find reasons for this absence, perhaps one was an attack on her by some upper-caste spokespersons. For example, a tract meant for Vaishya women critiqued the magical powers of Lona Chamarin: "From east to west UP, our women keep proclaiming the name of Lona Chamarin. They need to give up such practices at once; it is not only appalling, but such low-caste customs debase our women, for they are based in magic and superstition."[51]

Perhaps the more critical reason can be found in the increasing popularity of *sant* Ravidas (also known as Raidas, Rohidas) amongst Dalits, particularly the Chamars, especially from around 1900, and the appropriation and submergence of the power of goddesses, particularly Lona Chamarin, in his figure. The Chamkatiyas, a subdivision of Chamars, claimed to have produced both the saint Ravidas and the goddess Lona Chamarin.[52] Ravidas (*c.* fifteenth/sixteenth century) was a medieval poet and saint, a cobbler of the Chamar caste who believed in the *nirgun* form of *bhakti*.[53] Many anti-caste movements in North India invoked him while opposing institutionalized inequalities and hierarchies, and within their assertions of dissident ideologies.[54] Female figures have often emerged in narratives of Ravidas. For example, it has been repeatedly shown that his disciples included two Rajput women—Queen Jhali of the royal family of Chittorgarh, and the famous Mirabai.[55] Further, in some of the earlier Bhakti texts a female devotee called Jamana "Raidasani" is mentioned. A modern Dadupanthi commentary by Narayan Das suggests that this could

[51] Gupta 1907: 65.

[52] Briggs 1920: 26; Crooke 1896b, II: 172.

[53] Briggs 1920: 210.

[54] On Raidas, see Crooke 1896b, II: 185–7; *Rae Das ki Bani* 1908; Bakhsidas 1970 (1911); Briggs 1920: 207–11; Deming 1928; Kuril 1950 (1941); Schomer and McLeod 1987; Callewaert and Friedlander 1992; Schaller 1995; Callewaert 2000: 303–56; Gooptu 2001; Zelliot and Mokashi-Punekar 2005: 197–264.

[55] Callewaert and Friedlander 1992: 26; Omvedt 2003: 192–5; Crooke 1896b, II: 186; Mukta 1994: 37–45, 112.

refer to the wife of Ravidas, but either way it is without doubt a
reference to some female devotee of the same *jati* as Ravidas. He
goes on to say that the female devotee called "Prabhuta," referred to
in one of Ravidas' verses, was his wife. There are also early references
to how Ravidas and his wife were thrown out of the family home,
indicating that the tradition that Ravidas was married was current by
the late seventeenth century.[56] However, it appears that by the early
twentieth century it was Lona Chamarin who came to be seen as
Ravidas's wife or consort.[57] From this period, particularly, Ravidas was
conferred with a divine status and his memory reconstituted by being
endowed with a more aggressive social and religious history. He came
to symbolize a heterodox devotional alternative with an egalitarian
religious message, there coming into being many neighborhood
shrines in his name in the urban centers of UP.[58] This larger-than-
life picture of Ravidas was bolstered by attaching the figure of Lona
Chamarin to his stature. She was reconceptualized, sanitized, tamed,
and domesticated in Ravidas' hagiography, and made his wife or
consort. Crooke, Briggs, and the *Oudh Gazetteer* do not speak of
Lona as Ravidas' wife. However, in his study of the hagiographies
of Ravidas, Peter Friedlander says: "Anthropological data . . . shows
that Ravidas' community had a worldview in which the power of the
goddess was central . . . It is because of this importance of the goddess
for his community that Ravidas must come to an accommodation
with her and this he does by asserting his authority over her and incorporating her power into his own. Another instance of this is his
relationship with Lona Camarin, a kind of magical woman who shifts
in stories from human to witch to goddess and is often regarded as
Ravidas's wife."[59]

Present popular hagiographies of Ravidas published by Dalits also
sometimes state that Ravidas was married to Lona, who belonged to
the Chamkatiya subdivision of Chamars.[60] A change thus seems to

---

[56] Callewaert and Friedlander 1992: 25–6.

[57] For details, Parmar 2011: 119–22.

[58] Gooptu 2001: 148–52, 172; Bellwinkel-Schempp 2006: 24.

[59] Friedlander 1996: 114.

[60] Bains 1996: 3.

have gradually occurred in the ritual language around Lona. Wendy Doniger shows how "consort," though literally denoting a partner or a spouse, is a heavily loaded term in which, if the male principle is dominant, the union is regarded as auspicious; and if the reverse, it is perceived as perilous.[61] Lawrence Babb too has argued that goddesses are often viewed as dangerous and uncontrollable when they are single, but when they become wives they are seen as tamed and propitious.[62] While there have been criticisms of this model, Lona does appear to have been gradually classified as a consort of Ravidas, in the process becoming an appendage of his, inferior in power and status, and overwhelmed by the hagiographies and importance of Ravidas.

Today, a search for Lona Chamarin on the internet only reveals that she is a much-used phrase in *vashishikaran* and *mohini* mantras, used to attract women.[63] Goddess worship continues to be a noteworthy feature of the popular religious world of Dalits in North India, even acquiring new contours and shapes, this community having given it a new spin. In Bankagaon, a nondescript village near Lakhimpur Kheri in UP, the foundations of a temple dedicated to "English, the Dalit Goddess" was laid in 2010. The temple, a single-story structure covered with black granite, will have an over-three-foot-tall idol in black of "Dalit Goddess English," installed on a pedestal in the shape of a computer holding a pen, with a copy of the Indian Constitution, and donned in a gown and hat.[64] The representation of a goddess here is intricately tied to Dalit assertions and claims to dignity through education, employment, and political-public articulation. Such varying representations and shifting identities of goddesses amongst the low castes weave together the complex workings of caste, gender, and power, revealing the varied contexts in which they have been rehabilitated, marginalized, or given a new shape.

[61] O'Flaherty 1982.

[62] Babb 1975. Also Sax 1991: 31–2.

[63] http://www.prophet666.com/2013/09/lona-chamari-mohini-mantra.html accessed on November 15, 2013.

[64] http://articles.timesofindia.indiatimes.com/2010-05-09/special-report/28295913_1_english-medium-chandra-bhan-prasad-dalits and http://www.ndtv.com/article/cities/temple-for-goddess-english-focuses-on-dalits-62656 accessed November 20, 2013.

Performance and Print:
Enunciations of *Kajli*

Oral folk traditions and the public-popular cultural spaces of the marginalized have excited myriad viewpoints, with elites often regarding them as inferior in content and form to their own "high" culture. Some have seen popular culture as the imposition of hegemonic, mass-mediated ideas.[65] Others have celebrated it as a carnivalesque counterspace from "below," with a potential for dramatic eruptions against society's normative hierarchies.[66] One view is that popular culture is "a contradictory mix of forces from both 'below' and 'above,' both 'commercial' and 'authentic,' marked by both 'resistance' and 'incorporation,' involving both 'structure' and 'agency.'"[67]

Low-caste women's expressive genres have been used in Rajasthan and UP to invert proverbs, provoke songs, make jokes, and create folklores of pride that ridicule the upper castes and patriarchal values. As rhetorical strategies, it is argued, these signify oppositional discourses providing counter-hegemonic moods.[68] Such expressions have also been seen as Dalit commentaries, made consciously or unconsciously, on aspects of society and culture, and classified as "rituals of rebellion."[69] Yet others view conflicts over cultural meanings as inseparable from the struggles of survival among low castes.[70] Nevertheless, the popular, informal, cultural performances of low-caste women are not just languages of struggle or resistance but are embedded in their everyday lives. They embody a corner of fun and laughter, and tangentially sideline the painful emotions of living under constant oppression.

Scholars have noted the systematic attacks on such popular cultural articulations and folk traditions of the low castes, as well as of

[65] Gramsci 1971.

[66] Bakhtin 1981; Scott 1976. In the Indian context Banerjee 1989; Uberoi 2006: 3–11; Pinney 2004; Guha 1983; Raheja and Gold 1994.

[67] Storey 2014: 12.

[68] Raheja and Gold 1994: 27–9.

[69] Kolenda 2003: 33–78. Also, Sherinian 2005.

[70] Rege 2002: 1038.

women, in the colonial period, accompanied by a rising puritanism which, it is argued, often led to their gradual demise.[71] For example, particularly over this period the educated middle classes opposed *nautanki* in UP;[72] moralist strains emerged in the portrayal of women in the visual iconography of Bengal;[73] popular cultural festivals such as Holi, Ramlila, and Burhwa Mangal of Banaras faced the wrath of reformers;[74] women were forbidden from singing marriage songs, attending *mela*s, accompanying marriage processions, and participating in Holi;[75] there was an assault on the low-caste popular cultural forms of *lavani* and *powda* in Maharashtra;[76] and in early-twentieth-century Tamilnadu popular songs came to be seen as morally suspect and full of flaws, blunders, and grammatical errors which the well educated could not endure.[77] The practices of *devadasis* came to be attacked: "These arts, by their very social and political constitution, were trapped in class- and caste-inflected stratifications of taste . . . In the popular imagination, *devadasi* dance is understood as both aesthetically impoverished and morally dubious."[78]

Simultaneously, it has been remarked, there was a gradual reorientation of music and dance towards an urban, largely Brahmin, middle-class nationalism, which was part of a sanitizing mission that emphasized spirituality over sensuality.[79] Finally, the wider dissemination of print has been regarded as having a negative impact on oral cultures, performance traditions, and folklore, with particularly adverse consequences for women. However, "print, writing and oral traditions tend to coexist, although sometimes for different purposes, usually in different spheres and often with different consequences."[80] I place my discussion here in the context of these viewpoints.

[71] Banerjee 1989.
[72] Hansen 1992.
[73] Guha-Thakurta 2004.
[74] Kumar 1988: 138–9, 176–9, 190–3.
[75] Gupta 2001: 85–108.
[76] Rege 1995, 2002.
[77] Venkatachalapathy 2012: 130–68.
[78] Soneji 2012: 24–5.
[79] Weidman 2006: 149; Bakhle 2005.
[80] Blackburn 2003: 3. Also, Gupta 2001: 32–3.

In North India certain cultural realms and forms of folk songs were especially associated with particular castes, and they provided its best renditions. It was noted by the colonial historian of cultural forms W.G. Archer that much of the popular songs of North India were an expression of caste sensibilities, and the songs of Dalits were noticeably different from those of the upper castes.[81] Many Dalit men recited and sang *alha*s, celebrating the valor and stories of heroes like Alha Udal, giving them their own versions. *Birha* was mainly chanted by the Ahirs. If anyone in the Dusadh caste fell ill, an old man from the caste was called to sit next to the patient and, while singing *pachra*, pray to the goddess. It was believed that the continuous singing of *pachra* finally pleased the *devi*, who then cured the patient. Telis sang *kolhu ke geet*, which were extremely melodious. Boisterous singing and the use of drums provoked the active participation of the entire community. Dhobis played the *huruk*, a small drum in the shape of an hourglass; while the *daphla*, a tambourine, was the main instrument played by Chamars,[82] reflecting the heterogeneity of low-caste cultural practices and performances.

Low-caste women had a rich oral tradition of song and dance entrenched in their caste sensibility, labor, and everyday life. It has been remarked that "Songs, as people's oral traditions, illuminate the social construction of gender through which overarching caste and gender ideologies are transmitted and reproduced."[83] Women were pivotal to the singing of joyous and sad songs on varying occasions, articulating their pleasures and sorrows through imaginative narratives. They sang *kajli*s and participated in *sang*s, *swang*s, *lavani*s, *ragini*s, *kissa*s, and *katha*s, learning them from their mothers, sisters, and friends while cooking, washing, or stitching, and transmitting them over the generations.[84] *Kajli*—also known as *kajri*—was a favorite of low-caste women in eastern UP and was usually composed, performed, and

[81] Mss Eur F236/12, Archer Collection, OIOC.

[82] Upadhyay 1957: 29–30, 75–7. For folk culture of UP: O'Henry 1988; Onkar Prasad 1987; Srivastava 1974; Vatuk 1979; Pandey 1987.

[83] Jassal 2012: 2.

[84] Gupta 2001: 86–7; Wadley 2005; Mehrotra 2006: 59; Das 1991: 110. Das points out how a great corpus of songs was created partly, if not entirely, by women and that it was they who mainly preserved and transmitted it.

consumed by them. The word *kajli* was possibly a derivative of *kajal* (black kohl). In a country of sizzling summers, black monsoon clouds brought great joy. This was the moment for the playful *kajli* to be sung.[85] It epitomized a form of authorless local folk culture, classified by some as part of "little traditions," as against the classicism of "high" culture.[86] *Kajli* has also been regarded as a related genre of the *thumri* repertoire, which is identified as a "feminine voice" associated with the performance tradition of courtesans in North India.[87]

The origins and basis of *kajli* have been a subject of some debate.[88] Identifying *kajli* as a festival celebrated by Chamar and Dom women, Crooke stated: "In Mirzapur the chief Dom festivals are the *kajri* and Phagua or Holi. At the *kajri* in the month of Sawan they get drunk, dance and sing. It is the regular woman's saturnalia and on this occasion gross sexual license is tolerated."[89] *Kajli* was mainly cultivated in Mirzapur, from where it spread to other districts of UP, and later to the growing urban centers of Calcutta and Bombay.[90] Premghan, a prominent Hindi *rasik* of eastern UP, writing in 1913, authoritatively established *kajli* as a folk form of singing associated with low-caste women of the region. Fairs and festivals, he noted, were held around *kajli*, these being exclusively low-caste women's affairs. During *kajriya ka mela,* low-caste women sang *kajli*s near the river and, picking up soil from there, used it for the planting of barley. During *dhunmuniya ka mela* low-caste women played, danced, and sang *dhunmuniya kajri* uninhibitedly, all night long, on the streets.[91] Premghan stressed that just as Holi was a festival for men, *kajli* worked

---

[85] Onkar Prasad 1987: 66–93.
[86] Marriott 1955; Srinivas 1998; Jassal 2012: 72.
[87] Perron 2007: 16–17, 27; Rao 1990.
[88] Bhadeva 1967: 12.
[89] Crooke 1896b, II: 328. Also 185.
[90] Onkar Prasad 1987: 67.
[91] "Premghan" 1913: 1–2. Also Upadhyay and Upadhyay 1872. Shahid Amin shows how in some writings of the early nineteenth century, *kajli* was linked to expressing indignities that befell Hindu women due to the medieval Muslim conquerors of Hindustan. He however goes on to argue that it is the low-caste feminine erotic articulation of *kajli* that has reached us. I draw some of my arguments from his work. See Amin 2005b: 20–5.

for women in eastern UP.[92] He emphasized that singing *kajli*, and its associated playfulness and humor, were the domain of low-caste women, and that high-caste Hindu women were not a part of it. The language of *kajli* was not the language of "civilized" high-caste women.[93] Branding Kajli Teej as an exclusively women's festival, he remarked on how *kajlis* were composed by simple, low-caste rustic women with melodious, unadorned feeling, and sung "naturally" in "village" language. He argued that only low-caste village women could compose such impressive and unique songs, the power of which lay in singing and listening, not writing.[94] Premghan's entire effort was to establish *kajli* as an authentic, autonomous, rustic, low-caste women's folk rendition, surrounded by the feasts and festivals of this class of women, in which only they participated, played, and performed. Profanity was a part of the spectacular and unruly aspect of *kajli*, often giving vent to feelings taboo in everyday conversation.[95] Reveling in sexual banter, a *kajli* said:

My dearest lover, braid that coil of hair on my head.
After plaiting my hair, give me a hug,
And a nip and a bite on my cheeks. [96]

[*guhi de more mathe ki chutiya re baalam.*
chutiya guhat mohin garvan lagave,
galva mein kaat khai chikotiya re baalam.]

Another expressed flirtation and sexual innuendo:

I shall give twenty rupees to the police station in-charge,
and five rupees to the junior police officer;
These two breasts I shall offer my lover;
And to the non-commissioned officer I shall give nothing, oh my darling
     lover.[97]

[92] "Premghan" 1913: 2.
[93] Ibid.: 9–10.
[94] Ibid.: 11, 48.
[95] Kirin Narayan 1986. Unlike *thumri*, which was sung for the male gaze, *kajli* was performed amongst women. For *thumri* and its audience, Rao 1990.
[96] "Premghan" 1913: 12.
[97] Ibid.: 40. Also quoted in Amin 2005b: 24.

[*bees rupaya thanedarva ke debai,*
paanch rupaya jamadarva ke re;
ei duni jobna sipahiya ke debai,
angutha chataye dafadarva ke re sanvaliya.]

Low-caste women often ended *kajli* by uttering the names of their husbands to each other; often Muslim women followed suit, thus breaking the codes of etiquette and community boundaries.[98] Daphne Brooks shows how black women in America transformed the alienating conditions of marginalization into modes of self-actualization through performance, which she calls "dissenting methods of narration and aesthetic articulation."[99] While largely focusing on *prem* and *sringar*, *kajli* songs were not only a form of leisure activity but were quotidian, public, and creative embodiments of the social and cultural world of low-caste women, who turned the tables on normativity by creating unorthodox caste and gender epistemologies. These were among the ways of communicating fun, humor, irony, and satire, negotiating codified sexual relations, staging symbolic inversions, gleefully expressing deviances from codes of behavior, endorsing and contesting patriarchies and gender asymmetries, claiming sexual subjectivities, articulating relatively autonomous spaces, registering control over one's body and voice, providing a diversion from the accepted and the expected, and deploying an outlet from the inevitable frustrations of everyday tyranny.[100]

Such popular cultural expressions of low-caste women, and the sexual banter that often accompanied them, were used by some colonizers and reformers to reinforce the stereotypes of low-caste women as symbols of sexual excess. For example, M.A. Sherring was extremely contemptuous of *kajli*, regarding it as morally dubious and noting that female singers of a very low and abandoned character participated in *kajli melas*.[101] From the second half of the nineteenth century, and especially with the coming of mass print culture, the world and word of *kajli* saw reallocations, often entailing the effacing of low-caste

[98] "Premghan" 1913.
[99] Brooks 2006: 6.
[100] Jassal 2012: 73–5; Kirin Narayan 1995; Nilson 2001; Srivastava 1991: 270–310; Rao 1990.
[101] Sherring 1868: 220.

women's voice and body. Premghan lamented the fate of *kajli*, and the changes that had come about in its rendition as the consequence of a whole range of male folk creations. He even compared it to the "tragedy" of *lavani*, showing the way in which the "natural" melody of *lavani* had been destroyed by male singers who had adorned it with crests and plumes, linked it to *akharas*, and given it their own Marathi flavor. This manner of tampering had happened in UP too, so that *kajli* had been comprehensively ruined. In UP it had been appropriated by male *ustaads* and *akharas* and had lost its vitality at the hands of city-based male singing troupes.[102]

A look at some of the popular publications of *kajli* songs in the early twentieth century partially substantiates Premghan's claim. The urban-print male setting became a potent ground for altering the basis of *kajli*, and modifications found their way into slim, popular pamphlets. With this transmutation of *kajli* into a different milieu, a masculinist discursive strand appeared in its composition. Selectively appropriating and assimilating the rustic and unruly language of low-caste women, most of these pamphlets, variously titled *Kajli Surajmukhi, Kajri Mirzapuri,* and *Kajli Navabahar,* were compiled by urban, educated, upper-caste men.[103] The new language, techniques, and styles explored through the print medium signaled a normative male public sphere from which low-caste women were largely excluded, signifying male control over the voice, text, word, and meaning of *kajli,* with male authors now expressing women's desires. A distinctly collective participatory activity of Dalit women was now usurped by men who used it for their own fame and ends. One tract shows the picture of a male author on the cover, claiming to have "given the *kajli* of Mirzapur a new flavor."[104] In an attempt to retain zest, as well as make them commercially lucrative, many of these popular collections of *kajli* were written in a titillating style, with titles like "Colorful Kajri" (*Rangili Kajri*) and "Salacious Kajri" (*Chatpati Kajri*).[105] This variety of literature proliferated and made the *kajli* genre popular in urban milieux, except that it was

---

[102] "Premghan" 1913: 17–18.
[103] Vishvakarma 1927; Jagannath 1937; Pandey 1937.
[104] Maharaj 1937.
[105] Tiwari 1936.

now meant largely for the male gaze and consumption. As has been remarked, when the means of communication shift, the themes, forms, and characteristics of folk songs do as well.[106] The sensuous and the erotic were ironically reinstated and stylized, but there was a gendered impact of print technology: now *kajli* became a commercial venture, guided by urban tastes and markets, in the hands of upper-caste urban men. The alterations from oral to print form, and the shift from rural to urban circulation adversely impacted community production, impromptu improvisation, earthy vibrancy, and rich contextual variation.[107] In some of the new renditions, *kajli* lost its passion, exhilaration, and wanton abundance, in short perhaps its very essence, as it was reinvented and deployed with ingenuity as the means to promote reform, khadi, and nationalism,[108] and even to praise the imperial *darbar* and the royal visit to India.[109] The appropriation and subsequent sanitization of *kajli* was bemoaned by Premghan in his lament, which pointed out that even Madan Mohan Malaviya was using its style to compose political poetry.[110] *Prayag Samachar* from Allahabad carried an article in the form of a *kajli* in which the writer dwelt on an anticipated drought and the impending crop failure.[111] The flourishing print culture and the literary troupes around *kajli* were thus putting the genre to a variety of uses. However, the mixed ways in which *kajli* appeared in print shows that at times it was indifferent to reformist upper-caste endeavors and values, while at others it was endorsing them. New technologies and the growing vernacular literature around *kajli* expanded its popularity, but the context and social history of this genre, as a domain of low-caste women, was obliterated.[112]

[106] Blackburn and Ramanujan 1986: 25–9.
[107] Jassal 2012: 258.
[108] Shukl 1937: 4–5; Munnilal 1937.
[109] Sharma 1912.
[110] "Premghan" 1913: 43.
[111] *NNR*, July 30, 1891: 544.
[112] Later, there was also an appropriation and repopulation of this low-caste women's genre by a new class of classically trained women vocalists, performing on the concert stage, where *kajli* songs were either classicized or newly composed. See Perron 2007: 42, 105.

Dalit women, however, soon started making an entry into the decidedly "masculine" genre and world (including cast and audience) of *nautanki*, the most popular folk form of entertainment in UP in the early twentieth century. Gulab Bai, a poor Dalit woman of the Bedia caste, was the first female to enter this male space in the early 1930s, at the young age of twelve, followed by many such women who contributed immensely to its spectacular success.[113] Gulab Bai became the brightest star of the Kanpur style of *nautanki*, rising to dizzy heights within a few years. Many believed that her earnings were more than the district magistrate's income at the time.[114] Her expertise lay particularly in singing intimate, earthy folk songs full of erotic and sexual innuendo, originally collectively composed and sung in the intimate circles of women,[115] drawing also from the *kajli* genre. Thus she sang:

> When the soldier untied my blouse-strings,
> my breasts swung loose at night, O mother.
> When he caught hold of my skirt,
> Bharatpur city was ransacked at night, O mother.
> I feel scared alone, O mother.[116]

> [*jab re sipahiya ne choliband kholi,*
> *jovan dono dat gaye raat mori amma.*
> *jab re sipahiya ne mora lehenga pakdo*
> *bharatpur lut gayo raat mori amma.*
> *akeli dar laage raat mori amma.*]

In the words of one scholar, presenting such songs "to a wider audience meant shifting registers and moving into thorny terrain. What was quite routine when sung in all-women conclaves could sound explosive when sung in public, by a woman. It could shock and excite, at the same time establishing her [Gulab Bai's] reputation as seductive, attractive, desirable, and not quite respectable."[117] Moreover, *kajli* itself has continued to thrive in rural areas of eastern UP among low-caste

[113] Mehrotra 2006. This paragraph is drawn from her work.
[114] Ibid.: 115, 219.
[115] Ibid.: 121, 150.
[116] Ibid.: 150 (including translation).
[117] Ibid.: 153.

women, who have managed to creatively redeploy the genre. Many
kajlis sung mainly by low-caste women in the region over 2000–5
have been recorded, which highlights not only the resilience and
flexibility of this genre but also the ways in which the songs continue
to be marked by emotion, mirth, revelry, collective playfulness, and
spontaneity, and where migration and work experiences emerge as
important themes.[118] It appears that while in its printed and stage
form *kajli* has been appropriated by others, it continues to flourish
as an oral folk culture of low-caste women. At times reinstating, at
others inverting hegemonies and patriarchies, women have refused to
give up their sense of fun and ribaldry. Their sexual banter and wit,
especially amidst themselves, has found expression through varied and
fluid spaces. This was brought out well in a workshop of Dalit women
that I attended in Banda a few years back, where the *kajli* form was
repeatedly a template for satirical songs.[119] These mutations of *kajli*
reveal that while it acquired different contours, authors, and forms in
the print-urban-male environment of the early-twentieth century, it
continues to be the domain, albeit in a muted form, and a different
garb perhaps, of the creative genius of low-caste women.

Conclusion

The country's diverse cultures acquired new forms and meanings
in the colonial period, being now pitted against one another much
more intensely and sharply, often in unequal situations. Gendered
low-caste religious and cultural practices had to contend with assorted
fissures and slippages marked by marginalization, appropriation,
resilience, and re-enactment. Low-caste goddesses were sometimes
domesticated and marginalized, and at other times reinstated by Dalits
themselves. The conspicuous oral genre of *kajli* found new avenues
and forms through print, though now mainly in the domain of men,
with women continuing its oral-rural renditions. Print enabled new
uses for *kajli*, but as a genre of low-caste women it was kept alive
through orality. These diverse moves show that there were losses

[118] Jassal 2012: 71–114.
[119] Workshop on "Dalit Women and Popular Culture," Chitrakoot, Banda,
September 29–30, 2007, organized by "Nirantar."

and shrinkages in some arenas, resilience and malleability in others. We should be cautious of embracing any singular metanarrative about the explication of gendered Dalit cultural heritages. For if distinctly gendered caste-based spaces and practices were sometimes marginalized by upper-caste or Dalit men for nefarious reasons, there were also times when these rituals were successful in new creative avenues that reshaped their mythical symbols, religious idioms, and cultural articulations. Such incongruities suggest that amidst strains and erasures there was an element of incompleteness in the moralizing projects of modernization and civilization in the colonial period, as well as later, enabling us to witness the long afterlife of such religious and cultural realms.

7

Caste, Indentured Women, and the Hindi Public Sphere

Over the first three decades of the twentieth century a new and critical figure emerged in the public sphere of Hindi publications—the indentured subaltern woman. This coincided with the Indian nationalist campaign against indentured emigration. Reports, articles, editorials, letters, stories, and poems were composed about her in the vernacular. She came to be constructed by nationalists, reformers, writers, poets, elite women, and men in sympathetic yet contradictory ways which often compressed the layers of meaning of her migration. While there remains the virtual impossibility of disaggregating the caste composition of indentured women laborers, and thereby determining the specific percentage of Dalit women within this large category, this absence of precise statistical information is less significant than the fact of laboring women's oppression and its nature. I will therefore here discuss women who were marginalized and reduced to seeking escape through indenture on the plausible assumption that a significant number of such women were also from a Dalit background. A glance at the vernacular world of the period reanimates the histories of indentured women and shows how the issue came to be hotly discussed in colonial North India, giving it almost a popular and "mass" character. These writings also reveal how the emerging realignments of caste, class, labor, gender, family, and nation became enmeshed with emigration. The moralizing discursive practices of Hindi writers on the subject suggested serious attempts to rescue, rehabilitate, improve, discipline, police, and condemn the subaltern indentured woman—which

232

unveiled a tangle of arguments about national honor, women's chastity and respectability, manual labor, sexual anxieties, notions of morality and immorality, citizenship, and "sorry" sisterhood. Her simultaneous representation as an "innocent" victim and "guilty" migrant construed her as both part of the nation and outside it.

The emigration of women as indentured labor in colonial India has provoked important studies. The overwhelming focus has been on their conditions in the plantation colonies.[1] Broadly, we get two competing perspectives, although the division between them is not clear-cut. Some historians, especially those who adopt a nationalist, anti-colonial, humanitarian, or neo-Marxist paradigm, identify indenture with slavery and argue that emigration did not lead to a lessening of gender, caste, and class exploitation.[2] Rather, these patterns were retained, institutionalized, and strengthened in the new destinations.[3] Complementing this, others see migrant women "coolies" as victims of greed, deception, and colonial manipulation.[4] Emigration, they argue, not only compelled women into unfair contract regimes, it also subjected them to brutal sexual exploitation by overseers and competitive subjugation by Indian men.[5] A second group of researchers, particularly those identified with imperialist, colonialist, revisionist, and modernist schools, contend that emigration was a result of rational and informed choices on the part of migrant laborers, which led to considerable improvement in their living conditions. They equate indenture with free white labor. They argue that caste identities were greatly mitigated as a result of migration to new areas, as caste status in these places bore no implications for

[1] Carter 1994; Jain and Reddock 1998. For the contemporary context, Thapan 2005.

[2] Tinker 1974; Baak 1999: 124; Gupta 1992; Daniel, Bernstein, and Brass 1992; Breman 1989; Rajendra Prasad 2004.

[3] Klass 1961; Smith 1965; Moore 1995.

[4] Tinker 1974; Gillion 1962: 150; Mayer 1973: 3; Ahmed 1980: 16, 37.

[5] Kelly 1991; Beall 1990: 57–75; Lal 1985. For critique of these positions, see Carter 1996: 137. Carter offers a nuanced critique of the condition of indentured women. However, she occasionally falls into the trap of upholding the desire for a "tranquil" family life, as the most important one for these women. See Carter 1994: 5.

social mobility, occupation, and resource control.[6] In a similar way, some historians insist that emigration had liberating possibilities for women, particularly those belonging to the lower castes and classes. Stressing the dramatic changes brought about in the lives of women, they see emigration as the best thing that could have happened to them—such women they feel subsequently enjoyed greater freedom from patriarchal and caste demands.[7]

My present focus here is not on the condition of women in the plant-ation colonies, on which there is ample scholarship, but on how the figure of indentured woman came to be constructed and debated in the vibrant Hindi print-public sphere of early-twentieth-century India. By unpacking these voices one can discern the precedents of the positions just elaborated and interrogate such binaries as bad/good, moral/material, and fettered/free. Theoretically or paradigmatically weighted perspectives often lose sight of the contestory processes by which immigrant communities are formed.[8] They also tend to view the emigrant as an object of pity, overlooking the personal and cultural considerations involved in the process.[9] A recent poignant account by Gaiutra Bahadur underlines the mixed narratives of kidnap and escape, imperilment and empowerment, enslavement and liberation, and above all of the astounding spirit of "coolie" women.[10] Nuanced forms of revisionism can thus sometimes help bring out com-plexities,[11] and this is certainly true for indentured women.

I try to lend weight to these arguments, not only by examining cultural identity formations and the portrayal of women emigrants in the vernacular, but also by amplifying them with the writings of British officials and missionaries on the one hand, and on the other the actual experiences of women themselves, particularly Dalits, as they experienced recruitment and transportation. By focusing on, broadly, the Dalit-subaltern woman's subject position, and its inflections in the public sphere, I attempt to reformulate the gendered experiences

[6] Emmer 1986; Schwartz 1967; Jayawardena 1968; Nevadomsky 1980. For further explication, see Satyanarayana 2002: 90.

[7] Emmer 1985: 247; Reddock 1985, 1994; Mohammed 1995.

[8] Mohapatra 2006: 176–7.

[9] Satyanarayana 2002: 90.

[10] Bahadur 2013.

[11] Sarkar 2014: 148.

of indenture beyond victimhood/liberation and regulation/agency. When viewed through the optic of caste, the story of gendered migration gets redefined. This also helps break the existing restrictive rubric of continuity/change in caste structures and identities within indentured and plantation economies. Gender and caste identities were refashioned as much in the process of applying for migration as during the period of indenture. Although the discord between the voices and actions of Indians and those of the colonizers is loud and clear, there were nevertheless conjunctural echoes between them when it came to the question of control of women's labor and sexual flows. The actions of Dalit-subaltern women, however, carried far more ambivalent meanings, since these involved both free and indentured movement, voluntary and forced displacement, territorial bonding and transnational migration. This implicitly intersected with the larger Dalit critique of upper-caste progressivism and nationalism, which also found parallels in a section of indentured labor. In what follows I also underscore the deep social hierarchies within which Dalit migrants and potential migrants—especially single women—operated.

My arguments here are partly inspired by certain seminal works by feminist scholars who draw on contemporary ethnography to challenge the tendency to address women's cross-border movements and migration primarily within the framework of trafficking, and the conflation of trafficking with prostitution. The legal scholar Ratna Kapur argues that such positions not only portray the "disempowered" woman in a perpetual state of victimization but also reveal a deep reluctance to acknowledge consensual migration. This marginalizes the rights claims of migrants and denies the subtleties of their existence.[12] Another scholar of similar bent, Flavia Agnes, contends that any analysis of the complexities of the transnational female migrant must extend beyond the confining parameters of conceptual and operational work on cross-border movements. Rather than seeing these women solely as vulnerable victims, she terms them as risk-taking subjects.[13] A third, Nandita Sharma, challenges the conservative sexual morality of nation-states that legitimize the practice of criminalizing the migration of women. This has the effect

[12] Kapur 2010.
[13] Agnes 2008: 355–66. Also Kempadoo, Sanghera, and Pattanaik 2005.

of supporting a nationalistic consciousness of space and home.[14] And, finally, Samita Sen reflects on the diverse contours of women's migration from the nineteenth century, especially to overseas as well as to Assam plantations, signaling their mobility.[15]

I also draw upon scholarship on Dalits which stresses the attraction for them of "a place elsewhere," for transnational mobility, and for an oceanic, wider world of possibility. It has been persuasively contended that in colonial India the blandishments of colonial modernity and mobility held a much greater appeal among many Dalits than the condescending concessions of tradition and nation.[16] Provocatively, one prominent Dalit thinker has come out in support of foreign direct investment in present-day India on the grounds that Dalits do not succeed in traditional and local enterprises, and it is new, liberalized systems of trading that can provide them with opportunities.[17] While drawing upon, and differing from, these exciting methodological insights, debates around the indentured Dalit-subaltern woman in colonial India further enrich and complicate this scholarship, while also pointing to certain continuities and fractures in a colonial context. Many such women, for example, migrated to these colonies outside the family context. The subjective experiences of these migrant and potentially migrant women, particularly those who posed as single, illustrate the ambivalences of identity in particularly gendered ways. However, given the already existing stereotype about their sexual promiscuity among elites, they came to be derided as even more aberrant, and as personifying the breaking up of morality in the plantations.

Brief History of Gender and Indentured Emigration in Colonial North India

From the nineteenth century a new feature of colonial practice was the import of increasing numbers of Indian indentured laborers to the plantation economies of Fiji, the West Indies, Trinidad, Natal, and

[14] Sharma 2003: 53–65. Also Andrijasevic 2003: 251–70.
[15] Sen 2004.
[16] Menon 2006: 110–42.
[17] Prasad and Kamble 2012.

Mauritius, particularly following the abolition of slavery in 1838.[18] These workers called themselves *girmityas*.[19] Calcutta was one of the main ports of departure for these destinations. While such immigrants came from almost every region of India, the overwhelming majority, up to 80 per cent, in fact, was drawn from UP and Bihar, recruited by contractors especially engaged for the purpose who worked in the interiors of the region.[20] The social composition of immigrant labor often reflected the caste structures of rural North India.[21] Since most of the upper castes were prejudiced by their religion against overseas travel, a substantial portion of indentured laborers came from the lower castes.[22] Basing his findings upon their landing tickets, the largest number of emigrants, Brij Lal has argued, came from UP and belonged to the Dalit castes. Chamars alone totaled 13.4 per cent of all emigrants.[23] Furthermore, Dalits and tribals were perceived by the plantation owners as more submissive, malleable, manageable, hard-working, skillful, and reliable, with no taboos surrounding food or work.[24] Basti, Gorakhpur, Gonda, Bahraich, Azamgarh, and Banaras became important centers of emigration, the proportion of agricultural labor being high in these districts.[25] Emigration proved a

[18] By 1911, for example, there were 112,940 Indians in Trinidad and 40,438 in Fiji, which increased to over 60,000 in 1919: 478/1914, Industries Deptt, UPSA.

[19] The term *girmitya* was coined for those who signed an agreement (agreement>garment>*girmit*) to labor in the sugar colony, especially of Fiji. The pioneering work of Brij Lal is significant here; he uses quantitative data and statistical analysis to challenge stereotypes of *girmitiyas:* Lal 2001. Also Kelly 1991: 1.

[20] 478/1914, Industries Deptt, UPSA; 68/4–6/September 1873, General Deptt (Emigration), UPSA; 9/October 1873, Agriculture, Revenue & Commerce Deptt (Emigration), UPSA.

[21] Mohapatra 2006: 179.

[22] 478/1914, Industries Deptt, UPSA; Lal 2001: 100.

[23] Lal 2001: 106–7.

[24] Ghosh 1999: 8–48.

[25] For example, for Fiji alone 6415 recruits came from Basti, 3589 from Gonda, 2329 from Faizabad, 1747 from Sultanpur, 1716 from Azamgarh, and 1683 from Gorakhpur. Similarly, the largest number of laborers going to Trinidad and British Guiana between 1875 and 1915 were from eastern UP and Bihar: 81/1908, Industries Deptt, UPSA. Also Laurence 1994: 107–8.

kind of "safety valve" for the lower castes, especially in times of land scarcity, growing pressure on land, poverty, rural employment, loss of livelihood, natural disasters, and adverse seasonal conditions.[26] The main feature of the labor system that came into being was contractual servitude at fixed wages, usually for a minimum period of five years, on a plantation where the laborer was also obliged to live. After this period an immigrant could seek repatriation to India; this rider was added into the contract to separate indentured servitude from slavery.[27]

The gender composition of immigrant labor was skewed. Far more men than women migrated. They were usually single and in the active age group of twenty to thirty-five. Immigrants were also usually recruited individually rather than in groups.[28] Family migration was not the norm, with only 15 per cent of immigrants being married couples.[29] Nevertheless, between 28 and 40 per cent of migrants were women.[30] This number is far from insignificant, and yet women migrants have usually been depicted as dependents and spouses, disinclined to migrate, of negligible labor value, and of dubious virtue.[31] Their migration has been largely seen as associational, although 70 per cent of the women who migrated appeared to be single.[32] A high percentage of them were registered outside their

[26] Whitcombe 1972; Siddiqi 1973.

[27] Thomas 1985: 1; Mohapatra 2006: 178–9.

[28] Grierson 1883. Also 1–12/February 1883, Emigration, A, Revenue and Agricultural Deptt, NAI.

[29] Mohapatra 2006: 179. It was reported that often men migrated without the knowledge of their family. Economic pressures, low social status, and family bickering were stated as the reasons leading men to leave hearth and home. The wife was often left behind to fend for herself and the family: 344/1923, Box 256, Industries Deptt, UPSA.

[30] *Royal Commission on Labour*: 141.

[31] This position has been critiqued. See Carter 1994: 1; Thapan 2005: 11–12.

[32] Jain and Reddock 1998; Reddock 1994; Shepherd 1998; Kale 1998: 141. Brij Lal points out that of the total number of women who emigrated to Fiji, 63.9 per cent went as single women: Lal 1985: 57–8. Also Sanadhya 2012: 97.

home districts, as shown in records available from Basti, Gonda, Azamgarh, and Sultanpur. Most were women banished to the margins of society—prostitutes, widows, and Dalit women.[33] Many migrated to escape caste, class, and gender exploitation, abusive husbands, and the fetters of family.

However, the methods and processes of recruiting labor were highly gendered, favoring men over women. Recruiters constantly complained of the difficulty of getting female "coolies" in spite of an increase in the rates of commission for registering them. The recruitment of women was also opposed by the colonial planters, as they wanted more "able-bodied men." They resented the difficulty and expense of recruiting, transporting, and maintaining women laborers, since they were believed to introduce trouble and strife into plantation life.[34] The recruiters were also reluctant to bear the cost of reproducing a new generation of workers, maintaining women during pregnancy, and supporting other, non-productive family members.[35] At the same time, male claims to women's labor within the family were upheld; women were to be kept close to home and hearth.[36] Both structurally and institutionally, in spite of the rhetoric, it was made more difficult for women to emigrate.

In spite of these constraints, the recruitment of women from Basti alone, for example, continued to increase. It was reported that female recruits numbered 274 in 1904, and this number increased to 410 in 1905 and 696 in 1906. The percentage of women in the total number of people registered for emigration also increased during this period, from 22.20 per cent to 28.04 per cent.[37] The report of the protector of immigrants for the nine months ending December 31, 1915 revealed that there were more women than men among emigrants from UP to Trinidad aboard one ship, the *Ganges*—namely, 126 women to 81 men. On another ship, the *Dewa*, the number

[33] This however does not appear to be the case in Mauritius, where mostly married women migrated with their families and in groups. See Carter 1994: 34–9.

[34] Kale 1998: 161.

[35] Reddock 1994.

[36] Sen 2004: 77–104.

[37] 81/1908, Industries Deptt, UPSA.

of women emigrants was quite high—207 females to 352 males.[38] To give another example, from Banaras alone 128 men, 21 women, 6 children, and 5 infants migrated in one ship sailing to Mauritius as late as 1923.[39] Migration involved a profound transformation in the lives of all, but especially of women. It is in this context that positions and perspectives on women's emigration need to be placed.

Saving "Injured" and "Wronged" Bodies

While the indentured system began as early as the 1830s, it emerged as a significant issue in the writings and speeches of reformists, nationalists, and the Hindu middle-class intelligentsia only in the early twentieth century,[40] when it came to be overwhelmingly represented as a national calamity.[41] National newspapers lent their support to this position through detailed articles and letters on the subject.[42] Their emphasis on the figure of the subaltern indentured woman gave their viewpoint a particular color and a moral edge. For a section of Indian women, nationalists, and reformers in the early twentieth century, the physical body of the emigrant woman in particular became an evocative site on which stereotypes of morality, sexuality, national honor, citizenship, sisterhood, deceit, and exploitation could be promulgated in print and press. Leading women's journals lent strength to this perspective. Novels, stories, and innumerable poems were composed around the "suffering" indentured woman. While differing in their emphasis and perceptions, they were all deeply critical of the indentured labor policy, especially when it came to women.

[38] 73/1917, Box 49, Industries Deptt, UPSA.

[39] 344/1923, Box 256, Industries Deptt, UPSA.

[40] For example, the collectors of Balia, Banaras, and Ghazipur stated that "educated opinion on grounds of self-interest is opposed to the policy of emigration generally, though the outcry against particular abuses is fostered by persons who wish to bring the government into disrepute." It was reported that strong feelings of racial hatred were being created on this question, particularly in Gorakhpur, Azamgarh, and Banaras. See 344/1923, Box 256, Industries Deptt, UPSA; 478/1914, Industries Deptt, UPSA; 1–9/July 1922, A, Legislative Deptt, NAI.

[41] For details, Kumar 2011: 66–101.

[42] *Leader*, October 3, 14, and 26, 1923.

These voices were first articulated in the indictment of indenture by Gopal Krishna Gokhale in the Legislative Assembly, first in February 1910,[43] and more forcefully in March 1912. In 1912 he not only called it "Slave Traffic" but also strategically associated women, reputation, and national honor with the condemnation of indenture.[44] He noted that the system made the "adorable peasants immoral" through the inclusion of women of loose character in the quota of indenture, leading to "frightful immorality." He added: "It is a shocking affair altogether, a considerable part of the population in some of these colonies being practically illegitimate."[45]

The next weapon that fell into the hands of the nationalists was the account and report of C.F. Andrews (1871–1940) and W.W. Pearson on the conditions of Indian indentured labor in Fiji. Andrews gave extensive space in this report to the moral corruption and sexual degradation of Indian women in the plantation colony. He came to be viewed by Indian reformers and nationalists as a very "sympathetic" observer.[46] For example, in a speech by him to the planters in Fiji in 1915, Andrews remarked:

> In India the morals amongst Hindus are strict in the matter of marriage and the home and Hindus are very careful about their women. The women in India are very chaste but these women, well, you know what they are . . . Indians in India have some bad qualities, but the one thing that is truly noble in them and which has become almost a religion to them in India, is the very high marriage ideal and here you have about 9 out of every 10 in this colony, whose ideas of marriage have simply been shipwrecked . . . A degradation has taken place; something has happened—a serious moral degradation . . . These coolie lines are an apprenticeship of vice . . . The first thing is, that this bad system of

[43] On February 25, 1910, Gokhale moved a resolution in the Imperial Legislative Council for a ban on the recruitment of indentured labor for Natal. See Gokhale 1920: 509–18. Amidst various arguments given by him to support this move, he stated that "it has broken up families, it has driven men to crime and it has driven women to a life of shame."

[44] Gokhale 1920: 519–42. For an analysis of Gokhale's speech, see Kale 1998: 167–71; Kumar 2011: 71–7. I draw this paragraph from these works. Also 478/1914, Industries Deptt, UPSA.

[45] Gokhale 1920: 529.

[46] Andrews and Pearson 1916; Andrews 1937.

recruiting, especially of unmarried people, must stop. They must be brought out under family conditions, or not at all.[47]

At another place he stated:

> The Hindu woman in this country is like a rudderless vessel with its mast broken drifting on the rocks; or like a canoe being whirled down the rapids of a great river without any controlling hand. She passes from one man to another and has lost even the sense of shame in doing so—she who in India is modest, dutiful, home-loving and chaste . . . The Hindu woman in the coolie lines, having no semblance even of a Hindu home of her own and living a life in a strange land divorced from all the old ties and associations of Hindu religion, has abandoned religion itself . . . Indian women of loose character should be refused admission to the Colony under any State labour system . . . A third remedy would be to make illegal the present common practice of a Hindu wife obtaining by a written agreement (drawn up by a lawyer) a virtual divorce from her husband without resort to a court of law.[48]

Reverend John Weir Burton, a Methodist missionary, also pointed to the sexual exploitation of emigrant Indian women.[49] The Arya Samaj and the Marwari community of Calcutta became actively involved in the campaign, the former in UP and Bihar and the latter through the formation of an anti-indentured emigration league.[50] Gandhi lent his weight to the movement. Indentured emigration finally ended formally on January 1, 1920, as the result of a resolution moved in the United Provinces Assembly by Madan Mohan Malaviya in 1916, although discussions around its viability and morality continued.[51] Extensive popular writings in the vernacular, particularly in Hindi, gave the campaign against indenture a particular edge.

[47] Report of Andrews' Speech to the Planters' Association Executive Committee, Fiji, December 7, 1915, reprinted in Lal 1998: 147–9.

[48] Memorandum on indenture by C.F. Andrews, December 9, 1915, Suva, Fiji, reprinted in Lal 1998: 158–60.

[49] Burton 1910.

[50] Kumar 2013: 510–11.

[51] Notably, by the early twentieth century indenture had begun to outlive its purpose, as the growing number of indentured migrants who chose to settle rather than return home had equipped the plantations with an

Indentured Women and Hindi Writings

Indentured workers, particularly the figure of the subaltern indentured woman, became one of the hot topics of the dynamic Hindi print-public sphere in the early twentieth century, and this coincided with protests by reformers, nationalists, women's organizations, and the literati, who made extensive use of print and the press to disseminate their ideas among the wider public. Historians have written in great detail about the moving letter and account of Kunti, a Chamar woman from Gorakhpur who migrated to Fiji as an indentured laborer; her story gave the Hindi press and nationalists their first crucial claim to the righteousness of their campaigns.[52] In her letter Kunti alleged an attempted rape on her by a white overseer on April 10, 1913, while she was weeding a secluded banana patch. The format and composition of the letter indicated that it was designed for publication, and it was widely circulated in the media, with the anti-indenture Hindi newspaper *Bharat Mitra* taking the lead.[53] Kunti's letter sparked a fierce reaction and an intense campaign against outrages on the "indentured daughters of India," and was soon followed by Totaram Sanadhya's (1876–1948) Hindi book *Fiji Dwip Mein Mere Ikkis Varsh*, published in November 1914,[54] which

---

adequate labor workforce. This, combined with a persistent lobbying of the British Indian business community and provisional governments, brought indentured migration to an end, handing in the process a victory to Indian nationalists.

[52] Lal 1985; Kelly 1991: 45–65; Rajendra Prasad 2004: 48–9; Sanadhya 1915: 21–2. I draw my account and analysis of Kunti from these sources.

[53] *Bharat Mitra*, May 8, 1914. Also, *Leader*, April 10, 1913, and August 13, 1913. Letters have been regarded as particularly meaningful in transnational migrant histories, for they provide an unmediated voice of the ordinary immigrant in her/his own words, expressing the epic drama of migration. See Elliot, Gerber, and Shinke 2006.

[54] Sanadhya 1915. I am not going into this text as it has been recently analyzed comprehensively by Mrinalini Sinha, "Totaram Sanadhya's *Mere Fiji Dwip me Ikkis Varsh* and the Second Abolition," lecture at University of Maryland, Baltimore, April 4, 2012: www.youtube.com/watch?v=fMDS6iM8oWE accessed January 4, 2013.

went into its third edition by 1916 and was also translated into Gujarati, Bengali, Marathi, and Urdu.[55] Sanadhya, who had spent twenty-one years as an indentured laborer in Fiji, presented a moving, first-hand account, with poignant passages on the sexual abuse of women. Ghost-written for Sanadhya by Banarsidas Chaturvedi, this became a key Hindi text in the nationalist discourse on the abolition of indenture.[56] Unprecedented praise for the book was voiced by leading personalities like C.F. Andrews, Sir Henry Cotton, Ramanand Chatterji (editor of the *Modern Review*), Sridhar Pathak (president of the Hindi Sahitya Sammelan), and the eminent Hindi writer Maithilisaran Gupt; and eulogizing reviews appeared in newspapers and magazines like *Leader, Tribune, Vedic Magazine, Saraswati, Pratap*, and *Brahman Sarvasva*.[57] Baba Ramchandra, the famous peasant leader of Awadh, who had also returned from Fiji, added fuel to the fire with his writings. Soon after India's Independence, Bhavanidayal Sanyasi penned an autobiographical account of his life in South Africa, with an introduction by Dr Rajendra Prasad.[58] It appears to me that indentured workers who came back to India and became public spokespersons, whether Kunti, Sanadhya, Baba Ramchandra, or Sanyasi, soon began to appropriate and articulate a narrow language of nationalism instead of framing their polemics in a wider and more expansive notion of transnational rights. Hindi translations of Andrews' works soon appeared, and these had an even wider circulation and impact.[59] The newspaper *Abhyudaya* regularly carried such translations of Andrews' lectures and speeches.

Women's journals were not to be left behind, and it was one of the earliest, most respected, and leading Hindi women's periodicals of the time, *Stri Darpan*—edited by women—that seized upon the issue

[55] Sanadhya 2012.

[56] Sinha sees the writings of Sanadhya as signifying a rights discourse. However, others have argued that since the book was penned by Chaturvedi, his nationalist thought left a strong imprint on the work: Sanadhya 2012, introduction by the editors: 12.

[57] Sanadhya 1915: 1–18 (end pages of the book).

[58] Sanyasi 1947.

[59] For example, Andrews 1918: 1–35. The weekly Hindi newspaper *Bharat Bandhu* serialized Andrews' writings. See *Bharat Bandhu*, July 30, 1918.

emphatically. Supported substantially by several female members of the affluent Nehru family, Rameshwari Nehru, a Kashmiri Brahmin woman married to Brijlal Nehru, was its chief editor.[60] In 1917 and again in 1920 the magazine brought out at least four issues which gave extensive coverage to the subject of indenture, with a special focus on women.[61] Since the journal was also the mouthpiece of the Prayag Mahila Samiti, founded by Rameshwari Nehru in 1909, it covered speeches on the subject of indenture given in that forum, along with editorials, articles, and letters by prominent women associated with it.[62] Hindi translations of the lectures and letters of Andrews were carried alongside, building up a picture of terrible calamity.[63] Eminent poets and writers soon joined in to voice their protest. The celebrated "national poet" (*rashtra kavi*) Maithilisaran Gupt composed a poem, "Fiji," in which women once more became the critical focus, with implicit references to the plight of Kunti. Mannan Dwivedi "Gajpuri" wrote a novel, *Ramlal*, which also focused on the issue.[64] Premchand, the most prominent Hindi novel and story writer of the time, produced a story on the subject called "*Shudraa*."[65] Many anti-indenture Bhojpuri folk songs came to be composed at this time,[66] their particular focus being women.

Banarsidas Chaturvedi, a leading Hindi journalist, contributed immensely to the cause, not only by transcribing Sanadhya's book for

[60] For details on *Stri Darpan*, see Nijhawan 2012: 36–48; Mohan 2002.

[61] For example, C.F. Andrews, "*Kuli Pratha*" (Coolie Custom), *Stri Darpan*, February 1917: 63–4, 100–6; Nandrani Nehru, Editorial, "*Striyan aur Bharti*" (Women and Recruitment), *Stri Darpan*, March 1917: 114–17, 152–60; R. Nehru, Editorial, "*Striyan aur Bharti*," *Stri Darpan*, April 1917: 168–9; R. Nehru, Editorial, "The Women's Deputation," *Stri Darpan*, April 1917: 170; Editorial, "The Response of the Viceroy" (reprinted from *Abhyudaya*), April 1917: 171; Uma Nehru, "*Striyan aur Bharti*," *Stri Darpan*, April 1917: 200–4; Editorial, "*Upniveshon Mein Hindustani*" (Indians in the Colonies), *Stri Darpan*, March 1920: 174–5.

[62] Nandrani Nehru, Editorial, "*Striyan aur Bharti*." Also Nijhawan 2014.

[63] C.F. Andrews, "*Kuli Pratha*."

[64] Gajpuri 1917: 112–13.

[65] Premchand 1984, II: 338–60.

[66] Kumar 2013: 515–16.

him, but also by writing *Pravasi Bharatvasi* (1918) and *Fiji ki Samasya*
(1927), in which he condemned the indenture system from the point
of view of a committed nationalist.[67] Significantly, he was invited, as
guest editor, to publish special issues on oversees Indians by various
contemporary Hindi journals. *Pravasi Ank*s were taken out by some
important Hindi journals, including *Maryada, Vishal Bharat,* and
most of all *Chand,* with Chaturvedi as editor. For example, the April
1920 issue of *Vishal Bharat* carried a lengthy article by Sanadhya.
Long after indentured labor was formally abolished, the condition
of Indians overseas continued to provide fertile subject matter to the
Hindi press. The most formidable and voluminous collection on the
subject, running to more than 300 pages, came out as a special issue of
Chand in January 1926. As its specially invited editor, Chaturvedi used
his widespread contacts in colonies to bring a considerable number of
contributors into the issue. This unique collection contained diverse
articles on almost all aspects of indenture, including reports and
poems, mostly in Hindi but also some in English. Again, women
became a special focus here, with at least five long poems and four
articles published exclusively on them.

Certain features stand out in the extensive range of writings in
Hindi on the figure of the indentured woman, which suggests this
issue had now assumed a central role in the nationalist agenda. There
was, of course, a sense of deep pity for the "helpless," "broken"
woman, perpetually a victim, in all these contributions. Selectively
drawing from anti-slavery literature, the sentimental poem as a form
and device became particularly important, its melodramatic pathos
provoking tears. Maithilisaran Gupt mourned poetically:

> Behold the suffering woman in the distant fields,
> The helpless damsel fallen into the clutches of the wicked.[68]

> [*dekho, dur khet mein hai veh kaun dukhini nari,*
> *padi papiyon ke pale hai veh abla bechari.*]

It was not enough, however, to speak on behalf of the indentured
woman. She had to represent herself, in her own voice, even if

[67] For details, see Chaturvedi 1981: 55–6; 1993: 21–30.
[68] Gupt 2008 (1916): 94–5.

filtered through and mediated by men. As is known, it was Swami Manoharanand Saraswati—an Arya Samajist who had come to Fiji in 1912—who composed the letter for Kunti, written as if by Kunti herself.[69] Many men went a step further and wrote poems in the form of "testimonies" by women grieving over their pitiable condition. With liberal use of the personal pronoun (*main*), these were written as accounts in the first person. Though ostensibly meant to describe the first-hand experiences of indentured women, they were intended more to titillate than inform. One, called "The Overseas Damsel" ("*Pravasini Baala*"), cried:

> I, the overseas damsel, sit
> Distressed, lamenting, crying out for pity,
> Enduring unbearable hardships.[70]

> [*baithi main pravasini baala!*
> *karun vilaap "kalap" karti hoon,*
> *sehti kasht kasaala!!*]

Another poem, aptly titled "Overseas Indian Woman" ("*Pravasini Bharatvasini*"), mourned thus:

> Our heart breaks, our heads hurt, and we feel ashamed of speaking!
> But, oh Men of India, to whom else do we dare open our soul? . . .
> Oh! What I have gone through, hear with a strong heart . . .
> A dire battle was fought for the welfare of mother Sita,
> and the fruit of Mahabharat was the price to pay for one Draupadi's
>   honor . . .
> In the pure blood of the Aryans, is there no fire left today,
> For the brother stands and watches his sisters being shamed.[71]

> [*chaati phadti, sir dukhta hai, kehne mein aati hai laaj!*
> *kintu kahen man ki hum kisse, he bharat ke purush samaj? . . .*
> *ha! kya-kya maine bhoga hai, suno, karo pathar chaati . . .*
> *mata sita ka hit kitna, racha gaya bhaari sangram,*

[69] Kelly 1991: 45–6.

[70] Jyoti Prasad Mishra "Nirmal," "*Pravasini Baala*," *Chand*, January 1926: 253.

[71] Arvind Prasad Srivastava, "*Pravasini Bharatvasini*," *Chand*, January 1926: 451–3.

ek draupdi ki lajja ka, samar mahabharat tha daam . . .
aryon ke pavitra shonit mein, nahin ushnta hai kya aaj,
bhai khada dekh sakta hai, jaati jo behnon ki laaj!]

The poem evoked multiple metaphors and images. The indentured overseas woman was represented as a citizen of the Indian nation and yet outside it, completely disempowered as a result of her indentured status, and crying out for help from the men of her country. Her narrative was constantly interspersed with horror stories. Using the idiom of *dharm,* images of Sita and Draupadi were deployed to highlight the epic battles fought in their name, which were contrasted with the utter neglect of indentured women by the nation and its men. The application of tropes like the kidnapping of Sita and the "disrobing" of Draupadi allowed for myriad readings and could be metaphorically analogous with the condition of the indentured woman. An allegory of the brother–sister relationship was employed to make the plea stronger, mocking the brother's masculinity, for he stood mute witness to his "sister's" rape.

Using similar idioms, another poem expressed its derision thus:

Dear God, you lengthened the cloth draped over a single Draupadi,
And for a single sati Sita you waged a massive war.
Today lakhs of damsels are in the clutches of these villains—
Where are you today, O Krishna! The one with the naughty flute!![72]

[*ek draupadi ka prabhuvar tha tumne cheer badhaya,*
ek sati sita ke karan tha sangram machaya.
hai! aaj lakhon ablaen pari khalon ke pale—
kahan aaj ho he man mohan! natkhat veena vale!!]

In such poems these powerless, passive, abused victims without resource were enlisted by nationalist rhetoric to ridicule Indian/Hindu masculinity and issue a clarion call to Indian men, the nation, and the Hindu gods to come to their rescue and protect them. As has been shown in different contexts, the discourse of rescue and reform, while marking indentured women as victims, also contained them within a language of nationalist patriarchies.[73]

[72] Chaturvedi Ramchandra Sharma Vidyarthi "Visharad," "*Kuli Line Mein Pravasi Behnen,*" *Chand,* January 1926: 282.
[73] Soneji 2012; Sinha 2006; McClintock 1995; Sarkar 2001, 2009.

In order to lend flesh and blood to the misery of overseas women, some writers gave them faces and names, combining reality with fiction. Zahur Baksh (1897–1964), the prolific writer for *Chand* and famous for a series of sensational "first person confessions" under the heading "Wells of Fire in Society" (*Samaj ke Agni Kund*), in which he assumed the voice of the suffering woman, wrote a piece in the January 1926 issue titled "How I Was Degraded" (*Main Patit Kaise Hui*). Once again, he described the pain of a woman taken overseas by a recruiting agent (*arkati*). He even gave the name of the ship in which she was taken, and added such statements as "I had to satisfy the lust of 15–30 men every day."[74] The supposedly personalized nature of the account heightened the impact of an already melodramatic narrative.

In several of these narratives explicit links were made between emigrant women, water, and virtue. Beginning with Kunti, her account emphasized how, with much difficulty, she managed to free herself from the overseer and, to protect her chastity dived into a river, whereupon a boy on a boat close by rescued her.[75] In the emotional songs inspired by Kunti, the power of flowing water was perpetually present and audible:

> When evil forces resolved to shake the religion of the pure women,
> Kunti jumped into the seamless water.[76]

> [*satiyon ka dharm digane ko jab, anyayon ne kamar kasi;*
> *jal agam mein kunti kud pari.*]

Embedding Kunti in his poem, Maithilisaran Gupt repeated this connection:

> See who in that distant place, jumped suddenly into the water,
> Relieving herself from the evil world, she drowned herself in endless
>   waves.[77]

---

[74] Zahur Baksh, "*Main Patit Kaise Hui: Ek Satya Ghatna Par Aadharit*" (How I was Degraded: Based on a True Incident), *Chand*, January 1926: 273–88.

[75] Kelly 1991: 46; Lal 1985: 55.

[76] Chaturvedi 1985.

[77] Gupt 2008: 94–5.

[*dekho, kaun daur kar sehsa kud pari veh jal mein,*
paap jagat se pind chuda kar dubi aap atal mein.]

Choosing as his protagonist a low-caste *kaharin* woman, Gaura, Premchand's story "*Shudraa*" told how she was tricked and duped into going overseas, and once more the story ends with her suicide by drowning in a river. From Kunti to Gaura, from "real" to "mythical," there appeared a symbiotic relationship between indentured women, water, and virtue. Jumping into or drowning in flowing water was a metaphor for the preservation of the woman's chastity as well as the punishment of the "unchaste" woman. It was like a "trial by water" which signified both an escape for "innocent" victims, as in the case of Kunti, and drowning as "shame" for their apparent transgression, promiscuity, and sexual impurity. The "good" victims were assisted and protected by water while the "bad" women were punished by drowning. Water absorbed them, either to save their virtue or to "drown" their "disgraced," debauched, and tragic lives.

The sea was also borderless and unidentifiable, and in it certainties of place, nationality, and identity were dissolved. The turbulence of water, particularly the ordeals at sea, disturbed ideas of borders and national belonging and embodied the cruelties of indenture, loss of humanity, tears, struggle, and death. The sea passage, equated through mythology with Black Waters (*kala pani*) figured large in the arguments of the anti-migration lobby.[78] Its symbolic association with barriers, transitions, and journeys separated women from their family and drove them away from their land and nation. Water was also fluid, and no space was proof against its invasive power. While to the upper castes traveling overseas across the waters was a caste taboo, Dalits and women seemed to have had a much more ambiguous view about crossing the ocean: it was also identified as the passage to opportunity, jobs, emancipation, and positive hopes of a better life in an unseen world.[79] Some of them had long-established traditions of migration in search of employment.[80] Many folk songs of Dalit emigrants from North India represent their journey by sea as an

[78] Lal 1998.
[79] Narayan 2001; Menon 2006.
[80] Kolff 1990.

"escape" from the oppressions of caste, Brahmanic Hindu religion, economy, and nation.[81]

At the same time, latent biases against Dalits, particularly Dalit women, appeared within the movement. Kunti was, of course, applauded for her courage. Titled "The Cry of an Indian Woman from Fiji," *Bharat Mitra* wrote on May 8, 1914: "In spite of her [Kunti] being of the cobbler caste, she has surpassed many well-to-do (high class) ladies by the courage shown by her in jumping into the stream to save her chastity. This will gain for her a place in the list of honorable and brave ladies."[82] Sanadhya said: "Though being a *chamarin* by caste, Kunti protected her chastity by jumping in the river and in spite of being a subordinate she scolded the officer."[83]

While reflecting the pain of Kunti, such writings also depended upon stereotypes of caste, religious duty, and honor. The argument implied that "in spite" of being a Chamar woman Kunti deserved to be eulogized and applauded for her "bravery, patience and strength of mind."[84] The victimized Chamar woman was glorified and acquired subjecthood only when she emulated the virtues and ideals of upper-caste Indian womanhood and wifely devotion, thereby overcoming the perceived stereotypes about Dalit women.[85] The colonial authorities, however, called into question the character of Kunti by stating that she had concocted the incident. They saw in Kunti the image of the degraded Dalit emigrant woman who was partly responsible for her condition; they suggested she was immoral, amorous, and quarrelsome, implying that this was only to be expected from a woman of her class.[86] In a way, Kunti symbolized the "crisis" that beset women in the plantation colonies, where they were both victims and perpetrators, eliciting sympathy but also obscurely threatening.

The prominence given to the victimized woman also provided reformers and nationalists with a strong moral opportunity to condemn colonial rule, and more explicitly the overseer and the "beastly"

---

[81] Lal 2001: 114–16.
[82] Quoted in Kelly 1991: 51.
[83] Sanadhya 1915: 22.
[84] *Leader*, August 13, 1913; *Bharat Mitra*, May 8, 1914; Lal 1985: 55.
[85] Kumar 2013: 513.
[86] Kelly 1991: 49–53.

white-skinned man. Kunti had alleged attempted rape against a
white overseer. Baba Ramchandra expressed the view that beautiful
local women were constantly being molested by white men. Even
pregnant women were not spared, and were compelled into constant
intercourse, resulting in abortions.[87] Reiterating the cruelty of white
men, "*Pravasini Bharatvasini*" said:

> There are innumerable male demons here, and whites the destroyers of
> womanliness.[88]

> [*nar-pischach hain yahan bahut se, gore hain stritva ghaati.*]

Maithilisaran Gupt recapitulated this:

> Constantly striking as vultures over corpses, overseers
> Constantly molest our living frail women.[89]

> [*geedh mari lothen khate hain overseer nirantar*
> *haath chalate yahan humari jeeti ablaon par.*]

Describing the life of these women as a hell created by the white
man, another poem declared:

> If you want to see the hell of live misery on the surface of this earth—
> If you want to see the justice of these white demonic villains,
> Hold your heart witnesses, and come to "coolie" lane.
> See the misery of these sisters and shed many tears!! . . .
> What all will these unfortunate powerless women have to go through?
> Till when will they have to live in this painful hell?[90]

> [*bhutal par yadi jivit dukh ka, nark dekhna chah—*
> *in gorang pischach, khalon ka nyay dekhna chaho.*
> *hridya thaam lo zara vachakon, kuli lain mein aao.*
> *dekh durdasha in behnon ki do-do ashru bahao!! . . .*]

---

[87] Speeches and Writings, 2A/Notebook 10: 10; Speeches and Writings,
2A/Notebook 1: 19; "Complaint by Devkali—A Woman in Fiji," Subject
File 29/1914—all in Baba Ramchandra Private Papers, NMML. Also, Kumar
2011: 117.

[88] Srivastava, "*Pravasini Bharatvasini*": 451–3.

[89] Gupt 2008: 94–5.

[90] "Visharad," "*Kuli Line Mein Pravasi Behnen*": 282.

durbhagini in ablaon ko, kya-kya sehna hoga?
dukh purn is nark lok mein, kab tak rehna hoga?]

The "injured body" of the emigrant woman became a rhetorical trope that provided a legitimating structure within which to reinforce protest against the "illegitimacy" of British policies in relation to indentured labor.

Stri Darpan in particular took up the cause of their overseas "sorry" subaltern sisters, speaking on their behalf and attempting to establish bonds of diasporic sisterhood across region, caste, and class.[91] Women writers in the magazine took upon themselves the mantle of rescuing and saving the suffering emigrant woman.[92] This also enabled the journal to makes its voice heard in a more ample arena, with a vision not just for women but for the nation. In many ways it was speaking in harmony with other nationalists of the times and simultaneously representing moral feminists and nationalists. And it gave the periodical a political orientation. A deputation of prominent Indian women went to meet the viceroy about this issue, including Sarojini Naidu, who was actively associated with this campaign.[93] An Indian representative summed up the essence of telegrams sent to Lady Chelmsford, wife of the viceroy: "There was an intensely strong feeling of concern . . . [which included] ladies who lived in *purdah*, but read the news."[94] In a sense the campaign can be regarded as a precursor to the national movement, with women playing a critical role.[95] It has been remarked that the move to stop the degradation of Indian women on colonial plantations attracted more support among the Indian masses than any other movement in modern Indian history, more even than the movement for Independence.[96] These women and men revealed a "wounded attachment" to the subaltern emigrant

[91] Nijhawan 2014: 111–33.

[92] My arguments here are influenced by Brown 1995. Also Burton 1998: 338–61.

[93] Gillion 1962: 182; Kelly 1991: 48; *Speeches and Writings of Sarojini Naidu* 1924; Bahadur 2013: 159.

[94] Quoted in Tinker 1974: 353. Also Kelly 1991: 48.

[95] Nijhawan 2014: 111–33.

[96] Gillion 1962: 182; Lal 1985: 55.

woman and saw in a "damaged other" a justification for their own interventionist impulses.[97] Savitri Devi from Badaun in a meeting of the Prayag Mahila Samiti said, "Our simple women are duped into going to plantation colonies . . . In these times of crisis should we sit quietly? No, definitely not. We should unite and sympathetically teach our innocent sisters not to enter into the clutches of these evil people."[98]

In the process, indentured women's bodies grew central to the debate. Reformers and nationalists denigrated the laboring identity of these women by explicitly focusing on their sexual identity. They conflated indenture with prostitution, constantly reiterating the loss of women's honor (*izzat*) in the degradation of *girmit*. Rather than viewing them as exploited workers, women were seen as unwilling objects of exchange between unscrupulous men. Sympathy for indentured women was transformed into a concern over "moral filth" and forms of cohabitation consequent upon indenture. Issues of *Stri Darpan* repeatedly stressed the highly immoral lives emigrant women were forced to lead in the colonies and this often took priority over their dismal living conditions. The horror of a multiplicity of sexual partners or husbands was invoked and assumed to be true by all. Maithilisaran Gupt wrote:

> Three women behind every ten men, tired and afraid,
> See, are walking back as if carved in stone.[99]

> [*das nar peeche teen nariyan thaki aur shankit-si,*
> *dekho, laut rahi hain kaisi pathar mein ankit-si.*]

The poem "Emigrant Sisters in Coolie Lines" (*Kuli Line Mein Pravasi Behnen*) repeated the sexualized nature of exploitation, adding to the urgency and drama of the movement against indenture:

> Behind every four men, there is one helpless woman—
> And honor vanishes to save one's life.[100]

[97] The argument is influenced by Dozema 2001: 16–38. Also Andrijasevic 2003: 251–70.

[98] Nandrani Nehru, Editorial, *"Striyan aur Bharti"*: 115–16.

[99] Gupt 2008: 94–5.

[100] "Visharad," *"Kuli Line Mein Pravasi Behnen"*: 282.

[*chaar mard peeche hoti hai ek abhagini nari—*
apne praan bacha kar mano lajja kahin sidhari.]

In tandem, *Stri Darpan* stated with disgust that these women, mostly lower caste, were abandoning one man after another, or living simultaneously with many men, forsaking all shame, honor, chastity, and virtue. Any expression of non-conjugal female sexuality was seen by *Stri Darpan* as the highest form of moral degeneration to which indentured women could succumb. Potential women migrants were seen as prostitutes-in-waiting who had to be prevented from traveling at all costs. Endorsing Andrews and emphasizing Hindu *shastras* and religion, Nandrani Nehru wrote in an important editorial of the magazine: "Our *shastras* do not allow more than one husband and even widow remarriage is considered bad. How then can we tolerate such laws in which women constantly change husbands or have several? We will not allow any woman worker to be sent to these colonies."[101]It was also argued that the emigration of women often covered traffic of an undesirable character. The limited wealth and money that these women acquired was seen as sinful. Nandrani Nehru continued: "We do not need such money, which is earned after so much of disgrace . . . They just need such women in colonies who are either prostitutes or those who can be made into prostitutes. We strongly oppose any more women being sent to these colonies."[102]

The emphasis on the "immoral character" of such women gave the campaign a distinctly traditional, patriarchal tone. The alleged immoralities, obscene behavior, and lack of shame among emigrant women posed a serious threat to the moralities of middle-class, upper-caste reformers, and spread anxiety and panic among them, not least among the women. This also implicitly strengthened an "us–them" divide. From the late nineteenth century the social composition of prostitutes had also seen changes, with most such women now coming from the pauperized low castes.[103] The politics of branding immigrant women as prostitutes was intertwined with

[101] N. Nehru, *"Striyan aur Bharti"*: 156–9. For further analysis of these writings, also see Nijhawan 2014.

[102] N. Nehru, *"Striyan aur Bharti"*: 156–9.

[103] Banerjee 1989.

the alleged promiscuity of low-caste women, amplified in indenture. This was compounded by the loss of caste due to practices such as inter-caste sexual alliances and interdining, which were perceived as part and parcel of the experience of indenture.[104] The subaltern diasporic low-caste woman was the "outsider," a dim-witted woman who was not allowed to, and indeed could not, think or speak for herself; her "superior sisters" had to speak on her behalf and wean her away from the dangers lurking in unknown lands. The bonds of imagined sisterhood and citizenship, thus forged, were also deeply hierarchical. For immigrant women, such concerns represented a double-edged sword. They were targets of the moralizing impulses of nationalists, whose mission was to cleanse and sanitize the immorality of the colonies; but this could well encompass condemnation of the indentured woman herself, who had the audacity to indulge in such practices, whether voluntarily or involuntarily, since it indicated that she had forfeited all her moral moorings. In principle, however, the fact that there were many more men than women on the plantation may have empowered some women, who may have valued the right to "change husbands."

The migrant woman was always conceived of and depicted as duped, deceived, cheated, forced, coerced, abducted, or kidnapped.[105] It has been argued that while the deception argument may have been valid for an initial period, the notion that indentured migrants remained indefinitely ignorant of their destinations is untenable.[106] Similarly, while Brij Lal concedes that the recruitment process was sometimes based on fraud, he maintains that the extent of the deception has been exaggerated. He attributes emigration chiefly to the poor economic and social position of certain classes and castes in

---

[104] Both Sanadhya and Sanyasi, for example, were upper caste and expressed resentment at the mixing of castes, inter-caste sexual alliances, and interdining that took place at various depots. Sanyasi recalls how he was told: "Oh man, this is *Jagannath Dham*. Here why think of *chhut-chhat*? You have got yourself enrolled as a *girmit* for Natal. There, what say Chamar-Dom, you will have to eat from the hands of a *Habshi*": Sanyasi 1947: 15–16. Also Sanadhya 1915: 7–8; Bahadur 2013: 43–6.

[105] *Chand*, May 1932: 72.

[106] Carter 1995: 2.

India, rural poverty and dislocation, especially in times of famine, and explains that a new place outside India offered the possibility of moving out of the caste system.[107]

Yet numerous writings of the period pointed to the coercive nature of emigration, stressing that women in particular were always misinformed and misled by the recruiters, and often held captive against their will. It was repeatedly alleged that women were being abducted by emigration agents in UP and Bihar, for example in Azamgarh and Gorakhpur. Pilgrimages by women to shrines and temples, fairs, festivals, and railway stations were identified as the main sites of such kidnappings.[108] One educated native remarked: "The system of recruiting females is open to grave objection. Great atrocities are committed under its cover. Frequently the recruiters and their men entice away wives and daughters from poor and even respectable families, never mentioning to them the real object for which they are wanted."[109] Grierson, in his report, also pointed to the prevalence of this view in North India. The Hindi public sphere endorsed these opinions. Premchand's low-caste Gaura was thus tricked into going overseas. A poem said:

> Repeatedly stressing our miserable conditions, these scoundrels deceived us.
> Cheating us at many levels and then using force, they were able to send us here.[110]

> [*isi durdasha ko keh-keh kar, ha dushton ne behkaya.*
> *bahu chal karke, phir bal karke, humko yahan bhej paya.*]

The emphasis on the coercive aspects of women's migration was in some measure driven by sexually and morally conservative agendas, allied to the demands of the nation. It was meant to restrict and curtail women's migration, while increasing moral surveillance over their lives and reiterating their embodiment in nationalist ideologies. Any recognition of "voluntariness" on the part of woman was a threat

---

[107] Lal 2001: 229.
[108] 344/1923, Box 256, Industries Deptt, UPSA; Sanadhya 1915: 50–1.
[109] Grierson 1883: 30.
[110] Srivastava, "*Pravasini Bharatvasini*": 451–3.

to the nation's integrity. The resistance to emigration also relied heavily on the alleged cheating of such women and the suffering they endured. Although indentured women often found they had become the victims of forced labor and sexually exploitative conditions, it does not follow that they were recruited only through coercion or that they were all reduced to slavery. The possibility that the migration of women could at times occur voluntarily and with informed consent, to escape caste, class, and patriarchal oppressions, or as a way of bettering their situation, was not even perceived.[111] In the process, indentured women were shown as incapable of all independent decision-making and denied the possibility of self-representation.

Single Women, Caste, and the Colonial Administration

While stressing patriarchal authority, familial ties, and caste affinities, many writings evinced a particular horror at single women migrating on their own, unchaperoned by a male. Grierson had noted in his important report that troubled, abandoned, unfaithful, single, and destitute women would make the best women emigrants:

> Married women who have made a slip and who have either absconded from their husband's house with or without a lover, or who have been turned out of door by their husbands . . . I consider the most hopeful class for emigration purposes . . . I do not think that any one can say that the recruiting of these poor creatures is anything but good both for themselves and for the country . . . Even in the worst managed colonies, the material condition of women is far better than that of men . . . There seems to me to be everywhere too great a tendency to treat a native woman as an ignorant child . . . A native woman, married or single, has a perfect power to enter into a contract binding on herself and (to quote the Collector of Shahabad on this subject) "women have at law a right like men to go where they please and I would not take it away."[112]

[111] For example, Singaria, a tribal woman, migrated to Assam as indentured labor to escape social and patriarchal exploitation and physical coercion at home: Bates and Carter 1993: 162–4.

[112] Grierson 1883: 30–2.

Pitcher, who prepared another report, was also of the opinion that emigration accorded single destitute women a second chance.[113] However, single women became special targets of attack in the Hindi print sphere. An editorial of *Stri Darpan* argued: "We have to ensure that not even a single woman goes to these colonies on her own. Else she is bound to become corrupt. Men should come back from these colonies on a holiday, marry in their own *jati*, and take their wives with them. Till the protection of married men, women have no future or salvation in these colonies."[114]

Single and potentially migrant women were rendered suspect, not only by reformists and nationalists but also by British officials. While theoretically arguing that emigration to colonies offered an "escape to freedom," particularly to low-caste and widowed single women,[115] in actual practice and on the ground British officials were often pulled in different or opposite directions.[116] On the one hand many officials strongly refuted the allegations made by reformers and nationalists about the sexual exploitation of "coolie" women by European overseers,[117] stating that "immoral" relations were "not tolerated." On the other hand they reiterated the prevalence of immorality between Indians themselves, pointing out that "the trouble originated in the class of women who emigrated, since the majority of them were single women and some were even prostitutes."[118] Many officials and missionaries working in Fiji, for example the Methodist Cyril Bavin, deplored the fact that Indian women emigrating to Fiji were of a low character, and emphasized their "dark and degraded minds" and "moral degradation."[119] Single Dalit women came to be perceived as more liable to immoral sexual conduct; they were

[113] 1–12/February 1883, Emigration, A, Revenue and Agricultural Deptt, NAI.

[114] Editorial, "*Upniveshon mein Hindustani*": 175.

[115] Grierson 1883: 31; Geoghegan 1873; Comins 1892; 478/1914, Industries Deptt, UPSA.

[116] Faruqee 1996.

[117] Kelly 1991: 35.

[118] 478/1914, Industries Deptt, UPSA.

[119] Bavin 1914: 182, 193; Kelly 1991: 58–9.

habitually characterized as sexually deviant. The very construction of the idea of immoral single women was critically linked to the question of caste. There was also skepticism about the recruitment of single women due to its destabilizing consequences on family life, as control over their labor and sexuality went away from the arena of the household.[120] It was strongly recommended by many officials that "disreputable" single women not be recruited, and that recruitment be only of whole families.[121] Sometimes single women were forced to write of themselves as the partners of a man, a *joda*.[122] Arguments about labor and capital made by the colonial state came to be aligned with nationalist concerns to demarcate the territoriality of India.

The disdain with which single low-caste women migrants were seen was also reflected in the fact that they faced multiple difficulties when migrating. It was an unwritten rule that such women be scrutinized thoroughly and their credentials checked. Officials were inclined in favor of families' legal claims that women's migration was by definition involuntary, because women were incapable of consenting to the offers of recruiters, and therefore their compliance was meaningless and impossible.[123] There were continuous complaints regarding the arbitrary conduct of the registering officials, particularly in relation to low-caste poor women who arrived unaccompanied and reported themselves as single. They were often constrained, confined, harassed, and incarcerated, and their registrations delayed or refused.[124] Section 32(2) of the Indian Emigration Act allowed the detention for ten days of women who came alone but were believed to be married. It was the duty of the registering officer to register all such women emigrants within that period, but they were often detained for much longer. Often they were denied registration if there was even a slight suspicion that they were married and had left their husband behind.[125] Whenever a single woman was produced, the registering officer described the case as "suspicious" and deferred

[120] Sen 2004.
[121] 478/1914, Industries Deptt, UPSA.
[122] Sanyasi 1947: 16–17.
[123] Bahadur 2013: 26–39; Sen 2004: 79.
[124] 81/1908, Industries Deptt, UPSA.
[125] Ibid.

registration for long periods. Asked to define the word "suspicious," he usually had no specific answer; but some light may be shed on the interpretation of the term from the following remark in one of the sub-depot inspection books: "Inspected the sub-depot today. Only one female coolie admitted this very morning. She has got a little jewel on her, hence her case seems suspicious." This was far from adequate reason for the almost month-long detention to which the woman was subjected. Single women were not only kept for long periods of enquiry, but the process of obtaining certificates for them was lengthy and complicated. There is abundant evidence from the districts of UP that long and illegal detentions of single low-caste women, under the pretext of enquiry, were frequent.[126] And it was reported, for example from Basti, that many such women who had been refused registration were driven by want to become prostitutes in the region.[127]

Indian magistrates also hampered the registration of single women because they believed that such women were either being coerced into indentured emigration or fleeing the authority of fathers or husbands.[128] They also tried to discourage single women from migrating by using arguments based on what Duncan G. Pitcher described as "religious prejudices." A circular issued to all commissioners of divisions in the North West Provinces in 1879 stated: "In all cases where married women present themselves for registration, especially when they usually reside in another district, it should be ascertained in the best way available whether the husband is alive or dead and, in the former case, whether he has any objection to his wife becoming an emigrant."[129] The magistrate of Muttra (Mathura) stated that many of the detained single women who came for registration declared their husbands were dead. The truth of this had to be determined. "Free" and detached from parental, spousal, and male authority, these single low-caste women were demonized, and their emigration made virtually impossible. The prospect of such women working for

[126] "Difficulties alleged to have arisen in the registration of intending emigrants in NWP," L/PJ/6/6/265, OIOC.

[127] 81/1908, Industries Deptt, UPSA.

[128] Kale 1998.

[129] L/PJ/6/6/265, OIOC.

wages and the reproduction of their own labor, whether as laborers or prostitutes, was alarming, indeed threatening, to notions of order, virtue, and civility among both nationalists and colonialists. This significant restriction of single women's recruitment demonstrates that nationalist and colonial opinion, often quite unintentionally, worked in concert.

However, there are many examples, particularly of Dalit women from the Chamar and Pasi castes, posing as single women, falsifying their residences and names, and coming of their own accord to emigrate.[130] Of all women emigrants to Fiji, for example, 16 per cent belonged to the Chamar caste, a higher proportion than any other caste.[131] The high registration of women outside their districts proves that many women were quite mobile, contradicting the view that they were tradition/caste-bound and stayed at home;[132] this was particularly true of Dalit women. There were also instances of women eloping with their lovers, running away from their villages, and then meeting recruiters in order to be enlisted and escape the clutches of their families.[133] Many women used emigration to run away from violence in marital homes and escape abject poverty. Even while lamenting migration, we hear women's voices, indirectly and unintentionally, in some of the poems composed by nationalists:

> We were dying of hunger in India, what is our fault in this.
> Leaving that we came here, do not hold this against us.[134]
>
> [bharat mein bhukhi marti theen, ismen hai apna kya dosh.
> chod use jo hum aayi hain, isse kahin na karna rosh!]

It has been observed that Bhojpuri terms such as *gharkaili, dhenmani* or *rakheli* (a woman who lives with a man without marriage), *dolakarh, dolkarh* or *dolkarhi* (a woman who has gone to her husband's house without a marriage procession), and *urhari* (a woman who has been enticed away by a man who is not her husband), largely prevalent among emigrant workers of northern India, tell us something about

[130] Ibid.
[131] Lal 2001: 108.
[132] Ibid.: 131.
[133] Grierson 1883: 30.
[134] Srivastava, "*Pravasini Bharatvasini*": 451–3.

the mobility of migrant women, and that "These terms are indications of the desire and the ability of some Bhojpuri women to walk out of unhappy homes, whether natal or of the in-laws. The standard police reports about women getting lost in *melas*, never to return home, and the significant migration of single women to plantations in Assam and in Fiji make sense in terms of a pre-existing mobility of women, which cannot be reduced to the attractions and enticements of a distant labour market alone."[135]

Some women even used the recruiter to their advantage: they were clothed and fed, and once strong and healthy they changed their minds and walked away from him.[136] It is also significant that very few women returned to India, even after completing their compulsory term in the plantation colonies.[137] I will end this section by quoting from a revealing report of UP, which, while exposing the patriarchal bias of the colonial administration, also confirms that some single women, particularly Dalits, came of their own accord, minus their men, to migrate:

> Women came forward in abundance [for emigration] . . . Musammat Radhia, a Chamarin from Zillah Azimghur, Village Fatehpur was recruited by a person called Bhanjun. On an enquiry made through the Azimghur police it appeared that she had falsified her residence . . . Musammat Bachia, a Chamarin from Ghazipore, village Isripur was refused registration . . . I tried my best to trace out her home and to ascertain as to whether her husband was alive and willing to let her go and owing to her having given false information I could not trace her husband . . . Similarly Lakhia a Pasin of Ghazipore, village Paharpur was not registered because orders were sent to the police to enquire if the husband of the woman was alive and, if he was alive, to ascertain from him whether he was willing to his wife becoming an emigrant. No reply was received . . . Rukia a Chamarin of Ghazipore, village Karampore was refused registration because it was claimed that she had falsified her name.[138]

Dominant narratives of both nationalists and colonialists are at odds with such records of Dalit women's experiences, whose

[135] Amin 2005a: 47–8, 178–9.
[136] Grierson 1883: 31.
[137] Rajendra Prasad 2004: 15.
[138] L/PJ/6/6/265, OIOC.

needs were rendered invisible by the British and nationalists alike. These women perhaps occupied and negotiated ambiguous spaces represented by home and away, the national and the transnational, the inside and the outside. Emigration and indenture dramatically restructured their position, as well as their relationship to men. In constricting situations, and in a life filled with pressures and miseries, they sometimes left their husbands and family to carve out some little space for themselves. It cannot be denied that those women who managed to migrate did so in a highly gendered atmosphere. They faced sexual and economic exploitation, but with all its problems this may have also been for them an opportunity to better their social and material status.

Conclusion

Discussions by nationalists on the issue of migration, supported by virulent opposition to indentured labor, were rooted in an intensely privileged understanding of the Indian nation. They were also profoundly gendered, as the figure of the woman was called upon to play a particular role in the writings against indenture. She was represented in such a way as to burden her in public discussion with particular features, calculated to produce certain morally loaded meanings in any debate over indenture. She was also required as a symbolic figure in the nationalist armory against the colonial government. The Hindi print-public sphere in particular became a fertile ground for mobilizing gendered concepts of belonging, and for inflecting the campaign against indenture with middle-class reformist and nationalist idioms. These reformers, nationalists, and middle-class women undertook the task of thinking, speaking, and acting on behalf of the emigrant woman and deciding what was good for her.

While it had its roots in India, the campaign also proved an enabling discourse for middle-class women, who could represent their afflicted subaltern overseas sisters as in need of their urgent assistance, while failing to argue for any change in their subordinate position. Reforms around indentured women were altruistic acts, and in the discourse of "rescue" these women could only be marked as "victims." The gender of the women campaigners allowed them—it was believed—to feel for supposedly miserable indentured women, but since they were anchored to their superior caste/class position by their impeccable morals, this sympathy was prevented from becoming identification. The result was that their attitude was invariably patronizing or censorious. However, the vast majority of indentured women did not, indeed could not, be integrated into the moral economy of the middle class. In many ways, they remained the "other," leaving the safety of their home and nation, its boundary, and its sanctity.

The troubled, victimized, sexually exploited, and vulnerable figure of the emigrant woman became both metaphor and common rhetorical device for the crisis that beset indenture. Narrow and casual connections were drawn between prostitution and indenture. At the same time, regardless of the conditions of labor, distinctions between consensual, exploitative, and forced migration were elided. The condescending upper-caste commentary on migrant women, many of them Dalit, not only denied women any agency, but also saw migration purely as exploitation rather than as possible opportunity, even if deriving from circumstances of oppression and deprivation. Even when the subaltern indentured woman was seen sympathetically, the progressive edge of the anti-indenture movement was considerably blunted by its compassionate conservatism. While exposing the exploitation and inhumanity inherent in the system of indenture, deep-seated anxieties around "sexual slavery" also arose, since it presented a moral crisis of unprecedented proportions. This led to slippery statistics and hazy definitions which suggested that the dangerous, disruptive sexuality of the indentured woman required scrutiny and control. She was both a citizen of the nation and a hindrance to citizenship because of her "inappropriate" conduct, an insider and an outsider, a part of "us" and the "other," an innocent victim and a guilty migrant. Stranded between belonging and un-belonging, and inferiorized as both, she was seen as in need of both protection and punishment.

Representations of the indentured woman in the Hindi print world, while differing from colonial perspectives and official documents, often presumed and produced reciprocal gendered limits to migration. There were certain assumptions in the arguments of both nationalists and colonialists, particularly with regard to the migration of single women, which also determined not only the questions that were asked but also the responses to them. This also revealed intersections between different geographical areas, local, and transregional social hierarchies, and the wider power structures within which gendered subjects operated. Narratives and experiences of women, however, particularly those that were single and Dalit, make emigration appear more complicated, contradictory, and ambiguous than is commonly seen. These "unhomely" mobile women did not offer any simple moral tales, but demonstrated complex and multidimensional realities: they constantly negotiated regions, nations, and borders, and defied easy either/or alternatives. Occupying a liminal, untidy, "intimate public" space, their mobility disturbed received ideas of identity and confounded the gendered politics of belonging.

Conclusion

The poem "An Untouchable's Complaint" ("*Achhut ki Shikayat*") by Hira Dom, published in the September 1914 issue of *Saraswati*,[1] has become a cause célèbre, with scholars hailing it as one of the first published Dalit writings in Hindi. Occupying centerstage in the Dalit Hindi literature of colonial India, it has been described as an "epoch-making event."[2] It is meant to have drawn on a "language of national republicanism" and wielded a "two-pronged critique against both the upper castes and their colonial rulers."[3] Yet, less than a year later, in August 1914, Mohini Chamarin, a Dalit woman, wrote a story, "Thieves of the Subordinated" ("*Chhot ke Chor*"), which appeared in the August 1915 volume of *Kanya Manoranjan* (Girls' Entertainment),[4] a Hindi magazine for young girls and women, promoted as the most affordable monthly periodical in India.[5] Probably one of the first stories in Hindi by a Dalit woman to get into print—in a region where the illiteracy rates of Chamar women were as high as 99.99 per cent[6]—this was indeed a remarkable feat. Mohini Chamarin and her story, however, have been lost in the pages of history. Not only was the Dalit print-public-sphere in colonial North India largely coded as male, even its later narratives have been overwhelmingly male-centric.

This fragment of history, a story in a Dalit woman's voice, unlike Dalit male writings of the time, is neither centrally a critique of caste injustice nor a plea for recognition. It is also distinct from the

[1] Hira Dom, "*Acchut ki Shikayat*," *Saraswati*, September 1914: 512–13.
[2] Narayan and Misra 2004: 16.
[3] Gajarawala 2013: 33. Also, Brueck 2014: 73–4.
[4] Mohini Chamarin, "*Chhot ke Chor*," *Kanya Manoranjan*, August 1915: 307–8.
[5] Nijhawan 2012: 117–31.
[6] *Census, 1891, NWP*: 262.

literature by upper-caste, middle-class women, which, as we have seen over the course of this book, predominantly focused on social reform, nationalism, male patriarchy, and middle-class domesticity. Mohini Chamarin's is a narrative about extreme poverty, livelihood struggle, abject labor, backbreaking work, and the arduous everyday life of a woman-headed household—a widowed low-caste woman bringing up three sons on her own by working day and night in the fields. It is also a fantasy in which the figure of the thief is a metaphor for overcoming hardships of the family, told in a light vein of irony. Not penned in Khari Boli, the principal language of prose, it is in Awadhi, with the flavor of a "voice from below" coalescing the everyday language and lives of Dalit women.

This fragment is, naturally, a rare exemplar, but it is possible to anthologize the gendered narratives of Dalits in other ways: through the voices of colonizers, upper-caste writings, reformist magazines, missionary pamphlets, cartoons, Dalit literature, and the private-public experiences of Dalits themselves. Threading this book throughout have been the varying interfaces between these circuitous worlds of print journalism and Dalit actions, and together they have woven a social history of gendered Dalit representations. Interrogating earlier histories of an unmarked, undifferentiated Dalit, this book has tried to gather various threads that go into the making of the gendered Dalit. By centering on Dalit women, its endeavor has been to recast the meanings of existing studies on caste reform and Dalit politics in colonial UP, and redraw the margins of Dalit histories both literally and metaphorically.

A substantial part of this book has grappled with the biopolitics of caste and its specific modes of signification in mainstream Hindi print-visual cultures. I have tried to show how figurations of Dalit womanhood in partisan didactic and caste manuals encoded normative prescriptions that promoted casteism. How gestures of gender subordination were built into caste relations. And how collaterally, the writings of reformers, even when framed by liberal sympathy, subtly reinvented caste power in new ways in early-twentieth-century North India. Seemingly contradictory images of the Chamar midwife and Shabari, docile and dangerous Dalit male bodies, and discussions on inter-caste marriages, conversion, and indentured women, while revealing strains within Hinduism and reform, have also indicated how Dalit sexualities were intricately involved in realignments of family, gender, caste, community, religion, and nation. Though there were shifts in the moral contours of colonizers, reformers, and nationalists with regard to Dalit representation, which often resulted in ideological and religious ferment, it was seldom accompanied with, or extended to, changes in social and economic structures. Moreover, individual actions by Dalit women, their intimate desires, and the interface between sex and the social often motivated a collusion and consensus between high-caste and Dalit male reformers around gender regulation. The book has underscored this caste politics of compassion and compliance, and the limits of caste reform of gender by reformers, nationalists, and caste radicals in UP.

At the same time, disjunctive modes of socialization and identity politics, when aggregated, rupture singular, linear histories, and stimulate different and imaginative ways of gendering Dalits. While disparate representations of Dalits embodied condemnation of them, or at best a selective sympathy, they also opened up the possibilities for languages of rights and the acknowledgment of Dalit desires. It was in these fluid, in-between spaces and cracks that gender-caste categories were negotiated. While my book has underlined encoded and embedded constraints, it has also sifted out anecdotes of resistance and enabling moments of gendered Dalit agency. On the one hand, culturally entrenched templates, printed scripts, and representational conventions constructed Dalit women as vamps or victims, and Dalit men as defiant or deferential, which personified allegories of anxiety and the perfunctory camouflaging of caste hierarchies. On the other, Dalit performative modes—assertions by Chamar midwives, representations of heroic Dalit women of 1857, articulations of Dalit manhood, religious conversions by Dalit women, reconfigurations of goddesses and songs practiced by low castes, Dalit women posing as single women to migrate—all these embodied dignity and the desire for a better life. One attempted to reinstate power and dominance, the other contested it.

Through showing and discussing dialogical counter-representations, and dissonant voices and actions, this book has thus also ventured to decode the concealed scripts of Dalit agency. Distancing herself from oft-assumed synonyms for agency, i.e. "free will" and "resistance," the anthropologist Laura Ahearn describes agency as "the socioculturally mediated capacity to act."[7] Dalit women's and men's agency was grounded in, and determined by, material processes and specific contexts. It was inscribed in their everyday discursive practices and prosaic arbitrations at workplaces, cultural spaces, public-political engagements, print narratives, domestic and home turfs, religious and ritual customs, individual actions, and intimate desires. While these fragmented acts may not be interpreted as active agentive re-alignments, as overtly political moves, or as fully legible protests, nonetheless they signaled everyday Dalit agencies embodied in the interstices of these performances. They enabled Dalits to enact their scripts, and at times disarm the dominant cultures of caste, gender, religion, and nation.

In sum, my hope is that this book has taken the field of Dalit Studies some distance in the direction of gender sensitivity and aware-ness of the separate, separable lives of Dalit women. It is often all too clear, and sometimes dismayingly so, that the literature and cultural representations of a region a hundred years earlier lend themselves to a clearer appreciation of continuities as well as change, regressions as well as improvements, from those times to ours. The expectation of change for the better over time is all-too-often belied. Radical changes in technology, the socio-materialities of quotidian life, and the macro-economies of the political can often disguise fundamental continuities in certain underlying patterns of thought, practice, and behavior at the level of individual and community. There is no dearth of scholarly analysis showing that despite considerable alterations in caste practices as well as the new and varied purposes for which caste has been de-ployed over the past three decades or so, the limpet-like hold of caste prejudice in large swathes of the Gangetic belt is no weaker. What has been less clear in the literature is the specific nature of the difficulties of those at the very bottom of this seemingly bottomless pit—Dalit women. If this book has managed to cast the glimmers of a torchlight on how such women have been represented while living, suffering, resisting, and carving out meanings for themselves against all the odds, it will have served at least some of the purposes for which it has been written.

[7] Ahearn 2010: 28–9.

Glossary

achhut	untouchable, a term with negative connotations
achhutoddhar	caste-Hindu organizations' programme to uplift untouchables
Adi Hindu	original inhabitant of India. A social movement led by Dalits emerged by this name in UP in the 1920s
Ahir	pastoral caste of North India, also called Yadav, traditionally associated with the milk trade
akhara	gymnasium or club for wrestling and physical culture
alha	a rural song-story narrative
Arya Samaj	Hindu reform movement founded in 1875
Bania	used for members of castes associated with shopkeeping, trade, and money-lending
begar	forced unpaid labor
bhajan	devotional song
bhakti	religious devotion emphasizing the adoration of personified Hindu deities
bhangan	female sweeper
Bhangi	sweeper, a degrading caste term for the Valmiki Dalit caste of UP
bhatiyarin	woman bard singer
brahmacharya	(male) celibacy and chastity
Brahmin	member of the highest Hindu caste in the *varna* scheme, with priestly traditions

Chamar	major Dalit caste of North India, sometimes associated with leatherwork
chamarin	woman of the Chamar caste
chaprasi	peon
chhua-chhut/chhut-chhat	pollution taboos
Churha	another name for the traditional sweeper caste
dai	traditional midwife, mostly a Chamar/Dalit
dasi	woman servant or slave
devadasi	temple dancing-girl
devi	goddess; lady
Dhanuk	a Dalit caste of UP, traditionally regarded as cotton carders
dharm	religion; moral order
Dhobi	washerman, a Dalit caste of UP
dhobin	washerwoman
dola-palki	closed litter-palanquin
Dom	a Dalit caste of UP, traditionally workers at cremation places and makers of baskets and ropes; branded by the British as a criminal tribe
Dusadh	a Dalit caste of UP, traditionally seen as a community of pig-keepers and watchmen
dwij	twice-born; pure-caste Hindu. Twice-born indicates a physical first birth and a second spiritual birth upon performance of the sacred thread ceremony
ekkawallah	coachman
fakir	ascetic; beggar
gali	abuse

ghat	landing or bathing place at a riverside, sometimes with religious significance
goonda	scoundrel; evil character
halwai	maker and seller of sweetmeats
Harijan	term coined by Gandhi for Dalits; literally meaning "child of God"
havan	oblation with fire
Holi	prominent Hindu festival of color held in spring
jajmani	a system of mutual obligations among castes in a village
Jamadar	jobber; labor contractor; head sweeper
jamadarin	female sweeper
janeu	sacred thread worn by *dwij*s or caste-Hindus
jati	basic unit of Hindu caste; a subcaste
kajli	a folksong genre, especially popular in eastern UP
Kahar	a Shudra, OBC caste of UP, traditionally a community of water-drawers and palanquin carriers
kaharin	woman of the water-drawer caste
Kaliyug	in Hindu mythology the fourth and most degenerate age of human history
Kalwar	a Shudra, OBC caste of UP, traditionally liquor distillers
Khatik	a Dalit caste of UP, traditionally seen as keepers of pigs and dealers in hides
Kori	a Dalit caste of UP, traditionally weavers
Kurmi	Hindu cultivator caste of the eastern Gangetic plain
kutni	vamp; pimp

lathi	wooden staff, usually made of bamboo
lavani	popular folksong-dance of Maharashtra
lotah	small round pot, usually of brass or copper
Mali	a Shudra, OBC caste of UP, traditionally gardener and flower seller
malin	woman gardener and flower seller
Mallah	a Shudra, OBC caste of UP, identified as boatmen
maniharin	woman bangle seller
maulvi	Muslim religious teacher
Mehtar	another name for the sweeper caste
mehtarani	woman sweeper
mela	fair; large gathering
mem	madam; used often for a European woman
mohalla	(urban) neighborhood, often defined on caste and community lines
Nai	a Shudra, OBC caste of UP, traditionally barbers
nain	woman of the barber caste
naukari	employment
nautanki	a type of folk drama in North India
nirgun	formless
padri	padre; Christian missionary and preacher
panchayat	a council, usually of community elders
pundit/pandit	person (usually Brahmin) with knowledge of the Hindu scriptures
Pasi	a Dalit caste of UP, traditionally seen as watchmen and toddy tappers; branded as a criminal tribe by the British
pativrata	the devoted and ideal Hindu wife
pir	local Muslim deity or Sufi saint

pisanharin	woman who grinds corn
purdah	veil; seclusion
puri	a small round cake of wheat flour fried in oil
pyau	place where drinking water is distributed
roti-beti	food and marriage ties
sangathan	organization; a political movement to unite all Hindus
sati	widow immolation; also the term for a chaste woman
seva	to serve
shakti	activated power and energy, usually associated with deities, especially goddesses
shastra	a body of knowledge and writings, usually of the Hindu scriptures
Shilpkar	listed as a Dalit caste, prominent in the hilly areas of UP
shuddhi	purification; Hindu movement to purify and convert untouchables and others to Hinduism
Shudra	lowest Hindu caste in the fourfold *varna* scheme; caste with laboring traditions
Sitala	goddess of smallpox
telin	woman of the oil-presser caste
thakur	landed proprietor; a person of position
Vaishya	third in the Hindu fourfold *varna* scheme, usually designating a commercial livelihood
vanshavali	lineage
virangana	brave woman
zamindar	landlord
zenana	upper-caste women's area or compartment

Bibliography

Agnes, Flavia. 2008. "The Bar Dancer and the Trafficked Migrant: Globalisation and Subaltern Existence." In *The Fleeing People of South Asia: Selections from Refugee Watch*, ed. Sibaji Pratim Basu. Delhi: Anthem: 355–66.

Agnihotri, Angan Lal. 1905. *Lodha Rajput Mimansa* (A Treatise on Lodha Rajputs). Bulandshahr.

Ahearn, Laura M. 2010. "Agency and Language." In *Handbook of Pragmatics*, eds Jef Verschueren, Jan-Ola Ostman, and Jurgen Japsers. Online Version: 28–40.

Ahmad, Imtiaz. 1971. "Caste Mobility Movements in North India." *IESHR*, 8 (2): 164–91.

Ahmed, Ali. 1980. *Plantation to Politics: Studies on Fiji Indians*. Suva: University of the South Pacific.

Alavi, Seema. 1995. *The Sepoys and the Company: Tradition and Transition in Northern India, 1770–1830*. Delhi: Oxford University Press.

Allison, W.L., ed. 1969. *One Hundred Years of Christian Work of the North India Mission of the Presbyterian Church, USA*. Mysore: Wesley Press.

Alter, James P. 1986. *In the Doab and Rohilkhand: North Indian Christianity 1815–1915*, rev. John Alter. Delhi: ISPCK.

Alter, Joseph S. 1992. *The Wrestler's Body: Identity and Ideology in North India*. Berkeley: University of California Press.

———. 2000. *Gandhi's Body: Sex, Diet and the Politics of Nationalism*. Philadelphia: University of Pennsylvania Press.

Amardeep. 2012. "The Making of the Dalit Print Culture in Uttar Pradesh 1913–1978." Jawaharlal Nehru University: PhD Thesis.

Ambedkar, B.R. 1987 (1936). *Annihilation of Caste*. Bangalore: Dalit Sahitya Academy.

Amin, Shahid. 1984. *Sugarcane and Sugar in Gorakhpur: An Inquiry into Peasant Production for Capitalist Enterprise in Colonial India*. Delhi: Oxford University Press.

———. 2005a. *A Concise Encyclopedia of North Indian Peasant Life. Compilation from the Writings of William Crooke, J.R. Reid, and G.A. Grierson*. Delhi: Manohar.

————. 2005b. "Representing the Musalman: Then and Now, Now and Then." In *Subaltern Studies XII: Muslims, Dalits, and the Fabrications of History*, eds Shail Mayaram, M.S.S. Pandian, and Ajay Skaria. Ranikhet: Permanent Black: 1–35.

Anandhi, S. 1998. "Reproductive Bodies and Regulated Sexuality: Birth Control Debates in Early Twentieth Century Tamilnadu." In *A Question of Silence? The Sexual Economies of Modern India*, eds Mary E. John and Janaki Nair. Delhi: Kali: 139–66.

————. 1991. "Women's Question in the Dravidian Movement *c.* 1925–1948." *Social Scientist*, 19 (5–6), May–June: 24–41.

————, J. Jeyaranjan, and Rajan Krishnan. 2002. "Work, Caste and Competing Masculinities: Notes from a Tamil Village." *EPW*, XXXVII (43): 4397–406.

Anderson, Benedict. 1991 (1983). *Imagined Communities: Reflections on the Origin and Spread of Nationalism*. London: Verso.

Andrews, C.F. 1937. *India and the Pacific*. London: George Allen and Unwin.

————, and W.W. Pearson. 1916. *Report on Indentured Labour in Fiji: An Independent Enquiry*. Calcutta: Star Printing.

Andrews, Mr. 1918. *Fiji Mein Bhartiya Mazdoor* (Indian Workers in Fiji). Hathras: Bharatbandhu Karyalaya.

Andrijasevic, Rutvica. 2003. "The Difference Borders Make: (Il)Legality, Migration and Trafficking in Italy among Eastern European Women in Prostitution." In *Uprootings/Regroundings: Questions of Home and Migration*, eds Sara Ahmed, Claudia Castaneda, Anne-Marie Fortier, and Mimi Sheller. Oxford: Berg: 251–70.

Annual Report of the CMS for the Year 1901–2. 1902. London: CMS.

Annual Report of the CMS for the Year 1936–7. 1937. London: CMS.

Annual Report of the Meerut Mission of the CMS. 1864. Meerut: CMS.

"Anu," Ansuya. 1993. *Jhalkari Bai*. Delhi: Indian Government Publications.

Appadurai, Arjun, Frank J. Korom, and Margaret A. Mills, eds. 1991. *Gender, Genre and Power in South Asian Expressive Traditions*. Delhi: Motilal Banarsidass.

Appleby, Joyce, Lynn Hunt, and Margaret Jacob. 1994. *Telling the Truth about History*. New York: W.W. Norton.

Armstrong, D. 1983. *Political Anatomy of the Body: Medical Knowledge in Britain in the Twentieth Century*. Cambridge: Cambridge University Press.

Arnold, David. 1993. *Colonizing the Body: State Medicine and Epidemic Disease in Nineteenth-Century India*. Berkeley: University of California Press.

Arondekar, Anjali. 2009. *For the Record: On Sexuality and the Colonial Archive in India*. Durham: Duke University Press.

Baak, P.E. 1999. "About Enslaved Ex-Slaves, Uncaptured Contract Coolies and Unfreed Freemen." *Modern Asian Studies*, 33 (1): 121–57.

Babb, Lawrence A. 1975. *The Divine Hierarchy: Popular Hinduism in Central India*. New York: Columbia University Press.

Badaun: A Gazetteer, Vol. XV of District Gazetteers of UP. 1907. (By H.R. Nevill.) Allahabad: Government Press.

Bahadur, Gaiutra. 2013. *Coolie Woman: The Odyssey of Indenture*. London: Hurst.

Baijnath, Rai Bahadur Lala. 1905 (2nd edn). *Hinduism: Ancient and Modern*. Meerut: Vaishya Hitkari Office.

Bains, Pyara Singh. 1996. *Guru Ravidas Ji Ki Jeevni* (Biography of Ravidas). Dehradun: Ankan.

Bais, Bhagvan Vats Singh. 1931. *Bais Kshatriyatihas* (History of Bais Kshatriyas). Lucknow.

Bakhle, Janaki. 2005. *Two Men and Music: Nationalism in the Making of an Indian Classical Tradition*. Ranikhet: Permanent Black.

Bakhsidas. 1970 (1911). *Ravidas Ramayan*, ed. Ravya Ram Misra Syam. Mathura: Kasi Press.

Bakhtin, Mikhail. 1981. *The Dialogic Imagination*, trans. Caryl Emerson and Michael Holquist. Austin: University of Texas Press.

Baldevsingh. 1924. *Ahir Jati Mein 31 Rog* (31 Diseases of the Ahir Caste). Shikohabad.

Balfour, Margaret I., and Ruth Young. 1929. *The Work of Medical Women in India*. London: H. Milford.

Banaras: A Gazetteer, Vol. XXVI of District Gazetteers of UP. 1909. (By H.R. Nevill.) Allahabad: Government Press.

Bandhusamaj. 1927. *Hinduon ki Tez Talwar* (Sharp Sword of Hindus). Kanpur.

Bandyopadhyay, Sekhar. 1997. *Caste, Protest and Identity in Colonial Bengal: The Namasudras of Bengal, 1872–1947*. Surrey: Curzon.

———. 2004. *Caste, Culture and Hegemony: Social Dominance in Colonial Bengal*. Delhi: Sage.

Banerjee, Sikata. 2005. *Make Me a Man: Masculinity, Hinduism and Nationalism in India*. Albany: SUNY Press.

Banerjee, Sumanta. 1989. *The Parlour and the Streets: Elite and Popular Culture in Nineteenth Century Calcutta.* Calcutta: Seagull.

Banerjee, Swapna M. 2004. *Men, Women and Domestics: Articulating Middle-class Identity in Colonial Bengal.* Delhi: Oxford University Press.

Banerjee-Dube, Ishita, ed. 2010. *Caste in History.* Delhi: Oxford University Press.

Banerji, Chitrita. 2006. *Feeding the Gods: Memories of Food and Culture in Bengal.* Calcutta: Seagull.

Bankelal, Lala. 1909. *Kanyamanoranjan* (Entertainment for Girls). Morada-bad: Laxminarayan Press.

Bannerji, Himani. 2001. *Inventing Subjects: Studies in Hegemony, Patriarchy, and Colonialism.* Delhi: Tulika.

Banprasthi, Premanand. 1927. *Musalmani Gorakh Dhandha* (Fraud of Muslims). Awadh.

Banshidhar. 1939 (3rd edn). *Kshatriya Shilpkar Darpan* (Mirror of Kshatriya Shilpkars). Aligarh.

Barabanki: A Gazetteer, Vol. XLVIII of District Gazetteers of UP. 1904. (By H.R. Nevill.) Allahabad: Government Press.

Barnes, R., and J.B. Eicher, eds. 1992. *Dress and Gender: Making and Meaning.* Oxford: Berg.

Basham, Ardythe. 1980. *Untouchable Soldiers: The Mahars and the Mazhbis,* ed. Bhagwan Das. Bangalore: Ambedkar Sahitya Prakashan.

Basu, Monmayee. 2001. *Marriage and Hindu Law: Sacrament to Contract.* Delhi: Oxford University Press.

Basu, Raj Sekhar. 2011. *Nandanar's Children: The Paraiyans' Tryst with Destiny, Tamil Nadu 1850–1956.* Delhi: Sage.

Bates, Crispin, and Marina Carter. 1993. "Tribal and Indentured Migrants in Colonial India: Modes of Recruitment and Forms of Incorporation." In *Dalit Movements and the Meanings of Labour in India,* ed. Peter Robb. Delhi: Oxford University Press: 159–85.

Bauman, Chad M. 2008. *Christian Identity and Dalit Religion in Hindu India, 1868–1947.* Michigan: Wm. B. Eerdmans Publishing.

Bavin, Cyril. 1914. "The Indian in Fiji." In *A Century in the Pacific,* ed. James Colwell. London: Charles H. Kelly: 175–98.

Bayly, C.A. 1983. *Rulers, Townsmen and Bazaars: North Indian Society in the Age of British Expansion, 1770–1870.* Cambridge: Cambridge University Press.

———. 1988. *Indian Society and the Making of the British Empire.* Cambridge: Cambridge University Press.

————. 1986. "The Origins of Swadeshi (Home Industry): Cloth and Indian Society, 1700–1930." In *The Social Life of Things: Commodities in Cultural Perspective*, ed. Arjun Appadurai. Cambridge: Cambridge University Press: 285–322.

————. 1996. *Empire and Information: Intelligence Gathering and Social Communication in India, 1780–1870.* Cambridge: Cambridge University Press.

Bayly, Susan. 1999. *Caste, Society and Politics in India from the Eighteenth Century to the Modern Age.* Cambridge: Cambridge University Press.

Beall, Jo. 1990. "Women under Indenture in Colonial Natal, 1860–1911." In *South Asian Overseas, Migration and Ethnicity,* eds C. Clarke, C. Peach, and S. Vertovec. Cambridge: Cambridge University Press: 57–75.

Bean, Susan. 1989. "Gandhi and Khadi, the Fabric of Indian Independence." In *Cloth and Human Experience*, eds Annette B. Weiner and Jane Schneider. Washington: Smithsonian Institution Press: 355–76.

Bellwinkel-Schempp, Maren. 2006. "Social Practice of Bhakti in the Siv Narayan *Sampradaya.*" In *Bhakti in Current Research, 2001–2003,* ed. Monika Horstmann. Delhi: Manohar: 15–32.

————. 2007. "From Bhakti to Buddhism: Ravidas and Ambedkar." *EPW,* XLII (23): 2177–83.

Bennett, Michael, and Vanessa D. Dickerson. 2000. *Recovering the Black Female Body: Self-Representation by African American Women.* New Brunswick: Rutgers University Press.

Bhabha, Homi K. 1994. *The Location of Culture.* London: Routledge.

Bhadeva. 1967. "Varshageet *Kajli* ka Kal" (Songs of Rain during *Kajli*). *Aj Saptahik Visheshank*, August 26: 12.

Bhadra, Gautam. 1985. "Four Rebels of Eighteen-Fifty-Seven." In *Subaltern Studies IV: Writings on South Asian History and Society*, ed. Ranajit Guha. Delhi: Oxford University Press: 229–75.

Bharati, Vizia. 1995. "Hindu Epics: Portrayal of Dalit Women." In *Dalit Women in India: Issues and Perspectives,* ed. P.G. Jogdand. Pune: Gyan Publishing: 93–104.

Bharti, Anita. 2013. *Samkaleen Narivad aur Dalit Stri ka Pratirodh* (Contemporary Feminism and the Resistance of Dalit Women). Delhi: Swaraj Prakashan.

Bharti, Kanwal. 2006. *"1857 ka Bahujan Drishtikon." Vartman Sahitya,* 23, November–December: 79–83.

————. 2011. *Swami Achhutanandji "Harihar" aur Hindi Navjagran* (Achhutanand and Hindi Renaissance). Delhi: Swaraj Prakashan.

Bhartiya Hindu Shuddhi Sabha ka Sankshipt Itihaas tatha Vivran, 1923–1950
(Brief History and Description of Bhartiya Hindu Shuddhi Sabha).
1951. Delhi.

Bhattacharya, Shahana. 2013. "Rotting Hides and Runaway Labour:
Labour Control and Workers' Resistance in the Indian Leather Industry
c. 1860–1960." In *Working Lives and Worker Militancy: The Politics of
Labour in Colonial India,* ed. Ravi Ahuja. Delhi: Tulika: 47–96.

Bhave, Sumitra. 1988. *Pan on Fire: Eight Dalit Women Tell Their Story.* Delhi:
Indian Social Institute.

Blackburn, Stuart. 2003. *Print, Folklore, and Nationalism in Colonial South
India.* Delhi: Permanent Black.

———, and A.K. Ramanujan, eds. 1986. *Another Harmony: New Essays on
the Folklore of India.* Berkeley: University of California Press.

Blunt, E.A.H. 1931. *The Caste System of Northern India: With Special
Reference to UP.* London: Oxford University Press.

Boltanski, Luc. 1995. *Distant Suffering: Morality, Media and Politics,* trans.
Graham Burchell. Cambridge: Cambridge University Press.

Borst, Charlotte G. 1995. *Catching Babies: The Professionalization of Childbirth, 1870–1920.* Cambridge: Harvard University Press.

Bradbury, Rev. James. 1884. *India: Its Condition, Religion and Missions.*
London: John Shaw.

Brahmanand. 1934. *Khatre ka Danka: Ek Karor Harijan Musalman* (Drum
of Danger. One Crore Harijans Converted into Muhammadanism. A
Warning to Hindus to Take Care of the Untouchables who Should Not
be Allowed to be Converted to Islam). Banaras: Lakshmi Press.

Breman, Jan. 1989. *Taming the Coolie Beast: Plantation Society and the Colonial Order in Southeast Asia.* Delhi: Oxford University Press.

Briggs, Geo W. 1920. *The Chamars.* Calcutta: Association Press.

Brooks, Daphne A. 2006. *Bodies in Dissent: Spectacular Performances of Race
and Freedom, 1850–1910.* Durham: Duke University Press.

Brouwer, Ruth Compton. 1990. *New Women for God: Canadian Presbyterian
Women and India Missions, 1876–1914.* Toronto: University of Toronto
Press.

Brown, Wendy. 1995. *States of Injury: Power and Freedom in Late Modernity.*
Princeton: Princeton University Press.

———. 2006. *Regulating Aversion: Tolerance in the Age of Identity and Empire.*
Princeton: Princeton University Press.

Brueck, Laura R. 2014. *Writing Resistance: The Rhetorical Imagination of
Hindi Dalit Literature.* New York: Columbia University Press.

Burton, Antoinette. 1994. *Burdens of History: British Feminists, Indian Women and Imperial Culture, 1865–1915.* Chapel Hill: University of North Carolina Press.

———. 1998. "States of Injury: Josephine Butler on Slavery, Citizenship, and the Boer War." *Social Politics,* 5 (3), Fall: 338–61.

———. 2003. *Dwelling in the Archive: Women Writing House, Home, and History in Late-colonial India.* New York: Oxford University Press.

Burton, J.W. 1910. *Fiji of Today.* London: C.H. Kelly.

Callewaert, Winand M. 2000. *The Hagiographies of Anantadas: The Bhakti Poets of North India.* Surrey: Curzon.

———, and Peter G. Friedlander. 1992. *The Life and Works of Raidas.* Delhi: Manohar.

Campbell, Mary J. 1918. *The Power House at Pathankot: What Some Girls of India Wrought by Prayer.* Lucknow: Women's Christian Temperance Union of India.

Campkin, Ben, and Rosie Cox, 2007. "Introduction: Materialities and Metaphors of Dirt and Cleanliness." In *Dirt: New Geographies of Cleanliness and Contamination,* ed. Ben Campkin and Rosie Cox. London: I.B. Tauris: 1–10.

Cape, C. Phillips. 1924. *Prisoners Released: The Redemption of a Criminal Tribe.* London: Wesleyan Methodist Missionary Society.

Carroll, Lucy. 1977. "Caste, Community and Caste(s) Association: A Note on the Organisation of the Kayastha Conference and the Definition of a Kayastha Community." *Contribution to Asian Studies,* 10, 1977: 3–24.

———. 1978. "Colonial Perceptions of Indian Society and the Emergence of Caste(s) Associations." *JAS,* 37 (2), February: 233–50.

Carson, James P. 2010. *Populism, Gender and Sympathy in the Romantic Novel.* New York: Palgrave.

Carstairs, G.M. 1983. *Death of a Witch: A Village in North India 1950–1981.* London: Hutchinson.

Carter, Marina. 1994. *Lakshmi's Legacy: The Testimonies of Indian Women in 19ᵗʰ Century Mauritius.* Mauritius: Editions de l'Ocean Indien.

———. 1995. *Servants, Sardars and Settlers: Indians in Mauritius, 1834–74.* Delhi: Oxford University Press.

———. 1996. *Voices from Indenture: Experiences of Indian Migrants in the British Empire.* London: Leicester University Press.

Cawnpore: A Gazetteer, Vol. XIX of District Gazetteers of UP. 1909. (By H.R. Nevill.) Allahabad: Government Press.

Census of India, 1891, NWP, Vol. IX, Part XVI, Report. 1894. Allahabad: Government Press.

Census of India, 1901, NWP, Vol. XVI, Part I, Report. 1902. (By R. Burn.) Allahabad: Government Press.

Census of India, 1911, UP, Vol. XV, Part I, Report. 1912. (By E.A.H. Blunt.) Allahabad: Government Press.

Census of India, 1921, UP, Vol. XVI, Part I, Report. 1923. (By E.H.H. Edye.) Allahabad: Government Press.

Census of India, 1931, UP, Vol. XVIII, Part I, Report. 1933. (By A.C. Turner.) Allahabad: Printing and Stationery.

Census of India, 1931, UP, Vol. XVIII, Part II, Imperial and Provincial Tables. 1933. (By A.C. Turner.) Allahabad: Printing and Stationery.

Certeau, Michel de. 1984. *The Practice of Everyday Life*, trans. Steven F. Rendall. Berkeley: University of California Press.

Chakraborty, Chandrima. 2011. *Masculinity, Asceticism, Hinduism: Past and Present Imaginings in India*. Ranikhet: Permanent Black.

Chakravarti, Uma. 1989. "Whatever Happened to the Vedic *Dasi*?: Orientalism, Nationalism, and a Script for the Past." In *Recasting Women: Essays in Colonial History*, eds Kumkum Sangari and Sudesh Vaid. Delhi: Kali: 27–87.

———. 2003. *Gendering Caste through a Feminist Lens*. Calcutta: Stree.

———. 2004. "Women, Men and Beasts: The *Jatakas* as Popular Tradition." In *Subordinate and Marginal Groups in Early India*, ed. Aloka Parasher-Sen. Delhi: Oxford University Press: 210–42.

Chakravorty, Pallabi. 2008. *Bells of Change: Kathak Dance, Women and Modernity in India*. Calcutta: Seagull.

Chand, Tara. 1967. *History of Freedom Movement in India, Vol. II*. Delhi: Government of India.

Chandra Lila Sadhuni ka Vritant (Biographical Account of Chandra Lila, a Low-caste Female Convert). 1910 (2nd edn). Allahabad: Christian Literature Society for India.

Chandra, Kanchan. 2004. *Why Ethnic Parties Succeed: Patronage and Ethnic Head Counts in India*. Cambridge: Cambridge University Press.

Chandra, Sudhir. 1998. *Enslaved Daughters: Colonialism, Law and Women's Rights*. Delhi: Oxford University Press.

Chandrikaprasad. 1917. *Hinduon ke Sath Vishwasghat* (Treachery with the Hindus). Awadh.

Charitra Sudhar (Character Improvement). 1910. Allahabad: Christian Literature Society for India.

Chartier, Roger. 1989. *The Cultural Uses of Print: Power and the Uses of Print in Early Modern Europe*. Princeton: Princeton University Press.

Chatterjee, Indrani. 1999. *Gender, Slavery and Law in Colonial India*. Delhi: Oxford University Press.

Chatterjee, Partha. 1994. *The Nation and Its Fragments: Colonial and Postcolonial Histories*. Delhi: Oxford University Press.

Chatursen, Acharya. 1930. *Dharm ke Naam Par* (In the Name of Religion). Allahabad.

Chaturvedi, Banarsidas. 1981. *Nabbe Varsh* (Ninety Years). Delhi: National Publishing House.

———. 1993. *Samay ke Darpan Mein* (In the Mirror of Time). Delhi: Aakashwani.

Chaturvedi, J.P. 1985. *Fiji Mein Pravasi Bhartiye* (Overseas Indians in Fiji). Delhi: Bhartiya Sanskritik Sambandhi Parishad.

Chaturvedi, Jagpati. 1946 (2nd edn). *Humari Parivarik Vyavastha* (Our Familial Organization). Prayag: Matri Bhasha Mandir.

Chaturvedi, S.C. 1947. *Rural Wages in UP (A Study of the Material Collected During the Seventh Quinquennial Inquiry into Rural Wages, Conducted in December, 1944)*. Allahabad: Government of UP.

Chaudhuri, S.B. 1957. *Civil Rebellion in the Indian Mutiny*. Calcutta: World Press.

Chawla, Janet, ed. 2006. *Birth and Birthgivers: The Power Behind the Shame*. Delhi: Har-Anand.

Chitgopekar, Nilima, ed. 2002. *Invoking Goddesses: Gender Politics in Indian Religion*. Delhi: Shakti.

Chouliaraki, Lilie. 2006. *The Spectatorship of Suffering*. London: Sage.

Chopra, Radhika, Caroline Osella, and Filippo Osella, eds. 2004. *South Asian Masculinities: Context of Change, Sites of Continuity*. Delhi: Women Unlimited.

Chowdhry, Prem. 2007. *Contentious Marriages, Eloping Couples: Gender, Caste and Patriarchy in Northern India*. Delhi: Oxford University Press.

Clarke, Sathianathan. 1998. *Dalits and Christianity: Subaltern Religion and Liberation Theology in India*. Delhi: Oxford University Press.

Clayton, A.C. 1911. *Preachers in Print: An Outline of the Work of the Christian Literary Society for India*. London: Christian Literary Society.

CMS. 1926. *The Mass Movement in the United Provinces: A Survey and Statement of Needs*. Kottayam: CMS Press.

Cohen, Stephen P. 1969. "The Untouchable Soldier: Caste, Politics and the Indian Army." *JAS*, 28 (3): 453–68.

Cohn, Bernard S. 1987. *An Anthropologist among the Historians and Other Essays*. Delhi: Oxford University Press.

———. 1989. "Cloth, Clothes and Colonialism: India in the Nineteenth Century." In *Cloth and Human Experience,* eds Annette B. Weiner and Jane Schneider. Washington: Smithsonian Institution Press: 106–62.

Collin, Marcus. 2003. *Modern Love: An Intimate History of Men and Women in Twentieth-Century Britain*. London: Atlantic Books.

Collins, Patricia Hill. 2000 (2nd rev. edn). *Black Feminist Thought: Knowledge, Consciousness and the Politics of Empowerment*. New York: Routledge.

———. 2004. *Black Sexual Politics: African Americans, Gender, and the New Racism*. New York: Routledge.

Comaroff, John L., and Jean Comaroff. 1997. *Of Revelation and Revolution: Christianity, Colonialism, and Consciousness in South Africa*. Chicago: University of Chicago Press.

Comins, D.W.D. 1892. *Note on the Abolition of Return Passages to East Indian Immigrants from the Colonies of Trinidad and Tobago*. Calcutta: Bengal Secretariat.

Conference on Urdu and Hindi Christian Literature held at Allahabad, 24–25 February 1875. 1875. Madras: Christian Vernacular Education Society.

Connell, R.W. 1992. "A Very Straight Gay: Masculinity, Homosexual Experience, and the Dynamics of Gender." *American Sociological Review*, 57, December: 735–51.

———. 1995. *Masculinities*. Berkeley: University of California Press.

Constable, Philip. 2001. "The Marginalization of a Dalit Martial Race in Late Nineteenth-and Early Twentieth-Century Western India." *JAS*, 60 (2), May: 439–78.

Copley, Antony. 1997. *Religions in Conflict: Ideology, Cultural Contact and Conversion in Late-colonial India*. Delhi: Oxford University Press.

Crooke, W. 1896a (2nd edn). *The Popular Religion and Folklore of Northern India,* vols I and II. Westminster: Archibald Constable.

———. 1896b. *The Tribes and Castes of the North-Western Provinces and Oudh,* vols I to IV. Calcutta: Government Printing.

———. 1975 (1897). *The North-Western Provinces of India: Their History, Ethnology and Administration*. Delhi: Cosmo.

Cvetkovich, Ann. 2003. *An Archive of Feelings: Trauma, Sexuality, and Lesbian Public Cultures*. Durham: Duke University Press.

Daniel, E. Valentine, Henry Bernstein, and Tom Brass, eds. 1992. *Plantations, Proletarians and Peasants in Colonial Asia*. USA: Frank Cass.

Das, Bhagwan, ed. 1969. *Thus Spoke Ambedkar, Vol. II.* Jullundur: Bheem Patrika Publications.

Das, Bhikari. 1914. *Kayastha Varna Nirnaya* (Decisions of the Kayastha Caste). Etawah.

Das, Sisir Kumar. 1991. *A History of Indian Literature, Vol. III, 1800–1910: Western Impact, Indian Response.* Delhi: Sahitya Akademi.

Das, Veena, A. Kleinman, M. Ramphele, M. Lock, and P. Reynolds, eds. 2001. *Remaking a World: Violence, Social Suffering and Recovery.* Berkeley: University of California Press.

Dasgupta, Rohit K., and K. Moti Gokulsing. 2014. *Masculinity and Its Challenges in India: Essays on Changing Perceptions.* North Carolina: McFarland.

Davis-Floyd, Robbie, and Carolyn F. Sargent, eds. 1997. *Childbirth and Authoritative Knowledge: Cross-Cultural Perspectives.* Berkeley: University of California Press.

De, Rohit. 2010. "The Two Husbands of Vera Tiscenko: Apostasy, Conversion, and Divorce in Late-colonial India." *Law and History Review,* 28 (4): 1011–41.

Dehejia, Vidya, ed. 1997. *Representing the Body: Gender Issues in Indian Art.* Delhi: Kali.

———. 1999. *Devi, the Great Goddess: Female Divinity in South Asian Art.* Washington: Arthur M. Sackler Gallery.

Deming, Wilbur S. 1928. *Ramdas and the Ramdasis.* Calcutta: Association Press.

Derrida, Jacques. 1993. *Memoirs of the Blind: The Self-Portrait and Other Ruins,* trans. Pascale-Anne Brault and Michael Naas. Chicago: University of Chicago Press.

———. 1995. *Archive Fever: A Freudian Impression,* trans. Eric Prenowitz. Chicago: University of Chicago Press.

Deshpande, Anirudh. 1996. "Hopes and Disillusionment: Recruitment, Demobilisation and the Emergence of Discontent in the Indian Armed Forces after the Second World War." *IESHR,* 33 (2): 175–207.

Deshraj, Thakur. 1934. *Jat Itihaas* (History of Jats). Agra.

Devi, Devta aur Murtipuja (Goddesses, Gods and Idol Worship). 1923 (2nd edn). Allahabad: NICTBS.

Devi, Manvrata. 1948 (12th edn). *Nari Dharm Shiksha* (Teachings on Women's Duty). Banaras: Kashi Pustak Bhandar.

Devi, Rukmini. 1919. *Mem aur Saheb* (Madam and Sir). Banaras: Durga Prasad.

Devi, Yashoda. 1910. *Nari Niti Shiksha* (Teachings on Ethics for Women). Allahabad: Devi Pustakalaya.

———. 1925. *Kanya Kartavya* (Duties of Girls). Allahabad: Devi Pustakalaya.

Dimock, Jr., Edward C. "A Theology of the Repulsive: The Myth of the Goddess Sitala." In *The Divine Consort: Radha and the Goddesses of India*, eds John Stratton Hawley and Donna Marie Wulff. Berkeley: University of California Press: 184–203.

Dinkar, D.C. 1990 (2nd edn). *Swatantrata Sangram mein Achhuton ka Yogdan* (Contribution of Untouchables in Freedom Struggle). Lucknow: Triveni Press.

Dirks, Nicholas B. 1987. *The Hollow Crown: Ethnohistory of an Indian Kingdom*. Cambridge: Cambridge University Press.

———. 2001. *Castes of Mind: Colonialism and the Making of Modern India*. Princeton: Princeton University Press.

Disodiya, Rajni. "*Virangana Jhansi ki Jhalkaribai*." *Apeksha*, October–December 2004: 89.

Doniger, Wendy, trans. 1991. *The Laws of Manu*. Delhi: Penguin.

Dozema, J. 2001. "Ouch! Western Feminists' 'Wounded Attachments' to the "Third World Prostitute'." *Feminist Review*, 67: 16–38.

Dube, Saurabh. 1998. *Untouchable Pasts: Religion, Identity and Power among a Central Indian Community, 1780–1950*. Albany: SUNY Press.

———. 2004. "Colonial Registers of a Vernacular Christianity: Conversion to Translation." *EPW*, XXXIX (2): 161–71.

Dube, Sukhnandan Prasad. 1933. *Chhua-chhut ka Bhoot arthat Hinduon ki Dasha* (The Ghost of Pollution Taboos Meaning the State of Hindus). Lucknow: Awasthi Pustakalaya.

Duden, Barbara. 1993. *Disembodying Women: Perspectives on Pregnancy and the Unborn*. Cambridge: Harvard University Press.

Dudink, Stefan, Karen Hagemann, and John Tosh, eds. 2004. *Masculinities in Politics and War: Gendering Modern History*. New York: Manchester University Press.

Dwivedi, Manan. 1924 (3rd edn). *Humara Bhishan Haas* (Our Cataclysmic Decline). Kanpur.

Dyer, Richard. 1997. *White*. New York: Routledge.

Eagleton, Terry. 1992. *Ideology*. London: Verso.

Eaton, Richard M. 1978. *Sufis of Bijapur 1300–1700: Social Roles of Sufis in Medieval India*. Princeton: Princeton University Press.

———. 1993. *The Rise of Islam and the Bengal Frontier, 1204–1760*. Berkeley: University of California Press.

Ehrenreich, Barbara, and Deirdre English. 1973. *Witches, Midwives and Nurses: A History of Women Healers.* New York: Feminist Press.

Eisenstein, Elizabeth. 1979. *The Printing Press as an Agent of Change: Communications and Cultural Transformations in Early-Modern Europe,* 2 vols. Cambridge: Cambridge University Press.

Elliot, Bruce S., David A. Gerber, and Suzanne M. Shinke, eds. 2006. *Letter Across Borders: The Epistolary Practices of International Migrants.* New York: Palgrave.

Emmer, P.C. 1985. "The Great Escape: The Migration of Female Indentured Servants from British India to Surinam 1873–1916." In *Abolition and its Aftermath: The Historical Context 1790–1916,* ed. D. Richardson. London: Frank Cass: 245–66.

———. 1986. "The Meek Hindu: The Recruitment of Indian Indenture Labourers for Service Overseas, 1870–1916." In *Colonialism and Migration: Indenture Labour Before and After Slavery,* ed. P.C. Emmer. Dordrecht: Springer: 187–208.

Engels, Dagmar. 1996. *Beyond Purdah? Women in Bengal 1890–1939.* Delhi: Oxford University Press.

Erndl, Kathleen M. 1991. "The Mutilation of Surpanakha." In *Many Ramayans: The Diversity of a Narrative Tradition in South Asia,* ed. Paula Richman. Berkeley: University of California Press: 67–87.

Farrukhabad: A Gazetteer, Vol. IX of District Gazetteers of UP. 1911. (By E.R. Neave.) Allahabad: Government Press.

Faruqee, Ashrufa. 1996. "Conceiving the Coolie Woman: Indentured Labour, Indian Women and Colonial Discourse." *South Asia Research,* 16 (1): 61–76.

Fernandes, Walter. 1994. *Caste and Conversion Movements: Religion and Human Rights.* Delhi: Indian Social Institute.

Ferrari, Fabrizio M. 2007. "'Love Me Two Times.' From Smallpox to AIDS: Contagion and Possession in the Cult of Sitala." *Religions of South Asia,* 1 (1): 81–106.

———. 2010. "Old Rituals for New Threats: The Post-Smallpox Career of Sitala, the Cold Mother of Bengal." In *Ritual Matters: Dynamic Dimensions in Practice,* eds C. Brosius and U. Husken. Delhi: Routledge: 144–71.

———. 2014. *Religion, Devotion and Medicine in North India: The Healing Power of Sitala.* UK: Bloomsbury.

Final Settlement Report on the Bulandshahr District. 1919. (By E.A. Phelps.) Allahabad: Government Press.

Flemming, Leslie A. 1992. "A New Humanity: American Missionaries' Ideals for Indian Women in North India, 1870–1930." In *Western Women and Imperialism*, eds N. Chauduri and M. Strobel. Bloomington: Indiana University Press: 191–206.

Flueckiger, Joyce Burkhalter. 1996. *Gender and Genre in the Folklore of Middle India*. Ithaca: Cornell University Press.

Forbes, Geraldine H. 1986. "In Search of the 'Pure Heathen': Missionary Women in Nineteenth Century India." *EPW,* XXI (17): WS2-8.

———. 1996. *Women in Modern India*. Cambridge: Cambridge University Press.

———. 2005. *Women in Colonial India: Essays on Politics, Medicine, and Historiography*. Delhi: DC Publishers.

Forbes-Mitchell, William. 1893. *Reminiscences of the Great Mutiny 1857–59: Including the Relief, Siege, and Capture of Lucknow, and the Campaigns in Rohilcund and Oude*. London: Macmillan.

Forrester, Duncan B. 1979. *Caste and Christianity: Attitudes and Policies on Caste of Anglo-Saxon Protestant Missions in India*. Surrey: Curzon.

Foucault, Michel. 1977. *Discipline and Punish: The Birth of the Prison*, trans. A. Sheridon. New York: Pantheon.

———. 1978. *The History of Sexuality: Vol. 1*, trans. Robert Hurley. New York: Vintage.

Franco, Fernando, Jyotsna Macwan, and Suguna Ramanathan. 2000. *The Silken Swing: The Cultural Universe of Dalit Women*. Calcutta: Stree.

Frankenberg, Ruth. 1993. *White Women, Race Matters: The Social Construction of Whiteness*. Minneapolis: University of Minnesota Press.

Freitag, Sandria B. 1989. *Collective Action and Community: Public Arenas and the Emergence of Communalism in North India*. Berkeley: University of California Press.

———. 1991. "Crime in the Social Order of Colonial North India." *MAS*, 25 (2): 227–61.

Friedlander, Peter. 1996. "The Struggle for Salvation in the Hagiographies of Ravidas." In *Myth and Myth Making*, ed. Julia Leslie. Surrey: Curzon: 106–23.

Friedman, Sara L. 2006. *Intimate Politics: Marriage, the Market, and State Power in Southeastern China*. Cambridge: Harvard University Press.

Fuller, C.J. 1992. *The Camphor Flame: Popular Hinduism and Society in India*. Princeton: Princeton University Press.

Gaines, Jane, and Charlotte Herzog, eds. 1990. *Fabrications: Costume and the Female Body*. New York: Routledge.

Gajpuri, Mannan Dwivedi. 1917. *Ramlal: Gramin Jivan Ka Ek Samajik Upanyas* (Ramlal: A Social Novel on Rural Life). Prayag: Indian Press.

Gajarawala, Toral Jatin. 2013. *Untouchable Fictions: Literary Realism and the Crisis of Caste*. New York: Fordham University Press.

Galanter, Marc. 1997. *Law and Society in Modern India*. Delhi: Oxford University Press.

Ganga ka Vritant (The Story of the Ganges). 1905. Allahabad: NICTBS.

Gangaram. 1935 (2nd edn). *Mali Jati Nirnaya* (Decisions of the Mali Caste). Jaunpur.

Ganguli, Debjani. 2009. "Pain, Personhood and the Collective: Dalit Life Narratives." *Asian Studies Review*, 33 (4), December: 429–42.

Garg, Mahendulal. 1930. *Kalavati Shiksha* (Education for Women). Prayag.

"Gaur," Ganeshdutt Sharma. 1929. *Svapn Dosh Rakshak* (Protection from Nocturnal Emission). Banaras.

Gaur, Ramdas. 1927. *Kanyaon ki Pothi Ya Kanya Subodhini* (Text for Girls Retailing Appropriate Behavior for Them). Prayag: Gandhi Hindi Pustak Bhandar.

Gautum, S.S., comp. 2007a. *Bhartiya Lokoktiyon mein Jatiya Dvesh* (Caste Enmity in Indian Proverbs). Delhi: Gautum Book Centre.

———. 2007b. *Bhartiya Sahitya mein Mahilaon par Abhadra Kahavaten* (Indecent Sayings on Women in Indian Literature). Delhi: Gautum Book Centre.

Gayer, G.W. 1910. *Lectures on Some Criminal Tribes and Religious Mendicants of India*. 1910. Nagpur: Government Press.

Gazetteer of the Province of Oudh, Vol. II. 1877. Allahabad: Government Press.

Gazetteer of the Province of Oudh, Vol. III. 1878. Allahabad: Government Press.

Geetha, V. 2003. "Periyar, Women and an Ethic of Citizenship." In *Gender and Caste*, ed. Anupama Rao. Delhi: Kali: 180–203.

———, and S.V. Rajadurai. 1998. *Towards a Non-Brahmin Millennium: From Iyothee Das to Periyar*. Calcutta: Samya.

Geoghegan, J. 1873. *Note on Emigration from India*. Calcutta: Government Printing.

Ghai, R.K. 1990. *Shuddhi Movement in India: A Study of its Socio-Political Dimensions*. Delhi: Commonwealth Publishers.

Ghisaram, Chaudhry. 1920. *Bhajan Jat Kshatriya Jati Sudhar aur Jat Utpatti* (Songs on the Origin of Jat Kshatriyas and on the Introduction of Social Reform Amongst Them). Meerut.

Ghosh, Anindita. 2006. *Power in Print: Popular Publishing and Politics of Language and Culture in a Colonial Society.* Delhi: Oxford University Press.

Ghosh, Kaushik. 1999. "A Market for Aboriginality: Primitivism and Race Classification in the Indentured Labour Market of Colonial India." In *Subaltern Studies X: Writings on South Asian History and Society,* eds Gautum Bhadra, Gyan Prakash, and Susie Tharu. Delhi: Oxford University Press: 8–48.

Giddens, Anthony. 1992. *The Transformation of Intimacy: Sexuality, Love and Eroticism in Modern Societies.* Stanford: Stanford University Press.

Gillion, K.L. 1962. *Fiji's Indian Migrants: A History to the End of Indenture in 1920.* Melbourne: Oxford University Press.

Gilman, Sander L. 1985. *Difference and Pathology: Stereotypes of Sexuality, Race and Madness.* Ithaca: Cornell University Press.

Ginzburg, Carlo. 1999. *The Judge and the Historian: Marginal Notes on a Late-Twentieth-Century Miscarriage of Justice,* trans. Antony Shugaar. London: Verso.

Girdavar, Babu Sannulal Gupt. 1922. *Stri Subodhini* (Manual on Ideal Conduct for Women). Lucknow.

Gladstone, John Wilson. 1984. *Protestant Christianity and People's Movement in Kerala: A Study of Christian Mass Movements in Relation to Neo-Hindu Socio-Religious Movements in Kerala, 1850–1936.* Trivandrum: Seminary Publications.

Godse, Vishnubhat. 1974 (1907). *Majha Pravas* (My Travels). Pune: Venus Prakashan.

Gokhale, Gopal Krishna. 1920 (3rd edn). *Speeches of Gopal Krishna Gokhale.* Madras: G.A. Nateson.

Gooptu, Nandini. 2001. *The Politics of the Urban Poor in Early Twentieth Century India.* Cambridge: Cambridge University Press.

Gordon-Alexander, W. 1898. *Recollections of a Highland Subaltern: During the Campaigns of the 93rd Highlanders in India, under Colin Campbell, Lord Clyde in 1857, 1858 and 1859.* London: Edward Arnold.

Goyandka, Jaidayal. 1937. *Nari Dharm* (Woman's Duty). Gorakhpur: Geeta Press.

Gramsci, Antonio. 1971. *Selections from the Prison Notebooks.* London: Lawrence and Wishart.

Grierson, George A. 1883. *Report on Colonial Emigration from the Bengal Presidency.* Calcutta: Government of India.

———. 1923. *The Lay of Alha: A Saga of Rajput Chivalry as Sung by Minstrels of Northern India.* London: Oxford University Press.

Guha, Ranajit. 1983. *Elementary Aspects of Peasant Insurgency in Colonial India*. Delhi: Oxford University Press.

———. 1987. "Chandra's Death." In *Subaltern Studies V*, ed. Ranajit Guha. Delhi: Oxford University Press: 135–65.

Guha-Thakurta, Tapati. 2004. *Monuments, Objects, Histories: Institutions of Art in Colonial and Post-colonial India*. Delhi: Permanent Black.

Gundimeda, Sambaiah. 2009. "Democratisation of the Public Sphere: The Beef Stall Case in Hyderabad's *Sukoon* Festival." *South Asia Research*, 29 (2): 127–49.

Gupt, Maithilisaran. 2008. *Maithilisaran Gupt Granthavali, Vol. II* (Collection of Writings of Maithilisaran Gupt), ed. Krishnadutt Paliwal. Delhi: Vani Prakashan.

Gupta, Charu. 2001. *Sexuality, Obscenity, Community: Women, Muslims and the Hindu Public in Colonial India*. Delhi: Permanent Black.

———. 2007. "Dalit 'Viranganas' and Reinvention of 1857." *EPW*, XLII (19): 1739–45.

———. 2010. "Feminine, Criminal or Manly? Imaging Dalit Masculinities in Colonial North India." *IESHR*, 47 (3): 309–42.

———. 2011. "Writing Sex and Sexuality: Archives of Colonial North India." *Journal of Women's History*, 23 (4): 12–35.

———. 2012. "'Fashioning' Swadeshi: Clothing Women in Colonial North India." *EPW*, XLVII (42): 76–84.

Gupta, Dipankar. 1997. *Rivalry and Brotherhood: Politics in the Life of Farmers in Northern India*. Delhi: Oxford University Press.

Gupta, R.D. 1992. "Plantation Labour in Colonial India." *Journal of Peasant Studies*, 19 (3–4): 173–98.

Gupta, S.K. 1985. *The Scheduled Castes in Modern Indian Politics: Their Emergence as a Modern Power*. Delhi: Manohar.

Gupta, Sheo Dayal Sah. 1907. *Sri Vaishya Vansh Vibhushan* (The Ornament of Vaishya Community). Lucknow: Anglo Oriental Press.

Haggis, Jane. 2000. "Ironies of Emancipation: Changing Configurations of 'Women's Work' in the 'Mission of Sisterhood' to Indian Women." *Feminist Review*, 65: 108–26.

Hall, Stuart. 1980. "Encoding/Decoding." In *Culture, Media, Language: Working Papers in Cultural Studies, 1972–79*, eds Stuart Hall, D. Hobson, A. Lowe, and P. Willis. London: Hutchinson: 128–38.

Hancock, Mary. 2001. "Home Science and the Nationalization of Domesticity in Colonial India." *MAS*, 35 (4): 871–903.

Hansen, Kathryn. 1988. "The Virangana in North Indian History: Myth & Popular Culture." *EPW*, XXII (18): 25–33.

————. 1992. *Grounds for Play: The Nautanki Theatre of North India.* Berkeley: University of California Press.

Hardgrave, Robert L. 1968. "The Breast-cloth Controversy: Caste Consciousness and Social Change in Southern Travancore." *IESHR,* 5 (2): 171–87.

Hardiman, David. 1987. *The Coming of the Devi: Adivasi Assertion in Western India.* Delhi: Oxford University Press.

————. 2006. *Histories for the Subordinated.* Delhi: Permanent Black.

Harishchandra, Bharatendu. 1918 (2nd edn). *Agarwalon ki Utpatti* (Origin of the Agarwal Caste). Banaras.

Harit, Bihari Lal. 1995. *Virangana Jhalkari Bai Kavya* (Long Poem on Jhalkari Bai). Shahadra: Kirti Prakashan.

Harper, Susan Billington. 2000. *In the Shadow of the Mahatma: Bishop V.S. Azariah and the Travails of Christianity in British India.* Surrey: Curzon.

Hasan, Mushirul. 2007. *Wit and Humour in Colonial North India.* Delhi: Niyogi Books.

Hawley, John Stratton, and Donna Marie Wulff, eds. 1982. *The Divine Consort: Radha and the Goddesses of India.* Berkeley: University of California Press.

Halttunen, Karen. 1995. "Humanitarianism and the Pornography of Pain in Anglo-American Culture." *The American Historical Review,* 100 (2): 303–34.

Hebden, Keith. 2011. *Dalit Theology and Christian Anarchism.* London: Ashgate.

Heller, Agnes. 1984. *Everyday Life,* trans. G.L. Campbell. London: Routledge.

Henderson, Carol E., ed. 2010. *Imagining the Black Female Body: Reconciling Image in Print and Visual Culture.* New York: Palgrave.

Hiltebeitel, Alf, and Kathleen M. Erndl, eds. 2000. *Is the Goddess a Feminist? The Politics of South Asian Goddesses.* New York: New York University Press.

Hindu Dharm ke Phal (Fruits of Hinduism). 1905 (2nd edn). Allahabad: NICTBS.

Hinduon ki Nirdhanta (Causes of Hindu Poverty). 1909 (2nd edn). Allahabad: NICTBS.

Hobby, Elaine, ed. 2009. *The Birth of Mankind: Otherwise Named, the Woman's Book.* England: Ashgate.

Hoch, Paul. 1979. *White Hero, Black Beast: Racism, Sexism and the Mask of Masculinity.* London: Pluto.

Hoey, William. 1880. *A Monograph on Trade and Manufactures in Northern India*. Lucknow: American Methodist Mission Press.

Hollen, Cecilia Van. 2003. *Birth on the Threshold: Childbirth and Modernity in South India*. Berkeley: University of California Press.

Hollins, S.T. 1914. *The Criminal Tribes of UP*. Allahabad: Government Press.

hooks, bell. 1992. *Black Looks: Race and Representation*. Boston: South End Press.

Hosking, Geoffrey, and George Schopflin, eds. 1997. *Myths and Nationhood*. London: Hurst and Company.

Hukmadevi. 1932. *Mahila Manoranjak Prashnavali, II* (Entertaining Questionaire for Women). Lucknow.

Hull, Gloria, Patricia Bell Scott, and Barbara Smith. 1982. *All the Women are White, All the Blacks are Men, But Some of Us Are Brave: Black Women's Studies*. New York: Westbury.

Hunt, Sarah Beth. 2014. *Hindi Dalit Literature and the Politics of Representation*. Delhi: Routledge.

Hunter, Margaret L. 2005. *Race, Gender, and the Politics of Skin Tone*. New York: Routledge.

Ibbetson, D. 1916. *Punjab Castes: Races, Castes and Tribes of the People of Punjab*. Lahore: Government Press.

Ilaiah, Kancha. 1996. "Productive Labour, Consciousness and History." In *Subaltern Studies IX: Writings on South Asian History and Society*, eds Shahid Amin and Dipesh Chakrabarty. Delhi: Oxford University Press.

———. 2003. "Cultural Globalization." *The Hindu*. February 22.

———. 2005 (2nd edn). *Why I am Not a Hindu: A Sudra Critique of Hindutva Philosophy, Culture and Economy*. Calcutta: Samya.

Inden, Ronald. 1990. *Imagining India*. Oxford: Basil Blackwell.

Jaffrelot, Christophe. 2004. *Dr Ambedkar and Untouchability: Analysing and Fighting Caste*. Delhi: Permanent Black.

Jafri, S.N.A. 1931. *The History and Status of Landlords and Tenants in UP*. Allahabad: Pioneer Press.

Jagannath. 1937 (8th edn). *Kajri Mirzapuri*. Lucknow.

Jaghina, Deshraj. 1934. *Jati Itihaas* (History of the Jats). Agra: Kanti Press.

Jain, P.C., Shashi Jain, and Sudha Bhatnagar. 1997. *Scheduled Caste Women*. Jaipur: Rawat.

Jain, Parmeshthidas. 1937. *Vijatiya Vivah Mimansa* (Treatise on Inter-Caste Marriage). Allahabad.

Jain, Shobhita, and Rhoda Reddock, eds. 1998. *Women Plantation Workers: International Experiences*. Oxford: Berg.

Jalki, Dunkin. 2003. "Food for Thought." *The Dalit*, March–April: 24–7.

James, Joy, and T. Denean Sharpley-Whiting. 2000. *The Black Feminist Reader*. Oxford: Blackwell.

Jassal, Smita Tewari. 2012. *Unearthing Gender: Folk Songs of North India*. Durham: Duke University Press.

Jati ki Chhut-Chhat (Pollution Taboos of Caste). 1905. Allahabad: NICTBS.

Jati Panti ka Varnan (Explanation of Caste). 1924 (4th edn). Allahabad: NICTBS.

Jati Pariksha (Test of Caste). 1906. Allahabad: NICTBS.

Jayawardena, C. 1968. "Migration and Social Change: A Survey of Indian Communities Overseas." *Geographical Review*, 58: 426–49.

Jeffery, Patricia, Roger Jeffery, and Andrew Lyon. 1989. *Labour Pains and Labour Power: Women and Childbearing in India*. London: Zed.

Jeffery, Roger. 1988. *The Politics of Health in India*. Berkeley: University of California Press.

Jha, Brijmohan. 1925 (2nd edn). *Hinduon Jago* (Hindus Awake). Agra.

Jigyasu, Chandrika Prasad. 1941. *Bhartiya Maulik Samajvad: Srishti aur Manav Samaj ka Vikas Athwa "Bharat ke Adi Nivasi" Granth ka Pratham Khand* (Indian Authentic Socialism: Growth of Nature and Human Society or First Part of "Orignial Inhabitants of India"). Lucknow: Adi Hindu Gyan Prasarak Bureau.

———. 1965 (1937). *Bharat ke Adi Nivasiyon ki Sabhyata* (Civilization of India's Original Inhabitants). Lucknow: Bahujan Kalyan Prakashan.

———. 1968. *Sri 108 Swami Achhutanandji "Harihar."* Lucknow: Bahujan Kalyan Prakashan.

Jodhka, Surinder S., ed. 2012. *Village Society*. Hyderabad: Orient Blackswan.

Jogdand, P.G., ed. 1995. *Dalit Women in India: Issues and Perspectives*. Pune: Gyan Publishing House.

Jones, K. 1989. *The New Cambridge History of India: III.1—Socio-religious Movements in British India*. Cambridge: Cambridge University Press.

Jordan, W.D. 1968. *White over Black: American Attitudes toward the Negro (1550–1812)*. Chapel Hill: University of North Carolina Press.

Jordens, J.T.F. 1978. *Dayananda Saraswati: His Life and Ideas*. Delhi: Oxford University Press.

———. 1981. *Swami Shraddhananda: His Life and Causes*. Delhi: Oxford University Press.

Joshi, Badrinath. 1928 (2nd edn). *Vidhwodvah Mimansa* (Treatise on Widow Remarriage). Prayag.

Joshi, Chitra. 2003. *Lost Worlds: Indian Labour and its Forgotten Histories.* Delhi: Permanent Black.

Joshi, Janardan. 1918 (2nd edn). *Grh Prabandh Shastra* (Science of Household Management). Prayag.

Jotdar ka Brittant (Story of a Farmer). 1898. Allahabad: NICTBS.

Juergensmeyer, Mark. 2009 (1982). *Religious Rebels in the Punjab: The Ad Dharm Challenge to Caste.* Delhi: Navayana.

Junghare, Indira Y. 1975. "Songs of the Goddess Sitala: Religio-Cultural and Linguistic Features." *Man in India*, 55 (4): 298–316.

Kale, Madhavi. 1998. *Fragments of Empire: Capital, Slavery, and Indian Indentured Labor Migration in the British Caribbean.* Philadelphia: University of Pennsylvania Press.

Kannomal. 1923. *Mahila Sudhar* (Reform of Women). Agra: Mahavir Granth Karyalaya.

Kapadia, Karin. 1996. *Siva and Her Sisters: Gender, Caste and Class in Rural South India.* Delhi: Oxford University Press.

Kapur, Ratna. 2010. *Makeshift Migrants and Law: Gender, Belonging, and Postcolonial Anxieties.* Delhi: Routledge.

Kasturi, Malavika. 2002. *Embattled Identities: Rajput Lineages and the Colonial State in Nineteenth-Century North India.* Delhi: Oxford University Press.

Katyal, A., and N. Kishore. 2001. "Performing the Goddess: Sacred Ritual into Professional Performance." *The Drama Review*, 45 (1): 96–117.

Kedia, Baijnath. 1933. *Vyanga Chitravali, Part I* (Collection of Cartoons). Kashi: Hindi Pustak Agency.

Kelly, John D. 1991. *A Politics of Virtue: Hinduism, Sexuality, and Counter-colonial Discourse in Fiji.* Chicago: University of Chicago Press.

Kempadoo, Kamala, Jyoti Sanghera, and Bandana Pattanaik, eds. 2005. *Trafficking and Prostitution Reconsidered: New Perspectives on Migration, Sex Work, and Human Rights.* Boulder: Paradigm Publishers.

Kent, Eliza F. 2004. *Converting Women: Gender and Protestant Christianity in Colonial South India.* New York: Oxford University Press.

Khan, Rev. Munwar. 1911. *Jati ki Chhut-Chhat* (Pollution Taboos of Caste). Allahabad: NICTBS.

Khare, R.S. 1984. *The Untouchable as Himself: Ideology, Identity and Pragmatism among the Lucknow Chamars.* Cambridge: Cambridge University Press.

————, ed. 1992. *The Eternal Food: Gastronomic Ideas and Experiences of Hindus and Buddhists*. Albany: SUNY Press.

Kinsley, David. 1986. *Hindu Goddesses: Visions of the Divine Feminine in the Hindu Tradition*. Berkeley: University of California Press.

Kitts, Eustace J. 1885. *A Compendium of the Castes and Tribes found in India*. Bombay: Education Society's Press.

Klass, Mortan. 1961. *East Indians in Trinidad: A Study of Cultural Persistence*. New York: Columbia University Press.

Knorringa, Peter. 1999. "Artisan Labour in the Agra Footwear Industry: Continued Informality and Changing Threats." *Contributions to Indian Sociology*, 33 (1–2): 303–28.

Kolenda, Pauline. 1982. "Pox and the Terror of Childlessness: Images and Ideas of the Smallpox Goddess in a North Indian Village." In *Mother Worship*, ed. J.J. Preston. Chapel Hill: University of North Carolina Press: 227–50.

————. 1987. *Regional Differences in Family Structure in India*. Jaipur: Rawat.

————. 2003. *Caste, Marriage and Inequality: Studies from North and South India*. Jaipur: Rawat.

Kolff, Dirk. 1990. *Naukar, Rajput, and Sepoy: The Ethnohistory of the Military Labour Market in Hindustan, 1450–1950*. Cambridge: Cambridge University Press.

"Komal," Purshottam Das Gaur. 1934. *Achhut ke Patra* (Letters of an Untouchable). Allahabad: Gaur Pustak Bhandar.

Kooiman, Dick. 1989. *Conversion and Social Equality in India: The London Missionary Society in South Travancore in the 19th Century*. Delhi: Manohar.

Kshirsagar, R.K. 1994. *Dalit Movement in India and its Leaders (1857–1956)*. Delhi: MD Publications.

Kumar, Ashutosh. 2011. "Indentured Migration from Northern India, *c.* 1830–1920: Historiography, Experience, Representation." University of Delhi: PhD Thesis.

————. 2013. "Anti-Indenture Bhojpuri Folk Songs and Poems from North India." *Man in India*, 93 (4): 509–19.

Kumar, Mukul. 2004. "Relationship of Caste and Crime in Colonial India." *EPW*, XXXIX (10): 1078–87.

Kumar, Nita. 1988. *The Artisans of Banaras: Popular Culture and Identity, 1880–1986*. Princeton: Princeton University Press.

————. 2000. *Lessons from Schools: A History of Education in Banaras*. Delhi: Sage.

Kumar, Raj. 2010. *Dalit Personal Narratives: Reading Caste, Nation and Identity*. Hyderabad: Orient Blackswan.

Kuril, Ramcharan. 1950 (1941). *Bhagwan Ravidas ki Satyakatha*, ed. Mathukar Mishra. Kanpur: Krisna Press.

Lakhanpal, Chandravati. 1941 (3rd edn). *Striyon ki Stithi* (Condition of Women). Lucknow: Ganga Granthagar.

Lal, Brij V. 1985. "Kunti's Cry: Indentured Women on Fiji Plantations." *IESHR*, 22 (1): 55–71.

———. 2001. *Chalo Jahaji: A Journey through Indenture in Fiji*. Canberra: Suva Museum.

———, ed. 1998. *Crossing the Kala Pani: A Documentary History of Indian Indenture in Fiji*. Canberra: Division of Pacific and Asian History.

Lal, Cheda. 1919. *Kori Mahte Kshatriyon ki Vanshavali* (Genealogy of Koris). Farukhabad.

Lang, Sean. 2005. "Drop the Demon *Dai*: Maternal Mortality and the State in Colonial Madras, 1840–1875." *Social History of Medicine*, 18 (3): 357–78.

Langhamer, Claire. 2007. "Love and Courtship in Mid-Twentieth Century England." *The Historical Journal*, 50 (1): 173–96.

Langland, Elizabeth. 1995. *Nobody's Angels: Middle-class Women and Domestic Ideology in Victorian Culture*. Ithaca: Cornell University Press.

Lara Lari (Story of Quarrelsome Women).1905 (5th edn), trans. Rev.W.F. Johnson. Allahabad: NICTBS.

Laurence, K.P. 1994. *A Question of Labour: Indentured Immigration into Trinidad and British Guiana 1875–1915*. London: James Curry.

Laxman, R.K. 1989. "Freedom to Cartoon, Freedom to Speak." *Daedalus* 118 (4): 68–91.

———. 1990. *The Best of Laxman*. Delhi: Penguin Books.

Leavitt, Judith W. 1986. *Brought to Bed: Child-Bearing in America, 1750–1950*. New York: Oxford University Press.

Lebra-Chapman, Joyce. 1986. *The Rani of Jhansi: A Study of Female Heroism in India*. Honolulu: University of Hawaii Press.

Lele, Jayant, ed. 1981. *Tradition and Modernity in Bhakti Movements*. Leiden: Brill.

Leong-Salobir, Cecilia. 2011. *Food Culture in Colonial Asia: A Taste of Empire*. London: Routledge.

Leopold, Joan. 1970. "The Aryan Theory of Race in India, 1870–1920." *IESHR*, 7: 271–97.

Levine, Philippa. 2003. *Prostitution, Race and Politics: Policing Venereal Disease in the British Empire*. New York: Routledge.

Lloyd, H. 1882. *Hindu Women: With Glimpses into their Life and Zenanas.* London: Zenana Missionary Society.

Longer, Victor. 1981. *Forefront Forever: The History of the Mahar Regiment.* Saugor: Mahar Regiment Centre.

Lorenzen, D.N., ed. 1995. *Bhakti Religion in North India: Community, Identity and Political Action.* New York: SUNY Press.

Lubin, Alex. 2005. *Romance and Rights: The Politics of Interracial Intimacy, 1945–1954.* Jackson: University Press of Mississippi.

Lucas, J.J. n.d. *History of the NICTBS (1848–1934).* Allahabad: Mission Press.

Ludtke, Alf, ed. 1995. *The History of Everyday Life: Reconstructing Historical Experiences and Ways of Life,* trans. William Templer. Princeton: Princeton University Press.

Lutgendorf, Philip. 2001. "Dining Out at Lake Pampa: The Shabari Episode in Multiple Ramayanas." In *Questioning Ramayans: A South Asian Tradition,* ed. Paula Richman. Berkeley: University of California Press: 119–36, 376–79.

Lynch, Owen M. 1969. *The Politics of Untouchability: Social Mobility and Social Change in a City of India.* New York: Columbia University Press.

———. 1972. "Dr. B.R. Ambedkar: Myth and Charisma." In *The Untouchables in Contemporary India,* ed. J. Michael Mahar. Arizona: University of Arizona Press: 97–112.

MacRaild, D.M. 2008. "Review Article: 'The Moloch of Details'? Cycles of Criticism and the Meaning of History Now." *Journal of Contemporary History,* 43 (1), January: 113–25.

Maharaj, Markanda. 1937. *Kajlauta: Nai Kajli Mirzapuri* (A Pot of Kajli: New Kajli from Mirzapur). Banaras.

Mahasatveer, Swami Bodhanand. 1930. *Mool Bharatvasi aur Arya* (Original Inhabitants of India and Aryans). Lucknow: Nishad Printing Press.

Mahopdeshak, Shiv Sharma. 1927. *Stri Shiksha* (Women's Education). Bareilly: King Press.

Majumdar, R.C. 1963. *The Sepoy Mutiny and the Revolt of 1857.* Calcutta: Mukhopadhyay.

Mallampalli, Chandra. 2004. *Christians and Public Life in Colonial South India, 1863–1937: Contending with Marginality.* London: Routledge.

———. 2010. "Escaping the Grip of Personal Law in Colonial India: Proving Custom, Negotiating Hindu-ness." *Law and History Review,* 28 (4): 1043–65.

"Mani," Chintamani. 1935. *Manu aur Striyan* (Manu and Women). Allahabad: India Book Agency.

Marriott, McKim. 1955. "Little Communities in an Indigenous Civilization." In *Village India: Studies in the Little Community,* ed. McKim Marriott. Chicago: University of Chicago Press: 175–227.

Martin, Emily. 1987. *The Woman in the Body: A Cultural Analysis of Reproduction.* Boston: Boston Press.

Mayaram, Shail. 1991. "Criminality or Community? Alternative Constructions of the Mev Narrative of Darya Khan." *Contributions to Indian Sociology,* 25 (1): 57–84.

Mayer, A.C. 1973. *Peasants in the Pacific.* London: Routledge.

Mayer, Peter. 1993. "Inventing Village Tradition: The Late 19th Century Origins of the North Indian 'Jajmani System.'" *MAS,* 27 (2): 357–95.

McClintock, Anne. 1995. *Imperial Leather: Race, Gender and Sexuality in the Colonial Contest.* New York: Routledge.

McDermott, Rachel Fell. 2011. *Revelry, Rivalry, and Longing for the Goddesses of Bengal: The Fortunes of Hindu Festivals.* New York: Columbia University Press.

Meerut: A Gazetteer, Vol. IV of District Gazetteers of UP. 1904. (By H.R. Nevill.) Allahabad: Government Press.

Mehrotra, Deepti Priya. 2006. *Gulab Bai: The Queen of Nautanki Theatre.* Delhi: Penguin.

Mem Sahiba aur Ayah ki Katha (The Story of the Lady and the Ayah). 1896, trans. Rev. W. F. Johnson, from a story by Mrs Sherwood. Allahabad: Christian Literary Society.

Mencher, Joan P. 1974. "The Caste System Upside Down, or the Not-So-Mysterioius East." *Current Anthropology,* 15 (4): 469–93.

Mendelsohn, Oliver, and Marika Vicziany. 1998. *The Untouchables: Subordination, Poverty and the State in Modern India.* Cambridge: Cambridge University Press.

Menon, Dilip M. 2006. *The Blindness of Insight: Essays on Caste in Modern India.* Pondicherry: Navayana.

Metcalf, Thomas R. 1964. *The Aftermath of the Revolt—India, 1857–1870.* Princeton: Princeton University Press.

Mill, John Stuart. 1964. "Representative Government." In *The Dynamics of Nationalism,* ed. Louis L. Snyder. Princeton: Van Nostrand.

Mirzapur: A Gazetteer, Vol. XXVII of District Gazetteers of UP. 1911. (By D.L. Drake-Brockman.) Allahabad: Government Press.

Mishra, Jwalaprasad. 1911. *Dharuka Kshatriya Vanshavali* (Genealogy of Dharuka Kshatriyas). Moradabad.

Mishra, Shivnarayan. 1922. *Bahishkrit Bharat* (Outcasted India). Kanpur: Pratap Pustakalaya.

Moeschen, Sheila C. 2013. *Acts of Conspicuous Compassion: Performance Culture and American Charity Practices*. Ann Arbor: University of Michigan Press.

Mohammed, Patricia. 1995. "Writing Gender into History: The Negotiation of Gender Relations Among Indian Men and Women in Post-Indenture Trinidad Society, 1917–1947." In *Engendering History: Caribbean Women in Historical Perspective*, eds Verene Shepherd, Bridget Brereton, and Barbara Bailey. New York: St Martin's Press: 20–47.

Mohan, K. 2002. "Fashioning Minds and Images: A Case Study of *Stree Darpan* (1909–1928)." In *Breaking Out of Invisibility: Women in Indian History*, eds Aparna Basu and Anup Taneja. Delhi: Council of Historical Research: 232–71.

Mohan, Sanal. 2011. "Narrativizing the History of Slave Suffering." In *No Alphabet in Sight: New Dalit Writings from South India*, eds Susie Tharu and K. Satyanarayana. Delhi: Penguin: 534–55.

Mohapatra, Prabhu. 2006. "'Following Custom?' Representations of Community among Indian Immigrant Labour in the West Indies, 1880–1920." *Indian Review of Social History*, 51, Supplement 14: 173–202.

Mohar, Bhagwan Das. 1976. *The Impact of the 1857 Freedom Struggle on Hindi Literature* (in Hindi). Ajmer: Krishna Bros.

Moore, B.L. 1995. *Race, Power and Social Segmentation in Colonial Society: Guyana after Slavery 1838–1900*. Montreal: McGill.

Moore-Gilbert, Bart. 1998. *Postcolonial Theory/Contexts, Practices, Politics*. London: Verso.

Morris, Miss E. 1917. *Village Education: Its Goal and How to Attain It*. Ludhiana: Ludhiana Mission Steam Press.

Morrison, Toni. 1992. *Playing in the Dark: Whiteness and the Literary Imagination*. Cambridge: Harvard University Press.

Mujahid, Abdul Malik. 1989. *Conversion to Islam: Untouchables' Strategy for Protest in India*. Chambersburg: Anima Publications.

Mukherjee, Rudrangshu. 1984. *Awadh in Revolt 1857–1858: A Study in Popular Resistance*. Delhi: Oxford University Press.

Mukhopadhyay, Subrata Kumar. 1994. *Cult of Goddess Sitala in Bengal: An Enquiry into Folk Culture*. Calcutta: Firma KLM Pvt Ltd.

Mukta, Parita. 1994. *Upholding the Common Life: The Community of Mirabai*. Delhi: Oxford University Press.

Munnilal, Master. 1937. *Kajri ka Dangal* (Arena of *Kajri*). Howrah.

Nagar, Amritlal. 1981 (1957). *Gadar ke Phool* (Flowers of 1857 Revolt). Kanpur: Rajpal and Sons.

Nagaraj, D.R. 2010. *The Flaming Feet and Other Essays: The Dalit Movement in India*. Ranikhet: Permanent Black.

Naimishray, Mohandas. 1999. *Swatantrata Sangram ke Dalit Krantikari* (Dalit Revolutionaries of Freedom Struggle). Delhi: Nilkanth Prakashan.

———. 2003. *Virangana Jhalkari Bai*. Delhi: Radhakrishna.

———. 2014. *Hindi Dalit Sahitya* (Hindi Dalit Literature). Delhi: Sahitya Academy.

Nair, Janaki. 1996. *Women and Law in Colonial India: A Social History*. Delhi: Kali.

Nandy, Ashis. 1983. *The Intimate Enemy: Loss and Recovery of Self under Colonialism*. Delhi: Oxford University Press.

Narayan, Badri. 2001. *Documenting Dissent: Contesting Fables, Contested Memories and Dalit Political Discourse*. Simla: Indian Institute of Advanced Study.

———. 2006. *Women Heroes and Dalit Assertion in North India: Culture, Identity and Politics*. Delhi: Sage.

———. 2011. *The Making of the Dalit Public in North India: Uttar Pradesh, 1950–Present*. Delhi: Oxford University Press.

———, and A.R. Misra. 2004. *Multiple Marginalities: An Anthology of Identified Dalit Writings*. Delhi: Manohar.

Narayan, Kirin. 1986. "Birds on a Branch: Girlfriends and Wedding Songs in Kangra." *Ethos*, 14: 47–75.

———. 1995. "The Practice of Oral Literary Criticism: Women's Songs in Kangra, India." *The Journal of American Folklore*, 108 (429): 243–64.

Naregal, Veena. 2001. *Language Politics, Elites and the Public Sphere: Western India under Colonialism*. Delhi: Permanent Black.

Natarajan J., comp. 1954. *Report of the Press Commission, Part II: History of Indian Journalism*. Delhi: Press Commission.

Natyacharya, Pandit "Shaida." 1937. *Harijani Natak* (Harijan Play). Allahabad.

Neale, Walter. 1962. *Economic Change in Rural India: Land Tenure and Reform in UP 1800–1955*. New Haven: Yale University Press.

Nesfield, John C. 1885. *Brief View of the Caste System of NWP*. Allahabad: Government Press.

Neuman, Daniel M. 1990. *The Life of Music in North India: The Organization of an Artistic Tradition*. Chicago: University of Chicago Press.

Nevadomsky, J. 1980. "Abandoning the Retentionist Hypothesis: Family Changes Among the East Indians in Rural Trinidad." *International Journal of the Sociology of Family*, 10: 181–98.

Nigam, Aditya. 2010. "The Heterotopias of Dalit Politics: Becoming-Subject and the Consumption Utopia." In *Utopia/Dystopia: Conditions of Historical Possibility*, eds Michael D. Gordin, Helen Tilley, and Gyan Prakash. Princeton: Princeton University Press: 250–76.

Nigam, Sanjay. 1990. "Disciplining and Policing the 'Criminals by Birth': The Making of a Colonial Stereotype—The Criminal Tribes and Castes of North India," Parts I and II. *IESHR*, 27 (2): 131–64; 27 (3): 257–87.

Nijhawan, Shobna. 2012. *Women and Girls in the Hindi Public Sphere: Periodical Literature in Colonial North India*. Delhi: Oxford University Press.

———. 2014. "Fallen through the Nationalist and Feminist Grids of Analysis: Political Campaign of Indian Women against Indentured Labour Emigration." *Indian Journal of Gender Studies*, 21 (1): 111–33.

Nilson, Usha. 2001. "Grinding Millet but Singing of Sita: Power and Domination in Awadhi and Bhojpuri Women's Songs." In *Questioning Ramayans: A South Asian Tradition*, ed. Paula Richman. Berkeley: University of California Press: 137–58.

O'Connor, Percival C. Scott. 1908. *The Indian Countryside: A Calendar and Diary*. London: Brown, Langham & Co.

O'Flaherty, Wendy Doniger. 1982. "The Shifting Balance of Power in the Marriage of Siva and Parvati." In *The Divine Consort: Radha and the Goddesses of India*, eds John Stratton Hawley and Donna Marie Wulff. Berkeley: University of California Press: 129–43.

O'Hanlon, Rosalind. 1985. *Caste, Conflict and Ideology: Mahatma Jotirao Phule and Low-caste Protest in Nineteenth-Century India*. Cambridge: Cambridge University Press.

O'Henry, Edward. 1988. *Chant the Names of God: Musical Culture in Bhojpuri Speaking India*. San Diego: San Diego State University Press.

Oakley, Ann. 1984. *The Captured Womb: A History of the Medical Care of Pregnant Women*. New York: Basil Blackwell.

Oddie, Geoffrey A. 1969. "Protestant Missions, Caste and Social Change in India, 1850–1914." *IESHR*, 6: 259–91.

———. 1997. *Religious Conversion Movements in South Asia: Continuities and Change 1800–1900*. Surrey: Curzon.

Oesterheld, Christina, and Claus Peter Zoller, eds. 1999. *Of Clowns and Gods, Brahmans and Babus: Humour in South Asian Literature*. Delhi: Manohar.

Omvedt, Gail. 1994. *Dalits and the Democratic Revolution: Dr Ambedkar and the Dalit Movement in Colonial India*. Delhi: Sage.

————. 2003. *Buddhism in India: Challenging Brahmanism and Caste.* Delhi: Sage.

Orme, Robert. 1758. *A History of the Military Transactions of the British Nation in Indostan from 1745.* London.

Orsini, Francesca. 2002. *The Hindi Public Sphere 1920–1940: Language and Literature in the Age of Nationalism.* Delhi: Oxford University Press.

————. 2007. "Introduction." In *Love in South Asia: A Cultural History*, ed. Francesca Orsini. Delhi: Cambridge University Press, 1–39.

Ouwerkerk, Louise. 1945. *The Untouchables of India.* London: Oxford University Press.

"Pagal," Gupt. 1921 (2nd edn). *Grihani Bhushan* (Ornament of Household Mistress). Kashi: Pannalal Gupt.

Pai, Sudha. 2002. *Dalit Assertion and the Unfinished Democratic Revolution: The Bahujan Samaj Party in Uttar Pradesh.* Delhi: Sage.

Pandey, Govind. 1937 (3rd edn). *Kajli Navbahar.* Kanpur.

Pandey, Gyanendra. 1978. *The Ascendancy of the Congress in UP, 1926–34: A Study in Imperfect Mobilisation.* Delhi: Oxford University Press.

————. 2013. *A History of Prejudice: Race, Caste, and Difference in India and the United States.* Cambridge: Cambridge University Press.

Pandey, Ramtej. 1931. *Nari Dharm Shastra* (Treatise on Women's Duties). Kashi: Bhargav Pustakalaya.

Pandey, Shyam Manohar. 1987. *The Hindi Oral Epic Lorikayan.* Allahabad: Sahitya Bhawan.

Pandian, M.S.S. 2007. *Brahmin and Non-Brahmin: Genealogies of the Tamil Political Present.* Delhi: Permanent Black.

Panikkar, K.N. 1989. *Against Lord and State: Religion and Peasant Uprisings in Malabar 1836–1921.* Delhi: Oxford University Press.

Parmanand, Bhai. 1928. *Hindu Jati ka Rahasya* (Secret of Hindu Community). Lucknow.

Parmar, Shubha. 2011. "Gendering Dalit Identity in Colonial and Post-Colonial Uttar Pradesh, 1900–2001." Jawaharlal Nehru University: PhD Thesis.

Parshuram. 1921. *Kamdhenu Kahan Hai? Jahan Charkha Hai. Swaraj ki Kunji kiske Haath Hai? Abla ke Haath Mein* (Where is the Cow of Plenty? Where there is Spinning Wheel. In Whose Hands is the Key to Swaraj? In the Hands of Gentler Sex). Kanpur.

Pasi, Chetram. 1928. *Pasi Samaj* (Pasi Community). Allahabad.

Pasi, Raj Kumar. 1998. *Pasi Samaj ka Swatantrata Sangram Mein Yogdan* (Contribution of Pasi Community in Freedom Struggle). Lucknow: Pasi Shodh Evam Sanskritik Sansthan.

Pati, Biswamoy. 2003. *Identity, Hegemony and Resistance: Towards the Social History of Conversions in Orissa, 1800–2000*. Delhi: Three Essays Collective.

Peers, Douglas. 1991. "'The Habitual Nobility of Being': British Officers and the Social Construction of the Bengal Army in the Early 19th Century." *MAS*, 25 (3): 545–69.

Pemberton, J.F. and L.C. Perfumi. 1915. *A Century of Work in Meerut, 1815–1915*. Sikandra.

Perron, Lalita du. 2007. *Hindi Poetry in a Musical Genre: Thumri Lyrics*. London: Routledge.

Peterson, Indira Viswanathan, and Davesh Soneji, eds. 2008. *Performing Pasts: Reinventing the Arts in Modern South India*. Delhi: Oxford University Press.

Philip, Puthenveettil O. 1925. *The Depressed Classes and Christianity*. Calcutta: National Christian Council.

Phillips, Godfrey E. 1912. *The Outcastes—Hope or Work Among the Depressed Classes in India*. London: Young People's Missionary Movement.

Pickett, J. Waskom. 1933. *Christian Mass Movements in India: A Study with Recommendations*. Lucknow: Lucknow Publishing House.

———. 1938. *Christ's Way to India's Heart*. Lucknow: Lucknow Publishing House.

Pilibhit: A Gazetteer, Vol. XVIII of District Gazetteers of UP. 1911. (By H.R. Nevill.) Allahabad: Government Press.

Pinch, William R. 1996. *Peasants and Monks in British India*. Delhi: Oxford University Press.

Pinney, Christopher. 2004. *"Photos of the Gods": The Printed Image and Political Struggle in India*. London: Oxford University Press.

Pintchman, Tracy, and Rita D. Sherma, eds. 2011. *Woman and Goddess in Hinduism: Reinterpretations and Re-envisionings*. New York: Palgrave.

Pitman, Emma Raymond. 1906. *Indian Zenana Missions: Their Need, Origin, Objects, Agents, Modes of Working and Results*. London: John Snow & Comp.

Poddar, Hanuman Prasad. 1929. *Samaj Sudhar* (Social Reform). Gorakhpur: Geeta Press.

"Prakash," Ramgopal Shukla. 1934 (2nd edn). *Achhutoddhar Arthat Kattar Panthiyon ki Chillapon* (Upliftment of Untouchables: Meaning the Clamor of Conservatives). Kanpur.

Prasad, Bhagwandin. 1915. *Bhaichara* (Brotherhood). Allahabad.

Prasad, Chandra Bhan. 2004. *Dalit Diary, 1999–2003: Reflections on Apartheid in India*. Pondicherry: Navayana.

————, and Milind Kamble. 2012. "To Empower Dalits, Do Away with India's Antiquated Retail Trading System." *The Times of India*, December 5.

Prasad, Gajadhar. 1911. *Brahmankul Parivartan* (Changes in Brahmin Caste). Allahabad.

Prasad, Ganga. 1916. *Jati Bhed* (Caste Differentiation). Bulandshahr: Arya Pratinidhi Sabha.

Prasad, Mata. 1987. *Achhut Virangana Nautanki*. Lucknow: Cultural Publishers.

Prasad, Onkar. 1987. *Folk Music and Folk Dances of Banaras*. Calcutta: Anthropological Survey of India.

Prasad, Rajendra. 2004. *Tears in Paradise: A Personal and Historical Journey 1879–2004*. Auckland: Glade.

Prashad, Vijay. 2000. *Untouchable Freedom: A Social History of a Dalit Community*. Delhi: Oxford University Press.

Pratham Varshik Report. 1923. Agra: Bhartiya Hindu Shuddhi Sabha.

Premchand. 1984. *Mansarovar*, vols I to VIII (Collection of Premchand's Stories). Allahabad: Saraswati Press.

"Premghan," Upadhyay Badri Narayan Sharma. 1913. *Kajli Kautuhal arthat Kajli ka Tyohar, Uske Mele aur Kajli ke Giton ka Tatva, Bhed, Vibhed, Utpatti aur Tatsambandhi Itihaas adi ka Varnan* (An Essay on the Origin and Characteristics of *Kajli* Songs). Mirzapur: Anand Kadambini Press.

Rae Das ki Bani (Sayings of Ravidas). 1908. Allahabad: Belvedere Press.

Raghuvanshi, U.B.S. 1916. *Chanvar Puran* (Puranic History of the Chamars). Aligarh.

————. 1923. *Suryavansh Kshatriya Jaiswar Sabha* (Society of the Solar Dynasty of Kshatriya Jaiswars). Lahore.

Raheja, Gloria Goodwin, ed. 2003. *Songs, Stories, Lives: Gendered Dialogues and Cultural Critique*. Delhi: Kali.

————, and Ann Grodzins Gold. 1994. *Listen to the Heron's Words: Reimagining Gender and Kinship in North India*. Berkeley: University of California Press.

Rai, Amit S. 2002. *Rule of Sympathy: Sentiment, Race and Power 1750–1850*. New York: Palgrave.

Rai, Lala Lajpat. 1914. *The Depressed Classes and Our Duty*. Lahore: Arya Tract Society.

Rai, Vibhutinarayan. 2006. "*Kalkatiya Paltan ke Bahane 1857 ka Dalit Bhashya*" (Dalit Meanings of 1857 through the Bengal Army). *Vartman Sahitya*, 23, November–December: 25–31.

Rainwater, L. 1966. "The Crucible of Identity: The Lower Class Negro Family." *Daedalus*, 95 (1): 172–216.

Rajan, Rajeswari Sunder. 1993. *Real and Imagined Women: Gender, Culture and Postcolonialism*. London: Routledge.

———. 2000. "Real and Imagined Goddesses: A Debate." In *Is the Goddess a Feminist? The Politics of South Asian Goddesses,* eds Alf Hiltbeitel and Kathleen M. Erndl. New York: New York University Press: 269–84.

Ram, Kalpana and Margaret Jolly, eds. 1998. *Maternities and Modernities: Colonial and Postcolonial Experiences in Asia and the Pacific*. Cambridge: Cambridge University Press.

"Ram," Rameshwari Prasad. 1926. *Achhutoddhar Natak* (Play on Untouchables' Upliftment). Banaras: Nagari Pracharini Sabha.

Ramagundam, Rahul. 2008. *Gandhi"s Khadi: A History of Contention and Conciliation*. Delhi: Orient Longman.

Raman, Anuradha. 2012. "Put My View on the Table." *Outlook*, 14 May: 22–3.

Ramaswamy, Sumathi, ed. 2011. *The Goddess and the Nation: Mapping Mother India*. Delhi: Zubaan.

Ranciere, Jacques. 2009. *The Emancipated Spectator*, trans. Gregory Elliott. London: Verso.

Rao, Anupama, ed. 2003. *Gender and Caste*. Delhi: Kali.

———. 2009. *The Caste Question: Dalits and the Politics of Modern India*. Ranikhet: Permanent Black.

———. 2012. "Caste, Colonialism and the Reform of Gender: Perspectives from Western India." In *Gendering Colonial India: Reforms, Print, Caste and Communalism*, ed. Charu Gupta. Delhi: Orient Blackswan: 239–64.

———, and Saurabh Dube, eds. 2013. *Crime Through Time*. Delhi: Oxford University Press.

Rao, Vidya. 1990. "Thumri as Feminine Voice." *EPW*, XXV (17): WS31-9.

Ratnmala (Garland of Pearls). 1869. Allahabad: Christian Vernacular Education Society, Mission Press.

Rawat, Ajay S. 2002. *Garhwal Himalaya: A Study in Historical Perspective*. Delhi: Indus Publishing.

Rawat, Ramnarayan S. 2012. *Reconsidering Untouchability: Chamars and Dalit History in North India*. Ranikhet: Permanent Black.

Ray, Krishnendu, and Tulasi Srinivas, eds. 2012. *Curried Cultures: Globalization, Food, and South Asia*. Berkeley: University of California Press.

Raychaudhuri, Tapan. 2000. "Love in a Colonial Climate: Marriage, Sex and Romance in Nineteenth-Century Bengal." *MAS*, 34 (2): 349–78.

Reddock, Rhoda. 1985. "Freedom Denied: Indian Women and Indentureship in Trinidad and Tobago, 1845–1917." *EPW*, XX (43): 79–87.

———. 1994. *Women, Labour and Politics in Trinidad and Tobago: A History.* London: Zed Books.

Rege, Sharmila. 1995. "The Hegemonic Appropriation of Sexuality: The Case of the *Lavani* Performers of Maharashtra." *Contributions to Indian Sociology*, 29 (1–2): 23–38.

———. 2002. "Conceptualising Popular Culture: 'Lavani' and 'Powada' in Maharashtra." *EPW*, XXXVII (11): 1038–47.

———. 2006. *Writing Caste/Writing Gender: Narrating Dalit Women's Testimonios.* Delhi: Zubaan.

———. 2013. *Against the Madness of Manu: B.R. Ambedkar's Writings on Brahmanical Patriarchy.* Delhi: Navayana.

Report of the Adi Hindu Depressed Classes Kumbh Mela Conference, 15–16 January. 1942. Allahabad: Kumbh Mela Ground.

Report of the Benares Municipal Board Enquiry Committee. 1933. Allahabad: Government Press.

Report of the Committee Appointed by the Cawnpore Harijan Sevak Sangha in May 1933, to make a Survey of the Social and Religious Disabilities, Working Conditions, and the Standard of Life of the Harijans of Cawnpore. 1934. Harijan Survey Committee. Cawnpore: Harijan Sevak Sangh.

Report of the Conference of the Depressed Classes Committee, 9–11 October, Cawnpore. 1928. Lucknow: Methodist Publishing House.

Report of the Special Session of the All India Adi Hindu (Depressed Classes) Conference. Held at 11, Havelock Road, Lucknow, September 27–28, 1931. Lucknow: Ganga Fine Art Press.

Report of the Unemployment Committee UP 1935. 1936. Allahabad: Printing and Stationery.

Risalsingh, Chaudhari. 1928. *Pasi Panchayat Pranali ki Hindi Pustak: Pratham Bhag* (Hindi Book of Pasi Panchayat System: Part I). Prayag.

Rizvi, S.A.A., and M.L. Bhargava, eds. 1957. *Freedom Struggle in Uttar Pradesh, Volume I: 1857–59: Nature and Origin.* Uttar Pradesh: Publications Bureau.

Robb, Peter. 2011. *Sex and Sensibility: Richard Blechynden's Calcutta Diaries, 1791–1822.* Delhi: Oxford University Press.

Roberts, D. 1994. *The Myth of Aunt Jemina: Representations of Race and Region.* New York: Routledge.

Robertson, Alexander. 1938. *The Mahar Folk.* Calcutta: YMCA.

Rodrigues, Valerian, ed. 2002. *The Essential Writings of B.R. Ambedkar.* Delhi: Oxford University Press.

Ross, Robert. 2008. *Clothing: A Global History.* Cambridge: Polity.

Rountree, Kathryn. 2004. *Embracing the Witch and the Goddess: Feminist Ritual Makers in New Zealand.* London: Routledge.

Roy, Arundhati. 2014. "Introduction: The Doctor and the Saint." In *Annihilation of Caste: The Annotated Critical Edition, B.R. Ambedkar.* New Delhi: Navayana.

Roy, Kaushik. 2007. "The Beginning of 'People's War' in India." *EPW,* XLII (19): 1720–8.

Roy, Tapti. 1994. *The Politics of a Popular Uprising: Bundelkhand in 1857.* New York: Oxford University Press.

Roy, Tirthankar. 1999. *Traditional Industry in the Economy of Colonial India.* Cambridge: Cambridge University Press.

Royal Commission on Agriculture in India, Evidence taken in UP, Vol VII. 1927. London: Stationery Office.

Royal Commission on Labour in India, Evidence, Central Provinces and UP, Vol. III, Part I. 1931. London: Stationery Office.

Rozario, Santi, and Geoffrey Samuel, eds. 2002. *Daughters of Hariti: Childbirth and Female Healers in South and Southeast Asia.* London: Routledge.

Rusen, Jorn. 2005. *History, Narration, Interpretation, Orientation.* Oxford: Berghahn.

Sadhu, Deviprasad. 1907. *Nishad Vanshavali* (Genealogy of Nishad Caste). Lucknow.

Sagar, Pandit Sunderlal. 1929 (2nd edn). *Yadav Jivan* (Life of Yadavs). Agra: Jatav Mahasabha.

Sahay, K.N. 1998. *An Anthropological Study of Cartoons in India.* Delhi: Commonwealth Publishers.

Said, Edward. 1989. "Representing the Colonized: Anthropology's Interlocutors." *Critical Inquiry,* 15 (2): 217–25.

Sampath, Vikram. 2010. *"My Name is Gauhar Jaan": The Life and Times of a Musician.* Delhi: Rupa.

Sanadhya, Totaram. 1915 (2nd edn, 1914). *Fiji Dwip Mein Mere Ikkis Varsh* (My 21 Years in Fiji Island). Ferozabad: Bharti Bhawan.

———. 2012. *Bhootlane ki Katha: Girmit ke Anubhav* (Story of Bhootlane: Experiences of Indenture), eds Brij. V. Lal, Ashutosh Kumar, and Yogendra Yadav. Delhi: Rajkamal.

Sangari, Kumkum, and Sudesh Vaid, eds. 1989. *Recasting Women: Essays in Colonial History.* Delhi: Kali.

"Sant," Prasad Singh. 1933. *Harijan Gaan* (Song of Harijan). Azamgarh: Harijan Sevak Sangh.

Sanyasi, Bhavanidayal. 1947. *Pravasi ki Atma-Katha* (Autobiography of an Immigrant). Delhi: Sasta Sahitya Mandal.

"Saras," Thamman Singh. 1995. *Avantibai Lodhi: 1857 ki Amar Balidani.* Delhi: Hind Pocket Books.

Sarkar, Sumit. 1997. *Writing Social History.* Delhi: Oxford University Press.

———. 2002. *Beyond Nationalist Frames: Relocating Post-Modernism, Hindutva, History.* Delhi: Permanent Black.

———. 2014. *Modern Times: India 1880s–1950s.* Ranikhet: Permanent Black.

Sarkar, Tanika. 1999. *Words to Win: The Making of Amar Jiban, a Modern Autobiography.* Delhi: Kali.

———. 2001. *Hindu Wife, Hindu Nation: Community, Religion and Cultural Nationalism.* Delhi: Permanent Black.

———. 2009. *Rebels, Wives, Saints: Designing Selves and Nations in Colonial Times.* Ranikhet: Permanent Black.

———. 2013. "'Dirty Work, Filthy Caste': Calcutta Scavengers in the 1920s." In *Working Lives and Worker Militancy: The Politics of Labour in Colonial India,* ed. Ravi Ahuja. Delhi: Tulika: 174–206.

Sathi, Chedi Lal, ed. 1999. *Bhadant Bodhanand Mahasatvir: Jivan aur Karya* (Bodhanand: Life and Work). Lucknow: Buddh Vihar.

Satyanarayana, Adapa. 2002. "'Birds of Passage': Migration of South Indian Laborers to Southeast Asia." *Critical Asian Studies,* 34 (1): 89–115.

Satyanarayana, K., and Susie Tharu, ed. 2011. *No Alphabet in Sight: New Dalit Writing from South India, Tamil and Malayalam.* Delhi: Penguin.

———. 2013. *Steel Nibs are Sprouting: New Dalit Writing from South India, Kannada and Telugu.* Delhi: HarperCollins.

Satyvati, Kumari. 1932. *Stri Darshan* (Knowledge about Women). Chapra: Gyanodaya Prakashan.

Sax, William S. 1991. *Mountain Goddess: Gender and Politics in a Himalayan Pilgrimage.* New York: Oxford University Press.

Scarry, Elain. 1985. *The Body in Pain: The Making and Unmaking of the World.* New York: Oxford University Press.

Schaller, Joseph. 1995. "Sanskritization, Caste Uplift, and Social Dissidence in the Sant Ravidas Panth." In *Bhakti Religion in North India: Community, Identity and Political Action,* ed. David. N. Lorenzen. Albany: SUNY Press: 94–119.

Schomer, Karine, and W.H. McLeod, eds. 1987. *The Sants: Studies in a Devotional Tradition.* Delhi: Motilal Banarsidass.

Schwartz, B., ed. 1967. *Caste in Overseas Indian Communities.* San Francisco: Chandler Publishing.

Scott, James C. 1976. *The Moral Economy of the Peasant: Rebellion and Subsistence in Southeast Asia.* New Haven: Yale University Press.

Searle-Chatterjee, Mary. 1981. *Reversible Sex Roles: The Special Case of Banaras Sweepers.* Oxford: Pergamon Press.

Sehgal, Ramrakh Singh. 1922. *Samaj Darshan arthat Samajik Kuritiyon ka Digdarshan* (Observations on Society Meaning Inspection of Social Evils). Allahabad: Chand.

Semple, Rhonda Anne. 2003. *Missionary Women: Gender, Professionalism and the Victorian Idea of Christian Mission.* UK: Boydell Press.

Sen, Samita. 1999. *Women and Labour in Late-colonial India in the Bengal Jute Industry.* Cambridge: Cambridge University Press.

———. 2004. "'Without His Consent?' Marriage and Women's Migration in Colonial India." *International Labor and Working-Class History*, 65, Spring: 77–104.

Sethi, Rumina. 1999. *Myths of the Nation: National Identity and Literary Representation.* Oxford: Clarendon Press.

Shahjahanpur: A Gazetteer, Vol. XVII of District Gazetteers of UP. 1910. (By H.R. Nevill.) Allahabad: Government Press.

Shakya, Jagannath Prasad. 1999. *Jhansi ki Sherni: Virangana Jhalkari Bai ka Jeevan Charitra* (Lioness of Jhansi: Life Sketch of Jhalkari Bai). Gwalior: Mukesh Printers.

Sharan, Awadhendra. 2003. "From Caste to Category: Colonial Knowledge Practices and the Depressed/Scheduled Castes of Bihar." *IESHR*, 40 (3): 279–310.

Sharda, Chand Karan. 1925. *Dalitoddhar* (Dalit Upliftment). Ajmer.

Sharma, Chandrikanarayan. 1938. *Manavotpatti Vigyan* (Science of Human Origin). Kashi.

Sharma, Chotelal. 1928 (2nd edn). *Jati Anveshan* (Scrutiny of *Jati*). Jaipur.

Sharma, Jagardev. 1912. *Kajli Badshahi Jalsa Bahar.* Calcutta.

Sharma, Krishnanand. 1923. *Hinduon ki Unnati aur Achhut* (Progress of Hindus and Untouchables). Banaras.

Sharma, Nandita. 2003. "Travel Agency: A Critique of Anti-Trafficking Campaigns." *Refuge*, 21 (3): 53–65.

Sharma, Raj Bahadur. 1988. *Christian Missions in North India 1813–1913 (A Case Study of Meerut Division and Dehra Dun District).* Delhi: Mittal Publications.

Sharma, Satish Kumar. 1983. "Shuddhi: A Case Study of the Role of a Religious Movement in the Status Improvement of Untouchables." *Indian Journal of Social Research*, 24 (1): 70–7.

Sharpley-Whiting, R. Denean. 1999. *Black Venus: Sexualized Savages, Primal Fears, and Primitive Narratives in French*. Durham: Duke University Press.

Shastri, Shivkumar. 1916. *Varna Vyavastha par Vichaar* (Thoughts on the Caste System). Aligarh: Vishwavidya Pracharak Mahamandal.

Sheelbodh. "*Jhalkaribai: Ek Aitihasik Karvat*" (Jhalkaribai: A Historic Turn). *Apeksha*, April–June 2005: 85–9.

Shepherd, Verene A. "Indian Migrant Women and Plantation Labour in Nineteenth-and Twentieth-Century Jamaica: Gender Perspectives." In *Women Plantation Workers: International Experiences,* eds Shobhita Jain and Rhoda Reddock. Oxford: Berg: 89–106.

Sherinian, Zoe C. 2005. "Re-presenting Dalit Feminist Politics through Dialogical Musical Ethnography." *Women and Music: A Journal of Gender and Culture*, 9: 1–12.

Sherring, M.A. 1868. *The Sacred City of the Hindus: An Account of Benares in Ancient and Modern Times*. London: Trubner & Co.

———. 1872. *Hindu Tribes and Castes, as Represented in Benares*. London: Trubner & Co.

———. 1875. *The History of Protestant Missions in India from 1706–1871*. London: Trubner & Co.

Shilberrad, C.A. 1898. *A Monograph on Cotton Fabrics Produced in NWP.* Allahabad: Government Press.

Shraddhanand, Sanyasi. 1919. *Jati ke Dinon ko Mat Tyago arthat 7 Karor Dinon Ki Raksha* (Do not Abandon the Powerless in Castes Meaning Protection of 70 Million Powerless). Delhi: Sadharm Pracharak Press.

Shraddhanand, Swami. 1926. *Hindu Sangathan: Saviour of the Dying Race*. n.p.

Shukl, Umavaran. 1937 (3rd edn). *Kajli Sabrang Bahar* (*Kajli* for All Seasons). Kanpur.

Siddalingaiah (In conversation with Chandan Gowda). 2010. "Village Deities." *Seminar*, 612, August.

Siddiqi, A. 1973. *Agrarian Change in a Northern Indian State 1819–33*. Oxford: Oxford University Press.

Sikand, Yoginder Singh. 2004. *Islam, Caste and Dalit–Muslim Relations in India*. Delhi: Global Media Publications.

Singh, Jebaroja. 2004. "The Spotted Goddess: The Dalit Woman in Classical Brahminic Literature, and in Modern Fiction, Memoirs and Songs from Tamilnadu and Andhra Pradesh." Rutgers University: PhD Thesis.

Singh, Kuwar Lachman (Deputy Collector). 1874. *Historical and Statistical Memoir of Zila Bulandshahar*. Allahabad: Government Press.

Singh, Lakshminarayan, and Bhagwati Prasad Singh, eds. 1936. *Orh Kshatriya Chandrika* (Caste Tract on Orhs). Hathras.

Singh, Maina Chawla. 2000. *Gender, Religion and "Heathen Lands": American Missionary Women in South Asia (1860s–1940s)*. New York: Garland Publishing.

Singh, Mohinder. 1947. *The Depressed Classes: Their Economic and Social Condition*. Bombay: Hind Kitab.

Singh, Satnam. 2011 (3rd edn). *Chamar Jati ka Gauravshaali Itihaas* (Glorious History of the Chamar Caste). Delhi: Samyak.

Singha, Radhika. 1998. *A Despotism of Law: Crime and Justice in Early Colonial India*. Delhi: Oxford University Press.

———. 2007. "Finding Labor from India for the War in Iraq: The Jail Porter and Labor Corps, 1916–1920." *Comparative Studies in Society and History*, 49 (2): 412–45.

Sinha, Mrinalini. 1995. *Colonial Masculinity: The "Manly" Englishman and the "Effeminate" Bengali in the Late Nineteenth Century*. Manchester: Manchester University Press.

———. 2006. *Specters of Mother India: The Global Restructuring of an Empire*. Durham: Duke University Press.

Sitala Gungaan (Sitala's Praise). 1934. Gaya: Mahuri Pustak Bhandar.

Smarika: Virangana Uda Devi Pasi Shaheed Diwas. 2005. November 16. Lucknow: Virangana Uda Devi Smarak Sansthan.

Smith, Barbara. 1998. *The Truth that Never Hurts*. New York: Routledge.

Smith, M.G. 1965. *The Plural Society in the British West Indies*. Berkeley: University of California Press.

Soneji, Davesh. 2012. *Unfinished Gestures: Devadasis, Memory, and Modernity in South India*. Chicago: University of Chicago Press.

Speeches and Writings of Sarojini Naidu. 1924. Madras: G.A. Natesan and Co.

Spivak, Gayatri Chakravorty. 1988. "Can the Subaltern Speak?" In *Marxism and the Interpretation of Culture*, eds Cary Nelson and Larry Grossberg. Chicago: University of Illinois Press: 271–313.

———. 1999. "Moving Devi." In *Devi, the Great Goddess: Female Divinity in South Asian Art*, ed. Vidya Dehejia. Washington: Arthur M. Sackler Gallery: 181–200.

Srinivas, M.N. 1998. *Village, Caste, Gender and Method*. Delhi: Oxford University Press.

Srivastava, Anandi Prasad. 1928. *Achhut: Ek Samajik Natak* (Untouchable: A Social Play). Allahabad: Vishwa Granthavali.

Srivastava, I. 1991. "Woman as Portrayed in Women's Folk Songs of North India." *Asian Folklore Studies*, 1–2: 270–310.

Srivastava, Sahab Lal. 1974. *Folk Culture and Oral Tradition: A Comparative Study of Regions in Rajasthan and Eastern UP.* Delhi: Abhinav.

Stark, Ulrike. 2007. *An Empire of Books: The Naval Kishore Press and the Diffusion of the Printed Word in Colonial India.* Ranikhet: Permanent Black.

Stewart, Robert. 1896. *Life and Work in India.* Philadelphia.

Stewart, T.K. 1995. "Encountering the Smallpox Goddess: The Auspicious Song of Sitala." In *Religions of India in Practice*, ed. D.S. Lopez Jr. Princeton: Princeton University Press: 389–97.

Stokes, Eric. 1986. *The Peasant Armed: Indian Revolt of 1857.* New York: Oxford University Press.

Stoler, Ann Laura. 1995. *Race and the Education of Desire: Foucault's History of Sexuality and the Colonial Order of Things.* Durham: Duke University Press.

———. 2002. *Carnal Knowledge and Imperial Power: Race and the Intimate in Colonial Rule.* Berkeley: University of California Press.

Storey, John. 2014. *From Popular Culture to Everyday Life.* London: Routledge.

Subramanian, Lakshmi. 2006. *From the Tanjore Court to the Madras Music Academy: A Social History of Music in South India.* Delhi: Oxford University Press.

"Sumen," Sriramnathlal. 1933 (3rd edn). *Bhai ke Patra (Vivah Samasya aur Nari Jeevan)* (Letters of a Brother). Ajmer: Sasta Sahitya Mandal.

Summers, Martin. 2004. *Manliness and its Discontents: The Black Middle-class and the Transformation of Masculinity, 1900–1930.* Chapel Hill: University of North Carolina Press.

Survey of Evangelistic Work, Punjab Mission of the Presbyterian Church in the USA. 1929. Lucknow.

Swain, Clara A. 1909. *A Glimpse of India: Being a Collection of Extracts from the Letters of Clara A. Swain.* New York: James Pott and Company.

Tambe, Ashwini. 2009. *Codes of Misconduct: Regulating Prostitution in Late-colonial Bombay.* Minneapolis: University of Minnesota Press.

Taneti, James Elisha. 2013. *Caste, Gender and Christianity in Colonial India: Telugu Women in Mission.* New York: Palgrave.

Tarlo, Emma. 1996. *Clothing Matters: Dress and Identity in India.* Chicago: University of Chicago Press.

Tartakov, Gary Michael, ed. 2012. *Dalit Art and Visual Imagery.* Delhi: Oxford University Press.

Thakur, Keshavkumar. 1930. *Vivah aur Prem* (Marriage and Love). Allahabad: Chand.

———. 1932. *Grihasth Jeevan* (Family Life). Prayag.

Thapan, Meenakshi, ed. 2005. *Transnational Migration and the Politics of Identity.* Delhi: Sage.

Thapar, Romila. 2008. *Somanatha: The Many Voices of a History.* Delhi: Penguin.

Thapar-Bjorkert, Suruchi. 2006. *Women in the Indian National Movement: Unseen Faces and Unheard Voices, 1930–42.* Delhi: Sage.

Thomas, Timonthy N. 1985. *Indian Overseas: A Guide to Source Materials in the India Office Records for the Study of Indian Emigration 1830–1950.* London: British Library.

Thorat, Vimal. 2008. *Dalit Sahitya ka Strivadi Swar* (Feminist Voice of Dalit Literature). Delhi: Anamika.

Tinker, Hugh. 1974. *A New System of Slavery: The Export of Indian Labour Overseas 1830–1920.* London: Oxford University Press.

Tirathram. 1924. *Striyon ko Chetavni* (Warning to Women). Allahabad.

Tiwari, Chandrabhal. 1936 (3rd edn). *Rangili Kajri.* Banaras.

Trivedi, Lisa N. 2007. *Clothing Gandhi's Nation: Homespun and Modern India.* Bloomington: Indiana University Press.

Uberoi, Patricia. 2006. *Freedom and Destiny: Gender, Family, and Popular Culture in India.* Delhi: Oxford University Press.

Upadhyay, Gangaprasad. 1923. *Humari Desh Seva* (Our Service to the Country). Prayag: Arya Samaj Chowk.

———. 1925. *Padri Sahib se Bacho* (Beware of the Missionary). Prayag: Arya Samaj Chowk.

———. 1930. *The Arya Samaj and Depressed Classes.* Allahabad: Arya Samaj.

———, ed. 1941. *Dalitoddhar* (Dalit Upliftment). Allahabad.

Upadhyay, Krishndev. 1957. *Lok Sahitya ki Bhumika* (Role of Folk Literature). Allahabad: Sahitya Bhawan.

Upadhyay, P.P., and D.N. Upadhyay, eds. 1872. *Premghan Sarvasava* (Collection of Premghan's Writings). Prayag: Hindi Sahitya Sammelan.

Urban, Hugh B. 2003. "'India's Darkest Heart': Kali in the Colonial Imagination." In *Encountering Kali: In the Margins, at the Centre, in the West*, eds Rachel Fell McDermott and Jeffrey J. Kripal. Berkeley: University of California Press: 169–95.

"Vachanesh," Mishra. 1936. *Shabari.* Awadh: Hanumat Press.

Vaishya, Chimmanlal. 1924 (16th edn). *Narayani Shiksha arthat Grihasthashram* (Women's Education Meaning Family Life). Prayag.

Vajpeyi, Balkrishnapati. 1934. *Stri Sarvasava* (Essence of Women). Agra: Ratnashram.

Vajpeyi, Laxmidhar. 1941 (8th edn). *Dharmshiksha* (Religious Education). Prayag: Tarun Bharat Granthavali.

Varma, Bansidhar. 1916. *Ishvaku Kul Kshatriya Vanshavali* (Genealogy of the Isvaku Caste). Aligharh.

———. 1939. *Kshatriya Shilpkar Darpan* (Mirror of Kshatriya Shilpkars). Aligarh.

Varma, Kashiram. 1907. *Kurmi Kshatriya Darpan* (Mirror of Kurmi Kshatriyas). Lucknow.

Varma, Kumar Cheda Singh. 1904. *Kshatriyas and Would-be Kshatriyas*. Allahabad: Pioneer Press.

Varma, P.S., ed. 1992. *Dalit (Swatantrata) Pira* (Dalit (Freedom) Pain). Delhi: Vimukt Jati.

Varma, Ram Dayal. 1996. *Virangana Uda Devi*. Hardoi: Mahendra Printing Press.

———. 2004 (2nd edn). *San 1857 ki Amar Shaheed Virangana Uda Devi* (*Khand Kavya*). Hardoi: Manoj Printers.

Varma, Vrindavan Lal. 1987 (1946). *Jhansi ki Rani Lakshmibai*. Jhansi: Mayur Prakashan.

Vatal, Jagdish Sahai. 1923. *Report on the Industrial Survey of the Allahabad District of UP.* Allahabad: Government Press.

Vatsa, Rajendra Singh, Introduced by. 1977 (1912). *The Depressed Classes of India: An Enquiry into their Condition and Suggestions for their Uplift.* Delhi: Gitanjali Prakashan.

Vatuk, Ved Prakash, ed. 1979. *Studies in Indian Folk Traditions*. Delhi: Manohar.

Veeramani, K., ed. 1992. *Periyar on Women's Rights*, trans. Raju S. Sundaram. Madras: Emerald.

Venkatachalapathy, A.R. 2012. *The Province of the Book: Scholars, Scribes, and Scribblers in Colonial Tamilnadu*. Ranikhet: Permanent Black.

Verma, Mukut Behari. 1971. *History of Harijan Sevak Sangh, 1932–1968*. Delhi: Harijan Sevak Sangh.

Vijaisri, Priyadarshini. 2004. *Recasting the Devadasi: Patterns of Sacred Prostitution in Colonial South India*. Delhi: Kanishka.

Visharad, Bhawani Shankar. 1988. *Virangana Jhalkari Bai*. Aligarh: Anand Sahitya Sadan.

Vishvakarma, Nigamchand. 1927 (3rd edn). *Kajli Surajmukhi*. Kanpur.

Vishwanathan, Gauri. 1998. *Outside the Fold: Conversion, Modernity, and Belief*. Princeton: Princeton University Press.

"Viyogi," Nandlal Jaiswar. 1943. *Achhuton ka Insaf* (Justice of Untouchables). Allahabad: Jaiswar Seva Sadan.

Viyogi, Naval, and M. Anwar Ansari. 2010. *History of the Later Harappans and Shilpakara Movement, Vol. II*. Delhi: Kalpaz Publications.

Vyanga Chitravali (Collection of Cartoons and Caricatures). 1930. Allahabad: "Chand" Karyalaya.

Wadley, Susan S. 1980. "Sitala: The Cool One." *Asian Folklore Studies*, 39: 33–62.

———. 2005. *Essays on North Indian Folk Traditions*. Delhi: Chronicle Books.

Wakankar, Milind. 2010. *Subalternity and Religion: The Prehistory of Dalit Empowerment in South Asia*. Oxon: Routledge.

Wallace, Maurice O. 2002. *Constructing the Black Masculine: Identity and Ideality in African American Men's Literature and Culture, 1775–1995*. Durham: Duke University Press.

Wallace-Sanders, Kimberly, ed. 2002. *Skin Deep, Spirit Strong: The Black Female Body in American Culture*. Ann Arbor: University of Michigan Press.

Walsh, Cecil. 1929. *Indian Village Crimes with an Introduction on Police Investigation and Confessions*. London: Ernest Benn Limited.

Walsh, Judith E. 2004. *Domesticity in Colonial India: What Women Learned when Men Gave them Advice*. New York: Rowman and Littlefield.

Walton, H.G. 1903. *A Monograph on Tanning and Working in Leather in UP*. Allahabad: Government Press.

Wang, Joy. 2009. "White Postcolonial Guilt in Doris Lessing's 'The Grass is Singing'." *Research in African Literatures*, 40 (3): 37–47.

Wanzo, Rebecca. 2009. *The Suffering Will Not Be Televised: African American Women and Sentimental Political Storytelling*. Albany: SUNY Press.

Webster, John C.B. 1994 (2nd edn). *The Dalit Christians: A History*. Delhi: ISPCK.

———. 1999. *Religion and Dalit Liberation*. Delhi: Manohar.

Weidman, Amanda J. 2006. *Singing the Classical, Voicing the Modern: The Postcolonial Politics of Music in South India*. Durham: DUP.

Whitcombe, Elizabeth. 1972. *Agrarian Conditions in Northern India, Vol. 1: UP under British Rule, 1860–1900*. Berkeley: University of California Press.

White, David Gordon. 1996. *The Alchemical Body: Siddha Traditions in Medieval India*. Chicago: University of Chicago Press.

White, Hayden. 1987. *The Content and the Form: Narrative Discourse and Historical Representation.* Baltimore: Johns Hopkins University Press.

Wilfred, Felix. 2007. *Dalit Empowerment.* Delhi: ISPCK.

Wilkinson, Iain. 2005. *Suffering: A Sociological Introduction.* Cambridge: Polity Press.

Williams, Raymond. 1981. *The Sociology of Culture.* Chicago: University of Chicago Press.

Willis, Deborah, ed. 2010. *Black Venus 2010: They Called Her "Hottentot."* Philadelphia: Temple University Press.

WS 10 Class. 2009. *Isn't This Plate India? Dalit Histories and Memories of Food.* Pune: Krantijyoti Savitribai Phule Women's Studies Center, University of Pune.

Yadav, Baijnath. 1927. *Ahir Jati ki Niyamavali* (Rules for the Ahir Caste). Banaras: Gokul Press.

Yadav, Dilip Singh. 1914. *Ahir Itihaas ki Jhalak* (A Glimpse into the History of the Ahir Community). Etawah.

Yadav, Virendra. 2007. "1857 ka Mithak aur Viraasat: Ek Punarpaath" (Myth and Legacy of 1857: A Revisit). *Tadbhav*, 15, January: 125–54.

Yadavendu, Ramnarayan. 1942. *Yaduvansh Ka Itihaas* (History of Yadavs). Agra: Navyug Sahitya Niketan.

Yang, Anand A. 1985. "Dangerous Castes and Tribes: The Criminal Tribes Act and the Magahiya Doms of Northeast India." In *Crime and Criminality in British India*, ed. Anand A. Yang. Arizona: University of Arizona Press: 108–27.

Zelliot, Eleanor. 1992. *From Untouchable to Dalit: Essays on the Ambedkar Movement.* Delhi: Manohar.

———, and Rohini Mokashi-Punekar, eds. 2005. *Untouchable Saints: An Indian Phenomenon.* Delhi: Manohar.

Periodicals and Newspapers

For details, refer to the footnotes. Some of the most frequently consulted are:

Abhyudaya. 1925–8.

Abla Hitkarak. 1887.

Adarsh Hindu. 1926.

Bharat Mitra. 1914.

Chand. 1924–40.

Dainik Vartman. 1938.

Journal of the Association of Medical Women in India. 1930–2.

Madhuri. 1922–5.
Pioneer 1942.
Pratap. 1925–38.
Samta. 1942.
Saraswati. 1916.
Shuddhi Samachar. 1927.
Stri Darpan. 1917–27.
Sudha. 1925–8.
The Indian Social Reformer. 1912–40.
Native Newspaper Reports, UP.

Archival Sources

Oriental and India Office Collection, British Library, London

Public and Judicial Records (L/PJ Series), Military Deptt Records (L/MIL
    Series), Services and General Deptt Collections (L/SG Series), Records
    of the Board of Commissioners (F/4 Series).
George A. Grierson Collection. Mss Eur E223.
Hallett Collection. Mss Eur E251.
Indian Police Collection. Mss Eur F161.
Viscount Simon, Chairman of Indian Statutory Commission Collection.
    Mss Eur F77.
W.G. Archer Collection. Mss Eur F236.

Uttar Pradesh State Archives, Lucknow

Proceedings and Files of the Government of UP: General Administration,
    Judl, Industries, Agriculture, Revenue and Commerce Deptts (1891–
    1933).

Criminal Investigation Department Office, Lucknow

(Secret) Police Abstracts of Intelligence of UP Government, 1922–40.

National Archives of India, Delhi

Proceedings and Files of the Government of India and UP: Home Deptt,
    including Public, Jails, Police, Medical, Judl (1877–1933); Home Poll
    (1910–38); Legislative Deptt (1919–34); Foreign Deptt (1858–60);
    Revenue and Agriculture Deptt (1883).

Nehru Memorial Museum and Library, Delhi

All India Congress Committee Papers (AICC), Ist Installment, Part I, List 1.

All India Hindu Mahasabha Papers, 1930–50, List 8.

B.S. Moonje Papers, 1903–47, List 45.

Baba Ramchandra Papers, 1914–50, List 163.

Interview with Ganpat Rai by S.L. Manchanda, Acc. 330, Oral History Transcript.

Index

Numbers in italics denote pages with illustrations

321

kaharin, 29, 34–5, 40, 50n94, 250
Kahars, 124, 136, 159
kajli/ kajri, 4, 208, 221–30
Kaliyug, 18, 136
Kalwars, 20, 24
Kanpur, 24–6, 40, 79, 91n22, 122,
    127, 139, 143n144, 145, 150,
    152, 160–1, 177, 201–3, 205,
    229
Kanyaon ki Pothi, 33
Kapur, Ratna, 235
Kayasths, 12, 20, 83
khadi, 190, 197, 228
Khatiks, 22, 26, 42, 144, 161–2,
    179, 201–3, 213
Khatris, 12, 20
Kori, 95–6, 100, 142, 203
Kshatriyas, 18, 20, 41–2, 62, 126,
    129, 131, 135–6, 153, 179, 215
Kumaon, 25, 131–2, 159
Kunti, 243–5, 247, 249–52
Kuril, Ramcharan, 12–13, 24, 153,
    179
Kurmis, 42, 92, 179
kutnis, 29, 34, 41

labor/laborer, 2, 5, 18, 23–4, 171,
    210; Dalit male, 112–17, 143–6,
    151; Dalit women's, 36, 38–40,
    43–4, 49–50, 103, 162, 187,
    189, 232, 239; indentured,
    15–16, 233, 235–7, 240–1,
    243–4, 246, 253, 258, 264
Lakshmibai, the Rani of Jhansi, 94,
    96, 100, 102–4, 192
Lal, Brij, 237, 238n32, 243n52,
    249n75, 251n81, 256
language, 11, 26, 53, 62, 67, 71;
    of aspirations, 4; of benevolent
    paternalism, 171; of conversion,
    155; of *kajli*, 225; of manhood,

134, 164; of nationalism, 244,
    267; of nationalist patriarchies,
    248; of paternalism, 133; of
    prose, 268; of protest, 141,
    144–54, 221; of reforming
    practices, 163–4; of
    representation, 2; of rights,
    142, 168–9, 206; of sentiment
    and satire, 84; of suffering and
    sympathy, 73, 77
Lara Lari, 186
lathi, 138, 143; *akhara*s, 202
lavani, 222–3, 227
law, 28; colonial, 31; courts,
    17–18; legal cases, 70, 149; of
    Varnashrama, 83
Lawrence, John, 129
Leader (newspaper), 175n41,
    240n42, 243n53, 244, 251n84
leather, 129, 153; factories, 122;
    Muslim workers, 173; workers,
    5, 88, 144, 151, 213
literature, 1, 4, 11, 31–43, 50–1,
    68, 267
love, 14, 103, 117–18, 168, 174,
    180, 183, 198, 200, 202, 206
lower caste, 6, 18, 21, 32, 37, 63–4,
    66–7, 82, 88, 115–16, 163n237,
    170, 173, 192, 199–200,
    210–11, 214, 234, 237–8,
    255
Lucknow, 5, 10, 25, 40, 87, 91n22,
    96–7, 101, 131–2, 137, 139–40,
    150, 162, 185, 188
Lutgendorf, Philip, 73–4
Lynch, Owen, 5n7, 136n110,
    140n129, 163n237

Mahabharat, 30, 35, 247
Mahal, Begum Hazrat, 88, 94, 96,
    102

GLOBAL
SOUTH
ASIA

PADMA KAIMAL, K. SIVARAMAKRISHNAN,
AND ANAND A. YANG, SERIES EDITORS

Global South Asia takes an interdisciplinary approach to the humanities and social sciences in its exploration of how South Asia, through its global influence, is and has been shaping the world.

A Place for Utopia: Urban Designs from South Asia,
by Smriti Srinivas

The Afterlife of Sai Baba: Competing Visions of a Global Saint,
by Karline McLain

Sensitive Space: Fragmented Territory at the India-Bangladesh Border,
by Jason Cons

The Gender of Caste: Representing Dalits in Print,
by Charu Gupta